THE CUSTOMER RULES

The 14 Indispensable, Irrefutable, and Indisputable Qualities of the Greatest Service Companies in the World

C. BRITT BEEMER
ROBERT L. SHOOK

NEW YORK   CHICAGO   SAN FRANCISCO   LISBON
LONDON   MADRID   MEXICO CITY   MILAN   NEW DELHI
SAN JUAN   SEOUL   SINGAPORE   SYDNEY   TORONTO

The **McGraw·Hill** Companies

2 3 4 5 6 7 8 9 0   FGR/FGR   0 1 4 3 2 1 0 9 8

ISBN 978-0-07-160365-2
MHID 0-07-160365-4

McGraw-Hill books are available at special quantity discounts to use as premiums and sales promotions, or for use in corporate training programs. To contact a representative, please visit the Contact Us pages at www.mhprofessional.com.

This book is printed on acid-free paper.

Claire Jiang Beemer is an incredible gift from God. This book is dedicated to Claire's sweet spirit and her kind and gentle heart.

—C.B.B.

To Jacob, Jamie, and Jeremy, my sweet and beautiful grandchildren who I love so much.

—R.L.S.

Contents

Acknowledgments

This is the third Beemer-Shook collaboration, and once again, we had a wonderful support team. So while our names may appear on the cover, this book represents the combined efforts of many talented people.

One extraordinary person is Kathy Hilleshiem at ARG's corporate headquarters in Charleston, S.C. Kathy also worked on our two previous books, and here too, her multi talents served us well. Her assistance included collecting and organizing research data that appears throughout this book. She also helped us with the manuscript revisions that were necessary to keep our facts accurate and current. Kathy always remained cool and collected under pressure and met all deadlines.

We are also grateful to two other ARG employees, Angie Guyer and Glenda Morris, plus the entire staff of interviewers who conducted more than 9,000 interviews during the consumer research studies ARG conducted. Angie and Glenda were responsible for compiling this extensive data so Britt could interpret exactly what consumers were saying.

Another invaluable contributor is Debbie Watts, who transcribed our tape-recorded interviews that were conducted with the executives who are quoted throughout our book. It's always a joy to work with Debbie.

At McGraw-Hill, we were fortunate to have an exceptional editor, Knox Huston, who is a true professional in every sense of the word.

Knox is also a terrific person and a pleasure to know. McGraw-Hill's Jane Palmieri, the editing manager for *The Customer Rules*, did outstanding work, and she too is a delightful person to work with. We also thank Scott Amerman who copyedited our manuscript. We feel fortunate to work with Gaya Vinay, McGraw-Hill's marketing manager, and Lydia Rinaldi, the company's director of publicity. A special thank you to Phil Ruppel, who, early in his career as a promising editor, worked on several Shook books. Phil is now president of McGraw-Hill Professional Books. It was when Phil got involved in the acquisition stage that Bob couldn't resist the opportunity to work with a much admired, long-time friend.

We thank our literary agent, Al Zuckerman, whose advice and guidance is always appreciated. We also salute Barbara Burns, a top-notch publicist and a very lovely lady. Barbara got involved in the early stages of the writing of the manuscript and continues to work with us to help spread the word that the customer rules.

We met many wonderful people during our travels to conduct interviews, each of whom assisted us in various ways. They are: Maryann Aarseth, Joe Arterburn, Patti Carr, Patti Corrigan, Lana DuBois, Peg Falko, Mary Beth Heying, Raymond Jordan, Jeff Leebaw, Ginny Martin, Mark Marymee, Pam McClain, Chris Molineaux, Mol Marc Monseau, Kellie Mowery, Lisa Musante, Mark Schussel, Chuck Smock, Greg Thome, and Nan Wilkins.

We also thank our wonderful wives, Jan and Elinor, who never complained when we made a countless number of long-distance phone calls, early in the morning, late at night, on holidays and weekends to exchange ideas for our book.

Last and not least, we thank the executives that we interviewed for sharing their valuable time and consenting to share their thoughts on what it takes to win lifetime, loyal customers.

Introduction

As founder and CEO of America's Research Group (ARG), I conduct surveys on consumer and corporate behavior. The objective of my work is to give my clients a clear understanding about their customers, and in turn, provide them with a competitive advantage. You would think that business owners and managers already know all about their customers. They don't. If they did, there would be no reason for ARG to exist.

Over the 29 years since I started my company, I have conducted research for industry leaders such as General Electric, JCPenney, Sealy, Kohl's, and Warren Buffett's Berkshire Hathaway companies. I've observed one common denominator that is shared by these and other successful companies: their quest to serve their customers. They are never satisfied with the status quo. Everything they do evolves around the customer. They do it with zest and gusto. I have seen many marketing strategies throughout my career. So many, in fact, that it's as if there is an ongoing flavor of the month. But as far as my coauthor and I are concerned, unless the customer is the focal point of all its activities, a company is headed in the wrong direction.

In today's highly competitive marketplace, it's easy to be sidetracked and lose focus on one's customers. There are many distractions. For example, sales volume rapidly increases and the distribution department is unable to get merchandise out the door in a timely manner; or too little volume forces retailers to immediately cut prices to move the goods. We've witnessed executives who get so hung up with return on investment (ROI) that they start making their customers jump through hoops to return a purchase. We've seen managers become so wrapped up in information technology (IT) that they forget that its main purpose is to better serve the customer. Some managers are so influenced by their corporate law department that all their business decisions are based on legal ramifications. In other cases, companies invest so heavily in elaborate distribution and warehousing facilities that they lose sight that these facilities exist for the benefit of the customer.

We do not deny the importance of all parts of a business—each unit contributes to the overall success of the company. However, we do emphasize that all of these are tools to serve the customer. And when the customer is no longer the center of attention, it should serve as a red flag to management that the business is losing focus. As the adage goes: "*As you ramble on through life, whatever be your goal, keep your eye upon the donut, and not upon the hole.*" We elaborate in Chapter 1 that marketing is the responsibility not only of those employees in the marketing department. Everyone should be constantly thinking about the customer—the CEO, the people in the accounting department, the people in the warehouse—everyone. In order for a company to be a market leader, all employees must work in unison with a common goal to serve the customer.

To research this book, we visited the management of companies that were industry leaders and known to be customer-focused. For example, one of these companies exemplifying excellence in serving its customers is the Four Seasons Hotels and Resorts. According to such authoritative sources as Zagat, Condé Nast, Mobil Travel Guide, and Travel & Leisure, no other company in the lodging industry has received as much unprecedented recognition and accolades worldwide. While Four Seasons properties are palatial and provide lavish accommodations, it is the company's extraordinary service reputation that earns rave reviews. The graveyard of luxury hotels is filled with extravaganzas that were riddled with high vacancies. It wasn't that they didn't have high occupancy rates when they first opened. Their downfall was that customers didn't come back.

The Four Seasons competitive advantage is not its physical assets but its people who are trained to take a personal interest in making sure that each guest's stay far exceeds his or her expectations. Four Seasons employees do it in a way that seems as natural and effortless as a gracious hostess who makes a houseguest feel like a member of the family. However, there is nothing effortless about it; an enormous amount of effort is required. The kind of hospitality that is extended to Four Seasons guests by more than 30,000 employees in 73 locations around the world is a result of diligent management. During our research, we talked to founder, chairman, and CEO Isadore Sharp and other senior managers to find out how Four Seasons is able to instill a strong sense of pride in its people who seem to thrive on going beyond the call of duty to satisfy customers. What we discovered, we are happy to report, can be emulated by other companies when their management teams make a commitment to excel in customer satisfaction.

In all businesses, this effort has to start at the top. The CEO must be totally customer focused, and only then will this way of thinking permeate through the organization. All too often, however, CEOs give themselves credit for being in touch with their customers when, in fact, they are not. We spent a day accompanying a CEO of a large regional department store while he made his rounds visiting five locations, a mission that he boasted he repeats semiannually. We walked side by side with his entourage of eight senior managers while he stopped to personally chat with customers.

In one store, the CEO stopped a robust, grandmotherly shopper who was pushing a sparsely filled shopping cart through the women's lingerie department. He introduced himself as the company's CEO and chairman. Along with his managers, we crowded around the woman and the CEO questioned her about the store.

"What do you think about our selection?"

"It looks fine to me," she replied.

"Are you able to find what you're looking for?"

"No problem, sir."

"Do you think our store is well lighted?"

"Yes sir. I can see fine."

"Do you think we have an attractive store?"

"Yes sir," she said.

"Do you have any suggestions for improvements or any complaints?"

"Off the top of my head, I can't think of anything."

"Thank you for taking your time to talk to me."

"You're welcome."

One of the managers handed the woman a $10 discount coupon for any purchase made over $20 that day. "This is a token of our appreciation for your speaking with our CEO," he said. He, too, thanked her for her business.

The CEO walked away, his face beaming, and his team nodded in unison, agreeing with their leader. This procedure was repeated with several other customers, and then we and his entourage got into two limousines parked at the store's entrance and headed to another store. At the end of the day, the CEO boasted that he was not one to sit in an ivory tower, far removed from the action. "It feels good to get away from the office and mingle with customers," he said. "Being one on one with customers invigorates me. It enables me to feel the pulse of our business. I know what my customers want."

In truth, he had no idea what they wanted. Imagine yourself, dressed in your sweats in the middle of the afternoon on your day off, pushing your shopping cart and suddenly, out of nowhere, you're surrounded by a team of executives dressed in dark suits. Then an overbearing CEO starts drilling you with questions. Intimidating, isn't it? What are you going to say when he asks your opinion? In your mind, you'd be thinking, "I'll tell him what he wants to hear and I'm out of here." The last thing you want to do on your day off is have a confrontation with a group of executives.

"Yes sir," you would say, "I love your store." But inside, you'd be thinking, "This is the last time I'll ever set foot in this box."

Even more potentially harmful to his company than being out of touch with the customer is this CEO's belief that he is in touch when he clearly is not. It's not enough to get information on your customer; what matters is getting the right information and being able to objectively interpret it. Everyone already knows that it's a good thing for business owners and managers to listen to their customers. But if you get inadequate feedback and misread it, it will do a lot of damage.

The CEO cited above is an example of how misinformation can lead to misfortune. In this particular case, his stores looked worn and needed to be updated. Their appearances went downhill over a period of time, but they did so gradually, so that management had not noticed. With sales on a downward spiral, the CEO did not want to invest money in upgrading his stores. So when customers told him that the stores looked okay to them, he believed it. It's like being a guest in someone's home and being asked, "What do you think about our newly redecorated living room?" Are you going to say what's on your mind: "It reminds me of a bordello." Or will you tactfully reply to your host, "It's really you, and I hope you receive many years of pleasure from it."

We take the position that being in touch with one's customers is a good starting point, but just that—a starting point. But what good is it if one doesn't glean meaningful information to gain a competitive advantage?

ARG research discloses that large corporations tend to gather vast volumes of extraneous data on their customers. And while small companies may develop one-on-one relationships with customers, they lack the ability to collect and process useful information. Nearly everyone in business has taken the equivalent of Marketing 101, but most are unable to formulate a valid interpretation of what their customers are thinking. The failure to properly analyze data can cause as much damage as if nothing had been done.

While we start out sharing the philosophy that every business must be focused on the customer, it is not our intention to rehash old material. To set this book apart from the glut of garden-variety marketing books that have been published, ARG conducted consumer research in excess of $300,000 exclusively for this book, a first in trade book publishing history. This research appears throughout the book and provides current information on what consumers are thinking. Concurrently, we conducted interviews with CEOs and senior managers at companies that score exceptionally high marks in customer satisfaction. Each company that we feature is the leader in its industry for customer service. To collect this information, we visited the world headquarters of marquee companies such as Four Seasons, Chubb, Lexus, and Johnson & Johnson. This book is not based on theory. It is filled with solid data and information about what's happening in today's marketplace.

Not all of the companies we visited are multi-billion-dollar corporations with recognizable brand names. We also interviewed management at smaller companies. One was World Wide Technology (WWT), the largest African American–owned company in the United States. Founder and chairman David Steward, a man of faith, built his company based on biblical principles. Paraphrasing the Bible, Steward told us: "Our mission is to serve our employees and our customers. If we do this, we will succeed. We are here for each other." Steward believes that individual values should not be separated from corporate values, and this is evidenced in the way WWT does business. Steward's philosophy works and serves as a model for others. Founded in 1990, this St. Louis–based company had revenues in excess of $2.4 billion in 2007.

A small company that we fell in love with is Tom James Clothiers, a firm that specializes in selling tailor-made clothing. Everything this company does is totally focused on serving customers. Each member of its 600-plus sales force makes personal calls to the customer's office, and presenting his or her wares with swatches, offers an enormous selection of suits, sports jackets, slacks, and other garments in a wide assortment of beautiful fabrics that come in solids, stripes, and plaids in many colors. All in all, there is an endless combination of styles that can be custom-designed to match the customer's taste. The total number of items in the Tom James inventory vastly exceeds what a retailer might have in stock. The company's reps are expertly trained and considerably more knowledgeable than clothing salespeople in retail stores—that is, if you can even find one. If you have visited a department store lately, you have probably noticed that the number of salespeople on the floor has been substantially reduced. What we find so appealing about Tom James is the time that their customers are able to save by not having to shop at a retail store. This unusual company has found a way for the mountain to go to Muhammad.

Every chapter provides consumer surveys, and most importantly, explains what it all means. ARG has been doing these studies for 29 years, and, having talked to several million consumers, we have come up with objective analyses not only of what they say but of what they are thinking.

Sometimes not only do you have to get out there and talk to consumers, you have to come up with ways to really see them in a new light. Moen, the manufacturer of faucets and fixtures, did exactly that when they developed a new line of showerheads for the home. To find out more about their customers, they decided to go right into the showers and observe them in action. Surprisingly, it was not hard to recruit people to take showers in the privacy of their homes, with cameras located in the shower as well as the bathroom doorway, and be filmed from start to finish. This up-close-and-personal technique generated all sorts of revealing insights. Researchers discovered that people spent half of their time in the shower with their eyes closed, that they spent 30% of their time avoiding water, and that, because of poor shower design, they often risked slipping or otherwise being hurt. These and other findings shaped the design of Moen's Revolution showerhead, which became a bestseller. This unique research demonstrates that if you want to come up with a new product, one that differs from the competition, you have to see your customers in a new light. And what you see depends on how and where you look.

We structured each chapter to provide current research that reveals what consumers are thinking, and most importantly, what they want. This information is followed by examples about execution by the best companies that are the leaders in their industry in customer satisfaction. How high is their level of customer satisfaction? It is so high that they have raised the bar to another stratosphere. During our extensive interviews, a comment we heard on several occasions was, "A satisfied customer is not good enough. We want a *delighted* customer."

You may have a tendency to think that the costs of this high level of service will be a heavy drain on profits; on the contrary, your earnings will increase because, over time, your company will enjoy more revenues via repeat business and increased orders. Highly loyal customers will also refer business your way. This will result in lower customer acquisition costs and a healthy bottom line.

1

Everyone's Job

It's a simple premise. Everyone in the workplace has the same job—serving the customer. The sad thing is that many employees, and even their managers, don't understand it. Of course, if managers don't get it, their subordinates probably won't.

America's Research Group (ARG) conducted a survey in 2008 that asked, "Have you ever considered the notion that everyone has a job at your company that involves the customer?" We find it astonishing that *four out of ten working Americans think that neither their nor their coworkers' jobs have anything to do with customers.*

Sticking to the same theme, the survey dug deeper. Employees were asked, *"Does your supervisor talk to you about how your personal efforts affect the customer?"* Of those who responded, 51.5% answered "No." This is a sad commentary on the management of the American workforce.

To get more employees thinking about customers during their work-day, it would help if management arranged some conversations between the two. Hearing customers' needs and problems firsthand might allow employees to rethink their jobs. But mostly, this is not happening. In fact, *46% said that they never talked to customers.*

Making the Transition

Typically a business owner starts out caring for customers. Running a one-person operation, the owner is devoted to making sales calls, realizing that the best use of his or her time is being in front of customers. This is what generates revenues. Yes, the owner sweeps the floor, takes out the trash, and does the bookkeeping and inventorying—and does these chores in the evenings and on weekends when he or she can't call on customers. Hard-driven entrepreneurs don't need to take Marketing 101 to understand that the customer comes first.

When businesses grow, the owners must assume managerial responsibilities that make demands of their time and take them away from their customers. Some customers feel neglected. They complain that they miss the personal attention they used to receive. It is often difficult for a small business owner to make the transition to run a larger organization. It requires different skills. Hence, the single-minded focus on the customer, once the owner's strong suit, becomes less of a customer-winning advantage.

Often the newly hired staff has little or no contact with customers. While the business owner and sales force continue to make sales calls, others in the company are isolated from the customer. They have never been taught that their work too is customer related.

The owners who are able to make a successful transition from small to large are those who emphasize to their employees that the customer is the reason for the company's existence. These entrepreneurs have learned that taking exceptional care of the customer generates repeat orders. And most satisfied customers are the best source of referrals that generate still more business. Spending a good amount of their time in the field, these owners maintain firsthand knowledge of their customers' whims and needs. Their dedication to serving customers can become deeply ingrained in their company's culture, spreading into the consciousness and working habits of its employees. In a well-managed company, no matter its size, the sole proprietor's job, catering to the customers, becomes everyone's job.

To see how this works firsthand, visit a Four Seasons hotel and ask an employee where the coffee shop is. Ask a housekeeper, bellhop, or even a maintenance worker who's on a ladder changing a lightbulb. If the maintenance worker is asked, it's likely that he'll climb down and give you a friendly greeting. But he will not give you directions. He'll do better. He'll escort you to the coffee shop. "Just come with me," he'll politely say.

"Why does he do it?" you may ask. "Isn't his job to do maintenance and fix broken things?" Of course that's his job. But like all other Four Seasons employees, he knows that serving customers is his main job.

In many hotels, it's uncommon that a room attendant even says "hello" to a guest. That's because she's been trained to clean rooms. That's her job. A Four Seasons room attendant knows better. She's been trained to know that her job is to serve customers, and this obligation includes extending hospitality in the form of a warm greeting to guests.

Serving Others

The people at the companies we visited are driven by a desire to serve others. These women and men go to work every day with a desire to do good for their customers, employees, and communities. So where does such an attitude start? Our research has shown that the founder first aspired to these lofty goals.

David Steward is the chairman of World Wide Technology (WWT), a company he founded in 1990 with an initial investment of $250,000. Headquartered in St. Louis, WWT is now the largest African American–owned business in the United States, with sales in excess of $2.4 billion. A man of faith, Steward set out to run a company based on teachings from the Bible. He says that, like Jesus, his mission is to serve others.

"My serving starts with the 1,200-plus people associated with my company," Steward explains. "This means I must place the needs of our employees above my own. I am here to help them succeed. Consequently, a high percentage of my time and energy is spent coaching, advising, and supporting our people."

Steward disagrees with managers who believe their chiefdom entitles them to be served by subordinates. "They think that because they've worked their way up and have a corner office, they've earned the right to sit back and savor the perks they believe come with the job," he points out. "'I've paid the price,' they say. 'Now it's my turn to get what's due me.' They think their role in management is to be served. It's the other way around. It's a sign of trouble when a company has senior managers who expect to be placed on a pedestal while obedient subordinates scramble to serve them. Good leaders understand that their role is to serve their people. Serving others is not only the best way to get to the top, it's the best way to stay there. Once you've been promoted up the corporate ladder, your avenues to serve others are multiplied.

"My number one priority as chairman is to serve my people," Steward maintains. "If I am able to do this, it will permeate the organization and carry over to the customer. We believe that when this happens, our company will succeed."

World Wide Technology employees are reminded of their role in serving customers every time they receive a paycheck. On the check, the message is inscribed, "A satisfied customer made this check possible."

Harrah's, founded in Reno in 1936 by Bill Harrah, is one of the oldest casinos in Nevada. Today, it is known as Caesars Entertainment and is the largest gaming company in the world. Other well-known casinos that were once landmarks such as the Desert Inn, the Dunes, El Rancho, and the Sands are long gone. Harrah's survival and success are due in part to the high regard its people have for the customer. Its customer-focused policies trace back to Harrah himself, a man who, unlike David Steward, spent little time in church. Still, he too cared about treating customers well. Harrah is once known to have said to one of his senior officers, "I want you to understand this. The bottom line is the most important thing to most corporations. I still own 70% of this company, and the bottom line isn't that important to me. I do want shareholders to appreciate and join in our profits, but the three things I want done are: I want the customer treated properly; I want the employees treated properly (if we do that, we won't have to worry about the unions); and I want the place maintained and clean at all times. If we make money after that, fine. That's my philosophy."

Starting with his early days, Harrah put a system in place whereby each employee was rated especially for the attention he or she gave to pleasing the customer but without hurting the business. A perfectionist, Harrah constantly emphasized paying attention to the details. It was a big deal if a lightbulb was out; you had to change it. Adhesive tape was forbidden in public areas at Harrah's—no memos, licenses, or notes could be taped anywhere. "He was a nut for cleanliness," one long-time employee said. "You couldn't have an ashtray on a table for five or ten minutes before somebody came by, emptied it, washed it, and put it back. You couldn't have cigarette butts or stuff like that on the floor for a few minutes before some guy came around and swept it up. The keno girls and all the girls that wore the short skirts, they'd better have their seams straight on their stockings or they were in trouble. When you went to work, you wore black slacks, a white shirt, and a tie, and your pants had to be pressed. You walked on the floor and you'd better be in good shape or you weren't going to be on the floor for very long. You were going to be sent home."

When he built his first casino-hotel, the Lake Tahoe property, it was the world's first hotel with two bathrooms in every room. "I want to have two bathrooms so that when a gentleman and his wife are in the room, he can use one bathroom and get ready for dinner, and she can use her bathroom." Where did he get the idea? He said that it was what he would have personally wanted if he were a guest. Harrah died in 1978, but his emphasis on taking superlative care of his customers became his legacy. Thirty years after his death, his insistence on great customer service is still mandatory in the casinos that bear his name.

Put It in the Job Description

Don't keep it a secret. Spell out in every employee's job description how the job relates to the customer. This way, starting on day one, every employee knows that serving the customer is the company's top priority.

To our dismay, however, a survey conducted by ARG revealed that *only 59.2% of all working Americans have a written job description.* And yes, if a job description isn't in writing, it's not worth the paper it's written on! This research tells us that American industry is allowing 40% of its workforce to work as free agents.

At those companies where management has communicated to the workforce that everyone's job is customer related, there is a vast difference in the level of service. However, it's not the employees' fault when they don't know their job is to serve customers if nobody has ever told them that it is their first priority. It cannot be assumed that someone in the accounting or legal department would consider his or her job to be to take care of customers. It's not something taught in an accounting or law class. Unless it's specifically spelled out, people think that it's the marketing and salespeople's job—they are the ones who are on the firing line and in direct contact with customers. So in order to make it perfectly clear, it must be put in the job description. Let everyone see it in writing—at his or her time of employment.

Guiding Principles and Beliefs

Great companies have certain guiding principles and beliefs, or a mission statement that plays an everyday role in how people conduct their daily business. The best we've come across is Johnson & Johnson's. Founded in

1887, its credo was created in 1943 by CEO and chairman Robert Wood Johnson, the son of one of the cofounders. Introduced the year before the company became publicly traded, the document has been revised several times in accordance with Johnson's belief that it should evolve with the language as well as with the growth and development of the company. Here's the current version:

Our Credo

We believe our first responsibility is to the doctors, nurses and
  patients,
to mothers and fathers and all others who use our products and
  services.
In meeting their needs everything we do must be of high quality.
We must constantly strive to reduce our costs
in order to maintain reasonable prices.
Customers' orders must be serviced promptly and accurately.
Our suppliers and distributors must have an opportunity
to make a fair profit.

We are responsible to our employees,
the men and women who work with us throughout the world.
Everyone must be considered as an individual.
We must respect their dignity and recognize their merit.
They must have a sense of security in their jobs.
Compensation must be fair and adequate,
and working conditions clean, orderly and safe.
We must be mindful of ways to help our employees fulfill
their family responsibilities.
Employees must feel free to make suggestions and complaints.
There must be equal opportunity for employment, development
and advancement for those qualified.
We must provide competent management,
and their actions must be just and ethical.

We are responsible to the communities in which we live
  and work
and to the world community as well.
We must be good citizens — support good works and charities
and bear our fair share of taxes.
We must encourage civic improvements and better health and
  education.

We must maintain in good order
the property we are privileged to use,
protecting the environment and natural resources.

Our final responsibility is to our stockholders.
Business must make a sound profit.
We must experiment with new ideas.
Research must be carried on, innovative programs developed
and mistakes paid for.
New equipment must be purchased, new facilities provided
and new products launched.
Reserves must be created to provide for adverse times.
When we operate according to these principles,
the stockholders should realize a fair return.

This credo is cast in stone at Johnson & Johnson. Literally. As soon as you walk into the company's world headquarters in New Brunswick, New Jersey, you'll see this credo engraved in the limestone wall. The letters that spell "Our Credo" are 2¼ inches high; and underneath, the size of each individual letter is slightly larger than one inch. It's big and bold enough that you don't need your glasses to read it. The engraving makes it clear to employees and visitors that the credo is taken very seriously at Johnson & Johnson. The company goes much further than casting it in stone. To make sure that it's being adhered to, the company conducts annual surveys with its employees around the world addressing the important question: "How do you rate the company against the Credo?" So far, employees report that they and their coworkers follow it, and it plays a role in the decision making on day-to-day activities as well as major long-term plans.

There's still more to tell about the Johnson & Johnson credo. When we first sat down to interview the company's CEO, Bill Weldon, he immediately started off the conversation talking about the company's credo. Weldon spoke with passion, and in regards to the credo, he repeated the various responsibilities that the company has. "It's about treating people with dignity and respect," he emphasized. "Even if it means the company is reducing its workforce and has to let somebody go. You still treat them properly.

"We spend a lot of time making sure our employees have good working conditions," Weldon said. "But it goes beyond the employee; it's also about the employee's family, which includes paying good wages and good health benefits so they live well. This reflects the business we're in, which is providing products and services to people around the world that enhance their lives. The people who work here understand this, and they feel good about the commitment that we have to others as well as our commitment to them. The two feed off each other. This is why we talk a lot about our value system, which is embodied in our credo. We are here to do the right thing. That's a responsibility we have."

Ray Jordan, Johnson & Johnson's vice president of corporate communications, said that the company conducted some external research in 2007 to find out what people thought about the company. "What the study revealed," Jordan says, "is that they talked a lot about putting the needs of others first. When I read the report, I said, 'Wait a minute. That's the way the credo is written.' It's not about what we do but about our responsibility to patients, doctors, and nurses. We also have responsibilities to shareholders. I thought it was an interesting link that people outside the company were echoing what's reflected in our mission."

Today, having a mission statement is in vogue and most companies have one, but few place as much importance on theirs as does Johnson & Johnson. A 2007 ARG study reveals that *only 20.9% of American workers were ever told about the company's mission statement during a job interview. Knowing this, it comes as no surprise that only 21% of employees are able to recite their company's mission statement.* If a mission statement isn't important enough to be discussed during a job interview, why should it be expected to be made known after employment? Companies that are truly customer focused could never allow this to happen. They couldn't tolerate having four out of five of their employees not being united in the quest to achieve the company's goals.

In the same study, *only 47.4% of all working Americans have ever even seen their company's mission statement. Of those who have, 75.5% of them believe their employer truly adheres to its mission statement.* Compare this number to a survey reporting that 98% of all Japanese workers are familiar with their employers' mission statements. One manager of a major Japanese company was dismayed because 2% of his company's employees were unfamiliar with its mission statement. To him, 2% was a failing grade. "It means we have employees who think we're not working as a team," he sighed.

While it's important to have a written credo (mission statement), one company that goes beyond this is Four Seasons, where the unwritten credo of the Golden Rule (to treat others as you would want to be treated) is very much a part of its company culture. "Our founder, Isadore Sharp, has abided by the Golden Rule since the company was founded in 1961," says Ellen du Bellay, who is vice president of learning and development of the high-end hotel chain. "Mr. Sharp has always advocated treating our guests as we ourselves would want to be treated. Of course, this is what the Golden Rule tells us. Well, we talk about the Golden Rule so much that it is deeply engrained in the Four Seasons culture. Consequently, every employee knows that the Golden Rule should be applied at all times to the way our guests are served. Sure, it's a 2,000-year-old philosophy, but as far as we're concerned, it still works."

Edward Jones: A Business Model Built on Customer Relationships

Edward Jones, the financial securities firm, has more than 10,000 offices spread across the United States, Canada, and the United Kingdom. Edward Jones far exceeds industry leader Merrill Lynch in terms of total number of offices. Evidently, Edward Jones' large numbers haven't hindered its ability to serve customers because, according to J.D. Power and Associates and *SmartMoney* magazine, it ranks first in customer satisfaction among all full-service financial-service brokerage firms. In 1922 Edward D. Jones Sr. opened his own brokerage firm in downtown St. Louis, Missouri. During its early history, Edward D. Jones & Company operated as a conventional brokerage firm, underwriting stocks and bonds and selling securities to customers. In the 1940s and 1950s, Edward Jones' investment representatives were known as "TNT brokers" because they traveled the countryside surrounding St. Louis from Tuesday until Thursday drumming up business.

It wasn't until 1955 when the founder's son Edward D. Jones Jr. ("Ted") opened the firm's first branch office. Located in Mexico, Missouri (population 12,200), it became the prototype for other branch offices that were to pop up all over the Midwest. Ted who took over as managing partner in 1968 recognized an opportunity to focus on investors in small towns and farm communities that had been overlooked by the major firms. By meeting face-to-face with clients, building strong relationships, and by offering a conservative investment philosophy that focused on investing in blue-chip stocks and bonds, Ted believed his company would find a niche in the marketplace that would differentiate the firm from the competition.

In 1963, Edward Jones had 67 offices when John Bachmann, a 23-year-old man fresh out of college with an MBA, came aboard. Bachmann had worked part-time at Edward Jones for the past three years running messages, and when needed, he cleaned the basement and carried out the trash. As a full-time employee, Bachmann started out in a staff position but quickly realized that "to get ahead in this business, I would have to succeed in the sales side. I had to go out and meet the public." So after spending one year at the home office, the young man moved to Columbia, Missouri, and during the next seven years built a thriving one-man brokerage office. He then returned to company headquarters as a principal in the firm with responsibility for fixed-income product marketing. After several promotions, Ted Jones announced that Bachmann would succeed him as managing partner. At the time, Edward Jones had about 300 branch offices in 28 states. Following his predecessor's philosophy of serving serious long-term investors through one financial advisor offices, Bachmann introduced technology and training programs that spurred tremendous growth during his tenure. When he stepped down as managing partner to become a senior partner in 2003, under his guidance, Edward Jones had more than 9,000 offices.

Edward Jones' current head honcho is Jim Weddle, who, like Bachmann, started in the trenches. After graduating DePauw University in 1975, the psychology major with a minor in business turned down a position at Procter & Gamble to pursue an MBA at Washington University in St. Louis. His first contact with the firm was during a career day when he heard an Edward Jones representative speak about a part-time opening in the company's research department. "I put on the one suit I owned and went in for an interview," Weddle recalls. "When I handed my résumé to the director of research, he frowned and commented that I was attending a good graduate school but my undergraduate degree wasn't satisfactory. I was totally decimated, but quickly became suspicious and said, 'You must be from Wabash.'

"The man was John Bachmann, and he burst out laughing. He was a Wabash graduate, and a football rivalry between the two schools has been going on for about 100 years and at the time, the two schools were tied at 50–50. We kidded each other and by the end of the afternoon, he offered me a job and I started the next day."

Weddle worked in the research department while earning his MBA, and during this time, he regularly spoke to Edward Jones financial advisors. "I really enjoyed the industry," Weddle explains. "It was dynamic and fast-changing—it was different every day. By the time I finished graduate school and was ready to start my full-time career at Edward Jones, I concluded that I wasn't going to be a very good research analyst. I was enamored with the sales end of the business and realized I was on the wrong side of the phone. I wanted to be a financial advisor. So, as soon as I graduated I took the company's training program, sat for the Series 7 examination, and I was ready to go out and open a one-man branch office."

Weddle had grown up in Naperville, Illinois, a suburb of Chicago, and his wife Stacey was a native of Indianapolis. On weekends during his training program, the young married couple routinely packed their suitcase and drove through Illinois and Indiana in search of a small town that did not have an Edward Jones office. "We were looking for a place where we could settle down and call home," Weddle tells. "We'd visit the Chamber of Commerce, stop at the local mom and pop restaurants, and ask the locals a lot of questions about the town. We'd go into the pharmacy or hardware store and question people, 'Tell me why you think this town is so special?' On our fifth weekend, we stopped in Connersville, Indiana, a town 60 miles due east of Indianapolis with a population of 25,000. The town was the county seat, and its economy had a good mix of agriculture and business. Ford, Percolator, Dresser Industries, and Stant Manufacturing were the area's big employers. Stacey and I thought the town had a lot of charm, especially its courthouse square and the local businesses that surrounded it. We immediately knew that it was where we wanted to live."

Weddle was 23 years old when he opened the firm's two hundredth office. With the company's backing, he opened a one-person office, typical of nearly all Edward Jones brokers' offices. And like the firm's other branches, the firm helped him hire a branch office administrator (BOA) who would serve as his assistant. On day one, Weddle started introducing himself to prospective clients, making door-to-door visits, and getting involved in the local community meeting people. He did what other Edward Jones financial advisors were taught to do before him, and what thousands of others have since been trained to do. Today with more than 10,000 one-person offices strategically placed in strip shopping centers, small-town main streets, and suburban areas of large cities, Edward Jones blends in with the local community like a friendly neighbor. Edward Jones offices are everywhere, and today people recognize the name. They're next to the dry cleaners, the ice cream shop, and the beauty parlor. These 1,000-square-foot offices are informal and cozy. Clients feel comfortable about stopping in after work, even dropping by wearing bib overalls and work boots. And like Jim Weddle did for seven years in Connersville, today's Edward Jones advisors are just as apt to stop in at their clients' homes to review investment portfolios.

Having started their careers in the trenches, both Bachmann and Weddle had firsthand experience in working with clients, building their individual offices, one client at a time. It makes a huge difference when business owners, or in this case, a company's top dog(s), have an in-depth personal background in working with customers. Because, when a company's leaders are in tune with building lasting customer relationships, it sets the pace for the entire organization. Going forward, Edward Jones intends to stay close to its customers through its huge network of one-person offices. While plans are on the drawing board to eventually have 25,000 offices, the firm's future is premised on continuing to serve each customer on a personal basis. While Edward Jones engages in a rapid expansion program, none of its competitors is likely to follow suit with the opening of one-advisor offices. To copy Edward Jones, other firms would have to change their business model to accommodate large numbers of small offices. So while other firms' financial advisors are capable of establishing strong personal relationships with their clients, it's unlikely that a competitor can do it on a large scale quite like Edward Jones.

Hiring the Right People

It's been said, "No matter how much training you give an old gray mare, it ain't ever going to win the Kentucky Derby." This is why a company must carefully handpick the right people during the recruiting and hiring stages to maximize its ability to serve customers. This means putting in long, tedious hours conducting one-on-one interviews with job applicants. It's a slow process but it pays off down the road in double spades. How does this work? Interviewers must ask probing questions and listen intently.

"We developed a service index questionnaire," explains Phil Satre, former CEO and chairman of Harrah's Entertainment, Inc., which officially changed its name to Caesars Entertainment Corporation in late 2008. "It provides insight about our job applicants, about whether they like people. We want to know such things as: Do they like to communicate with people? Do they smile and make eye contact when they greet somebody? Are they 'people people'? The questionnaire is designed to let our recruiter know if the interviewee is service driven. With some people it's a natural thing. With others it's not."

Marilyn Winn, former senior vice president of human resources at Harrah's, explains: "You can't take someone who doesn't have the right attitude or personality and make him into a different person. We look for people who have what we refer to as a hospitality personality. This begins with people who like people, and by this I mean they've got to care about them. In this business it takes a special type of person who is willing to work weekends and holidays, our busiest times. This is an individual who enjoys serving others so much that he is willing to sacrifice his own well-being to benefit others.

"In the gaming industry, a company enjoys a competitive advantage if its employees excel at building personal relationships with customers," adds Winn, currently president of Rio, Paris, and Bally's hotel-casinos in Las Vegas that are owned by Caesars Entertainment. "In our restaurants, it might be the maître d' or a waitress that keeps a guest coming back. In the casino, it might be a dealer or cocktail waitress that a customer looks for on his next visit."

Winn points out that it's important to attract the right types of people from the start; otherwise employee turnover will be high. "The gaming industry has a 40% turnover rate on the casino floor," she says, "and in a business like ours where relationships are so important, high turnover has a negative effect."

An in-depth and thoughtful hiring process is crucial to the company's success. Winn explains: "During an interview we'll ask probing questions such as, 'How would your most recent supervisor describe your personality?' 'Can you tell me of a time when you personally improved a guest's experience?' 'Give me an example about how you changed a particular customer's bad experience into a pleasant experience.' We rate them by their answers to direct questions that are specially prepared for specific jobs. We want people with certain qualities, and if they don't have what we're looking for, we quickly eliminate them from consideration."

Winn says that if an applicant gets past the structured interview process, he or she will be invited to spend time on the floor to take a look at the job as performed by a model employee. "For example, if a woman wants to be a cocktail server," Winn explains, "she is told 'We would like you to watch one of our servers for a short period of time. You can see what she wears, and in particular, look at her shoes because she's on her feet for long periods. Notice, too, that she carries a heavy tray and has to maneuver through the aisles. She's constantly bending over to pick up beverage glasses.' We want a job candidate to see what the job actually entails, because she might be under the impression that the position is much more exciting than it really is. It's better that she come in with both eyes wide open, knowing that this job is hard work."

✳   ✳   ✳

In addition to hiring people with a specific aptitude for a particular job, great marketing companies search for people with passion. This is what the biotech company Centocor, a wholly owned Johnson & Johnson unit, did when building its team in the mid-1980s and throughout the 1990s to launch Remicade, a drug to treat immune-mediated disorders such as Crohn's disease and rheumatoid arthritis. Today Centocor is the maker of Remicade, Johnson & Johnson's top-selling medicine. But throughout the 1990s, the biotech start-up struggled, at times teetering on going under. During these turbulent times, it was its passionate scientists that kept the company afloat. One individual who came aboard is Thomas Schaible, Ph.D., who today serves as vice president medical affairs, immunology at Centocor. When asked what made him leave a top-notch position to join Centocor, then in the doldrums, Schaible responds, "Two words: Monoclonal antibodies!" He explains, "Monoclonals were first discovered in 1976, and due to their exquisite specificity for identifying a biological target and their promise to serve as either diagnostic or therapeutic agents, they had extraordinary potential. It all seemed like Star Wars. I wanted to be a part of it. It was an incredibly exciting opportunity. . ."

Joe Scodari received a call from a headhunter in 1996, the same year that Remicade was approved by the Food and Drug Administration. He had been running a billion-dollar unit of Rhone-Poulenc Rorer. Why would he leave a top position to join a company that in the previous year had only $22 million in revenues? "My friends and colleagues told me that I had to be crazy to risk joining a small company with an iffy future," he explains. "But I wanted to be part of building something that had tremendous potential. That's what turns me on. Any time you make a career transition, you put your family through hell. I met with Dave Holveck, who was Centocor's chairman, and when he explained what he envisioned with the company's biotech medicines, I wanted to be a part of it. I told Dave that as long as I didn't have to take a pay cut that would cause my family to sacrifice, I'd come aboard."

Julie McHugh also joined Centocor in 1996 as director of marketing and later served as the company's president. Julie previously worked at SmithKline Beecham and was also attracted by the excitement she could feel when she first visited the small biotech. "I was intrigued by the incredibly passionate scientists I met here," she tells. "They fervently believed in what they were doing, and their enthusiasm was contagious. The company had suffered setbacks with potentially promising drugs, and I admired their tenacity. Yes, they had failed, but were not folding up the tent. It was exhilarating to be around these people. I consider it a blessing to be part of such a team and know that when I come to work every day, we are making an important difference in so many people's lives."

When you meet Johnson & Johnson people like Tom Schaible, Joe Scodari, and Julie McHugh who are so motivated to do good for others, you can understand why their company is so successful. They want to make a difference. Money is not their god.

Interestingly enough, in an ARG survey that asked Americans which was the driving force of the companies they worked for, profits or doing good for their customers, 33% said that profits came first.

Goodwill Ambassadors

An ARG survey revealed that 54% of American employees have contact with customers who buy from their company. Of these employees, only 43.8% associate their job with marketing. What astonished us was that 55.6% had never in their lives considered their jobs as marketing positions. This is a sad commentary. These employees do not understand that they can directly affect, in a positive or negative way, what customers think about their company. They are oblivious to how they can either help or hinder their company's success by enhancing the customer's experience.

Looking beyond the workplace, employees are relatives, friends, and neighbors, and in these roles, they can serve as goodwill ambassadors for their employers. When they think of their jobs as marketing positions, they are more apt to spread the word about the good things their company does. Remember, all employees spend considerably more time away from the company than on the job. With this in mind, let's hope they are saying positive things about the company.

It's the Vendor's and Temp's Job Too

Every organization must take management responsibility for *all* the people on whose productivity and performance it relies—whether they're temps, part-timers, or employees of its outsourcers, suppliers, and distributors. This means they must be on the same page as the company's own employees—with a clear understanding that their job is to serve the company's customers. Growing numbers of businesses today outsource, and all too often companies overlook these distant hires, neglecting to make sure they are as customer driven as their full-time people. As a consequence, customers are often neglected and even mistreated. But rarely, if ever, does a customer distinguish these outsourced folk from "company" employees. To the customer, poor service is just that—poor service. How is she or he to know that the person behind the counter or the voice on the phone is a temp?

Of course, it shouldn't matter whether customers know who is or who is not an employee. Nor should it matter that work is outsourced. Your customers should receive the same high level of service and quality of goods simply because they are *your* customers, and they should get it regardless of whether or not an outside vendor or temp is involved.

Over the years, we have taken many trips to Aspen, Colorado. We usually fly on United Airlines to Denver with a connecting flight to Aspen on a commuter plane. Although we purchase a round trip Columbus–Aspen ticket from United, the Denver–Aspen leg is on United Express, operated by Mesa Airlines. The service to and from Denver on Mesa can be horrendous. For example, if there are only a handful of passengers booked, the flight is likely to be canceled due to so-called mechanical problems. The passengers are then made to wait for the next flight, an hour or two later. This happens with such regularity that passengers who frequent this route recognize that Mesa intentionally cancels partially booked flights to save money. But the passengers are never informed. Passengers should never be given false information.

Each time we complain to United, we are told by a ticket agent or manager, "We apologize, but that part of your trip is not operated by United. It is operated by Mesa." And each time we hear that, we say, "We bought our ticket from United. We are your customers. It is your responsibility to assure that your customers receive the same quality of service from your partner as your company provides." No excuse is acceptable, yet we may as well be talking to a brick wall.

We believe that United Airlines should be held accountable for poor service rendered by its partner. The company should put pressure on Mesa Airlines to either provide the same quality of service that United does, or it will find a new partner. This is true with any company that partners with another company. A hotel that has an independent restaurant on its premise must demand the same service and quality of meals that the hotel extends to its guests. The same is true of the hotel's health club, gift shops, and other retailers run by independent contractors. Even within the confines of a home office or distribution center where employees don't have daily personal contact with customers, there are areas of the company where employees of outsourcers are prevalent. You'll find these outsourced workers in the company's computer systems or call centers.

So how does a company get its temps, outsourced employees, and vendors to deliver outstanding service to customers? For starters, these workers must be effectively indoctrinated to fully understand that taking care of customers is everyone's job.

2

Sell Your Employees First

In 2001, Kmart, the nation's second largest retailer at the time, filed bankruptcy. Five years earlier, an ARG study uncovered shoppers' thoughts about the giant discount retailer. *An astounding 77% said when they shopped at Kmart, they sensed that store employees didn't want to be there.*

Kmart customers wondered, "Why should I want to be in this store when even its employees don't like being here?" No wonder Kmart's revenues plummeted.

It's not only Kmart employees. Across the United States, consumers gave the nation's workforce poor marks when it came to exhibiting a high level of enthusiasm. A 2008 ARG survey points out that *only 19.3% of American consumers thought retail workers exhibit a high level of enthusiasm. A mere 23.8% gave high marks to restaurant workers, and barely 22.9% spoke favorably of office employees.* In our opinion, an approval rating under 70% represents a failing grade.

When questioned about how they were able to gauge employee enthusiasm, 74% said they saw it in their body language. This tells us that even when a supervisor instructs them to act positively in the presence of customers, employees can't fake it. Incidentally, the word *enthusiasm* comes from the Greek word *entheos*, meaning "having god within." The Greeks got it right: many an actor has tried, but enthusiasm must be genuine.

Who's responsible for a company's reputation? Its CEO? President? The head of public relations? Another ARG consumer survey revealed that *48.9% of Americans base a store's customer-service image on the attitude of the cashier at the checkout counter.* Disgruntled cashiers can't hide their discontent. It shows in their unwillingness to extend themselves when encountering a customer. Wal-Mart is aware of this, hence their one-question survey on the credit card slider when checking out, "Was your cashier friendly?" Cashiers frequently display their true feelings to customers. Are they genuinely pleased to be of service or just plain annoyed? Since the last person the customer deals with before heading out the door is the cashier, that's who's responsible for that final lingering impression.

All of this shouldn't surprise anyone. We've all had to deal with disgruntled employees. You sense a store clerk feels he's doing you a favor by speaking to you. An airline ticket agent stares at a computer, never glancing up to acknowledge your presence although you stand there five minutes. We all know that even a busy person can make eye contact or offer an acknowledgment, "One moment please," to keep the customer from feeling invisible.

In our role as a customer, we're treated with disdain so often that we become oblivious to it. The receptionist at the dentist's office continues to talk on a personal call while you stand waiting to let her know you arrived promptly for your appointment. A long line of customers waits where only one teller is on the job. Several others talk on the phone, do paperwork, and generally avoid eye contact. You almost have to get up your nerve to interrupt them!

With so many apathetic people in the workforce, it comes as no surprise that a 2006 ARG *study disclosed that one-third of consumers feel that employees at stores where they shop don't like their jobs.* This apathy drives away customers in large numbers. Sadly, many employers are clueless as to the effect of poor morale on their revenues. Managers who care whether employee morale is good or bad know it is the direct result of their own people management skills.

A Good Place to Work

The facts are clear. One out of three employees is unhappy at work, and consequently large numbers of customers take their business elsewhere. No company can afford a mass exit of customers. A logical solution to the problem is to treat your employees well, and that can begin by enhancing their work environment. For any company weak in this area, evidence shows a correlation between the influence of employee attitudes on customers and that company's bottom line. This is reported in *Fortune's* "100 Best Companies to Work For," an annual cover story since 1998. Obviously these companies get it, and so do others that do good things for their employees but did not make the top 100 list.

Many factors go into making a company's workplace desirable. The companies on the *Fortune* list offer benefits that run the gamut. Of course, nothing beats a good day's pay, which can include performance incentives, employee bonuses, stock options, health-care coverage, and contributions to retirement plans.

It is also a boost in morale when people work in a pleasing environment. In this department, some companies on the *Fortune* list shower their employees with over-the-top amenities. Let's take a look at Google, number one on the 2006 list. The company operated out of its founder's garage in 1998, but just eight years later, in 2006, company sales exceeded $10 billion. Sitting with more than $10.4 billion in cash at the end of the third quarter in 2006, the Silicon Valley Internet company is one fat cat. Speaking about fat, many of its employees at company headquarters in Mountain View, California, are also adding inches to their waistlines: the company's 11 cafés serve free gourmet meals so delectable that employees write home about them. Google employees say anticipating the Irish oatmeal with fresh berries makes their mouth water during morning rush-hour traffic. At lunchtime, someone with a more sophisticated palate might opt for the raw bar, roast quail, or roasted black bass served with parsley pesto and bread crumbs. With such delectables, during their first year of employment new people are warned to expect to put on the "Google 15."

Of course, when it comes to America's best company to work for in 2006, the food simply whets the appetite for the additional services they have to offer. At Google you can do your laundry; drop off your dry cleaning; get an oil change; have your car washed; work out in the gym; attend subsidized exercise classes; get a massage; study Spanish, French, Japanese, and Mandarin; and ask a personal concierge to arrange your dinner reservations. Go ahead, get your hair cut on the premises. Thinking of buying a hybrid car? Let the company donate $5,000 toward your environmentally friendly purchase. Naturally, under those conditions, you might refer someone to work at Google, and after hiring your buddy, the company rewards you with $2,000. Just have a new baby? Congratulations! To ease new mothers' first four weeks at home, Google reimburses them up to $500 in take-out food. Time for a checkup? Visit one of Google's five on-site doctors free of charge. And it should be no surprise to learn there is usually a band playing at Google's weekly TGIF party.

Many Silicon Valley companies provide shuttle-bus transportation from area train stations. Google operates free Wi-Fi–enabled coaches from five Bay Area locations. Lactation rooms are common in corporate America, but Google provides breast pumps so nursing moms don't have to carry the equipment to work. Although there are an unlimited number of sick days at Google, who would ever call in sick without good cause? The fact is, work is such a cozy place, it's sometimes difficult for employees to leave the office—which is precisely how the company justifies the expenses for its vast array of perks. It's smart business to indulge employees by creating an environment where they want to come to work early, stay in during lunch breaks, and stick around past quitting time.

As an added bonus, a reputation for treating their employees well allows companies to be more selective in hiring new people. Why? Because excessively large numbers of people line up at their doors seeking jobs. For example, at Google, the number one–ranked company by *Fortune* in its February 2008 list of the top 100 companies to work for, 761,799 applicants sought jobs at the Mountain View, California–based company. Those people were competing for a mere 3,039 job openings. The same *Fortune* article ranked Edward Jones as the fourth best company to work for. At Edward Jones, 422,102 job applicants vied for 1,182 job openings.

In addition to being able to hire the cream of the crop, these companies enjoy low employee turnover that reduces recruiting and training expenditures. Turnover for number 48 on the *Fortune* list, SAS Institute, has never exceeded 5%—remarkable anywhere, but even more so in an industry where turnover averages 20%. SAS saves about $85 million a year in recruiting, training, and other turnover-related costs, while spending considerably less than $75 million on benefits. What's more, its people are productive and its customers loyal. A 2005 study by the Society for Human Resource Management reported that 18% of all employees change jobs each year. And companies spend about 1.5 times employees' salaries replacing them, according to Spherion, a recruiting and staffing company based in Fort Lauderdale, Florida.

So how does all this relate to taking care of customers? Remember that employees with years of tenure have had more time to build relationships with customers and become familiar with their preferences. No wonder high turnover annoys customers. They don't relish having to repeatedly start afresh building relationships with recently hired employees. Just as customers feel comfortable dealing with a favorite waiter at a fine restaurant, it's the same in every business—whether someone buys a car, stocks and bonds, or the services of a consulting firm.

Good Pay

Providing a slew of perks at the office is terrific, but it doesn't replace a substantial paycheck. Remember, people spend more time off the job than on, and they want an enjoyable lifestyle away from the office—for both themselves and their families. To make them happy campers, you must provide both a good work environment *and* a good paycheck. It can't be "either or." One without the other doesn't cut the mustard.

Among major full-service brokers, Edward Jones is the only remaining private partnership. Instead of being publicly owned, the firm opened the partnership to its brokers and employees, giving right of ownership in the company to those who meet certain requirements. In the 1960s, Ted Jones began to assume more and more of the leadership of the firm. Under his guidance, the firm enjoyed a period of rapid expansion, and by the early 1970s it had become a sizable regional securities firm. In 1974, Ted transformed the family-owned business into a limited partnership through which employees could acquire ownership in the company. Jones thought those who contributed to Edward Jones' success should be its owners. Partners would be financial advisors, branch office administrators, and home office associates at all levels. Depending on one's position and performance, an individual could become a limited partner or a general partner. Of an estimated 35,000 Edward Jones employees, about 12,000 are limited partners.

Ted Jones was adamant that the only people permitted to become partners would be those who helped build the company. He believed this so strongly that he did not permit his two sisters to have ownership, and in a heated debate with his father, threatened to quit the company if his siblings were given an interest. His father reluctantly submitted to Ted's wishes, and even now, the company is owned only by those who contribute to building it.

Had Ted Jones elected to sell the company with a public stock offering or to another company, it would have made him one of the richest men in America. Certainly selling at a multiple based on book value or company earnings would have generated a tremendous sum. Instead, he allowed his associates to buy ownership in the company at book value. Likewise, to this day, when a partner cashes out, he or she receives book value. Note that as the company's equity increases, so does each partner's equity position. Back in the late 1990s when offers for the company were up to 10 times book value for the firm, nearly every employee at Edward Jones insisted the firm remain independent as a privately owned business.

Edward Jones is one of America's best companies to work for, *and* it provides opportunities for its people to acquire ownership and enjoy hefty earnings. Based on performance, every associate is eligible to become a limited partner. "When people are owners, they don't act like employees," says Jim Weddle, the company's managing partner. "We want lots of owners in our firm. It makes us happy to share the fruits of ownership." But does offering a great place to work and ownership in the company benefit customers? Evidently so. For the third straight year, in 2007, J.D. Power and Associates ranked Edward Jones as the number one firm for investor satisfaction. Investors satisfied with their investment firms tend to recommend those places to family and friends. Positive word of mouth pays off for firms, and happy, active investors also serve them well. Investors highly committed to their full-service investment firms generate 12 times more new investment dollars per year than do clients with lower commitment, representing $900,000 per account each year in new assets under management, according to the study. They're also more loyal, use additional services, and are more likely to recommend their financial institution, J.D. Power and Associates says.

✳   ✳   ✳

When Dave Liniger started RE/MAX in 1973, he founded his Denver-based company on a concept that eventually revolutionized the real estate industry. His company specializes in seeking out top-producing independent agents who worked for local brokers. The brokers provide a desk, office support, advertising, and so on. A broker with the best reputation generally attracts the top-producing agents in the area. These agents believe the broker's image is the big drawing card, so why not work with the most prestigious firm? In exchange for these services, commissions are split 50-50 between broker and agent.

"An estimated 80% of all agents failed during their first year," Liniger points out, "and a high percentage of the successful remaining 20% would eventually leave a small broker to work for a larger firm. It didn't take long for a top agent to conclude, 'Why should I pay half of my commissions to someone? I'll just start my own company. While I'm at it, I'll put on some agents to help with my overhead and keep 50% of their commissions.' Our concept is radically different. We are more like a co-op. We model our offices after a group of doctors or lawyers who share the expenses of running the business, pay their personal expenses, and keep the vast majority of their income for themselves.

"Our business model means that beginners can't afford to work on this arrangement," Liniger tells. "Our average agent has been in the business for 8 years before joining the RE/MAX organization. Our average agent has 13.8 years experience in the business. This means we don't have the beginner. Instead, we attract an agent who has already been successful. This experienced agent has established a reputation in his community. We have very few beginners without a track record, because we don't know if they have what it takes to succeed or not."

To illustrate why a successful real estate agent would join RE/MAX, Bill Echols, the company's vice president of public relations, tells about his earlier days in the field. "In 1978, my partner and I opened a RE/MAX office in Albuquerque, the first in New Mexico. We were new in the area and didn't know anyone, and no one there knew us. To meet real estate agents, every Sunday I went to open houses, talked to them about their listed house, and handed out my card. It was a very low-key approach, and soon they'd say, 'I've been hearing about RE/MAX, what's the story on it?' So I'd tell them. I was quite impressed with one particular agent, Deanna Dunn, who was working for the number one broker in town. Every weekend that she had an open house, I showed up, and eventually I started talking to her about our company. During the week, we'd have lunch, and while Deanna recognized the advantages of joining RE/MAX, like many people, she did not look forward to making a change.

"She also resisted having to pay a fixed monthly bill rather than simply splitting her commissions with the broker. Like other agents, her fear was that she'd have to shell out money for expenses even during those months when she had no sales. Of course, I explained that over time she'd be many dollars ahead on our arrangement, but she couldn't understand how that could be.

"Finally, I said, 'Okay, Deanna, I'll quit talking to you about RE/MAX.'

" 'Please don't stop telling me about it, Bill.'

" 'I want you to do yourself a favor, Deanna. Go back through every one of your listings and sales that you've made during the past two years. I don't care how long it takes you, but go through all your files. Then, be honest with yourself and figure out where this business came from. Did it come from your broker, or did it come from your personal efforts? I'm curious, so when you've figured it out, please call me with your findings. That's all I want to know.'

" 'I'll do that, Bill.'

"Four days later Deanna called. 'Bill, you are not going to believe this, because I can't believe it myself. Ninety-nine percent of all the business I did during the past two years was all my own doing. My broker had nothing whatsoever to do with it.'

" 'That doesn't surprise me,' I answered. 'So when are you coming over?'

" 'I'll be there next week, and I'm bringing three agents with me!' "

RE/MAX's Mike Reagan, senior vice president, brand marketing, says, "We are not in the real estate business. We are in the business of improving the lives of real estate professionals." By providing an opportunity that allows real estate agents to make more money, the company has been a huge success. Today, there are more than 120,000 RE/MAX agents worldwide.

✳　✳　✳

Toyota had long established a reputation for reliable, sturdy cars and trucks when it introduced the Lexus in 1989. Former group vice president Bob Carter explains: "It took everyone by surprise when we came out with a luxury car. This marked a first for a Japanese company. The media banter was that an Asian manufacturer couldn't compete with European manufacturers designing this kind of car. Back then, our top vehicle was the Cressida. People who were attracted to Toyota products walked in and became loyal customers, but then a significant number left us because we didn't have a vehicle positioned in the luxury arena.

"Our goal was to take what we knew from making Toyota cars and produce the world's finest product," Carter continues. "Our research with car owners in this market revealed that their traditional values were based on performance, content, size, and other qualities associated with luxury goods in general. Our intention was to carve a niche within the high-end market by adding attributes not typically associated with luxury goods, attributes that would set Lexus apart from the competition. So in addition to high-level luxury features such as smooth ride, comfort, and quality, we'd provide a high level of durability. But our real differentiator would be a high level of personalized service that would assure maximum customer satisfaction. We were committed to creating a brand based on what we at Lexus refer to as the customer experience. It wouldn't happen overnight, but that was our goal. The Japanese have a word for it, *kaizen*, a philosophy that dictates constant improvement. We would continually strive for perfection, a target that can never be achieved."

In 1987, David Wilson signed a letter of intent with the company, making him one of the first Lexus dealers. His dealership opened in Orange County, California, in the autumn of 1989 when the 1990 model was introduced. At the time, Wilson owned the number two Toyota dealership in the United States.

Wilson is an only-in-America success story. Raised on a farm in Iowa, he was 14 when his family first installed indoor plumbing. He inherited a strong work ethic from his father, who, after his day job at the John Deere factory, devoted his weekends to working the family farm. "Growing up on a farm in Iowa was a wonderful experience," Wilson says. "You observe what happens when you plant in the spring and you can reap in the fall. It teaches you to dream and set a goal, because even though you can't see the corn, if you plow in the spring, harrow in June, and there's rain in July, and you detassel in September, come October, you're going to have a crop. So I learned you must have a plan, and if you work that plan, with a little bit of luck, you'll get corn—either a little or a lot, depending upon the weather. It's not all subject to whim or fancy—you have to have a plan. It reminds me of a sea captain whose ship pulls out of the harbor in New York and plans to arrive in a French harbor in seven days. The captain's goal is to get from here to there, and when his voyage starts, he can't see anything but water. It's like that for seven days, but if he does this and that on Monday, Tuesday, and the rest of the week, come Saturday morning when the sun comes up, he's going to be looking at the French harbor. Even though he couldn't see it for seven days, if he works his plan, he'll eventually reach his destination. This is what happens when you have a plan."

The oldest of five children, Wilson saw his mother work full-time to set aside money to pay for each child's tuition for the first year of college. "Mom wanted us to have some exposure to college," Wilson tells. "I liked my freshman year and was determined to get a degree. I worked my way through my first two years by pumping gas, selling shoes, and later working at a car dealership that paid $5 an hour, three times the minimum wage I had been earning. The dealership had a contract with the local telephone company to wash its vans inside and out and to change the oil and filter on a regular basis. The telephone company had Ford Econoline vans that had the engine between the two seats. After I washed them, I'd put the van up on the hoist, drain the oil, lower it back down, and change the filter while I put in five quarts of oil. A few months into this job, I got in a hurry and neglected to put the drain plug back in and drove the van to the telephone company. The next day, the driver drove the van with no oil in it, and the engine fried. Today, we wouldn't expect an employee to pay for the damage, it would be just the cost of doing business, but back in 1968, the dealer held me responsible.

"'How do you intend to pay for the damages?' my boss asked me.

"'You can take out half of the $100 I make each week,' I said.

"We did that for two weeks and then I told him that we had to work out another arrangement. 'I am my sole support,' I told him. 'I can't live on half of what I make. You're open seven days a week, 18 hours a day, and I only have 16 hours of classes. So let me be a salesman.' The guy liked me and put me on the floor. I was the dealership's top salesman my first month, and for the next two and a half years, I sold cars. When I graduated, I became his sales manager."

In 1971, Wilson moved to Phoenix to take a job as a car salesman at a Lincoln-Mercury dealership, where, six years later, he received a 25% equity position. "While I had a 25% interest in the Phoenix dealership, the senior partner never respected me as a minority stockholder. I vowed that some day when I was in a position to offer an interest in my business, I'd treat him the way I would want to be treated."

In 1982, Wilson migrated to Orange, California, and this time he became a 25% owner in Toyota of Orange. His agreement with the majority owner gave him the right of first refusal. Since the 67-year-old owner was in poor health, as general manager, Wilson ran the business. Within six months after assuming its management, the dealership's monthly profits jumped from $25,000 to $250,000, and within two years it became the sixth largest Toyota dealership in the United States. This caught the attention of Toyota's top management. With a contract that had built-in salary increases based on performance, Wilson saw his annual earnings bolt to $1 million. In 1985, Wilson was able to buy the remaining 75% interest in the dealership.

The Orange County Toyota dealership became the company's second largest, and at this writing, Wilson owns 15 dealerships that consist of six Toyotas, three Lexus, three Hondas, and one Acura, Mazda, and Ford dealership that in total generate revenues in excess of $2 billion. "Every one of my dealerships has a 25% partner," Wilson stresses, "and none of them has ever had to put in any money. All of our growth has come from within. I've created a lot of millionaires, and, in fact, make that multimillionaires. I treat them as if they're majority partners. Had I been treated this way, I'd still be working for the guy in Phoenix selling Lincoln and Mercury cars."

In June 2006, Wilson opened a new Lexus dealership in Newport Beach, California, which, at a cost of $75 million for the land and building, is said to be the most expensive automobile dealership in the United States. A one-purpose building, with a Mercedes-Benz dealership right down the street and with every other major brand within a 10-mile radius, Wilson's investment represents his tremendous faith in Lexus. "I am financing the property," Wilson says, "and I am personally guaranteeing it. I wouldn't have done this with any other automobile manufacturer, but my 25-year relationship with Toyota makes me believe the company won't let me fail. They can't go out and ask 50 guys to put up this kind of money in land and building and make a car that won't succeed. If the car doesn't do well, the company will do something different. It gets back to the company's commitment to *kaizen*. Toyota keeps coming up with better products. I remember back in '86 when my Toyota dealership sold 3,900 new trucks and 3,600 cars. Those were little trucks, the 8100 model, which were a lot of people's second cars or their kids' first cars. A small business owner had a fleet of five or six of them and he drove a Mercedes or a BMW. Those same small truck owners who bought luxury cars were putting 150,000 miles on their Toyotas and they didn't require any maintenance. None. You hardly had to change the oil. They just kept on going. Their reliability was legendary. Now those same owners know that Lexus is a luxury car that will give them the same performance. We don't sell vehicles per se. We sell transportation. This is why I have so much faith in Lexus. We're in the luxury transportation business."

Bob Carter emphasizes that Lexus can't succeed unless its dealers do. "The traditional thinking in the industry has long been that the lower the number of dealerships an automaker has, the fewer cars that will be sold," the automobile executive explains. "However, our business model was to have a relatively small number of dealers, and today, we have 182 owner locations with 223 total rooftops, meaning some dealers have more than one location. As a comparison, in 1989, Mercedes-Benz and BMW had an estimated 400 to 450 dealerships each. Today, they have 325 to 350 dealers. We have by far the smallest number, and even now, some states don't have a single dealership. Our dealers are responsible for a larger geographical area, and today they are the industry's highest in revenues per dealership in vehicle sales and service sales. They also enjoy the highest return on their investment. That's our business model. We want them to make a lot of money, because when they do, they can provide more amenities and service than other car dealers. It all passes on to the customer. This enhances our brand's reputation. The Lexus Division success is dependent on our dealers' success."

Who Comes First, the Employee or the Customer?

A wise old man once said, "Happy wife makes happy life." This same advice could apply to companies that strive for high customer satisfaction and long-term loyalty. A happy employee makes a happy customer. As we mentioned earlier, when Kmart customers sensed the retailer's employees were unhappy, they defected en masse to other stores.

There are times when a company has its customers' interests in mind and acts with good intentions yet fails to recognize its actions might inadvertently upset its employees. This happened in mid-2006 when Macy's introduced a dress code requiring employees at its East Coast stores to wear black. Pinstripe suits were allowed, but the stripe had to be thin and only in one color—black. Employees in the casual wear departments were permitted to wear black denim. The objective was to make it easy for customers to identify sales clerks, even from a distance, and know whom to ask for help.

Since the number of department store salespeople on the floor has drastically reduced in recent years, we all know how difficult it is to track an associate down when looking for service, so the dress code seemed like a good idea at the time. Customers and management loved having store associates on the floor dressed in black. The problem was, the employees themselves didn't like it. The new dress code required them to buy more clothes, and even with steep store discounts, having to put together an entire wardrobe in black posed a financial burden for these modestly paid store employees. This was especially true for part-time help. One national analyst said the dress code could make it difficult for Macy's to hire part-time temporary help during the Christmas shopping season because of the added expense. It also meant long-time employees could no longer wear many of their favorite outfits. Even female employees who loved black clothing didn't want to wear it every day. Apparently, variety is the spice of life. And what happens when black is no longer in fashion? As everyone in the fashion industry knows, styles (and colors) change. Still another problem is that when employees begin to think of their black outfits as uniforms, they'll start disliking their everyday clothes, and this will cause them to buy fewer black outfits. As a result, over time they will wear the same "uniforms" every day, and these clothes will become frayed and worn. This is not the image a company wants its employees to present.

With its focus on improving customer service, Macy's did not anticipate the negative reaction the dress code could generate with its employees. Management was focused on helping customers find someone to serve them, indeed a fine objective. However, in its zeal to take care of its customers, Macy's failed to ask its salespeople how they felt about wearing black clothes. Had the company asked and listened, it could have been quickly known: the staff would balk. With this knowledge, Macy's would have a choice. Should it enforce the dress code so that customers can more readily identify sales associates? Or should the modus operandi be abandoned because employees opposed it? We think the dress code was doomed before it was started. While the benefits to the customer were obvious, employee ire negated the advantages.

We feel Macy's failed to address the real problem that its shoppers have. There simply aren't enough salespeople on the floor to serve them!

✳   ✳   ✳

Bill Pulte is founder and chairman of Pulte Homes, one of the nation's largest home builders, a company selling around 25,000 homes each year. Pulte puts it in perspective when he says that his company has three audiences: customers, shareholders, and employees. "Our employees are our number one consideration," he emphasizes. "When we get the right people, and we give them the right training and support, good results follow from the other two groups. However, if we focus only on customers or only on shareholders and don't have the right employees, we can't sustain what we're working to accomplish. It starts with the employees. When we do that right, our efforts with our customers and shareholders fall into place."

By treating Pulte people right, the company has kept its customers and shareholders happy. In 2004, Pulte Homes received J.D. Powers and Associate's inaugural Platinum Award for Excellence in Customer Satisfaction. It was 1950 when Bill Pulte built his first home, a $10,000 Detroit bungalow, and in 2007 a customer bought the five hundred thousandth Pulte home. The shareholders have done well too. Pulte Homes has been named several times to *BusinessWeek*'s 50 Best Performing Companies.

✳   ✳   ✳

Howard Schultz, CEO of Starbucks, likes to say, "We're not in the coffee business serving people. We are in the people business serving coffee."

It helps that people doing the serving are well treated. Staff turnover is lower at Starbucks than at similar establishments, not least because the company provides full health benefits for even part-time workers. In fact, it spends more on health care than on coffee.

Promoting from Within

One of the most demoralizing blows to employees occurs when a company fills senior and middle management positions with outsiders. Not only is this a sign that the company failed to build its people, its workforce is put on notice that no matter how hard anyone works, he or she can advance only so far within the organization. Be assured that this doesn't happen in a Dave Wilson dealership. "We don't hire sales managers and general managers," Wilson stresses. "We hire salespeople. Every general manager starts with us as a salesperson. It doesn't matter what job you've had before. If you are going to be with our company, you start by selling in the showroom. We have a chain. You move from sales to finance and insurance, which involves the paperwork completion part of a deal. Next you go to the sales desk and then to general sales manager, and in this position, you attend dealer candidate academy. It takes 8 to 12 years and when you're ready, we find a dealership for you. As a dealer, you become a 25% partner and never have to put a dime into it."

Wilson's two sons-in-law are general managers and partners at two Wilson-owned dealerships in Scottsdale, Arizona. Both are college graduates, one a University of Indiana law school graduate. "Both fellows wanted to be in the car business," Wilson says, "and they started by selling cars for several years. Neither one ever complained. They both understand a saying that's often repeated around here, 'The bigger the foundation, the taller the building.' My daughters asked me, 'How come when we have a picnic this Sunday, our husbands have to work?' My stock answer is, 'Well, because for six years my day off was Wednesday. That's why.' If I treated my sons-in-law differently than our other employees, not only would it hurt them, it would hurt the morale of all our employees."

It's the same at Edward Jones. While earning his MBA, for two years John Bachmann worked as a summer intern there. After his 1962 graduation, he accepted a staff position, and the following year he opened a broker's office in Columbia, Missouri. He spent seven years there before returning to the St. Louis home office as a principal with responsibility for fixed-income product marketing. After Bachmann earned a series of promotions, Ted Jones announced that Bachmann would succeed him as managing partner. Today's managing partner, Jim Weddle, also started his career with Edward Jones as an intern in 1976 while working on his MBA, and he too worked as a financial advisor, running his own office in Connersville, Indiana, before returning seven years later to the home office to assume a management position in sales training—at the age of 30. Like Bachmann, Weddle worked in several areas of the company before being named managing partner in late 2005. The firm's only other managing partner besides Edward Jones and Ted Jones was Douglas Hill, who briefly held the position after Bachmann stepped down in January 2003 and until Weddle replaced him. Hill also had a successful broker's office, having spent 10 years in Dodge City, Kansas, before taking charge of the firm's first formalized training program for financial advisors. He later headed the firm's sales and marketing division for 16 years.

In addition to learning the business from the ground up, all of Edward Jones' top leaders have spent years personally working directly with investors. No one can accuse Edward Jones managers of working in ivory towers far removed from the client. Every financial advisor knows it's possible for him or her to some day head the firm, for unlike many other investment firms, Edward Jones doesn't routinely seek senior management from outside. Many of its leaders are home-grown employees who excel and work their way to top echelons of the organization. So, in addition to being one of the best places in America to work, Edward Jones also offers exceptional opportunities for advancement.

✳   ✳   ✳

When a job opens at Caesars Entertainment (formerly Harrah's Entertainment), employees are given the opportunity to apply for the position prior to the company recruiting someone from the outside. Ron Beronio, former director of recruiting, explains, "We'd post the position on bulletin boards and on our internal Web site, so any interested employee can apply. Only if we didn't find a qualified internal person did we look elsewhere."

Tom Jenkin has been president of the gaming company's Western Division since 2004. Jenkin signed on with the company in 1975 as a fry cook at Harrah's flagship hotel on the Strip in Las Vegas. Jenkin worked at many entry and lower-level positions with the company prior to moving into middle management and eventually advancing up the corporate ladder. Now in a senior position, he identifies with employees working in many different areas of the company.

Similar success stories can be found at Four Seasons. Rob Hagelberg started his career with the company as a front desk manager in Palm Beach. Today, he is hotel manager of the Four Seasons hotel in Westlake Village. "I believe that the opportunity to be promoted by hard work and desire is a key strength for Four Seasons," Hagelberg says with pride.

An ARG study reveals that 88% *of Americans think it hurts morale when their company hires a manager from the outside versus promoting somebody from within to the position.* "It makes us feel that no matter how hard we work, we won't be rewarded for it" was the most common statement expressed to ARG interviewers.

Bring in the Customers

Johnson & Johnson's Remicade is a biomedicine that treats several immune mediated inflammatory diseases, including rheumatoid arthritis. Back in the early 1990s, a clinical physician filmed the progress of one of his patients being treated by the medicine. One member of the clinical research team recalls seeing the video. "It showed a young woman who could barely walk down stairs. Then, she was filmed walking down the same steps two weeks later, and again in another two weeks after taking her first two infusions of Remicade. It was remarkable. I hardly believed it was the same woman. Later on, she actually pranced down those steps. The corresponding data confirmed that her joints had vastly improved. These initial tests demonstrated that Remicade worked on rheumatoid arthritis and showed an acute benefit." At the time it was not known how long benefits from the drug might last, but the results encouraged the team of scientists and others who had labored on Remicade's development for years. The video confirmed their hard work was not in vain.

Remo Colarusso, Johnson & Johnson's vice president in charge of worldwide manufacturing, says that the company regularly invites patients to talk to a group of employees to describe their response to a particular medicine. "We generally assemble in the cafeteria," Colarusso says. "These informal talks reinforce how important our work is. One girl in her early teens came from Texas, accompanied by her parents, to tell us she had been stricken by rheumatoid arthritis when she was 11 years old. An early symptom was that she had dislocated her hip after merely getting up from a sofa. Not only was it painful, she could barely walk and it sapped her energy. She explained that she loved to sing and wanted to someday be a professional singer. Then the girl told us her doctor had put her on Remicade. 'I was wheeled into the hospital on a Sunday,' she said, 'and after having my first infusion, by Tuesday, I was doing aerobics.' She talked about how she now is able to do everything and has since released two music albums. Her father gave me a big bear hug, and said, 'Thank you for what you've done for my daughter.'"

In January 1999, a few months after the Food and Drug Administration (FDA) approved Remicade to treat Crohn's disease, Joe Scodari, former head of Johnson & Johnson's pharmaceuticals business, says he received a telephone call. "'Mr. Scodari, I want to thank you for what you did for my younger brother. He's 27 years old and has had Crohn's disease since he was 19. He hadn't had a firm bowel movement for nine years. He couldn't control his bowels and always had to be near a bathroom. Anywhere he went—out with friends, to a restaurant, at a movie, anywhere—he had to stay close to the bathroom. Until he started Remicade, it was impossible for him to live a normal life. Thank you for helping my brother live a normal life.'" Scodari relates this telephone conversation again and again with Johnson & Johnson employees. "Hearing a story about how one of our products benefits a patient lets all of us know how important our work is. This is why we bring patients in to talk to our drug reps, scientists, and plant workers. It is one thing to work on a medicine in the lab, and quite another to hear firsthand from a patient who has benefited from it. Putting a face on a patient is far better than quoting a statistic."

✳   ✳   ✳

Based in Dallas, Texas, Mary Kay was founded by Mary Kay Ash in 1963, and today there are more than 1.7 million Independent Beauty Consultants in well over 30 global markets. These Beauty Consultants purchase Mary Kay products at wholesale from the company and sell them at retail to millions of consumers. Mary Kay's son, Richard Rogers, the company's executive chairman, explains, "The Beauty Consultants are our customers. They are independent contractors, and they, in turn, sell to end consumers."

According to Rhonda Shasteen, senior vice president of corporate brand strategy and sales support, Mary Kay sells two things to its customers—products and a business opportunity. "Each Independent Beauty Consultant is self-employed, and her business income is derived primarily from the profit on her personal sales of Mary Kay products. However, she may also be entitled to a commission calculated on the wholesale value of products purchased from Mary Kay Inc. by other independent contractors whom she has introduced to the Mary Kay opportunity.

The company often offers women within the independent sales force the opportunity to tell their success stories at company-sponsored events. (In fact, outside speakers are rarely brought in.) Such testimonies happen regularly at small meetings held by members of the independent sales force. On a larger scale, five back-to-back conventions known as Seminars are held in Dallas during the summer. Each runs for three days and can have as many as 10,000 people in attendance. Altogether about 50,000 of the independent sales force attend from across the United States and around the world. Annual Seminars are also held in other countries where the company does business. To motivate audience members just getting started in the business or needing a pep talk, successful Independent Sales Directors deliver inspirational speeches about their personal achievements. In the world of Mary Kay, these personal profiles are known as "I stories." One speaker's story tells that she considered herself an extreme introvert before becoming a Mary Kay Independent Beauty Consultant, and now, lo and behold, in less than one year, she addresses a huge audience with total self-confidence. Another relates how her success in her Mary Kay business allowed her husband to leave a career he despised. Some stories tell of single mothers struggling to support their families while working traditional jobs as assistants, nurses, and teachers. Becoming a Beauty Consultant has allowed them to enjoy extra incomes, and with the flexible hours this business offers, they can schedule their work around their children's needs. "I can personally send my kids off to school each morning, attend little league games and school plays, pick them up after school, and at the same time, make money," one speaker tells.

✳   ✳   ✳

Having customers talk to employees about their positive experiences using a product or having received excellent service is something every company can do. Lexus sends its dealers to visit its plants in the United States and Japan so factory workers can hear firsthand that their fine workmanship is appreciated. Owners of fine restaurants invite guests to visit the kitchen to thank the chef and his staff for preparing and serving an exceptional meal. A number of companies do this, and every company can. It's an easy and effective way to reinforce to people that their work is appreciated.

A Matter of Integrity

Many companies talk about their values and beliefs, but exceptional companies incorporate them into the very fabric of the organization. As Ralph Waldo Emerson wrote, "What you do speaks so loud I cannot hear what you say." Your employees watch you, and they judge you by your actions rather than the slogan on your wall. In recent years, in the highest echelons of major companies, we've witnessed many business leaders motivated by greed. To cash in on high-priced stock options and justify multi-million-dollar bonuses, they have misstated corporate financial data to hide losses and exaggerate profits for personal gain. Some have traded securities in their own companies, profiting from inside information unavailable to the public. In doing so, they have put their self-interest ahead of their shareholders. These individuals in leadership positions have violated the trust investors and employees had put in them. As a consequence, hundreds of thousands of employees have lost their jobs at major companies such as Enron, Tyco, Global Crossing, Adelphia, WorldCom, and Arthur Andersen. Many of these employees have also lost some or all of their savings from retirement plans. Imagine the resulting morale of the people who continue to be employed by these companies. How humiliating to have to defend the misdeeds of their company leaders to their families and friends.

Most leaders are not involved in scandals, but there are still far too many who, while abiding by the letter of the law, are guilty of behavior that taints their company's reputation. We have heard many employees express feelings of shame because their companies make shoddy products, provide poor customer service, or don't honor their warranties. What do employees think about working for a company that makes false claims in its advertising? Or a company that encourages its salespeople to oversell, unfairly knock a competitor, or pressure customers to buy more than they can afford? Companies promoting these tactics ultimately gain bad reputations, and their employees feel it's a reflection on their own character in the eyes of the general public. At the very least, these employees feel less pride in working for such companies. As one Lexus employee told us, "When I worked for [another automaker], I used to be embarrassed to hand out my business card, but here at Lexus, I'm proud to give it to everyone."

No question, working for a company known for its integrity is a source of pride to its workforce. In Chapter 1, we talked about a company's mission statements, and saw that great companies like Johnson & Johnson survey its employees to make sure its credo is being adhered to. More recently, Lexus, since its founding in 1989, has hired people who are committed to what is now known as the Lexus Covenant:

> *Lexus will enter the most competitive, prestigious automobile*
> *race in the world.*
> *Over 50 years of Toyota automotive experience has culminated*
> *in the creation of Lexus cars.*
> *They will be the finest cars ever built.*
> *Lexus will win the race because Lexus will do it right from the*
> *start.*
> *Lexus will have the finest dealer network in the industry.*
> *Lexus will treat each customer as we would a guest in our home.*
> *If you think you can't, you won't...*
> *If you think you can, you will!*
> *We can, we will.*

The Lexus Covenant is uncomplicated and concise. It is not a clever slogan created by a public relations committee; this statement, proclaimed when Lexus was in its infancy, has ever since been the basis for every decision the company makes, from cars designed with the driver in mind to dealers who make customer satisfaction their most important goal. "Every single person in this organization has the Lexus Covenant on his or her desk," says Nancy Fein, the division's former vice president of customer satisfaction, the position she now holds with the Toyota Division. "It's on a card they carry in their wallet. It's at the front door when you walk into our headquarters. When we hire young people at our call center, they can recite it by heart. It's what we live by and breathe. It isn't just a bunch of words. It's all about the best product, the best dealers, and the best customer experience in the industry."

The company demonstrated quickly that its covenant was more than idle words. "When we came out with the first Lexus," Fein explains, "we heard two customer complaints—problems with the rear-window brake light and a sticky cruise control. At the time, we had an estimated 8,000 such cars on the road when our people met to decide what should be done. The consensus was: We either stick by our word or we don't, and the problems were fixed immediately. But it wasn't just the cars of the two customers who complained. We did a recall on all 8,000 cars on the road. Every customer was personally contacted. We brought in mechanics from Japan and along with our people in the U.S., more than 300 Lexus people went out to see those customers. On many occasions they actually repaired cars in the customer's driveway. Our service people also washed and gassed their cars. And when cars were returned to customers, we apologized profusely for the inconvenience. Now generally, a recall is a negative in this industry, but the way we did it, those customers became more loyal and supportive of Lexus than before the problem. The company's swift, decisive action sent a message to our employees and dealers: Lexus was going to do business according to its covenant. And to this day, nearly 20 years later, we react the same way when a problem occurs."

When the company launched the 2007 Lexus IS, the 250 IS models had a problem with the accelerator pedal on the all-wheel drive. Because the accelerator was shaped differently than it was on the rear-wheel drive, there was a possibility it could get caught on the carpet. Although no incidences were reported in the United States, the company made the decision to recall every IS. Most of these customers were first-time Lexus owners, and the company was anxious to get off to a good start with them. "We brought them all in," Fein says, "and like we always do, we washed the cars and filled up their tanks. And to show our sincerity to our brand-new customers, we sent a $200 iPod Nano to each of them. The iPod has the name Lexus on it and connects directly to their vehicle. We apologized for the inconvenience we caused them and said, 'Welcome to the Lexus family.' As a side note, I didn't have a single complaint about that condition in my call center, but piles of thank you letters came in. It's all about putting the customer first. That's our company's philosophy based on the Lexus covenant. It permeates everything we do. Yes, there will always be problems. It's how you react that counts."

Using the Company's Products

If the product is good, make it available to your employees. We can think of no better way to sell them on its merits. We think the company that does this best is Four Seasons. Each employee goes through an initial orientation program that ends with a complimentary stay in the hotel. "It's called a familiarization stay," explains Ellen du Bellay, vice president of learning and development. "Every new employee, from chef to parking lot attendant, is eligible for free lodging. Many employees who work at Four Seasons properties in such places as Bangkok, Damascus, and Jakarta would never otherwise be able to afford a room at a five-star hotel.

During their stay, they receive the same VIP treatment given to every hotel guest. Through the company's complimentary room night policy, after six months' employment, every employee is entitled to 3 free nights at any available Four Seasons hotel in the chain, and after his or her first anniversary with the company, 5 free nights. After two years, it's 7 nights a year, and after five years, 10 nights. Twenty-plus year veterans are entitled to 20 free nights a year. During their stays, employees receive a 50% discount on food and beverages. All-expense-paid trips are awarded to employees of the month, and managers of the month, quarter, and year. Winners of these awards receive free airfare, plus a spending allowance.

"Having our employees stay free at our hotels is all a part of who we are," says du Bellay. "We want them to appreciate the customer experience. We think it will enable them to better serve our guests and give them pride in what they do."

Du Bellay points out that every Four Seasons has a Heart of the House, an employee cafeteria located in the back of the hotel. "The surroundings are nice and comfortable," she explains. "We serve free meals, and that food is prepared the same as the food we serve our customers, and it is prepared by the same chefs that serve our guests. Each hotel also has employee appreciation events that are either monthly or quarterly. At these events, managers serve the employees or do other special things. Each hotel has a children's party, usually a Christmas event with Santa Claus, games, and a gift for every child. There is also an employee party that includes music and dancing. These are only a few of the opportunities for employees to be a guest at their hotel.

"In some countries, the developer of a new hotel has shown us plans and said, 'This is management's dining room and this dining room will be for employees.' We always reply, 'No, we won't have two dining rooms. We'll have one room and everyone sits in the same room.' The fact that we don't have a hierarchy comes as a shock to some people; still, we will not compromise on that, even if it means not doing a deal."

✳   ✳   ✳

Cabela's, the Sidney, Nebraska–based direct marketer and specialty retailer of hunting, fishing, camping, and related outdoor merchandise, is hailed as the World's Foremost Outfitter. A vast majority of its employees are outdoor enthusiasts, and a company program encourages them to field-test its products. "We have a saying," explains Michael Callahan, a former senior vice president of business development and international operations. "If it's not good enough for us to use, it's not good enough.

Period. We encourage employees to field-test Cabela's merchandise, and in particular, our own Cabela's brand products. This applies to everything we stock. For example, an employee can check out a thousand-dollar pair of Swarovski binoculars so he can understand how to use them. Yes, they have to bring the binoculars back, but we feel it's important for them to personally know the product so they can speak with authority when they talk to a customer."

"We require them to submit field-test reports," adds Dennis Highby, Cabela's president and chief executive officer. "We encourage them to take brand-new merchandise right out of stock, use it, and, yes, get it dirty. We just ask that they complete the field-test reports in a timely manner. We want them to know what they're selling."

While it's good for morale to give free merchandise and services to employees, at the very least, we believe a company should give its employees a generous discount when they buy its products. By using the products, they become more familiar with what you sell, and second, they can say to a customer with conviction, "Yes, I use it." It also enhances employee loyalty. An ARG survey uncovers that *75.7% of employees who receive a discount express it boosts their morale.* Some said that it shows the company cares for them, and others went as far as to say that it makes them feel special, like family.

3

The Company Culture

At some companies, their culture is an internal matter, off-limits to outsiders. At others, it's acknowledged but given minimum attention. Each of the 14 companies we visited regards its culture as an integral part of its everyday affairs. It's who they are and what they stand for.

For the record, a company's culture isn't decided by a committee when somebody suggests: "We ought to have one." On the contrary, it evolves over a period of time and becomes a chemistry that makes the organization go. We view it as the character of an organization, much like a person's character, and similarly, company cultures run the gamut. A company's culture traces back to its early roots, starting with its founder. Over time, however, it may change when different key people come and go, with some leaving a lasting mark. A company's culture may also change by the collective beliefs of individuals. A majority of today's management gurus place much credence on the widespread influence a company's culture projects both internally and externally.

The best-managed companies celebrate their heritage, letting all employees know how the company was founded, accentuating the values and principles of its founder(s). This emphasis instills a source of pride in their people, akin to national patriotism. Early on, for example, American schoolchildren are indoctrinated with stories about our nation's founding fathers. Our history books expound the courageous pioneers who sailed across the ocean to the New World, driven by a desire for religious freedom and a spirit of adventure. Tribute is paid to the brave men who signed the Declaration of Independence, a document that declared war against the British, then the world's most powerful nation. Inking one's signature was analogous to signing one's death warrant—failure to defeat the British meant that every signer would surely be hanged, cut, and quartered. We rejoice in living in a land founded on the premise that grants each of us the right to life, liberty, and the pursuit of happiness. Our nation is rich with heritage that makes us rejoice to be Americans.

Good managers also enlighten employees. Yet, according to a study we conducted, *42.2% of American workers do not know when or how their company was started.* We relate this to living in a country where its citizens are uninformed with no knowledge of its history. In the same study, *46.8% said that nobody had ever taken the time to inform them about the company's founder and his or her early inspirations and ambitions.* Then there are other cases when companies are acquired or merged together and people are let go. In such situations, it may be that the surviving management team intentionally chose to play down its "former" history. That could very well be a major mistake. However, in those cases where there has been no merger or acquisition, we think this approach is sheer negligence.

The same survey revealed that *25% of the American workforce doesn't think their company is committed to its employees.* With one out of four Americans thinking that they work for a company that has no loyalty to them, we concluded that these people are unlikely to have any loyalty to their employers. We believe this situation violates everything about having a customer-service hierarchy.

When the survey asked participants if their companies give people a chance for job advancement, *25.2% said that they are working in a dead-end job.* How's that for taking the wind out of a person's sails! It's a sad commentary that one out of four people is going to work knowing he or she has no chance for a better job. You can bet that they only go through the motions, doing just enough to keep their jobs. As a consequence, they have no incentive to serve customers. They are strictly there to collect a paycheck.

The survey also revealed that *10% of all Americans believed that their company culture made no demands on treating customers with respect.* On the surface, 10% may sound low, but we find it hard to fathom that a company founder did not institute a policy from the beginning declaring that the customer always comes first. We believe this should be the essence of a company's existence. The survey showed that *24.3% of the participants said that their company culture did not call for them to consider serving the customer above and beyond the call of duty*. This situation suggests that such a company is willing to accept mediocrity as its norm.

Upon reviewing the surveys taken on company cultures, it came as no surprise to learn that *48.3% of Americans believe that their employers place profits ahead of everything else*. It's a sad commentary that so many employees are convinced that making a profit is their company's number one priority. This response implies that they think their employer would reduce quality of product and service to enhance their bottom line.

This chapter highlights companies with cultures that place a high priority on treating customers well, and how it ultimately contributes to a healthy bottom line.

The Founder's Legacy

It's hard to fathom that 42.2% of the American workforce doesn't know when or how their company was founded. We believe companies that don't communicate this information to their employees fail to take advantage of a potentially valuable tool, one that can be used not only to motivate employees but to create strong customer loyalty. An example of one that does is Mary Kay, the renowned Dallas-based cosmetics company founded by Mary Kay Ash in 1963. Currently, there are more than 1.7 million Mary Kay Independent Beauty Consultants in well over 30 global markets who have their own Mary Kay business, and their numbers are increasing exponentially year after year. By the time the company celebrates its fiftieth anniversary, its sales force could be 2 million strong. Although Mary Kay Ash died in 2001 at age 83, her legacy lives on. It will continue in years to come, in part, because Mary Kay's corporate leadership team has been perceptive to keeping the founder's heartwarming life's story known. Consequently, women around the world are drawn to the company to both use and sell its high-quality skin care and color cosmetics products.

What makes the story such a good one is that the life and times of Mary Kay Ash are inspiring and wholesome. It's a tale about a woman who was driven by a desire to help other women believe in themselves and aspire to achieve their maximum potential. Her success illustrates how a woman coming from modest means can realize considerable wealth and fame, even after starting late in life. At age 45, Ash had retired after a 25-year career in direct sales. Soon thereafter, the energetic mother of three started her own company. And as they say, the rest is history. Having lived her life to the fullest, Ash has since served as a role model to millions of aspiring women.

Mary Kay Ash was a smart, attractive, five-foot, two-inch blonde with a dynamic personality. She radiated enthusiasm. A gifted speaker, she charmed and excited large audiences that attended the company's annual Seminars held in Dallas every summer dating back to the company's first anniversary in 1964. Ash recruited her son, Richard Rogers, then 20 years old, to handle the business end of the company while she sold, recruited, and taught others how to sell her line of skin care products. The company had a humble beginning and one that was based on the principle "the more you give, the more you receive." The business was profitable from the start, generating $198,000 in wholesale sales in its first year. Sales climbed to $800,000 in the company's second year. Ash built her company around her desire to enrich women's lives. She did it by giving lots of recognition, motivation, and support, and by providing excellent financial opportunities.

Mary Kay's first name is instantly recognizable when mentioned, as are only a handful of famous celebrities such as Elvis, Madonna, and Oprah. No other businessperson's first name has become as identifiable as Mary Kay's. This recognition is remarkable considering that the company does very little advertising. Even so, the company is one of America's most recognizable brand names. This situation can be attributed to the image that Mary Kay, the woman, projected during the course of her career—an inspirational image that carries on to this day.

Ash was dedicated to providing opportunities to the large legion of women who began their own Mary Kay businesses. She was determined that they and future Independent Beauty Consultants would follow in her footsteps after her demise. To assure that this would happen, she wrote her autobiography, *Miracles Happen*, as well as two other books, *Mary Kay on People Management* and *Mary Kay: You Can Have It All*. All three books were instant bestsellers, with the most recent one reaching the number one spot on the *New York Times* Best Seller List. Additionally, her timeless messages are captured in hundreds of hours of video and audiotapes, which she made while enjoying good health. Insightfully, Ash wanted her beliefs shared with future Mary Kay Independent Beauty Consultants. Her message never wavered from the two tenets upon which the company was based. She lived her personal and business life by the

Golden Rule and a philosophy that dictated: God first, family second, and career third. She strongly believed that when a person kept life's priorities in this order, everything else would fall into place.

In 1993, the company opened a Mary Kay museum that was housed at its world headquarters in Dallas. Later in 1995, when the company moved across town to a magnificent new 600,000-square-foot building, the museum was relocated inside a soaring glass lobby. Occupying more than 3,500 square feet, it has become a tourist attraction in its own right in the Dallas area.

Rogers, the company's executive chairman, always joked that his mother saved everything, refusing to discard old possessions. "Someday, we'll have a use for all these," she'd tell him. Perhaps she was thinking ahead, because today, many of those very items are on display at the museum, including an old pan that she used to mix some of the original skin care products. One popular item on exhibit is a large diamond pin in the shape of a bumblebee that Ash personally wore. The reason for the pin's popularity is the story behind it. In speeches, Ash talked about how aerodynamics engineers had studied the bumblebee and concluded that it was simply impossible for it to fly. "Its wings are too weak and its body too heavy for flight," she'd say. "The study showed that the bumblebee could not be airborne. The word got out and everybody knew this—but they forgot to tell the bumblebee, and he went right on flying!" For Ash, the bumblebee was a symbol for the countless women she hoped to help "become all they could be." Ash had replicas made of her diamond bumblebee pin that are still awarded to the star performers in the independent sales force. Consequently, it has become a badge of merit, signifying that those wearing it are indeed VIPs within the independent sales force.

"Our company thinks it's important to let people know what we stand for," explains Yvonne Pendleton, director of corporate heritage at Mary Kay. "The museum is a way of telling our story."

Pendleton recalls that when Mary Kay was listed on *Fortune* magazine's Best Companies list, an accompanying article was very telling. Its premise was that most great companies have three things in common: (1) a founder whose beliefs permeate the organization; (2) a larger purpose as its mission; and (3) its people having fun at what they do. "Mary Kay was truly an inspirational leader whose mission was always about more than cosmetics. And, as she would frequently say," Pendleton points out, "'Laugh at yourself, have some fun.' It was as if the article was describing our company."

According to an ARG study, Mary Kay has a clear understanding about the importance in keeping the Mary Kay Ash legacy intact.

A recent study reveals that *71% of Americans want to do business with a company that has a worthy heritage and promotes the founder's legacy tracing back to the company's infancy.* We believe that many Wal-Mart customers are loyal to this day because they had positive feelings toward its founder, Sam Walton. Wendy's customers have similar feelings toward its founder, Dave Thomas, who came across in television commercials as a sincere and humble man.

Doing What's Good for the Customer

Our research shows that those company cultures focused on serving the customer usually trace back to the founder's beliefs, and years later after management has changed, these bedrock values remain intact. Undoubtedly it helps if the company maintains well-organized archives and its history is repeatedly communicated to its people. Otherwise, no matter how principled its founder was, over time his or her virtue will become unknown.

By delving into company founders' personalities, we discovered that while they were determined and ambitious, it was not the desire for wealth that motivated them. On the contrary, they were preoccupied with a desire to provide a value or service to their customers. We believe this is a good lesson for "wannabe" entrepreneurs. Too often, we hear young people say, "I want to start a company because I want to be rich." As numerous case studies of successful people reveal, obtaining wealth is a wrong reason for starting a business. Good business objectives are focused on what one can do for the customer, not one's personal gain. And if providing value to the customer is achieved, profits and eventual wealth will follow as a by-product.

Isadore Sharp was only 25 when, in 1960, he opened the Four Seasons Motor Hotel in Toronto, the forerunner to Four Seasons Hotels and Resorts. His first location was on Jarvis Street, one of the city's main thoroughfares and not far from the central downtown area. At the time, Sharp was a building contractor, a business he learned starting at an early age having worked for his father, a Polish immigrant, who owned a plastering contracting company. "I spent much of my high school and college days working part-time as a laborer doing carpentry, laying pipes, doing small electrical jobs, and digging ditches," Sharp tells. "I literally learned the business from the ground up, and upon graduating college, I built homes.

"The first hotel I built was strictly as a real estate investment. At the time, I had no intention of being in the hotel business. It was located in a red light district and provided ease of parking that wasn't readily available at Toronto's downtown hotels. I had a friend who operated a thriving motel out on the highway, and his business gave me the idea that we could do the same thing downtown. We'd give them convenient parking, but instead of being far out, guests would be in the heart of the city. Architecturally, it was a gem, and not having much money, I built it on a strict budget. Still, it was done in a pleasing aesthetic style. To guests, it was a little diamond in the rough. My objective was to combine the benefits of what a motel offered with what an out-of-town businessperson looked for when he stayed at a hotel. I didn't know anything about running a hotel, but instinctively I had this idea that a hotel is where you welcome guests for a night or two. My objective was to be a good host. I wanted to treat guests the same way I'd treat them had I invited them to be a guest at my home. I was young, and I didn't articulate my beliefs in a formal way. Back then, I hadn't conceptually thought about luxury. I just had a standard of service in my mind about what a good host should extend to a guest."

The 126-room hotel was an instant success. Believing that front desk clerks made an important first impression on guests, Sharp paid twice the going rate for their services in order to attract and retain good ones. Early on he initiated a profit-sharing plan, and he scheduled two "stress breaks" every day for his employees. Over time, he created an environment that cultivated employee loyalty.

So, exactly what transpired from Four Seasons unpretentious beginning that served as the catalyst for the metamorphosis of what was to become the world's premier hotel organization? We believe it began when Isadore Sharp decided that his company's modus operandi would be to treat people by the Golden Rule. "I wanted to be a good host," Sharp explains. "It's as simple as that. Let's treat the people who come through those doors, whoever they are, and for whatever reason, as a welcomed guest. It doesn't matter what they look like. Don't question them. Don't prejudge. Let's just say, 'Welcome.' I repeat, I never articulated that we'd follow the Golden Rule, but that's what we were doing, and it's what we will always do." The beautiful part of Sharp's philosophy is that it is not the least bit complicated. It was simply a matter of starting with the best of intentions and never—ever—wavering.

✳ ✳ ✳

After spending two summers in between semesters doing carpentry work for a small contractor, Bill Pulte was convinced he wanted to build houses for the rest of his life. A high school honor student, he took correspondence courses to learn how to build houses. Following his graduation in 1950, Pulte built his first home. He used a floor plan from a House-of-the-Week blueprint that appeared in the local *Detroit Times*. His mother bought it for one dollar. He built the house on a lot that his aunt owned near the Detroit City Airport. Upon completing the house, he sold it for $10,000. At age 19, he built a second house, this time for his parents who had never owned one. He describes the experience as "a labor of love."

While all of his friends were in college, Pulte was honing his skills as a tradesman builder. Like other qualified tradesmen, he relied on a carpenter's square, a flat metal square tool used to lay out such things as stairways and rafters. "There were 20 different things you can do with a carpenter's square," Pulte explains, "and back in those days, every guy in the crew knew how to use one in almost every way you could. Today, I'll bet you can't find a guy that can do even 10 of those things, and most wouldn't even know what a carpenter's square is.

"Pride of craftsmanship was very important to tradesmen in those days," Pulte continues. "I personally never wanted to do anything slipshod. I think when you're brought up in the trades with an emphasis on quality, it always stays with you. That's because you have great respect for your craft. However when you start as an entrepreneur, your goal is to make money. From very early on, mine was to build a good house.

"In those days I couldn't afford one of those machines that bangs in nails, continually recocks, and bangs the next nail," Pulte adds. "However after getting my hands all black-and-blue from hitting my fingers while holding oak flooring nails, I decided I wasn't going to be a tradesman builder for the rest of my life. After that first house, my goal was to become the best custom builder in Detroit."

Pulte spent the next five years building custom homes. Then, for a few years, he worked as a general contractor building commercial properties, including a shopping center, a factory, two schools, and two churches. "While the commercial building projects were larger," he explains, "the profit margins were lower. In those days, contractors tended to do a minimum of what they had to do. They cut corners to be competitive pricewise. In comparison to custom home building, there was no teamwork among the tradesmen. That's because you rarely worked with the same subcontractors. Jobs went to the low bidders. As a consequence, commercial tradesmen were driven by price rather than the quality of their work."

In 1959, Pulte decided he wanted to build homes and bought 50 lots to develop; his first subdivision was Concord Green in the Detroit area.

The subdivision had two model homes so prospective buyers could walk through to inspect the quality of the craftsmanship of a Pulte home. At the time, a builder with a model home was considered market savvy. In 1959, a Pulte home sold for $29,000. The following year, the company expanded to Washington, D.C., and the next year Pulte entered the Chicago market. The company has since built homes across the country as well as in Mexico and Puerto Rico. In 1995, Pulte Homes became the largest homebuilder in the United States. In spite of its growth, the company never forgot where it came from. Pulte says that the company's culture traces back to his years as a carpenter who took pride in his craftsmanship. To this day, having pride in workmanship is deeply ingrained in Pulte's company culture. "Early on I recognized that if you gave quality to start with," Pulte explains, "you had fewer service problems later on. Customers really get upset when they move into a new home and have to call the builder to come back to fix things that should have worked in the first place."

Walk the Talk

Rick Germain is a third-generation car dealer. His grandfather had been an accountant for Ford Motor Company, and when he retired in 1947 he bought a Mercury franchise in Columbus, Ohio. In 1967, his father, Robert, who operated a Lincoln-Mercury dealership, attended a meeting where Lee Iacocca talked about Toyota, a Japanese automaker that was planning to come to the United States. After hearing Iacocca's comments, Robert called Toyota upon returning to Columbus and made an appointment to visit the company's regional office in Chicago. He opened a Toyota dealership in Columbus in 1969. Today, Rick with his brothers, Steve and Bob, own 15 dealerships in the Columbus and Naples, Florida, markets that include two Lexus locations in Columbus and one in Naples. They have been with Lexus since the beginning, starting in 1989 when the first models were launched.

"It was exciting to start a new franchise, and be there on the ground floor, coming out with a new brand as opposed to an existing one," Germain explains. "My brothers and I had more than 20 years of experience with Toyota, so we believed in the company. But Lexus was its first luxury brand, and we were up against the European luxury carmakers such as BMW and Mercedes. We knew going in that it was not going to be a walk in the park. I remember going to dealership meetings that Lexus held, and they kept telling us how they'd listen to us and how much they'd depend on us for our feedback. Now I've heard a lot of car companies talk about hearing what their franchisees had to say, but it was all talk. I served on the Lexus dealer advisory council for years and even chaired it for a while. I remember the first meeting with some of Lexus' executives attending. All of us dealers had a list of concerns about products, parts, service, and marketing that we discussed with them. At the end of the meeting, they agreed to get back to us on each item on our list. At our next meeting, I was blown away with their response. One by one, they covered each item on the list, and they thoroughly discussed everything. They followed up on many of our suggestions, demonstrating that they respected our opinions. There was no 'we're looking into that,' or 'we're sorry but that can't happen.' When they didn't always do what we requested, they made it perfectly clear why they couldn't. Afterward, we were able to go back to our associates and customers that had similar concerns. We were then able to explain to them why the car was engineered a certain way, what we were unable to do, and why Lexus has a certain policy."

Germain found out how well Lexus really listens to its dealers when he attended an advisory council meeting at which the company talked about a new model that it would soon introduce in the United States. "The company wasn't too far from launching it," Germain recalls, "however we [the dealers] didn't think it was necessary. Based on what we told the company, they pulled the plug on the model. I'm sure the company had poured huge sums of dollars into it, but without our approval, they dropped it. I've been around many different car companies, but this was a definite first."

✳　✳　✳

Executive Jet Aviation, the forerunner to NetJets, Inc., was founded in 1964 in Columbus, Ohio, by a group of retired Air Force generals. General O. F. "Dick" Lassiter served as the company's first CEO. Paul Tibbets Jr., who piloted the Enola Gay, the airplane that dropped the atomic bomb on Hiroshima, was the company's president, and an early board member was General Curtis LeMay. Entertainers Jimmy Stewart and Arthur Godfrey also served on the board. Executive Jet was the first private jet charter company in the United States. At the time when Richard Santulli acquired the company in 1984, it had a five-plane fleet. A former mathematician at Goldman Sachs, where he headed the firm's quantitative analysis division, Santulli devised the first-ever fractional aircraft ownership plan that provided all of the convenience, access, and time advantages of owning a jet aircraft but at a lesser cost. Making use of his extensive math background, Santulli spent five months studying flight logs used by his predecessors. "They were military guys, and they never threw out a flight log from the day they went into business. So here I am, a math guy, trying to figure out a distribution plan. What I discovered in 1985 was that people flew exactly as they did in 1980, '75, '70, and so on. Same places, same time of day, same day of the week. It did not change. And the business was practically all east of the Mississippi. People still fly the same time of day. It makes sense. But I had to prove it. Where do they go? How long do they stay? I bought eight planes, and I sold people fractional ownership in them. I'd tell them, 'Buy an eighth of an airplane. I'll guarantee that whenever you want it, you'll get it.' People were saying, 'Santulli has gone crazy.' I'd say, 'Listen, you buy a share and if you don't like it, I'll buy it back. I'll guarantee your money back.' I had a reputation of being an honest guy. That's how I built the business."

Hindsight tells us that Santulli's concept was right on the money, and today NetJets operates more than 700 jet aircrafts worldwide through its subsidiaries, making it the largest private fleet in the world. A list of NetJets' customers reads like a Who's Who in corporate America combined with a register of the World's Most Rich and Famous. Owners (what customers are called) include such sports celebrities as Tiger Woods and Pete Sampras. (Many show business people and Fortune 500 companies are owners; however, NetJets never reveals names without the owners' permission.) Catering to this elite clientele demands exceptional service. NetJets doesn't disappoint its customers. Catered gourmet meals are served with the finest available foods and wines. Chauffeured limousines are available to scuttle owners to their destinations immediately following their exit from a plane only minutes after it lands. Every owner's request within reason is granted. Above all else, NetJets has a flawless safety record.

"We are selling a certain percent ownership in an airplane," Santulli tells, "and yet, we make owners feel very special, as if they owned the whole thing. Above all else, safety always comes first. All of my people know there is nothing we won't spend or do to make traveling by NetJets safe. Safety is our number one priority. Now, there are times when some of our services are not perfect. For instance, if an owner who's in Duluth calls us on short notice for a trip in the early morning, we might not be able to stock a particular brand of wine or his favorite caviar. Or perhaps someone on the previous flight took a DVD movie because he didn't get to finish watching it. So there are times when we're not perfect. Please forgive us. However, we'll always be safe. And this is what our customers are buying."

James Christiansen, president of NetJets Aviation, says, "Many companies give a lot of lip service about how people are treated as family, but here, that's exactly how Richard feels about employees and owners. He's compassionate and is interested in what's going on. As we grow bigger—we now have 7,000 employees worldwide—he's still focused on that. When a customer signs a contract, we say, 'Welcome to the family.' It's not a contrived phrase. It's really the feeling here."

"Family and safety are integral parts of our culture," concurs Matt Harris, executive vice president of owner and employee services. "Incidentally, we don't have customers, we have owners, because that's exactly who the people are that travel on NetJets planes. And their safety is always our number one priority. Everyone in every department is focused on safety. At any time, anyone can raise his or her hand and say, 'I don't feel that this is safe to do,' and that person will be heard. Every single employee feels empowered to speak out on a safety issue."

"Richard is incredibly supportive of the people who work here," Christiansen tells us. "He always says, 'Just go do the right thing.' To explain how this works, I have a good story but I can't use real names. One night, our dispatch manager received a phone call from one of our captains. 'Mr. Smith is upset because we're not going to operate this trip due to the weather. He wants to speak to the dispatcher, so here he is.'

"'These guys won't fly tonight and I disagree with them,' Smith said. 'I see other planes flying out of here, but your pilots refuse to fly. They say it's a safety issue. I don't think it's true. And I want to fly now.'

"'I'm sorry but it's the captain's decision, and I'm looking at what looks like bad weather. I agree with him,' the dispatcher replied.

"'Let me tell you something,' Mr. Smith shouted at the dispatcher. 'I know Richard Santulli, and if your pilots don't fly me to where I want to go right now, I'll have them fired. And you'll lose your job too.'

"'Just a minute,' the dispatcher said, and he dialed Santulli's home phone number, placing him into a three-way conference call. 'I've got Mr. Smith on the phone, and he's very upset with us,' the dispatcher told Santulli.

"After [the dispatcher explained] the situation to his boss, Santulli asked to speak to Mr. Smith.

"'Mr. Smith, first thank you very much. We appreciate your business. Now regarding your flight tonight, here's the deal. I think the captain made the right decision. We will not fly you anywhere tonight, but tomorrow morning, we will take you home. And when you get to your office tomorrow, you'll find a check on your desk. We are refunding your money. You are out of the program. You obviously don't understand the value we put on safety as well as the value we place on having our people treated with respect. So thank you very much, but we can no longer do business with you.'

"Let me remind you that we are in the service business, and we will do whatever it takes to serve our customers," Christiansen explains. "We will jump through hoops. But we expect our people to be treated with respect, and we will never compromise on safety matters."

Warren Buffett, founder and chairman of Berkshire Hathaway, had flown Executive Jet for years before he bought the company in 1998. In Buffett's 2006 chairman's letter to Berkshire Hathaway shareholders, the world's second-richest person said, "There's a reason NetJets is the runaway leader: It offers the ultimate in safety and service. At Berkshire, and at a number of our subsidiaries, NetJets' aircraft are an indispensable business tool. I also have a contract for personal use with NetJets, and so do members of my family and most Berkshire directors. (None of us, I should add, get a discount.) Once you've flown NetJets, returning to commercial flights is like going back to holding hands."

✳ ✳ ✳

David Steward, founder and chairman of World Wide Technology (WWT), the largest African American–owned company in the United States, built his business based on serving others. He invested his life savings in WWT in 1990, and during the company's early years, the company struggled to stay afloat. Many times when the company was in its infancy, after covering his weekly payroll, there was no money left in the till for Steward to draw a check for himself. "When your company is down to its last $300," he says, "and you're the owner, guess who doesn't get paid? Ultimately, it was my responsibility to make sure everyone else gets a paycheck, and I always met my payroll. Never, that is, except those times when I was unable to take a check home. Believe me, it's not easy to think of everyone else and make sure their morale is high while inside you're thinking about how you've got to go home and tell Mama that we don't get paid this week. 'Honey, we've got to figure out a way to feed our children, pay the mortgage, and get gas money so I can get back to work.'"

And there were occasions when aggressive bill collectors pounded on the door at Steward's home, demanding their money. "One afternoon in 1993, I suffered the humiliation of having my car repossessed from our parking lot," Steward tells. "A lot of our employees saw how I had to run out to grab my papers from the backseat as they towed the car away. Instead of arguing with the tow truck man and demanding that he let me keep the car, I didn't make a big deal out of it. There was no panic. I just went right back to work as if nothing had happened. I had a business to run and more important things to concentrate on. Had I allowed the incident to upset me, my employees could have lost their confidence in me and the vision we had for the company. That night, my wife picked me up and I used her car until I was able to replace mine. Back when my business was hanging by a thread, I kept focused on my mission to serve others, believing that our employees, vendors, and customers would someday benefit. As we are told in 2 Corinthians 1:3–4: 'Blessed be the God and the Father of our Lord Jesus Christ, the Father of mercies and the God of all consolation, who consoles us in all our affliction, so that we may be able to console those who are in any affliction with the consolation with which we ourselves are consoled by God.' The Good Book tells us to do good deeds, even though we ourselves are enduring difficult times. I refused to be consumed with feeling sorry for myself. I know that I would gain strength by doing well for others. This is God's will, and it is my mission, both in periods of prosperity and adversity."

By demonstrating his faith during the most severe circumstances and refusing to cave in when faced with adversity, Steward earned the loyalty of his people. Seeing that he lived by his deep beliefs, he won the admiration of his employees, vendors, and customers. "A lot of people are afraid to speak out and talk about their faith," Steward says. "They separate their beliefs from their business and won't come out and say what they think is wrong. But to me, my business is my platform for me to announce that I am a Christian and express my views."

When WWT first started, David Steward was a one-man sales force. He spent the vast amount of his time calling on customers; his office work was done during those times when he was not able to sell his services. To this day, Steward spends a minimum of 50% of his time with customers. How well his employees know his priorities. Recently, a regional sales manager invited a prospective representative from Florida to visit the WWT headquarters in St. Louis. The manager happened to walk by Steward's office and seeing that the door was open came in with the job candidate and said, "Hi, Dave, just thought if you had an extra minute, I'd like to introduce you to this young lady." Steward welcomed the two visitors and spent 20 minutes with them. "I'm always available to go on calls with our reps," he told her. "I want to do everything I possibly can to help you be successful." At the end of the meeting, Dave gave her a signed copy of his book, *Doing Business by the Good Book*. "Take this book with you," he said. "It tells you about our company and what I believe."

The woman was so overwhelmed with Steward, she sat there and cried. Afterward, she told the sales manager, "I can't believe such a company exists. I want this job so badly I'll work here for nothing. I'll work strictly on commissions. You don't even have to put me in the health program because I'm covered under my husband's."

✳ ✳ ✳

When you talk to managers at Johnson & Johnson about the management of the company, eventually they'll talk about their credo and how it influences their work and decision making. "With the recent corporate governance scandals," Joe Scodari says, "a lot of companies are beginning to realize the importance attached to the principles and values that were instituted years ago but are rarely, if ever, mentioned. It's really different here at J&J because our credo is truly woven into the culture, and it's been this way for the past 60-plus years. In every interaction with employees, our CEO, Bill Weldon, talks about wanting to win in the marketplace, but doing it the right way. I think this is rare in corporate America, and it's fundamentally part of the fabric of this company."

✳ ✳ ✳

A common denominator of customer-focused companies is that they have a strong heritage, often tracing back to the founder for wanting to do what's in the best interest of the customer; if they do this with consistency, it has a positive effect on everyone, and in particular, employees. Conversely, an ARG study reveals *when a company puts making a profit ahead of acting in the best interests of the customer, 77.5% of its employees are less motivated to work there.* Again and again, we heard comments such as, "When a customer has a complaint and management doesn't make a sincere effort to solve it, it's a real downer." Others expressed: "It's as if the company is saying, 'Now that we got your money, you're on your own.'" Feelings of this nature make employees feel shame in their work when, ideally, their jobs should be a source of pride.

If we suggested to you that a company would prioritize profits over the best interests of its customers and be openly obvious about it, you'd probably think it was preposterous, no company would do such a thing. Well, have you been to a movie theater lately? If so, chances are that you, like others in the audience, have a strong dislike to spending your hard-earned money on a ticket only to be forced to watch several minutes of commercials before the movie starts. You feel like the theater is taking advantage of you because it has a captive market—and, of course, it does. We think this is a perfect example of how a company will do something strictly for profit, even though it clearly knows its customers don't like it. Moviegoers are there to escape from their daily lives. They have no interest in watching commercials. When they're at home, they take bathroom breaks and food breaks, or simply mute the voice on their TVs. But just before the movie starts, they have nowhere to go. "Well, they can come five minutes late and avoid the commercials," one theater owner told us, knowing full well that most people will get there early to assure having a good seat.

A Never-Compromise-on-Quality Philosophy

Cabela's president and CEO, Dennis Highby, recalls joining the company in 1976 at age 27 and how its two founders always insisted on quality merchandise. "I worked at Herter's, an outdoor catalog company in Mitchell, South Dakota," Highby tells. "Back then, Herter's annual sales were around $35 million, compared to $4 million at Cabela's. When I joined the company, Cabela's didn't carry imported goods nor was its brand on any of our product line. Dick and Jim were so intent on quality that they were paranoid about selling a product that didn't appear to be up to our standards. 'Everything we sell has to be first-class merchandise,' they'd say over and over. 'We don't sell junk.'

"I convinced them that we should at least talk to exporters," Highby continues, "and I had made contact with a man named Charlie Chan, who owned Snowbound, a clothing manufacturer in Taiwan. I sent Chan samples of some goose-down vests and coats along with our specifications and requested him to make up some samples for us to consider.

"Chan sent us some samples, and upon receiving them, Jim Cabela said, 'How do we know these are really goose down and not just old chicken feathers?'

"'It has to pass federal government requirements,' I replied.

"My answer didn't assure Jim that the garments were what they were supposed to be. He wanted to know about the loft, which is a measurement that determines the thickness and resilience of the goose down. For example, a high loft batting is thicker and fluffier. To determine the quality, Jim had me take the garments apart so we could measure one ounce of down. I did what he requested, and let me tell you, there were feathers floating all over the place. After placing the down in a tube, we were able to determine how many cubic inches of down equaled one ounce. The competition was selling garments with 400 to 500 fill power per inch. These samples were 600. 'It looks pretty good,' I said to Jim.

"'Well, these are only samples,' Jim answered. 'Get out your passport. We're going to Taiwan to see their factory.'

"I had already been there and saw it, but before Jim would consider putting these garments in the catalog, he wanted to personally see the factory. So we went to see Charlie Chan's factory. Jim liked what he saw, and upon our return to Sidney we purchased a teletype machine. It was costly, but in the days before e-mail, this is how we'd communicate with vendors in that part of the world. We placed an initial order of 300 vests and 300 garments. Chan sent a teletype reply: 'I can't make them in such small quantities. You'll have to place a larger order.' The price was reasonable and the margins were excellent, so Jim agreed to increase the order. When the merchandise came in, he still wasn't 100% convinced of the quality, so we randomly tore apart several of them to make sure their quality met our standards. They did, and this merchandise was the first items we carried under the Cabela's brand. The customers loved it. So the next year, we added more products with our brand, and we began placing our brand on items in different categories."

A tall, handsome man with snow-white hair and a thick mustache, Highby has a rugged appearance that could easily appear on the cover of a Cabela's fishing or hunting catalog. He is soft-spoken and laid-back. A Hollywood casting agency would have picked him to play the role of president of an outdoor catalog company. A warm smile lights his face when he affectionately recalls another story about the company's chairman and cofounder. "Do you know anything about fishing?" Highby asks. Then without waiting for a reply, he continues, "There's what we call a swivel that a fisherman puts on the end of his monofilament line so your lure doesn't twist. It's still used today. Years ago, I was sitting in Jim's office and a Japanese vendor's samples arrived. Jim was excited and wanted to compare them with the swivels we had been selling. To test them, he had two pieces of monofilament with weights attached which he hung from a board. Then we would turn each swivel and we watched them go around and around and around. While we were in the middle of our tests, he'd have me teletype the company in Japan that its swivel's quality had to be better. 'It is not up to our standards, and our customers would be disappointed,' my message read. A few weeks later, another sample came in, and again Jim would conduct the spin test. Finally, he was convinced that the product was a good enough quality to put our brand on it.

"These examples illustrate how we've grown this company," Highby adds, "and it's ingrained into our merchants who do our buying today, many of whom have been here for 25 years or more. And like all of our people in every department, they know that Jim Cabela personally reads every customer comment sent to this company. He does this every day. Every letter goes from his office to my office. My assistant, Tracie, sorts them, and she gives me the ones she feels I should read."

"You can call in an order and make a passing comment to the operator," says Ralph Castner, Cabela's chief financial officer, "and she's trained to type what you say on your file. For instance, you might say, 'I love my waders. They're the best I've ever had,' or you might remark, 'Your product really sucks.' Or someone might send in a letter or express an opinion online. Every one of those goes to Jim's office, and he'll take the time to read every one of them. Then he'll have them passed on to the appropriate person in the area where the comment(s) should be addressed. In my case, as the chairman of our subsidiary, World's Foremost Bank, I'll respond to inquiries and complaints regarding credit card issues. For instance, when a new customer doesn't put down his income on a credit card application, his credit limit is $500. So the other day I received a complaint from a customer who bought something for $700, and I had to explain to him why he had exceeded his limit. Often Jim will handwrite a note on a letter that reads, 'Ralph, make sure you get this fixed.' I estimate Jim spends two hours a day going through customers' letters. Knowing that this is so important to one of our founders sends a message to all our people. It's a tremendous source of pride to know that Jim values customers so much. He also sets the pace on how Cabela's customers are treated."

Employees also take pride in how Cabela's reputation was built on a policy of unconditionally accepting returns from catalog customers. Castner says, "I've seen cases where someone bought an electronic collar to train his dog, and after the dog has been trained, a worn collar is sent back with a request for a refund. Yes, there are people who take advantage of our return policy, and our database system can spot those rare individuals who clearly abuse it. So every now and then we'll send them a letter that says we are not capable of meeting their expectations and suggest they shop elsewhere."

"It's built into our system that when someone talks to someone at our call center or e-mails a complaint, it will be brought to the attention of the appropriate person," explains Michael Callahan, former senior vice president of business development and international operations. "If it's about a defective product, it may be one of our buyers who's notified, and the chances are he will personally call the customer. Imagine that—getting a call from the buyer. Our customers really appreciate it. 'Can you tell me a little bit more about what happened?' the buyer will inquire. 'Well, that shouldn't happen, so I am going to send you a brand new one. In fact, I'm going to send you a better one than that.' When I was responsible for the retail side of the business, many times I'd call a customer, and I know our general managers and regional managers did too. This is part of who we are. It's our company culture."

The Right Thing to Do

When Thomas C. Chubb and his son Percy founded Chubb & Son in 1882, they opened a marine underwriting business in New York City. They collected $1,000 apiece from 100 prominent merchants and began insuring ships and cargoes. The company has since become one of the world's most respected insurance companies, best known for comprehensive homeowners insurance for clients that own yachts, fine jewelry, and valuable art collections. The company is also a major player in the commercial property and casualty industry and a leading provider of director's and officer's insurance. Chubb has received accolades for its swift and fair handling of claims, a reputation tracing back to its early roots.

On several historical occasions Chubb has demonstrated its willingness to do the right thing. One such time was when an earthquake registering 8.3 on the Richter scale devastated San Francisco on the morning of April 18, 1906. The destruction was so severe an estimated 80% of the city was obliterated. As many as 300,000 residents of its 410,000 population were left homeless. An estimated 3,000 people perished. Within minutes after the earthquake struck at 5:12 a.m., flames burst from the ruins, rupturing all the main lines, leaving the city with no water to put out the ensuing fire that raged for three days.

That same day, on the other side of the country, Percy Chubb and his younger brother, Hendon, who joined the company in 1895, sat in their office behind their facing roll-top desks, pondering what action they might take. They quickly decided that one of them should immediately travel to San Francisco. In their minds, there was no substitute for seeing with one's own eyes what was at the time the worst natural disaster in the nation's history. Knowing that Chubb policyholders in the Bay Area would be in need of quick claim settlements, the younger Chubb boarded a train the following day and headed west carrying a suitcase filled with cash. Altogether, Chubb paid out $750,000, a huge sum of money at the time, depleting the company's reserves to a mere $100,000. The fledgling company took a big hit, one that nearly put it on the brink of bankruptcy. It was the only insurance company on record to have paid all of its claims that resulted from the earthquake. The Chubb brothers had no regrets. They were doing their job, which was to help Chubb policyholders the best way they could. The Chubb's never hesitated because they knew it was the right thing to do.

Years later, during World War II, Hendon Chubb made another bold decision. This is when the company consented to insure cargo shipped by sea between the United States and Europe. No other insurance company was willing to assume the risk, but Chubb believed it was vital to the nation's security because America desperately needed to continue its trade with Europe. A lot of cargo ships were sunk by the Germans, and here too, the company lost substantial sums of money. Again, it was the right thing to do.

In more recent times, Chubb took a leadership role when terrorists struck the World Trade Center on September 11, 2001. Thomas Motamed, Chubb's former vice chairman and chief operating officer, vividly recalls the infamous day: "I was in my office when someone came in and said, 'A plane has crashed into the Twin Towers.' My first reaction was that some pilot didn't know what he was doing. We went into the investment conference room and that's when we watched a second plane hit. Shortly thereafter, a group of 14 of us went into the boardroom. We discussed what happened, knowing that our claim exposure would be great. Someone declared, 'It's an act of war,' which would have been excluded from coverage. We discussed what constitutes a war. Was this a declared or undeclared war? Was it an attack by a foreign nation or some other group? We had all sorts of discussions. We realized that none of these questions could have been answered at the time because we didn't have enough facts to support a decision.

"We all sat there, and that's when our chairman said, 'Well, we've got to do the right thing. And what is the right thing? Let's start paying the money.' The claims people in the room got the message. This wasn't a typical case where you determine, 'Okay, is it covered?' Then you read the contract, and you say we cover it or we don't cover it. We effectively put the contract aside and took the position: 'Okay, we are going to pay.'

And there was no further discussion. Go pay. Start writing the checks. That second plane crashed into the building at 9:03 a.m., and we made our decision before lunchtime. Done. End of it.

"Our position was that it was the right thing to do, so just do it," Motamed asserts. "Our competitors were horrified. Again, Chubb is going out there and saying they are going to pay. We had to go to our reinsurers to get the money that they owed us, but they had no obligation to pay us. So when we made our decision, it was not a financial decision. We said that we'd fight with the reinsurers later. Our interest was in doing what was right for the customers, and that was to give them the money, which we did."

Mark Korsgaard, a senior vice president and the company's worldwide casualty claim manager, explains the remarkable way in which Chubb took immediate action in what has since been hailed as unprecedented in the insurance industry. "We have a lot of clientele in the New York financial district, which meant we had major exposure in the World Trade Center Towers," Korsgaard tells. "We are also a large underwriter of worker's compensation insurance. Much like we would assemble a team in the event of a major hurricane, we brought in people from across the country. We had the information we collected from our agents, and in other incidences, from payroll records, on who was covered by our worker's compensation. But in some cases, we didn't know if they were injured, nor if they had been killed. We took it upon ourselves to make outbound calls to people's homes, which was somewhat uneasy for our adjusters because they didn't know if the individual was actually deceased or injured. Just the same, we had to talk to spouses or other family members so we could get enough information to know what had to be done at our end.

"Once we had a viable claimant," Korsgaard continues, "we were able to make an advanced payment that covered a two-month period. State law required one check every two weeks, but we wanted to make the advance payment so we wouldn't have to bother them after our initial discussion. Our people worked overtime, and it was a difficult, stressful task, one that required a lot of empathy. We were dealing with individuals who were enduring horrendous circumstances, and consequently it was a traumatic ordeal for our people as well as the victims and their families. Subsequently, we had to bring in counseling for our people during and afterward."

In the end, about 1,000 out of the 2,750 people killed at the World Trade Center Towers were Chubb claimants. The company paid nearly $3 billion in claims, considerably more than any other insurance company.

When we visited Chubb, we kept hearing a certain phrase repeated by several of the senior executives we met with at Chubb. They quoted to us what Hendon Chubb used to say: "We are a company that goes beyond the four corners of the contract to find ways to pay claims." This is very different from what many insurance companies do. Remember now, an insurance policy is a contract, and as such, a legal document that specifies the exact obligation of the insurer. For an insurance company to look for ways beyond its legal obligation is indeed a rarity in the business, or for that matter, in any business. But this is exactly what Chubb did when it indemnified its policyholders that suffered losses at the World Trade Center Towers. Of course, its people were following a tradition that was established years before when Hendon Chubb took a suitcase filled with money to San Francisco. It's interesting how matter-of-factly they did it. Why? Because it was part of their company culture.

Changing the Culture

"You can't mandate a culture," says Four Seasons founder and CEO, Isadore Sharp. "You have to create it, believe in it, and although the world is not going to be the same year after year, you must be prepared to stick with the game, without altering your culture as times change."

Yet, like every facet of a company, its culture may at times be subject to change. This is to be expected, particularly when it's a merger and acquisition of two entities with completely different cultures. If the differences are extreme, the merger and acquisition is in jeopardy. Many billion-dollar acquisitions have failed due to culture clashes. When Daimler-Benz acquired Chrysler in 1998, many industry experts expressed that it was only a matter of time before the two giant automakers would split. Nine years later, Chrysler was sold. When the breakup occurred, few were surprised.

✳ ✳ ✳

Caesars Entertainment Corporation is the world's most successful gaming company. It is also one of the industry's oldest, with roots tracing back to 1937, when Bill Harrah opened a bingo parlor in Reno, and nine years later, Harrah's Club opened on North Virginia Street, the casino's present location in Reno. The company expanded, and Harrah's later built a hotel in Reno and a casino resort in Lake Tahoe. Bill Harrah stayed away from Las Vegas, wanting nothing to do with a town known at the time for its ties to the Mafia. Following his death in 1978, the company was acquired by Holiday Inns International, and shortly afterward, Harrah's was operating in Atlantic City and Las Vegas. While Harrah's was managed as a separate unit, apart from Holiday Inns, its management was soon emulating its parent company's capacity to manage far-away properties. As a consequence, Harrah's moved into other markets during the 1980s. In 1990, Holiday Inns was acquired by Bass PLC, and the remaining company included Harrah's, Embassy Suites, Hampton Inn, and Homewood Suites. Its new name was the Promus Companies. Philip Satre was named president and chief operating officer. Satre had joined the company full-time in 1980 as vice president and general counsel. Many years before, he worked for Harrah's during the summer as an undergraduate student at Stanford. As a young attorney, Satre had met Bill Harrah and had firsthand exposure to the company founder's insistence on providing exceptional customer service. While Harrah's had enormous expansion under Satre's leadership, he was determined to assure that the company culture remained intact.

In 1995, the Promus Companies spun off its hotel brands, and the remaining company that consisted of the Harrah's brand was renamed Harrah's Entertainment. In 2002, the year of the company's sixty-fifth anniversary, the company operated 26 casinos. In 2003, Phil Satre stepped down as chief executive officer and was replaced by Gary Loveman, a Harvard Business School professor who had been retained as a consultant by Harrah's during the mid-1990s. In 1998, Loveman had joined the company when Satre named him chief operating officer. In 2004, the company acquired Horseshoe Gaming for $1.45 billion, and casinos located in Indiana, Louisiana, and Mississippi became members of the house of Harrah's. The following year, the company made a monster-sized deal when it acquired Caesars Entertainment for $9.4 billion, making Harrah's Entertainment the largest gaming enterprise in the world. At the time of the acquisition Caesars had 27 properties, including such illustrious brand-name casinos as Caesars, Bally's, Flamingo, Grand Casinos, Hilton, and Paris Las Vegas. The company changed its name to Caesars Entertainment in late 2008.

Under the leadership of Satre, and then followed by Loveman, Harrah's invested heavily in information technology (IT), and launched a marketing plan that was focused on rewarding customers with unparalleled customer-service experience. Three decades have passed since Harrah's was a "local" casino resort company owned and operated by Bill Harrah in Reno and nearby Lake Tahoe. The company's sheer size has transformed it into a far different enterprise than the one that for years was identified by Bill Harrah's strong personality. Still, in spite of its size and heavy reliance on IT, its legacy of service remains intact. "Our culture is ingrained in the company," explains David Norton, senior vice president and chief marketing officer, Caesars Entertainment. "While a bit of science has been added over the years, the company has a strong foundation that emphasizes service. True, management has become more analytical and today we use data that helps us make informed decisions versus the old way of operating by gut feel. Still, having said that, today's frontline employees deal with customers, day and night, and when they are face-to-face with our customers, they're delivering the same high quality of personal service just like the company always did under Bill Harrah's leadership."

"Loveman is very visible in the organization, and I refer to him as the keeper of the culture," says John Bruns, former vice president of customer satisfaction and chief operating officer of Harrah's London Clubs International subsidiary. "He's constantly visiting our properties, talking about the value proposition to our customer that we refer to as our customer promise that vows your visit to Harrah's will be better than your last visit, and it will be better than the competition."

Acquiring a Company

In 1979, Centocor was founded in Philadelphia, Pennsylvania. Three years later in 1982, the company raised $21 million with its initial public (stock) offering, the same year that it introduced its first product, a diagnostic test used to detect the rabies virus. Centocor was founded with the premise that monoclonal antibodies could be used to treat a variety of illnesses in a specific manner. Centocor's drugs were laboratory-produced antibodies that can locate and bind to specific substances in the body. They can target, for example, an exact antigen such as a foreign protein, bacteria, virus, or pollen. Unlike small molecules made from chemicals through chemical synthesis, monoclonal antibodies had fewer side effects and were hailed as the wave of the future.

Centocor had some small successes during the 1980s; by 1988, its revenues hit $72 million. Like most start-up biotech companies, Centocor invested heavily in one medicine; its promising drug was Centoxin, a human antibody drug designed to treat gram-negative sepsis, a bacterial infection that was killing an estimated 80,000 Americans out of approximately 200,000 cases in the United States. Sepsis is the most common cause of death in the intensive care unit. The costs of the clinical trials and setting up a manufacturing plant were staggering; the years 1991 and 1992 generated a combined loss of $300 million. Then a disaster happened. Centoxin failed to pass the clinical trial and the drug never saw its way to the marketplace. Within four months, Centocor's stock plummeted from $60 in December 1991 to $6. With little money in the till, it would bet the company's future on Remicade, a promising drug for treating immune-related diseases. Operating on a shoestring, the company put its entire energy into making Remicade work. In August 1998, the drug was approved by the FDA for the treatment of Crohn's disease. In November 1999, the FDA approved Remicade for a second indication for the treatment of rheumatoid arthritis. It has since been approved for other diseases such as psoriasis, ulcerative colitis, and ankylosing spondylitis. Today Remicade is considered a major breakthrough medicine. It is the bestselling biotech medicine in the world.

"In late 1998, when Centocor was still an independent company," Joe Scodari explains, "we had begun to realize that we would become an acquisition target. So we went to our investment banking firm, Morgan Stanley, and they did an analysis to determine the fundamental value of Centocor. We also wanted to determine that if an unfriendly takeover attempt occurred, what company might be our preferred white knight. We came up with a value, but as far as we were concerned, the most important topic was who the white knight would be. It was Johnson & Johnson. We believed Centocor had tremendous growth potential and was an organization with many greatly talented people. Our team consisted of Dave Holveck, Dominic Caruso, Harlan Weisman, and me. Our priority was to build a prominent biotech company, a real business that made a profit. We wanted to be able to afford to hire the best people. And third, we wanted to build a company with values where people felt good about what they were doing, and were contributing to patient care. We studied the Johnson & Johnson corporate culture, and although it was a much larger company, it had a value system that we felt was very similar to our small company."

"Once we made the decision," explains Dave Holveck, Centocor's CEO at the time (who later served as president of Johnson & Johnson Development Corporation but left the company in early 2008), "we didn't sit passively waiting to be acquired. We were very aggressive. You might say we attacked the process. Our goal was to be acquired by the best company out there."

Meetings were conducted with several investment banking firms. A meeting was set up between Johnson & Johnson's vice chairman,

Robert Wilson, and Holveck. "At the time I wasn't too familiar with J&J," Holveck says, "but like everyone, I was aware of their famous brand products such as baby powder. Right off the bat, before we even sat down to talk, Wilson said to me, 'Dave, this discussion may end in two hours or it may continue, and if so, bigger and broader agreements will be constructed. I want to make it clear right from the beginning that if we get to that latter stage, I want a commitment from you that you can bring your people along. The people are the most important aspect in this field.'

"When he put an emphasis on the fact that people is what it is all about, I liked him immediately," Holveck continues. "Everyone else was talking about the product or the financials. With Wilson, number one was the people. All along with the talks we were having with different pursuers, my biggest concern was the people. I had to make certain that our people would be able to continue with their mission—they had to be included in the equation. Although Wilson didn't know it, he won me over with his opening statement. After hearing that, I was at ease talking to him and I sensed this was the company that would be right for us."

After meeting with Wilson, Holveck reviewed what had transpired with Scodari. "We identified J&J as our preferred white knight," Scodari says. "Number one, we liked their decentralized operating model. At the time, J&J had more than 100 separate units that were run autonomously, and with this corporate structure, we could continue to operate independently, as we had all along. Of course, we realized all the problems we faced if we remained a stand-alone company, so this represented an opportunity to have our cake and eat it too. And obviously there were some advantages of being under the J&J umbrella. J&J had the financial strength that would help us develop future products, and second, the company had some of the smartest people in our industry, who [would be] available when we needed to draw upon their expertise."

Interestingly, Johnson & Johnson used similar criteria in its decision to acquire Centocor. "The starting point when we do due diligence to acquire a company," William Weldon explains, "that's high on our checklist is its corporate culture. There have been many times when we've walked away from companies that looked like good acquisition candidates but we didn't think the cultures would meld together. So we look for companies that we feel have good values—values that we think are consistent with our values. And we talk to them about our credo. We describe it as the fabric that holds us all together and gives us a management direction and a philosophy that we all subscribe to."

In 1999, Johnson & Johnson acquired Centocor for $4.9 billion. As parties on both sides agree, it was a "good fit."

✳   ✳   ✳

Today, Mark Templin is group vice president and general manager of Lexus. He originally joined Toyota Motor Sales, U.S.A., Inc., in 1990 and held several marketing and sales management positions within the Lexus division. Then, prior to being promoted to his current position, Templin served as vice president of Scion, responsible for all Scion activities. Scion is Toyota's lowest-priced car division; Lexus is the company's highest-priced product with sticker prices of its top-of-the-line model in the $120,000 range. To an outsider, viewing Templin as a rising star at Lexus and then being transferred to the Scion division, one might suspect that he was demoted, akin to a major league baseball player being sent back to a minor league farm team. We assure you that in Templin's case that is not what happened. On the contrary, his years at Scion groomed him well for his present high-ranking position.

"Did you know that the word *scion* means 'descendant'?" Templin explains, referring to his career at Scion, which has been sandwiched in between his work at Lexus. "I feel very passionate about the Scion group, having helped build it from scratch and looking at what we were able to accomplish. At Toyota, Scion is viewed as a laboratory, a place where we can try new things. It's a place to experiment and step out of the normal course of our business and to find new ways of doing things. When the Lexus was introduced in 1989, it was all about changing the world and the way we do business."

Scion is a U.S.-only division of Toyota that was founded in 2003 and currently has three models, the xD, xB, and the tC. "Scion's target audience is a young generation of people that is now coming up, especially Generation Y," Templin points out. "The division is now concentrating on Gen Z, the group of young people that will soon be getting their driver's license and adding millions of drivers to the U.S. roadways for the next 13 years. This is our attempt to reach an entirely new group of people who we anticipate will want to do business in a whole different way. We have three brands, Scion, Toyota, and Lexus. The goal of Scion is to bring new people into our family and then keep them by having them grow up through the family by eventually selling them Toyota products and then Lexus products.

"When I came over to Scion," Templin continues, "people would comment, 'Oh, it must be a really big change from the luxury car division to the entry car division of your company.' My reply to them was, 'We are selling different products to a different group of people, but what we are trying to accomplish is the same. We are trying to figure out a way to do business that is friendlier to our customers. So, in this respect, Lexus and Scion are trying to accomplish the same thing—they're just doing it with a different group of people with a different product. We are the same company, all adhering to the same company culture.'"

Company Cultures Transcend Borders

"We worked with the London School of Business for several years," explains Jim Weddle, managing partner at Edward Jones, "studying the U.K. market prior to entering it in 1997. We looked at the competition, the infrastructure—everything, including the British culture. Next, we announced that we were looking for volunteers, and we conducted extensive interviews with dozens of folks who expressed an interest in working abroad. We selected eight financial advisors, and we gave them extensive cultural training."

The company's strategy was to bide its time. It would take a while before its eight financial advisors would get a foothold in the United Kingdom. To ease the burden, a five-year guarantee of the broker's previous year's earnings would be paid, plus a generous cost-of-living stipend.

"'You don't want to go over there and offend people,' we told them," Weddle says. "'You want to respect their culture, and unlike how Edward Jones does it in the States, the British will be offended if you go knock on their doors at their homes, or for that matter, at their place of business. They will consider it an interruption of their day, an invasion of their privacy. So that's something you can't do in the U.K.' We anticipated that it would take a while for our financial advisors to develop relationships, but eventually, they would; and once they did, they would succeed."

In the United States, Edward Jones' modus operandi had been a direct approach where its brokers knocked on doors, introduced themselves to prospective investors, and were subsequently invited in to transact business, usually at the kitchen table. This approach worked remarkably well for the company in thousands of small communities across America, and this is how the eight financial advisors had built their businesses prior to their move to England. But the British were a reserved people, and hence it was anticipated that this approach would be ineffective. With this thinking, the Edward Jones transplants were instructed not to employ the tactics that had accounted for their successes back home, and consequently, they performed poorly abroad.

One of the eight Edward Jones transplants, Katie Bass, became tired of doing badly in a newly established office in Harpenden, a 25-minute train ride from London. The 28-year-old broker, the daughter of a cattle rancher in Tarkio, Missouri, had joined Edward Jones right out of college, and she didn't accept the fact that the Britons were so much different. Katie wasn't convinced that she couldn't do what she did back home that had worked so well in Union, Missouri, where she had enjoyed previous success. "Katie did what she was told she shouldn't do," Weddle explains. "She said, 'I started from scratch in the U.S. I know how to introduce myself and explain to people what I do, plus what I can do for them. I have to start doing that here in England. To heck with all this cultural training.' So Katie went out and introduced herself to people. She's very engaging and has a high level of energy. Very self-assured."

Bass went back to the basics as she was trained to do in the States. She'd approach a British housewife who might be busy with her children at the time, and she'd say, "Hi, nice to meet you. My office will be right down on Station Road. If I can ever be of service to you, please let me know." She'd leave a business card and a brochure, and a few weeks later, she'd invite the couple to a seminar that she would conduct at a local conference center. It took a little time, but eventually she opened accounts. In her first nine months she had 100 clients.

Rolling his eyes, Jim Weddle says, "Thank heavens Katie took the initiative to do it the Edward Jones way like we did it in the U.S. We should have never deviated from our culture, which is a friendly, small-town approach. When the other seven brokers saw what Katie did, they quickly followed suit. We discarded the training that advised them not to make calls that might risk offending the British. And sure enough, our people received a response just as positively to a personal handshake and a warm introduction as they received back home in the Midwest."

4

Being Big, Thinking Small

Being big and thinking small sounds like an oxymoron. In America, we are taught to think big. It's synonymous with business success. For the record, we do not oppose thinking big. We believe, however, that business owners must continue to do the little things they did when they were small businesses that wooed customers in the first place.

An ARG survey revealed that *51% of consumers think big companies care less about them than do smaller companies*. They feel this way because they sense a void in the personal interest that small business owners have in their customers. In the same survey, *48% of Americans think big companies are less interested in taking care of them*. Big companies must figure out how to get closer to the customer. This endeavor requires tearing down walls that have been constructed by bureaucrats, changing systems that make customers feel like numbers. We note that an ARG study uncovers that *89.5% think big companies are more likely to treat them as a number*. Over time, companies set up procedures and support them with rules and regulations. It enables them to process orders, control inventories, manage invoices, and so on. While these systems are meant to serve customers efficiently, over time they become transactional, not personal.

We discussed in Chapter 1 how a small business owner must constantly be in front of the customers, always aware that this is the best use of his or her time. For a small enterprise, this is the top priority. As a company grows, this focus should never waver.

All things being equal, people choose to do business with the small company. An ARG study shows that 78.6% *would buy at the small store if it could match the big store's price.* This study makes it clear that people have a definite preference to do business with small businesses. It's the human touch that's missing in big business. In the same study, 90.2% *said that they feel overwhelmed at a large store when there is nobody there to take care of them.* Retailers that are making large investments in big box stores should take note. If these stores are not adequately staffed, shoppers will head toward smaller stores such as hardware stores where they will find assistance — and find relief from feelings of being overwhelmed.

Small-Town Values

There are times when we crave for the "good old days" when people didn't bother to lock their doors to their houses and they left their car windows down and their keys in the ignition. It was even safe to hitchhike. Everyone knew all their neighbors on their street. On a slow day, the pharmacist at the corner drugstore made sundaes and ice cream cones at the soda fountain. The hardware store owner spent 10 minutes searching through a bin of nuts and bolts for a two-cent screw because the customer couldn't find it. The family doctor even made house calls. Now and then you might travel through a small town and experience traces of the good old days, and when you do, it gives you a warm feeling.

We won't debate the merits of the past and the present. But we do acknowledge that it makes us feel good to reminisce about those times. And the same thing applies to being familiar with a company's roots that trace back to its humble beginnings in a small town. That also makes us feel good. Americans appreciate a company that didn't grow too big for its britches and abandoned its roots. We value those that remained loyal to the hometown folk.

One of the secrets that Cabela's credits for its success is that the company has maintained its small-town roots by staying in Sidney, Nebraska, population 6,000. As a small catalog operator selling flies to fishermen, the company could have been based anywhere. Sidney is located a few miles north of the Colorado border in the western part of the state known as the Nebraska Panhandle. Sidney is more than five hours due west from Omaha via automobile. It's about as rural America as it gets—visiting Sidney one is reminded of the movie *Back to the Future*. A visitor feels as though he's traveled back in a time capsule to a bygone era. Life moves on at a slow pace in Sidney, and you have to love living in a small town or the place isn't for you. There are a couple of restaurants that serve a good steak dinner—after all, Nebraska is cattle country. But other than Cedar Lanes, the local bowling alley with 12 lanes; Fox Theater, a two-screen movie house; or Stewie's, a downtown watering hole, that's about as much nightlife as you'll get in this town. Daytime activities include a shooting park that opened in 2006 that features skeet and trap shooting as well as an archery range. There's also Hillside, an 18-hole public golf course, where the green fees are only $20. Until 2005, when a Wal-Mart opened, there was virtually no place to shop for food other than the Safeway or Sonny's grocery store. The nearest large metropolitan areas are Cheyenne, Wyoming, which is two hours directly west, or Denver, a 3¹/₂-hour drive southwest.

So what do people do for excitement in Sidney? When we interviewed Ralph Castner, the company's chief financial officer, he told us, "Last night I helped my kids with their 4-H calf. We were castrating cattle. Now if I told somebody from New York that, he would look at me as if I were from a different planet. An exciting time around here is when wild turkey season begins in mid-April. Half the people in this building will go turkey hunting that first weekend. That's what our customers do. Of course, we're close to Colorado and Wyoming, where there's great hunting for larger game and world-class fly-fishing. A high percent of Cabela's people share my passion for hunting and fishing, so living in Sidney is a good place for us to be."

Sidney is also a good place for Cabela's to be. The people who work for the company are, with few exceptions, avid outdoors people. They love the products that the company sells because fishing, hunting, camping, and archery are their passions. We met many Cabela's employees when we visited its headquarters, and their enthusiasm can be felt in the air. Working there is their dream job. Second, Sidney is in the nation's heartland. It is a place of the world where outdoor living is an important part of the culture. Their fathers, grandfathers, and great-grandfathers hunted and fished. Their favorite childhood memories are those times they spent with family members and good friends wading in rivers, hunched over in a blind, and sitting around a campfire telling stories—bonding with one another. And with their own children, this is the kind of quality time they spend with them. It's a wonderful, wholesome life, and one that builds character.

Today, Cabela's is a $2 billion company, one that is growing at an annual rate of 15% to 20%. "When you ask Jim Cabela how we're going to keep up that growth rate, he answers, 'Exactly like we've been doing it for the past 44 years,'" Castner says. "The only difference is that it now takes opening up to eight stores a year when it used to take one when we were just a catalog business. By being here in Sidney, we are close to the customer. I'm convinced that being in a small town is a major plus. Part of the culture of living out here is that we love doing what our customers love doing. We stay close to our product. I think that if we lived in a place that was more urban, there would be more options, and you'd have more people who didn't enjoy this lifestyle. So what we've got here are a bunch of people who love to use our products, and they're on a mission to communicate across the country a message about what they love. As we grow, our management team has to put additional infrastructure in the company. That's required when you get bigger, but honestly, it pains me every time I do it."

CEO Dennis Highby concurs that being headquartered in Sidney is an important part of what makes Cabela's tick. "Out of the 6,000 people who live in this town, 1,250 of them work in this building," Highby points out. "There's a lot of camaraderie here. People know each other. Perhaps they go to the same church, or their children go to the same school. Nobody puts on airs around here, so there is a lot of interaction between our people, regardless of one's position in the company. Jim Cabela comes to work every day, and like everyone else, he parks his car in the same lot wherever he can find a space. There are no reserved parking spots."

Highby explains that Dick and Jim Cabela started to think long term to the time when they wouldn't be around to head the company. "About 10 years ago, the three of us took a trip to Minneapolis to discuss our future with some consultants. They asked some good questions. 'What do you want to do with this company?' 'Are you going to sell it?' 'No,' Dick and Jim answered. 'Why not?' 'Well, we would be worried about what the buyer would do with our company. It's our company. It would be devastating to the community.' 'What do you think your company's worth?' The meeting made Dick and Jim think about what if something were to happen to one of them and how difficult it would be for the surviving brother. This prompted them to seek the counsel of others, one of whom was Warren Buffett. Selling to Berkshire Hathaway was an option, and Buffett expressed an interest. But we decided that being a public company was the right choice, and so we did our initial public offering in June 2004.

"As long as Dick and Jim are around, we'll always be here in Sidney. And as long as I'm CEO, that's how I feel," Highby states. "Of course, depending upon who the CEO might be in the future, anything is possible. Our board members are concerned about succession planning, and they feel strongly that our culture must be maintained. So staying here is the right place, but as we expand, it becomes more challenging to attract large numbers of people. So far, we've been able to surround ourselves with great people."

❋   ❋   ❋

After visiting Cabela's in Sidney and Mary Kay in Dallas where they, too, continually talk about their founder's rags-to-riches story, ARG conducted a survey unlike any other. This study revealed that *56% of Americans say that knowing about an owner's values and early struggles to overcome adversity positively influenced their desire to do business with the company.* Interesting, although both Cabela's and Mary Kay today are big companies, Americans will identify with the owner, decades earlier, when he or she was just getting started in business. Again, this kind of storytelling puts a face on a business.

❋   ❋   ❋

Edward Jones is another company with traditional town values. Its past three managing partners all began their careers in small towns where they ran their own one-person brokerage offices prior to being brought back to St. Louis where they were promoted to managerial positions and went on to rise through the ranks to the number one spot. To this day, the 10,000-plus Edward Jones offices are run by a financial advisor and an assistant, who is called a branch office administrator (BOA). During its early days of expansion, the company opened branch offices in small towns throughout the Midwest and eventually expanded coast to coast. Typically the broker built his business by spending his time away from his office, meeting with prospects and clients at their homes and places of business. "We expect our financial advisors to spend 80% of their time away from the office when they're getting started," senior partner John Bachmann explains. "The time spent in the office is for writing thank you notes and looking up information for clients. A year or two later, the business will quickly transition itself to the financial advisor spending 80% of his time in the office. Sure, he or she still puts in one-on-one time with clients in their homes and the office, but he or she is also communicating with them by telephone."

Peter Drucker was invited by Bachmann to consult the company, and it turned out to be a brilliant move. Edward Jones had built its business by being the antithesis of security firms on Wall Street, and Drucker had a reputation of being an anticonsultant, who sometimes referred to himself as an "insultant" who chided clients for fees. Drucker was known for asking questions rather than providing answers. "Peter challenged us on our assumptions," managing partner Jim Weddle points out, "and that's what a good consultant will do. One of our assumptions was that we were most competitive in smaller communities. Peter said, 'You are going to be competitive wherever you find individual investors.' He then asked us if there were any metropolitan areas where we had succeeded, and we told him that the two exceptions were in the St. Louis and Kansas City markets. We explained that we avoided metropolitan markets to stay away from competing with the big brokerage firms that didn't have representation in the rural areas where we operated. At a 1981 meeting we had with him, Peter asked if our offices in St. Louis and Kansas City were more productive than our small-town locations and it turned out that they were. His insight opened our eyes to see things differently."

Four years before Drucker's arrival, Gary Reamey joined the company and opened an office in Morris, Illinois, a town of 11,000 that is 61 miles southwest of Chicago. After running one of the company's most successful branches, Reamey in 1982 was named regional leader, responsible for branches in northern Illinois. Reamey believed that Edward Jones could succeed in the small communities surrounding Chicago, and in a meeting with Bachmann, he noted, "If we carefully select the right people, we can open successful branches in places in the western suburbs of Chicago such as Downers Grove, Elmhurst, and Naperville." "There was a lot of doubt," Weddle tells, "but Gary proved the model would work just as effectively in larger suburban locations, and we started to aggressively open branches in those markets. The successes of these offices confirmed what Drucker had said about how we would do better in areas where we had competition. It might have been that due to the competition, our financial advisors had to work a little harder or had more focus. Whatever it was, they definitely did better."

Today, Edward Jones has branch offices in all U.S. major metropolitan areas and throughout Canada, where, incidentally, Gary Reamey is now the firm's country leader.

While Edward Jones has entered large metropolitan markets and has moved into Canada and the United Kingdom, it still sticks to the format of having branch offices consisting of one financial advisor and a

BOA. The company has as many as 300 or more branches in large metropolitan areas such as Dallas and Seattle, and today, the total number of such offices is about 75% of the total offices of Edward Jones. Having said this, the company has not abandoned its small-town values. Financial advisors still make in-person sales calls, and their offices can still be found in strip shopping centers next door to barber shops and dry cleaning establishments. Being close to their customer is ingrained in the company's culture, no matter the size of the community.

* * *

Today, Ashley Furniture Industries is the fastest-growing company in the furniture industry. Based in Arcadia, Wisconsin, the $3 billion–plus company has 350-plus stores and is opening as many as 50 new stores a year. Ashley Furniture is also one of the largest furniture manufacturers in the United States; in addition to selling its extensive line in its 350-plus stores operated mainly by licensees, another 6,000 independent furniture retailers with 12,000 outlets across the country sell Ashley furniture. Ashley Furniture is growing by leaps and bounds and has become one of the giants in the furniture industry. Still, the company thinks small and caters to the needs of the small independent furniture operator. Chairman Ron Wanek, who grew up on a dairy farm in Minnesota, started as a cabinetmaker in 1945, and he has never forgotten his small-town roots. His company, Arcadia Furniture, was acquired by Ashley in 1970. Its first year as an Ashley unit, it had 35 employees and a product line of 11 simple occasional tables that generated $360,000. Although it was a small part of Ashley, Arcadia quickly grew and soon became one of the parent company's top lines. In 1976, Wanek along with other investors bought controlling interest in Ashley.

Under Wanek's leadership, Ashley was somewhat of an anomaly in the furniture industry. Located in a remote small town in Wisconsin, it was far removed from North Carolina and Virginia, the hub of the furniture manufacturing industry. "We were small and out in Wisconsin," he explains. "They didn't think we knew anything about the furniture business because we applied some nontraditional manufacturing processes. We didn't abide by the traditional thinking, and instead, invested heavily in new technology and equipment to make furniture while they stayed with the old ways. We didn't inherit anything and didn't have the luxury of a recognized name. With our constant improvement program in place, we were always in debt, so we couldn't afford to make mistakes. We were in a different position than those guys, and it took a street fighter's mentality for us to survive.

"We were also able to identify with the independent retailer in small towns across the country," Wanek continues, "and we catered to their needs. For example, the biggest complaint furniture dealers have about the industry's manufacturers is that they're required to place a minimum order. This means that they warehouse their merchandise or pay a premium by buying through a distributor. We acquired expertise in transportation and designed a distribution system to serve these independent retailers. With us, they can place a small minimum order and mix 22 different product categories in their order that allows them to realize a good gross margin return on their investment. Other manufacturers didn't want to do this, and it gave us the opportunity to open 6,000 accounts across the country."

Wanek believes that there will always be a need for the traditional mom-and-pop furniture retailer in America. "The independent retailer who stays current and close to his customer will survive," he says. "Consumers might search the Internet to see what's out there, but they will want to visit a store to see, feel, and smell the furniture."

Ashley Furniture caters to middle America. "We do furniture for 70% of the market," Wanek emphasizes. "We don't do it for the very bottom, and we don't do it at the premium end. It's a great satisfaction in giving the customers furniture that they can afford. For us to do it right, we must have a product that people like. In other words, it has to appeal to them. Second, the quality must be right. Third, the price must be right. And finally, they want it now, so it must be available to purchase. To make all this happen, you must have a passion for what you do. I think that's the most noticeable thing you observe when you visit our headquarters. In my opinion, the furniture industry is the greatest business to be in because you can touch so many people's lives and give them really good values."

Less Is More

When Dave Liniger founded RE/MAX in 1973, his premise was to seek out the top-producing real estate agents. Knowing that 80% of all agents fail during their first year, he decided he would recruit only seasoned agents. "Homeowners list with the biggest companies that are best known in the area," Liniger explains. "But after five or six years in the business, their top producers start thinking, 'I'm giving half my commissions to my broker, and it isn't that expensive to start my own real estate office.' This is not true today with costs at nearly a half a million to start a decent-sized office because you'll need about 10,000 square feet of space, plus some costly technology. Plus, advertising costs have skyrocketed."

Liniger grins when he says, "At a press conference when I first started my business, I told some reporters, 'I'm not in the real estate business. I'm in the real estate agent business.' I planned to build my company on something I read in a book some 40-plus years ago purporting that the companies with the best employees had the highest customer satisfaction. My take on that was by treating your employees and your sales associates as your customer, you will get the best ones. This was an unusual comment back then, but I took it to heart. In my business, it meant that if I get the best agents, they will deliver world-class service to their customer, who is the real estate customer. We modeled our offices on the same order as a group of physicians or a group of dentists who share expenses of running the business, but they pay their own personal expenses and keep the lion's share of their earnings for themselves.

"What we did right off the bat was a defining moment," Liniger continues. "It meant beginners couldn't afford to come to work for us. We had no intention of being a training mill. We weren't going to bring people in, get them licensed, and nurse them. Today, our average agent has been in the business for eight years before he or she even joins the RE/MAX organization. Our average agent today has 13.8 years experience in the business. Our approach eliminated the weak ones, and we only got those who were already successful. Every real estate agent who's been selling real estate in a particular area in town for an average of eight years has a reputation in the business. Everyone in the area knows each other and they know a real estate's reputation. Unlike taking a beginner who's an unknown factor, and you don't know if he or she is good, or for that matter, ethical, you go with somebody with maximum potential. By the way, that's how we got our name. I didn't want to call it Dave Liniger Realty. We came up with real estate maximums, and this meant maximum service for the customer because they weren't dealing with beginners or part-timers. We offered maximum recruiting ability for the broker as well as maximum commissions. Well, because all of that would take up too much room on a sign, we initially decided to call ourselves RE.MAX, but that looked too much like somebody's name. So we took out the period, put in a slash, and we came up with RE/MAX as an acronym. That's how it all started."

In the beginning, it seemed like an impossible task for Liniger to persuade the top agents in the Denver area to sign up with him. "I made over 1,000 phone calls, did 204 face-to-face interviews in my first month," he tells, "and I signed up four. The two biggest companies in town only hired men. In 1973, if you were a woman, you could be a secretary or bookkeeper at a real estate office. That was it. At the time there had been a big backlash against all the women who came into the business as part-timers in the '60s and early '70s. The two top companies in town only had men working for them. I wanted their top producers. I kept hearing, 'This sounds good on paper, but I'm already with the biggest and best. I'll wait and see if you make it, and then we can talk again.'"

Liniger's new company was by no means an overnight success story. He signed up 21 agents in his first full year in business, and in the second year, another 21. The number doubled to 84 by the third year, and hit 135 in the fourth year. At the end of his fifth year, he had 289 agents. "Seventy-five percent were female, and they were good agents and they realized that the two big firms in town wouldn't hire them. The agents who signed up loved the RE/MAX concept. In our sixth year, we had a track record and 200 men from the all-men companies joined my ladies. In our market, we were the number one real estate company in Denver.

"We decided that unlike the franchisors such as Century 21 and ERA, we would not be all things to all people," Liniger continues. "We focused on the top 20% of the agents who were doing 80% of the business. We realized that if we could get 50% of the top 20, we'd capture 30% to 35% market share. Of course, there would be some we didn't want because they were unethical. We also didn't want the prima donnas. Then there were those who would never leave their broker. Some had a sweetheart arrangement or perhaps a personal relationship. We eventually got half of the top 20%, and since the industry has become so much more professional during the past three decades, our goal is to now get half of the top 30%. When we hit those numbers such as we have done in Colorado, we will run 30% to 40% market share."

✳   ✳   ✳

With 4,400 brokers and agents in the United States, Chubb is the nation's tenth largest property and casualty company; another 4,000 brokers can be found in 29 countries around the world. Its domestic sales force is relatively small in comparison to other large insurers that have as many as 15,000 domestic representatives peddling their wares. However, Chubb isn't interested in selling a product line that offers "something for everybody."

"In the late 1970s, we made a conscious decision that we would serve a more affluent client," explains Tom Motamed, former vice chairman and chief operating officer. "We chose to excel in the services we provided that would include such things as appraising client's properties and informing them about how they could mitigate losses. We would look for ways to pay claims and do it more expediently than our competition. To implement this strategy, we'd carve a niche in the marketplace whereby we'd pick certain industry segments, and we'd be recognized as *the* company with the most expertise in underwriting risks. By specializing, we have a better understanding about the exposures which, in turn, boosts the confidence of our brokers and agents that sell our products and services. As a result, we hear clients say, 'Chubb is quite knowledgeable about my industry and they understand my company.' For those who are paying money to us in the event they will incur a loss, they feel as though they are not just paying for a piece of paper. Having said that, many of them don't actually believe something catastrophic will happen to them."

With a strategy of covering selective risks with highly informed brokers and agents, plus a team of highly qualified home office and field people, Chubb's niche has earned it a reputation for insuring high-priced articles ranging from expensive jewelry to luxurious yachts. Indeed, its wealthy and discriminate clientele own fine possessions. They are wealthy and enjoy superior quality and they are willing to pay for exceptional service. The company estimates that it insures a majority of U.S. homes worth more than $5 million. With extensive experience in covering high-value properties, Chubb has more savvy than other insurers in determining fees charged by decorators, landscape designers, and lighting and sound consultants. If someone owns a masterpiece oil painting, chances are the owner will want to have it insured by Chubb. As a leader in insuring privately owned fine art, Chubb is also equipped to insure a collector's costly possessions that are on loan to a museum or cultural institution. Chubb art authorities will furnish information to such collectors on everything from valuation to what they need to know about packing and shipping.

"Back in the '70s we were a small company," says Frances O'Brien, a senior vice president, "and to be competitive, we needed to develop a different strategy than the bigger underwriters. That's when we came up with this idea of providing total service to our brokers, agents, and customers. It meant we were going to have broad policies. We were going to have quick and accurate policy issuance. We were going to be the best-in-class claim service. We would provide loss control advice. And we would help clients decide how much they should insure their homes for. By providing more service and, in turn, by being likely to cost more, it became a natural progression that people who were less price sensitive tended to be wealthier. So, over time our business migrated to what we are today. But initially, it was more about what could we provide that would be different. This thinking helped us develop a niche customer. We were able to move from there to where we were developing products and services that our customer wanted."

Today Chubb is known for being staffed with highly trained people who have specialized technical skills. Going back to its early days, on the commercial side of the business, the company continues to be an industry leader in the ocean cargo field. It has since expanded into other markets, and due to the unique nature or complexities of certain claims, the company has specialists who are devoted exclusively to handling claims for such segments as directors and officers liability, environmental liability, surety, information and network technology, and worker's compensation. Other company professionals specialize in underwriting coverage for attorneys, financial institutions, and nonprofits. More recently, Chubb has moved into the life science business.

"We view life sciences as a growth area," explains Mark Korsgaard, senior vice president and worldwide claim manager, "so we assembled a team of underwriters, claims people, and loss control people all of whom work together on product development and the execution of claim service. For instance, one person in the home office works in claims and has biology and law degrees. She spent years in the life science field and has an excellent understanding of FDA regulations. Our customers feel at ease talking to such a person with this depth of expertise."

As a niche player, Chubb must pick and choose brokers and agents that can effectively sell its products and services to an elite clientele. In some areas, this may require an insurance brokerage to be knowledgeable in fine art, and if not, hire a broker who is. And if the company is insuring $5 million homes, its brokers and agents are likely to live in the same communities as do their clients, or nearby, and serve on the same community and civic boards. As an insurer of an elite clientele, Chubb has assembled an elite force of brokers and agents as its representatives. Of the 39,000 brokers and agents in the United States, with the vast number of them representing many property and casualty companies, only 4,400 sell Chubb products. Is there a touch of snob appeal to be one of this small corps of brokers and agents? While Chubb might not comment on the subject, we think there is. Note for example that Chubb has a U.S. market share of 2.3%, but in affluent Westchester County in New York, the company's penetration is impressive with an estimated 40% to 50% of the homes insured in its target market. On the commercial side of the business, you'll find an equally impressive penetration in certain market segments such as law firms, technology firms, museums, and cultural institutions.

"We're not doing construction," says Tom Motamed, "nor do we do long-haul truckers, and we're not doing restaurants or pizza parlors. However, in the places where we choose to play, we have penetrated those markets, and this is how a company establishes brand. I'm the first to say that we can't provide any value to a car wash or a pizza parlor. But we can in certain segments because we positioned ourselves in these niches as the brand they want. They come to us because they know we understand their business and stuff. From our standpoint, we can provide quality service to these segments, but if we have 10 million customers, I can tell you, we can't provide quality service to anybody.

"If you are Coca-Cola, as long as the can looks good and it tastes the same as it did last week, people are buying it. But that's not insurance. We are not all things to all people. If you have a $200,000 house and drive a Ford Taurus, you're going to get a better value by going somewhere else rather than coming to Chubb."

Motamed concludes by saying, "We probably could have been a bigger company if we wrote business outside our sweet spot. A lot of people out there are insurance generalists; we view ourselves as specialists. We aren't all things to all people, and we are perfectly happy with that."

One Customer at a Time

There are no shortcuts for developing relationships with customers, and that's done one at a time. A lot of retailers thought they could reduce the number of salespeople on their sales floor by putting a greeter at the front door. They thought that this employee would give customers a big, warm greeting when they walked in the door and it would be an inexpensive way to reduce the sales force and keep the customer happy. The greeter would appear to save customers time by directing them to the department where they wanted to shop. The problem was that customers didn't save time because when they got where they wanted to go, there was nobody there to serve them. ARG did a survey to find out what the American consumer thinks about store greeters, and 60% *emphatically stated that they believed greeters were only figureheads, not much different than having a stooge at the door.* This shows that bells and whistles don't cut it. You've got to give them substance.

Great companies never forget that customer loyalty is earned one customer at a time. And as they grow bigger they don't become spoiled by their success. They focus on doing what they did best when they were small: they remain close to the customer. Bob Carter, former Lexus group vice president and general manager, says, "I am confident that if you talk to any Lexus associate and ask what the brand stands for, he or she will say, 'The brand is about the ownership and retail experience.' Not to downplay the product, we do fireside chats with every dealer, general manager, and all the dealers' management staff, and we keep reminding ourselves what really matters. We tell them, 'Yes, we sold 329,000 last year. But in the eyes of the customer, he or she doesn't care about that. It doesn't matter to that one customer. That customer is concerned about the car he or she is buying, or his or her car that's being serviced.' Our goal is to provide each customer with a superb product, and with it, a retail ownership experience that's effortless."

Lexus, a brand that stands for high quality, is a perennial winner of awards presented each year to the best of the luxury class of cars. In one study, Lexus ranked the best in fewest problems with only 93 per hundred reported by new car owners. That's less than one problem per car, an amazingly low number. In years past, the Big Three had a dozen or more problems per new car. "We are very proud of this achievement," says Nancy Fein, former vice president of customer satisfaction, "but it is still not good enough. If your car was one that had a problem, you'd only be concerned about it, so we are working hard to do better. I am part of a team that goes to Japan with our Initial Quality Survey results and we review them with every one of our plants that builds our vehicles. Then they commit to what they will do to achieve specific goals that will lower those numbers the following year. Actually, they have their own internal targets and they compete with each other to be the number one plant in having the lowest problems per 100 vehicles. Sure, if we had zero per 100, we'd probably be happy. But right now, we continue to try to address that because we know that you have to get it right the first time."

Like Carter, Fein stresses that each Lexus owner is only interested in his or her car. "It's about that one car," she says, "that one customer. As long as we continue to personalize and maintain a personal relationship with each of our customers and treat each one as an individual and as a valued customer, we will be able to meet our objective. It doesn't matter how many cars we sell, we tell our customer service organization, we must never lose sight of the fact that it's only that customer and his or her concerns that count."

* * *

Tom James epitomizes a company that was built one customer at a time. While less than 3% of their new customers had previously purchased custom clothes, once accustomed to Tom James merchandise, a high percentage become lifetime customers. While Tom James clothes are high quality, it's the personal attention that the customers receive that wins their loyalty.

Jim McEachern joined Tom James Clothiers in 1966 as the company's second employee when he was hired by its founder, Spencer Hays. McEachern has been with the company until his retirement in 2008. He was named vice president, director of sales in 1969 and president in 1973, and he served as chairman and CEO from 1984 to 1998. His most recent title was senior executive officer, and he serves on the board of directors. With more than 40 years of experience under his belt, McEachern is a top authority on custom-made clothing.

"It used to be that there were a lot of good clothing salesmen in the department stores," McEachern tells. "In fact, back when I started with the company in 1966, many prospects would say, 'I like your merchandise but I've been dealing with the same salesman at XYZ Department Store for years.' Well, we rarely hear anyone say that today. That's pretty much a thing of the past.

"It's the individual attention we give that they won't find when they're browsing in a department store," McEachern says. "I once called on a banker who was disinterested in what I was saying. To get his attention, I said, 'I bet you have a problem with every shirt that you buy.' He looked at me quizzically and I continued, 'You have a fairly large neck in proportion to the rest of your body so when you wear a suit, the shoulders come down on you like this, don't they?' I said, demonstrating to him what I meant. 'Yes, they do, but how did you know?' 'Well, I know all ready-made shirts are purchased according to a man's neck size, and so the shirts you're buying are going to be too wide for your shoulders.' Of course, he knew I was right.

" 'From now on,' I said, 'We're going to make your shirts so they fit your neck size, but they'll be customized for your yoke size and your sleeve length.' Once he realized the service I could give him that he wasn't getting when he bought off the rack, he listened intently to my presentation and that was the beginning of a long relationship between the two of us. Once I can politely point out a prospect's problems, I am able to establish myself as something of an authority, and of course, this is an added value that I bring to the table."

"You can buy a blue suit anywhere," explains Naresh Khanna, who, year after year, is one of Tom James' top clothing professionals. "There are thousands of stores that sell them across the country. But part of the service that Tom James provides is to help a client coordinate his suit, shirt, and tie so everything comes together in the right color, pattern, and the fabric so he looks and feels his best. Speaking of feeling his best, a custom-made suit feels better. It reminds me about when kids get dressed up for Sunday school. When they've got their best Sunday clothes on, their manners are also better. Adults are the same way. We not only act better, we have more confidence and feel everything is going to go the way we want it to go."

Never Hide Behind Policy

A mysterious $2,000 deposit appeared on my checking account at Fifth Third Bank in Columbus. My wife, Elinor, called to notify the bank of the error. "There is $2,000 in our account that doesn't belong there," she explained. The woman thanked Elinor and assured her that the $2,000 would be removed from the account.

"Would you please send us a corrected monthly statement?"

"I will, but we will have to charge you for that."

"But it was the bank's fault, not ours!" Elinor replied. "Why will we be charged?"

"Because it's our policy. I'm sorry. I don't make the rules."

Because it upset us so much, we did an ARG survey to find out how other people feel about being told "It's against our policy": *59.2% of Americans are so infuriated by being given this lame excuse that they take their business elsewhere.* That's a lot of customers to lose—and far more than any company can afford to lose. With this knowledge, never—ever—say this to a customer. If your company has a policy on why it has a certain procedure, be up front and explain it. Customers might not agree with you, but they'll be far less likely to walk out enraged!

✳   ✳   ✳

For the record, we feel it is inexcusable to tell a customer, "It's against company policy." A customer is entitled to a full explanation. As Barbara Talbott, executive vice president, marketing, Four Seasons Hotels and Resorts, explains, "I would hope that a guest at Four Seasons is never told, 'It's against our policy.' Our attitude is, 'Anything is possible. Our job is to delight our customer.' I loved it when a guest in a focus group said, 'Four Seasons is in the business of saying yes.' That's just how he felt what we do.

He went on to say that even when Four Seasons says no, it starts with a yes. And the yes is about what's possible. We feel it's about offering choices."

Susan Helstab, also a Four Seasons marketing vice president, concurs with Talbott: "We can't get it perfect every time. What we deliver is a human interaction, a service experience, and none of us is perfect. It's inevitable that there are times when we can't live up to your expectations or even the promise that we've made. But what we work on very hard is to ensure that you feel good about how we tried to address that with you, and how we made it up to you. Then it becomes a matter about how we try to recover the trust and confidence that we lost by disappointing you in that moment."

✳   ✳   ✳

Lexus' former vice president of customer satisfaction, Nancy Fein, explains, "We don't have a whole lot of policies. We don't have a matrix that says, 'If a customer says this, this is what you do for her.' Lexus associates are empowered to do what we call 'case managing each customer.' This means that if you call in and I take the call, I am the only one that will call you back. You are going to deal with me, and I am going to take you through this process. I will not refer it somewhere else. I am not putting you in the system. I am taking care of you. I have the responsibility as well as the authority to take care of you."

Crunch Time

We heard lots of stories about how top executives pitch in during crunch times—when things get hectic and they roll up their sleeves and work side by side with low-entry employees to better serve customers. Arnold Block, the former general manager of Harrah's in St. Louis, talks about how he helps guests check in and out of the hotel when there are long lines at the counter. Block has done the same thing when he's in the restaurant during busy times. "It's in my blood," he says, "that when I see the waiters and waitresses are swamped, I'll quickly eat my dinner and help them clear tables."

Arnold Block was the company's top dog in St. Louis. As the general manager, Block earned his stripes, and he didn't have to work on weekends or on major holidays such as Thanksgiving, Christmas, and New Year's. But you can be sure you would see this general manager in the casino, mingling with customers, on most weekends and all holidays, especially when there would be a full house. "I feel that I have to be here, not that I want to because I enjoy being with my family just like everyone else does. I think it's important for my people to see me here. I tell them, 'This is the business we are in. And we get paid well. There's a lot of enjoyment and satisfaction you'll get out of it. But if you don't, then you probably picked the wrong career.'"

At the Four Seasons, they actually refer to it as "The Crunch." As Rob Hagelberg, hotel manager in Westlake Village, California, explains, "If there's a crunch in the front drive and the cars are backed up, who-ever's available will pitch in and do everything from driving cars to pulling the tickets. I do this sort of thing on a daily basis. I'll pour coffee for guests and I'll help check in guests at the front desk. If there's a changeover in the ballroom where there's a limited amount of time before another event begins, we'll all move chairs and flip up tables. It's a team effort and good for everyone's morale. When I do it, nobody can say, 'It's not my job.' We need to get it done for the guest. So whatever it takes, we're going to do it."

At Cabela's, Ralph Castner, the chief financial officer, talks about attending a grand opening of a new store in April 2007. "The store was packed with customers," he says, "so one of the store managers yelled over to me, 'Ralph, we need help bagging stuff at the checkout.' I had never bagged in my life, so my first reaction was that he wanted me to get some-body to pitch in. Then I thought to myself that I was available so I'll do it. So there I was, one of the five highest paid guys in the company, and I'm helping a cashier so her line would move faster. I was thankful I wasn't asked to run a cash register because I didn't know how. It was a good expe-rience because I realized how many items weren't tagged, and that's what really slows up the line. Along the same line of thinking, we had every salaried employee in our headquarters building spend three days working in the distribution center. This experience gave them a clear picture about serving our customers. My job for three days was to stuff envelopes with a gift certificate for anyone who ordered one."

Show the Customer How Much You Care

There's a constant danger that threatens every growing company that its management gets too removed from the front lines and customers resent it. Customers start to think management is getting too big for its britches, and they begin to think the company is no longer hungry for their busi-ness. When customers feel neglected, the timing is ripe for a competitor to woo them away. This is what could have happened at NetJets when Ray Catena was thinking about switching from NetJets to a competitor. Catena owns one of the nation's most successful automobile dealerships that consists of franchises with Lexus, Mercedes, Aston Martin, Jaguar, Porsche, and Infiniti, all located in New Jersey. Known for providing superior service to his customers, Catena expects it from others.

"Back in 1998, I received a call from Steve Eisman, my top salesman," Richard Santulli, NetJets' CEO, says. "He called on a Saturday morning around eleven to say that Ray Catena was talking to FlexJets and we might lose the account.

" 'Catena lives near me,' I said, 'Come on, Steve, I don't want to lose him.'

" 'He thinks we're getting too big,' Steve said, 'and we don't care about him.'

" 'That's not true,' I said. 'Tell Ray to call me. I'll wait for his call.'

"The exact date was March 7, 1998, and a few minutes later, the phone rings and it's Catena. I walked outside with the phone. 'Look, I know you guys are safe, and all that, but look, Rich, I'm in the service business too. I like the fact that Flex is much smaller, so I think I'd be better off with them. You're so big, and I don't think you care about your customers.'

" 'I'll tell you what, Ray, I'll give you a million dollars if you can tell me what I am going to do in one hour from now. I'm serious—one million dollars.' He made a few guesses, like I'm playing golf, going fishing, and so on.

" 'Okay, I give up. What are you doing?'

" 'I'm getting married.'

" 'You're getting married?' he asked in surprise.

" 'That's right, I'm getting married in my house. I'm outside on the lawn. Say, Ray, would you like to come to the wedding? In one hour the priest will be here.'

" 'You're serious, aren't you?'

" 'Absolutely. And you said we don't care about customers.'

" 'Rich, please tell Steve to send me the contract. And congratulations on your marriage.' "

A Big Company That Thinks Small

In Johnson & Johnson's 2006 annual report, Bill Weldon, J&J's chairman and CEO, clearly states the company's mission: "As the world's most comprehensive and broadly based health-care company, Johnson & Johnson is privileged to play a role in helping millions of people be well ... and stay well."

We like the simplicity and clarity of his message. When you meet Weldon and other senior J&J men and women, you feel comfortable talking to them because they come across as humble people with a strong passion to do the right thing. You quickly appraise them as dedicated workers who know they have a responsibility to serve others. Although J&J is a company with 122,200 employees, its people act as if they were with a much smaller company, one that might still be run by its original owner, or perhaps a family business.

"When you talk to the leaders of J&J's different businesses," Ray Jordan, vice president of public affairs and corporate communications, points out, "they express how they value their autonomy because it allows them to run their businesses. They also talk about how their autonomy creates a lot of energy. There's always a balancing act going on between a sort of efficiency and the effectiveness of that autonomy, in particular as it relates to being close with the customer."

Remarkably, Johnson & Johnson, a giant international company with $53 billion in annual revenues that earned $11 billion in 2006, has managed to be extremely light on its feet. J&J is able to do this by being a decentralized organization that consists of 250-plus different operating companies all around the world, each operated as an individual business unit. Unlike the business model of Warren Buffett's Berkshire Hathaway, where each company is managed totally independently and separately from the others, J&J units (as they are internally referred to) do interact, and corporate management provides resources including financial assistance, research, and advisory services.

Johnson & Johnson has leadership presence in three distinct segments of the health-care industry: consumer health care, medical devices and diagnostics, and pharmaceuticals. While each of these segments as a separate company would be an industry leader in its own right, these segments consist of many companies, and this permits its people to remain close to customers. It also promotes entrepreneurship and a sense of ownership. This decentralization serves as a magnet for talent, because it offers opportunities for individual advancement and growth. "With 250 companies, an individual can aspire to be president of a company," Weldon states, "and he or she can learn and grow and thereby move into different areas such as diagnostics devices, pharmaceuticals, and so on. People don't realize it but our medical device business by itself is the largest medical device company in the world. So is our consumer health products company. And our pharmaceutical company would be the world's fifth or sixth largest pharmaceutical company. And if you take the biotech part of it, it would be the second or third largest biotech company. So when I talk to the summer interns and our MBA students who work here, I always say, 'You can come to Johnson & Johnson and have a career. You never have to go anyplace else, and you will always be challenged and excited with the opportunity that presents itself.'"

Joe Scodari, former worldwide chairman, pharmaceuticals group, believes the company's decentralization offers significant competitive advantages. "Being broadly based in human health care," he explains, "gives us the capability within the walls of J&J to link together technologies that can provide benefits not available at many other companies. The Cypher Stent, manufactured by J&J's Cordis, is an example of how the company has been able to bring drugs and medical devices together. Likewise, progress is being made to bring diagnostics and drugs together. For instance, a collaboration is being done on a predictive diagnostic that could accurately forecast the outcome in cancer therapy. Imagine being able to know the outcome of how a patient will respond to therapy prior to the treatment. Being able to forecast the side effects, and most importantly, identify those patients that would not have benefited are incredible things to know in advance."

5

The Total Customer Experience — Before, During, and After the Sale

The total customer experience is analogous to the different stages of a long relationship of two people in love. First, there is the initial attraction, and if a mutual interest develops, they date. Likewise, the customer is initially exposed to a company by advertising or perhaps a third-party referral. Both sexes "advertise" their goods by the way they dress and talk on the phone and by the messages via Internet dating services. They also meet through a third-party referral, also known as a blind date. As consumers, we shop around. When we seek a mate, we play the field. Shoppers browse. The courtship can be likened to a sales presentation. The engagement period is a trial period prior to matrimony. A customer may also request a trial period, an "engagement period," before making a commitment. With consumers, the "marriage ceremony" is the close of the sale. After a marriage, a honeymoon follows, and for a while there is bliss. Likewise, immediately following a purchase, a customer has a "honeymoon" with no reason to be dissatisfied—it's usually too soon for anything to go wrong.

Sooner or later, the honeymoon is over. After the customer has had an opportunity to use the product, it's only a matter of time before something needs to be serviced. Both bad business relationships and marriages result in divorce. For either to succeed, a lot of work is required.

There are many ways that a buyer is initially attracted to a seller. Interest could be sparked by an advertisement, a salesperson's call, or perhaps a referral by a third party. An ARG study determined that *90% of consumers are influenced by advertising; 39% said that they are strongly influenced by advertising.* But the companies had better have what they advertise in inventory. Our studies showed that *77.6% of consumers will go back to a store that advertises an item in the newspapers but doesn't have it in inventory. However, if it happens a second time, only 56.3% will still shop there. If the store doesn't have advertised merchandise the third time, only 29.5% will return again.*

What kind of advertising works well? Put the business owner in the commercial: *73.4% of Americans believe what a business owner says in a commercial.* When Dick and Jim Cabela started selling fishing flies in 1961, they personalized their mimeographed catalogs by writing folksy messages to their customers. Later, photographs of the two brothers began to appear in catalogs. "You would not believe the letters we receive from people who act like they know our founders," says Ron Spath, vice president of customer relations. "Some will write personal stories to Dick and Jim about their families, their jobs, their fish stories. They feel as if they know the brothers because they were very visible right from the get-go. It is more than the Cabela's brand that our customers identify with—it's Dick and Jim Cabela, two down-to-earth guys who started this business in their kitchen."

There are many examples of brands that have been developed based on a company's founder's unique personality. Wendy's company founder, Dave Thomas, appeared in Wendy's commercials. Even though *Advertising Age* panned his appearance in the early ads, declaring that Thomas' inarticulate speech made him America's worst corporate spokesperson, the company ignored the critics. Time proved that the Wendy's marketing team was right on the money—Dave Thomas was indeed an incredibly effective spokesperson. America identified with his down-to-earth mannerisms, and sales of Wendy's square-shaped hamburgers soared. Similarly, those homey Smucker's "With a name like Smucker's, it has to be good" ads are also folksy and ooze with sincerity.

If you're going to put color inserts in the Sunday newspaper, we advise not cutting corners by using a poor-quality paper. In fact, *72.5% of consumers will judge the quality of your merchandise based on the quality of the insert's paper.* The same survey also revealed that *80.3% will determine that your store does or doesn't carry the latest styles based on your four-color inserts, and 52% of all consumers will judge how reputable your store is based on your inserts.*

Another of our studies revealed that *80.9% of consumers read private-sale mailers that they receive from a store they have patronized. Only 48.7% of consumers think that the stores they frequent make shopping fun for them.* This has become a serious problem for retailers.

It has always been costly to get new customers, so when you have them in your store, you've got to make the most of it. Since not every customer who looks actually buys, you want to make sure to keep the ones who do place an initial order. So what makes them walk away? ARG research found that *33.4% of shoppers will stop shopping a store where the checkout lines are too long and too slow; 47.3% will go somewhere else because they didn't like employees' attitudes; 56% said they would stop shopping a store that made it difficult to return merchandise. Incidentally, 62% believed certain companies make it difficult to return something.* Remember: your competition wants to take away your customers. It's hard enough to get customers through your door and make a sale. At this stage, you don't want to lose them by doing something dumb. As we mentioned earlier, Cabela's reputation is partially built on its return policy, which augments the company's loyal customer base.

Build It and They Will Come

Cabela's former senior vice president of business development and international operations, Michael Callahan, says, "Build it and they will come." This is said in reference to the huge outdoor goods stores averaging 150,000 square feet that the company has been opening, as many as eight new units a year. These are huge stores—about the size of three football fields. In 1998, the company opened the first store outside Nebraska in Owatonna, Minnesota. It chose Owatonna on the company's CEO Dennis Highby's recommendation. Highby is a native Minnesotan. "In the beginning, we didn't say we'd build *x* number of stores a year, or even one store a year," Callahan explains. "Our expansion program was more opportunistic than anything else. If we saw an opportunity, say, in Mitchell, South Dakota, where we opened an 80,000-square-foot store in 2000, we'd take a look, and we'd say, 'Let's put a store there.'"

As the company installed advanced information technologies, Cabela's management became more sophisticated in selecting locations for its retail business. "Based on our catalog sales," Castner, the company's chief financial officer, explains, "we can determine the number of active Cabela's customers in a given market. Knowing we have a built-in base of loyal customers means that we'll have a following whenever a new store opens. With an annual mailing of 150 million catalogs, our customers are spread across the U.S. and Canada. We analyze where our catalog revenues are strong according to zip codes, and this influences where a new store opens. We think it's an advantage we enjoy versus a retailer that doesn't have a catalog business."

"We became accustomed to a 15% to 20% annual growth rate," Callahan tells, "and for it to continue, the brick-and-mortar side of our business will be our primary growth vehicle. While the catalog business was growing at a fairly steep trajectory, over time it began to taper off, although still a long way from plateauing. Furthermore, we have long known that only 20% of the world buys mail order while the other 80% still want to go to a store."

Its strong reputation has earned Cabela's a loyal customer base that drives herds of avid outdoors people into its stores. Certainly, being known for its high-quality goods, enormous selection of merchandise, and 100% satisfaction guarantee draws satisfied catalog shoppers to attend a Cabela's grand opening. But it goes even further than having a large list of catalog customers. Unlike other catalog companies that have opened satellite stores in outlet malls across the country, Cabela's opened 150,000-square-foot stores, and these are not your typical big box stores. There is nothing boxy about a Cabela's store. While each has a common theme and likeness to the others, no two stores are alike. Almost all are free-standing structures, what's known in the retail industry as a destination store, meaning it's the place you plan to go from the time you get in your car and leave your house to shop. Cabela's draws its customers from near and far, from all directions. Customers are willing to drive hundreds of miles to visit a Cabela's. It's not unusual for a family to drive 200 miles and plan a mini–weekend vacation around a visit at Cabela's. The day we went to the store in Sidney, Nebraska, we counted license plates from 32 states.

In Chapter 1, we describe a visit to Cabela's as an outdoors person's paradise. There are activities for the entire family, and with so much going on, the average customer visits for $3^1/_2$ hours. The high quality and selection of outdoors merchandise is beyond anything they have ever seen under a single roof. Displays such as antique rifles and museum-quality taxidermy mounts of game animals from around the world make shopping at Cabela's a unique experience.

Also available to serve customers are enthusiastic outfitters (what salespeople are called) who specialize in such areas as hunting, fishing, and camping. These product specialists are avid outdoors people who love their work because it allows them to talk about their favorite pastime with customers who share the same passion.

Ten years ago, ARG research identified that *90% of Americans would browse when they shopped.* We called it retail therapy. *Today, nearly 63% of shoppers who formerly liked to browse said it is no longer a fun activity.* Why not? *Well 67% of them said that it was harder to find a salesperson to help them, and 89% of this group said the lack of capable help is why they no longer browse.* We assure you that this is not what the customer experiences at Cabela's.

The larger stores have 120,000 to 140,000 stock keeping units (SKUs). The Cabela's catalogs are known for their vast selection of quality goods, but rarely does a retailer carry such a large inventory. To see, touch, and try out real merchandise is an experience no catalog can match. A survey taken at Cabela's in Lehi, Utah, just south of Salt Lake City, revealed that the average customer comes to the 165,000-square-foot store 12 to 14 times a year and makes a purchase on 10 of those visits. What happens on the other two visits? "Well, we had out-of-town visitors," surveyed customers typically said, "so I wanted to show them the store, and they bought something."

An ARG survey disclosed that *71.4% of consumers shop a store due to its unique appearance.* The same survey revealed that *54.3% said they have driven by a store but didn't shop it because the outside was so unpleasant.* These figures illustrate that when a retailer like Cabela's does something special, its appearance will draw them inside.

Prior to a grand opening, local ads combined with a strong publicity campaign spread the word that Cabela's was coming to town. The large crowds of tens of thousands attract politicians and local celebrities. For example, speakers at the 2005 grand opening in Utah were Senator Orrin Hatch, Governor Jon Huntsman, and U.S. Congressman Jim Matheson. Speaker of the Utah House Greg Curtis was the master of ceremonies. It's a real coup for a local government to bring a Cabela's to the community. After all, the giant-sized store is a magnet for drawing hoards of tourists. The Cabela's in Utah is one of the state's most popular tourist attractions. One might think, "Well, Utah has a small population and is off the beaten path." If so, try explaining why Cabela's is the number one tourist attraction in Michigan, ahead of the Henry Ford Automobile Museum, as well as in Pennsylvania where it's drawing bigger crowds than Hershey's. Not only do stores employ a staff of 300-plus, but restaurants, motels, and gasoline stations also open at nearby locations. Besides, Cabela's is fun, wholesome entertainment for people of all ages. And the store contributes to the community. On any given day during the school year, you'll spot a bus full of students on a field trip coming to see the taxidermy, aquarium, and the African diorama. "Obviously, the kids don't spend anything," Callahan says, "but we give them a tour as a service to the community because it's an educational experience. We also make conference rooms available for local charitable and conservation meetings."

Since its regular mail order customers are among the most enthusiastic people to visit a new location, catalog sales in the area initially drop. "In Utah, our annual catalog sales were running at $11 million," Highby explains, "and after the new store opened, sales dipped to $10 million. But we picked up $60 million in store sales. It then took about 12 to 15 months before our catalog sales got back to where they were, and continued to climb ever since."

"We have that initial drop in our catalog sales," explains Ron Spath, "but within a year or so, our catalog sales exceed what they had been before we had the store because we get new customers, many who go to our Web site to shop."

A "Wow" Experience

Again and again during our interviews, we kept hearing about giving customers a "wow" experience. "Everyone makes a big fuss about customer satisfaction," Bill Pulte, founder and chairman of Pulte Homes, explains. "At Pulte, we work on the premise that we don't want to satisfy the customer, we want to delight the customer. Here's what I mean. When a husband and his wife go to a restaurant for dinner and have a nice meal, they are satisfied with it. So they go home and that's the end of it. They forget about it. On the other hand if they had a fabulous meal and extraordinary service, what do they do? They tell their friends about it. With this in mind, we don't think that just being satisfied is good enough."

Eric Pekarski, former national vice president of strategic initiatives at Pulte, adds, "Bill differentiated a long time ago when he said, 'People who are satisfied when they buy a home are those who get a home.' The difference is that delighted people get an experience by having a company that supports the home they bought well beyond the time when they get the keys to their house. I think the level of comfort is when you continue to serve them after they've closed on their house. Pulte takes great care of its customers and, as a result, they talk about how great their experience was with Pulte. It was so fantastic that they'd talk about it when they were around the water cooler at work. They'd tell everyone, 'If you're thinking about a new home, see Pulte.'"

Prior to joining Pulte Homes in 2001, Pekarski was director of operations for Sandcastle Resorts and Hotels, a company that owns and operates full-service hotels in the United States, including several Hilton flagship properties. "In the lodging industry, hotel employees ask how you are when you register at the front desk, and at a good hotel, they might even ask if everything is okay once you've settled in your room," he explains. "But if you're there for three or four days, the chances are nobody will inquire about your well-being until you check out. On your way out the door, you'll hear, 'How was everything?' By that time, if it wasn't good, it's too late. Of course, this attention to customers goes beyond the hotel business. I always thought, 'If we could just get to customers before they're on their way, then if something wasn't right, we'd have an opportunity to fix it.' In many ways, a seven-day stay in a hotel is like a seven-year stay in a house. In the housing business, it is not acceptable to simply hand the keys to somebody and say, 'Here's your house. Thanks so much for buying.' There is a lot that goes on after the close, ranging from educating them on how to take care of their home to just walking a couple through the house during the first month when things are really hectic."

✳ ✳ ✳

Although Lexus scores the highest marks in the luxury car brand for customer satisfaction, Bob Carter, the division's former group vice president, says, "I'm really not in business to satisfy you. I am in the business of making you an advocate. If you're in the market for another car and you are just satisfied, you may consider another brand. But if I can offer you the product *and* the services that give you a "wow" experience, this is what will make you an advocate. That's why it goes much further than having a great product. It's the service *after* the sale that makes true advocates of customers. And in our business, this includes getting you in and out in an expeditious manner.

"We survey Lexus car owners and ask questions such as, 'Did you like the salesperson?' 'Did you like the car?' But getting customer satisfaction isn't necessarily a predictor of customer loyalty. It doesn't predict who is going to buy another car from us. I can go to a Marriott, and if I'm asked, 'Are you satisfied with the service?' I will say that I am, but it doesn't mean I'm going to be an advocate of Marriott like I would be of the Four Seasons. Marriott gave me what I wanted, but nothing exceptional to get me so excited that I want to go back to Marriott again. Now the Four Seasons—that's different."

A thoughtful expression appears on Carter's face. "I'll tell you what I call advocacy," he says, and quickly adds, "Harley Davidson. I defy you to find customers more passionate than Harley Davidson owners. The ultimate advocacy is when you get people tattooing your brand on their arm!"

Nancy Fein, former vice president of customer satisfaction, points out, "Advocates are the customers that talk about us at their golf clubs and cocktail parties. Their loyalty is to the Lexus brand as opposed to their car. They may buy a different vehicle from us the next time, but they keep coming back. Based on their past experience, they have high expectations, and our job is to keep trying to exceed those expectations. We want them to say, 'Wow, I can't believe they did that!' And that's what they tell their friends, 'Wow, did they take care of me.'"

Lexus has a 59% loyalty rate as compared to the luxury car industry that averages about 40%. Seventy percent of Lexus customers come back to their dealerships for service, again far above the industry average, also at 40%.

✳   ✳   ✳

Four Seasons' reputation for excellence is so intact that its guests expect an excellent experience every visit. "Our guests are accustomed to our personal service and attention to detail," Susan Helstab, senior vice president of corporate marketing, explains, "and consequently a high percent of them make special requests with their reservations. It's our goal to fulfill every request."

And special requests run the gamut. As Barbara Talbott, executive vice president of marketing, tells, "It could be stocking the private bar with specific items. For instance, a guest might request hand-squeezed orange juice, and another might want a particular brand of scotch or vodka. A guest with allergies might have special requirements for the room. Another guest might ask us to book a reservation at a recently opened 'hot' restaurant in town. Other times, guests with a package plan want to exchange a spa treatment, for example, for a round of golf or vice versa. Our guests believe that we have the ability to shape their stay in a way that's very personal to them, and the view of the employee is, 'How can I meet or even exceed the expectations of this guest?' Each employee takes this as his or her personal responsibility—one guest at a time."

Typically, travelers experience stress when away from home, and since the events of September 11, 2001, travel has become even more stressful. Flight cancellations, delays, and the security process have given travelers a sense of being less in control. In addition, increased traffic congestion has added to a traveler's stress. "There is more aggressiveness to all interactions," Susan Helstab says, "and Four Seasons is an anecdote to that. We provide a calming, reassuring, serene environment. When you travel, people with whom you interact expect the worst of you: you feel you have to prove that you are worthy of respect. At Four Seasons, every guest is worthy of respect the moment he or she walks through our doors—they feel it immediately. Travelers are on the go from the time they get up, and we provide them with some time to enjoy the moment. They can relax by taking in the visual beauty that exists at our hotels, whether it's the flowers, the architecture, the décor of the room, or some of the amenities we provide. And if they're traveling with a loved one, they get to focus on each other because we're taking care of all the details for them."

Four Seasons is famous for its exquisite properties, ultradeluxe spas, marble floors, lavish furnishings, and rooms with breathtaking views. Each hotel's physical radiance is a joy to behold. However, Four Seasons does not have a monopoly on these attributes; they are available at other hotels and resorts around the world. It's these luxuries combined with the warm hospitality that each guest receives that makes Four Seasons stand out above the crowd. It's a series of hundreds of small touches, each by itself that might go unnoticed, that makes the total guest experience a special happening. It's being given a cold towel by a doorman when you arrive back at the hotel after a jog in a nearby park, or the refreshing feeling of having a pool attendant spray cool water on you while you sunbathe. Or it might be the ice cream bar, frozen grapes, or fruit skewer. And it's so many little things that most guests never notice. For instance, the clock on the bed stand that faces out during the day is turned by the chambermaid to face the bed at nighttime.

Helstab tells about her own personal experience while staying at the Beverly Wilshire on New Year's Eve. "To celebrate the occasion, each guest was given an eight-ounce bottle of champagne called 'Pop.' One bottle was rosé that came in pink neon packaging, and another bottle was regular champagne in a blue nylon bottle. Each bottle was in a champagne bucket with a matching colored straw. It was the presentation that made this so special. It had a real sense of fun. It also acknowledged that since you are in the hotel, you've already figured out what you wanted to do for New Year's Eve, so how could Four Seasons do something for you that you haven't already done for yourself? This was just the right touch to help you celebrate the occasion one last time. It was done in such good taste that it took the expected to another level. It just put a smile on my face and made me feel special."

"It's also the thoughtfulness," Talbott adds, "the sense of generosity because you know you're not paying extra for it. It was just given to you. It's the unanticipated gesture that is just perfect at this moment. What could be nicer?"

Four Seasons' reputation didn't happen overnight. It evolved over a period of time, starting with its founder and CEO, Isadore Sharp, who, to this day, keeps thinking from a guest's prospective. "What would you want as a guest who is traveling," Sharp explains, "what would you need to make your business more successful and more pleasant? You are away from your office and your home. What's the support you need?

"From the beginning, I was only thinking as a guest, and I would come up with ideas. We never did anything because we were trying to impress people, and there were never any gimmicks. We wanted our customers to think of Four Seasons as a value for what they spent, and if we earned that reputation, we could charge more and people would be willing to pay for it. With this thinking, we had many innovations over the years, but they didn't happen overnight. Just a lot of little ideas. It was not rocket science. At our first hotel in 1961, we put shampoo in the bathroom. This idea came to me because I grew up with three sisters and I knew women would never wash their hair with soap. So we put it in the shower and in the bathtub. At first, the shampoo was in a little package that you'd open in the shower with wet hands, and you'd use your teeth to tear it open. Well, you'd end up drinking the shampoo. Over time, we kept improving the package. We were the first to have two telephones in the room, and we had remote controls before there was remote control television.

"We were the first to put very comfortable mattresses in our rooms. After all, how can you expect to get a good night's sleep if you're not on a comfortable mattress? Consequently, when we opened our first hotel in London, we found a German manufacturer to make a special mattress for us, and every guest that flew across the Atlantic from the States who arrived at six or seven in the morning would be assured that a comfortable bed was waiting for him. Later we developed a special pillow top. In 1963, we were the first to build a first-class fitness facility in a hotel, and in 1986, we were one of the first companies to build a full-scale spa. That was in Dallas. I saw the trend of lifestyle that focused on the food we eat and exercise we did. We've also renovated older properties so they too have spas.

"We've initiated many innovations, and always with the idea in mind that this is what the guest wants. It delights me when the industry adopts what we started. Everything from shampoo to workout rooms has become a standard in the industry. This is fine with me because it's good for people who travel."

Customer Service Behind the Curtain

Sometimes the "wow" results from what a company does in the back room that the customer never sees. For example, at NetJets hundreds of employees work in a service area that looks like a large trading floor of a securities firm. Lined up in this big room are hundreds of desks and computers used by account managers organized into teams of six that are assigned to designated owners. These individuals personally serve owners. They book flights, arrange the food catering during the flights, set up ground transportation, and cater to every customer whim to ensure that NetJets exceeds the customer's expectations. In another section of the same room, the company has invested heavily in a state-of-the-art in-house technology system called IntelliJet that is operated by highly skilled technology people. This elaborate computer system was designed and built exclusively for NetJets. It does such things as schedule trips, check all the performance numbers with the company's licensed dispatchers, bill owners, and manage flight crew duty time.

There are many interesting statistics involving NetJets' stellar performance, among which is its amazing record for safety. Its fleet of 700-plus aircraft has never had a fatality. Another fascinating statistic is the company's recovery time when one of its planes is down due to a mechanical problem. "What would you want as a customer who is traveling?" Jim Christiansen, NetJets' president, queries enthusiastically. "I've run corporate airplanes for many years, and I have to tell you, it makes your stomach sink when the phone rings and Mr. Big is stuck in Broken Pelvis, Montana, and says, 'My plane is broken, Jim, what are you going to do about it?' In the past, you'd go, 'Uhh, let me think about it . . .' Our average recovery time means that once we get that call from an owner, in an average of 56 minutes he's in the air on his way on another airplane. Remember, now we have to get the plane from Place A to Place B, get the crew squared away, get the plane fueled, and get it moved around. If you understand this business, you know how astounding this statistic is."

"When you buy into NetJets," explains Matt Harris, executive vice president, "you buy into our safety culture. And you buy into the service delivery. You don't need to necessarily know what's going on behind the curtain, but it's our infrastructure that allows that 56-minute turnaround to happen.

"Here's what happens," Harris continues. "With over 700 planes worldwide operated by the NetJets subsidiaries, we have a critical mass that allows us to park a plane rather than have it fly back empty to our base in Columbus. Our technology system then schedules the plane to pick up another nearby owner. It's like having the pieces of a giant puzzle fit together, and with as many planes as we have, we're able to match up our airplanes and crews. Another company with a small fleet can't possibly do this, so it's one of our competitive advantages."

In other parts of the large room, NetJets has licensed dispatchers. "As an added safety precaution," Harris tells, "we have a dual release system for every flight. This requires both the pilot and our Federal Aviation Administration (FAA) licensed dispatcher to agree that the trip can be accomplished safely. Our dispatchers are responsible for such things as running flight plans, flight releases, and checking the aircraft's performance data. Then they communicate with the flight crews to make sure that all systems are a go."

With weather conditions being such an important factor, NetJets employs eight full-time meteorologists who also work in the big room. Why meteorologists? "We're interested in aviation-specific weather at airports that aren't necessarily traveled and serviced by major metropolitan areas," Harris points out, "because we go to off-the-beaten-path places. One of the jokes around here is that we have more satellite dishes on our roof than CNN does for the weather channel. And yes, we ingest the same data that the major airlines and the weather centers use, but we also tailor it to the missions that our aircraft are flying, which is what our owners' needs are."

Al Peters, NetJets' vice president of its systems operation control center, is responsible for scheduling where the company's airplanes go every day. The center, also in the big room, orchestrates where maintenance people and crew services personnel are needed. "We're constantly modifying schedules due to such things as weather delays and traffic control delays," Peters explains, "so there are always daily challenges. Then too, we have compression problems because everyone wants to leave at certain peak times of the day and during certain times of the year such as around Thanksgiving and Spring Break. Then there are special events that a lot of our owners go to such as the Cannes Film Festival, the Masters, and the Super Bowl."

Of course companies in other industries also have a lot going on in their back rooms that the customer never sees or, for that matter, needs to know. Nonetheless, it is a vital part of the customer experience—before, during, and after the sale.

When a Product Is Much More Than a Product

In the 1980s when the automobile tire business was engaged in a price battle to win customers, Michelin recognized that it couldn't compete on those terms. Instead, the company made the decision to sell safety as its number one feature, and its advertising campaign informed consumers that when they drove on Michelin tires, their children would be safe. Their timing was perfect because at the time more women were becoming chief decision makers for buying their family's tires. Michelin became the undisputed leader in tire safety, a position the company holds to this day. And by selling safety, Michelin sells a lot of tires.

✳   ✳   ✳

A hotel's basic product is a good night's sleep. Four Seasons does it to an extreme. In addition to its top-of-the-line mattress, a guest sleeps on down pillows or can request hypoallergenic pillows. Every room has blackout curtains to eliminate all outside light, which eliminates wearing eye shades for those sleepers who are light sensitive. The rooms are also soundproofed. And of course, the thermostat can be adjusted by the guest to get an exact desired room temperature.

✳   ✳   ✳

To an outsider, a Mary Kay Independent Beauty Consultant sells the same cosmetics that can be purchased in a department store, and on the surface, one cosmetics line seems pretty much like another brand. We won't debate the merit of different cosmetics brands, but what sets Mary Kay apart is the personal attention given by the Beauty Consultant to each of her customers. For starters, Mary Kay Independent Beauty Consultants are more knowledgeable and are able to provide more personalized service than their counterparts at department store cosmetics counters. This is evident by the skin care classes they conduct for small groups of women, who, in turn, become knowledgeable in using Mary Kay products. Mary Kay also offers opportunities for women to be independent business owners, and in this arena the company truly excels. There are an estimated 1.7 million Beauty Consultants worldwide today, and this number is growing by leaps and bounds. "The business opportunity is the foundation of our company's success," Rhonda Shasteen, senior vice president of corporate brand strategy and sales support, explains. "It's a business that's dependent upon more than a one-time sale. Beauty Consultants want their customers to come back time and time again over the years, and that's what provides a successful business opportunity for them.

"Many people think of us as a cosmetics company, first and foremost, that just happens to distribute and sell its products through a direct sales organization," Shasteen confides. "But that, in fact, is not the case. We are first and foremost an organization that provides a business opportunity for women, and that just happens to sell cosmetics as the vehicle to support that opportunity. This is why we say that our independent sales force—our Independent Beauty Consultants—are our customers."

✳   ✳   ✳

"My people know how much I care about this company that they sometimes think I'm an evangelist," Richard Santulli, NetJets' CEO, asserts. "I love this company. But the bad news about this company is that we've never had a perfect day. It can't happen in our business. That's terrible when you think about it. Take one weekend this past March, for instance, when we had an ice storm in New York. So many people canceled their trips from Friday night to the next morning that our owners booked 130 more trips for Saturday. What happens is that I can't get airplanes in, so Saturday was not a great day. And it happens every day. Airplanes break. When you have a company that doesn't allow you to ever have a perfect day—and I mean *ever*, the owner service person's job is even that much more critical. It's easy to deal with people when it's a wonderful trip, and when this happens, we tell you everything is right. That's simple. When there is a problem, what's important is how we communicate with that owner.

"I tell my people every day that anybody can buy a plane," Santulli continues, "and anybody can fly an airplane. We have to be the safest people in the world, which we are. And we have to let people know we care. As long as they know we care, we will win because not everything is going to be perfect."

Added Value, Plus, Plus, Plus

You receive added value when a company gives you more than you bargained for. There are hundreds of subtle ways that Four Seasons provides added value. As we mentioned, it's that cool spray of water that refreshes a sunbather, or a chambermaid's turning a clock radio toward the bed in the evening. It's the accumulation of many services that make a stay at Four Seasons a memorable experience, and it's what keeps bringing guests back.

In a totally different business, Chubb does the same thing but with a less glamorous product than a five-star hotel and resort. Most people consider insurance a mundane product, one that we must have and hope never to use. It is also an intangible product—a contract on a piece of paper that can cost a lot of money. As Senior Vice President Frances O'Brien puts it, "People mostly get a letter from their insurance company that's either an invoice or a policy, and they don't want to have to deal with it. Our client could have homeowners or automobile coverage and he receives a bill from us every month or quarter for years, and he might not have a claim for a long time. Maybe never. To win his loyalty, we look for ways to provide more than just a promise that if something horrible happens we'll be there for him. So our service goes beyond providing a written agreement that we'll indemnify a client in the event of a loss."

During our visit at Chubb, we heard several people say how the company goes beyond the four corners of the contract. This is a philosophy initiated by Hendon Chubb, one of the original family members who started his career with the company in 1895 and served as CEO from 1911 to 1946. We randomly talked to Chubb policyholders and brokers, and the consensus was that there are other companies that offer coverage at lower premiums but none match the service that Chubb consistently delivers. In an industry where aggressive agents are always prevalent to sell their wares but hard to find when a claim occurs, Chubb marches to a different drummer.

There is a slew of services that Chubb provides that makes it the company of choice for discriminate shoppers. Mark Korsgaard, who heads Chubb's worldwide casualty claims, says, "We seek out people who can solve problems, and we give them a fair amount of autonomy. We expect them to resolve issues. During their training, we emphasize that prompt and quality contact is essential. 'As soon as you get a claim, call the insured,' they are told. We differ from other companies because we train people to find coverage for the loss. That's right. Find ways to make sure that loss is covered and should be paid. We put aside fraud-type scenarios and we give our customers the benefit of the doubt. We have created an aura of responsiveness to the customer. It starts with our responsiveness to our agents and it permeates throughout the organization. Our claims people are lifetime learners. They have a desire to learn because every claim can be very different than any other previous one.

"We used to have an ad that referred to insurance claims," Korsgaard continues. "The ad read, 'They are not like fine wines.' We often refer to that ad to remind ourselves that no claim gets better with age. Someone once said to me that insurance claims all go away eventually. However, my job is to figure out how to make them go away as quickly and as efficiently as possible. We do this by thinking, 'What can we do from the customer's viewpoint?' The customer is thinking, 'Get my car back to me,' and, 'I don't want to be hassled.'"

"We are the product," Frances O'Brien, Chubb's senior vice president, says. "It's our job to fulfill the promise our agents make to their clients, so we have to make sure we are always there for them. We also have to be easy to do business with. From the agents' perspective, they are businesspeople and need to operate efficiently. We must make sure we don't create any cumbersome processes that make it difficult for them to do business with us. We've spent a lot of time working on how we can better service our agents."

Paul Krump, Chubb's senior vice president and chief operating officer for Chubb Commercial Insurance, underscores the fact that "the company has 400 loss control engineers around the globe who are working with clients to mitigate losses and make recommendations to improve the risk. Customers appreciate this, but now and then someone will say, 'You're really doing this to lower your losses.' 'Yes,' I'll reply, 'and those are also affecting you by lowering your premiums over time. It's a win-win situation.'"

It's a given that Chubb will pay every claim according to the terms in the policy, but there are still other services not in the contract that the company provides—ones that are over and beyond the call of duty. "For most people, they have never experienced a loss," Korsgaard explains, "and consequently, they don't know who to call, for example, to come in and clean up. They don't know the steps involved, or what to expect. Our people are very good at explaining the process and setting up the expectation in what has to be done. We're constantly surveying our claimants and I'm always amazed at their comments about our individual people, about how they tell us how so-and-so had so much empathy."

On October 19, 1991, an incompletely extinguished grass fire in Berkeley/Oakland Hills, just across the bay from San Francisco, became one of the nation's most destructive wildland and urban interface fires in history. The following day the fire spread southwest driven by wind gusts up to 65 miles per hour and were too much for the regional firefighting resources to handle. Television viewers watched the 49ers football game aghast as the cameras kept turning away from the field to focus on the thick black smoke. Flames destroyed power lines to 17 pumping stations in the Oakland water system, thereby inhibiting the firefighters from containing it. By the end of the day, 25 people died and nearly 3,000 homes were destroyed. "We insured so many homes that were destroyed by the fire," Korsgaard tells, "and it left a lot of people without a place to stay. In order to contact them, we placed ads in the paper and we summoned their brokers to attend a two-day session we conducted in a local hotel where we brought in every type of resource that they might need that was insurance-related to help get life back on track. This included bringing in architects, engineers, and other restoration people, plus we included people who could offer financing advice." Again, Chubb went beyond the four corners of the contract. For the record, there was no obligation to do anything until a policyholder reported his or her losses.

Follow-Up Service *After* the Sale

Aaron Brown, former head of customer relations at Pulte Homes, says, "Most home builders have a customer service department that's responsible for serving the homeowner after the sale. Now, I'm referring to what happens after there is a signed contract and a down payment, because it could be as long as a year before the house is constructed and occupied. A lot of things can happen during this period, and when there is a problem, the typical homeowner calls the service department to fix his problem. That is a very reactive approach. Pulte takes a proactive approach. In fact, the company changed the name from customer service to customer relations. Of course, it goes way beyond a name change. The objective is to have someone be in contact with the new home buyer within days after the contract is signed. This person served as a liaison the home buyer could count on. While the customer could always contact the salesperson, the customer contact continually communicated with the homeowner from that point on."

As a production home builder, customers visit a model home on a site where Pulte develops a large residential tract, and what they ultimately purchase is a replica of the house on display. The house is built after the customer signs a contract and makes a down payment. Customers make certain selections such as the color of carpeting and cabinets, and so on. They choose a specific lot. Pulte is not a custom home builder. There are certain standard features but not a lot of options. It's not like selecting a meal off the menu at the Cheesecake Factory. The customer benefits from this standardization because certain economies of scale reduce Pulte's buying and building costs. There are also no surprises. It's not like buying a car with a sticker price of $20,000 that ends up costing $38,000 with all the extras.

The focus of Pulte's customer relations includes a definite routine that ensures that Pulte homeowners receive exceptional service from start to finish—and beyond, because the service continues even after the home is occupied. The company has specific procedures to make certain that no customer gets short-changed. The goal is to delight every customer.

There is a seven-step progression that follows the purchase of the home starting with a preconstruction meeting that typically happens just before the ground is broken. "Here you are told what you can anticipate experiencing," Brown explains. " 'Here are some key things you need to know about your lot.' 'This is going to be your timeline.' Pulte lets people know what to expect and then finds a way to exceed their expectations. The goal is to build a foundation of trust. The next time they meet with the customer is right before the drywall goes up—at this point, the house has been framed, insulated, plumbed, and the heating, ventilation, and air-conditioning have been installed. The purpose is to help the customer understand what's behind the walls. Not only is this good information for homeowners to know, but you want them to see that you aren't hiding anything. Naturally, the company is quite proud of the quality. Along with the homeowners, the building superintendent and the salesperson are present. That's a very positive experience that relieves any anxiety buyers may have. Unfortunately, some builders hide behind a veil that has made the public skeptical. Pulte wants to assure customers that they are getting what they paid for. You are contributing to someone's American dream, and you want it to be a wonderful experience. Knowing that a home is the most expensive purchase the average American will ever make, Pulte believes it should also be the best experience he or she has ever had."

The next step is the inspection process by the customer relations contact, which doesn't include the homeowner. This is an inspection with a 400-point checklist, covering everything from basement to roof. Does the bathtub hold water? Does the water get hot? Do all the lights work? Do all the outlets work? Are the windows opening and closing easily? Are paint touch-ups needed? The objective is to make sure everything is in order prior to the owner seeing the finished product.

Next the customer relations contact takes the homeowner on a tour of the house, which is the preclosing orientation. This generally occurs a few days before the actual house closing. A question-and-answer session is conducted, in which questions are answered about topics ranging from maintenance to what's the best pizza shop in the neighborhood. Other information about the community includes fire department and police department locations, recommended dentists and doctors, and so on. "This is a celebration," Brown tells, "and Pulte wants to make sure that the homeowner is totally comfortable with the house. The company's promise to homeowners is that it will never send them to a closing unless they feel their house is 100% complete. Pulte is so confident about its quality that it won't let customers close on their house if they feel that there is an open item. In any other industry, it is totally unacceptable to buy an unfinished product. You wouldn't buy a $40,000 car that didn't have its final coat of paint on it. But in the housing industry, people typically move into houses that still need cabinets installed, walls painted, and all other things. That's something Pulte won't tolerate."

Thirty days later, the customer relations contact makes another visit, this time to check with the homeowner to see if there have been any problems that have only been apparent after the house has been lived in. "There may be a paint touch that you never see because no one has been in the house at eight in the evening but it's visible when a light hits a wall a certain way. Whatever the problem, they want to fix it. Then, there's a 3-month walk-through involving a full inspection of the house. They examine windows, the paint, the furnace, and homeowners are encouraged to change the filter. There's a long checklist to make sure everything is right. Again, it's a proactive approach. Finally, there is the 11-month inspection. Here they look for things such as if there was any settlement or movement in the foundation, any shrinking of the paint or drywall, and a lot of other things to make sure the house is in as good condition as it was on the first day."

Eric Pekarski says that what Pulte customer relations contacts do is definitely not the norm in the house building industry. "Pulte does it because it's the right thing to do," he asserts. "It's a part of the total customer experience. This is why they get the customer relations contact involved right from the beginning. For more than a year, he or she is in constant communication with the customer. They're constantly calling and e-mailing customers to keep them updated on what's going on with their house. For instance, the contact might call to say, 'I wanted to give you a head's up that if you're coming by the house this weekend, we had a little accident. A workman broke a window and a new one has been ordered. It's nothing to be concerned about.' There's an old saying in the building business that a house is built by one thousand hands with 100,000 pieces. This means there is bound to be some things that go wrong."

Pulte invests a lot of money in its customer relations program. We think it's an excellent investment because the company's customers are more than satisfied, they're delighted. How do we know? After our interviews at Pulte, ARG conducted a study that addressed home buying: 51% *said that they never had a real estate agent follow up after they moved into their home. Of those who did, 91.1% said that they would recommend that agent!* How well Pulte Homes knows this. An estimated 40%-plus of Pulte's annual sales come from referrals and repeat customers.

✳   ✳   ✳

Edward Jones has what's known as the "Goodknight" program. Successful, veteran financial advisors volunteer to share with a newer financial advisor. They temporarily take these new advisors into their offices and turn some of their not-so-active client accounts over to them. This way, veterans can refocus their business on fewer accounts, while newer advisors can give more attention to their new clients. "The program is named after Jim Goodknight," Jim Weddle explains, "who had an office in Joplin, Missouri, a town of 50,000. Jim invited a new broker to work out of his office, and to get him started Jim turned over many of his smaller accounts. Not only did these leads help the new broker get started in the business, it was a good way for Jim's smaller clients to get more service. It also freed Jim and allowed him to concentrate on his bigger clients. Before he retired, he set up four Goodknight plans. His second broker, Dan Stanley, implemented two Goodknight plans. We think it's a win-win-win situation because it's good for the original broker, the new broker, and the client."

Correcting a Mistake

Customers judge companies on how its people react when they make a mistake. We like what Eric Pekarski, formerly of Pulte, had to say on the subject. "It's a given that we're all going to make mistakes," he asserts. "What's important is how we recover from them. Having once been in the restaurant business, I remind people about my observations from earlier in my career. We've all seen a waiter disagree with an upset customer who wants something for free. The waiter disagrees and an argument pursues. The waiter argues and the customer argues and they quarrel back and forth. The manager comes over, and the bickering continues. Finally, 20 minutes later, the manager says, 'Okay, I'll buy dessert for the table.' Well, talk about a horrible management situation. If the customer is right, he is right. Let's acknowledge it and let's do it fast. Then, let's try to recover as quickly as we can. You don't have to get the manager involved. You know what's right and you know what's wrong. And there are gray areas in everything.

"If the warranty says you cover a certain width of a crack in the garage floor, then fix it, and if it's a narrower width, don't. Of course, there are also some judgment calls that have to be made. Just remember that when you do it, do it quickly. Back to the example of the restaurant customer who was finally given a free dessert. By the time he got his dessert, he had lost his appetite. As a result, the restaurant gave away money but got nothing in return because the customer will never come back."

* * *

World Wide Technology's founder and chairman, David Steward, says, "We're not infallible and we do make mistakes. But when we do, we'll do whatever it takes to get it right. We'll take whatever resources we have to assure that we make it right for the customer, even if it costs us money to give the value that's expected of us and of ourselves, which is above and beyond. Our attitude is we're only as good as the last deal we did.

"Some of the best salespeople we have in the marketplace are our customers who are saying good things about us," Steward adds. "They sell our company better than any salesperson we have. That's because they can say things that we can't say about ourselves. They're sending customers to us by talking about our willingness to go over and beyond on their behalf. They're telling others about how we put their interest first ahead of our own. And they're talking about our willingness to fix a problem at whatever it costs to satisfy our customer."

* * *

Many companies tend to be quick at delivering good news but slow to tell customers about the bad news. It's obvious why people are eager to talk about good things. That's easy. And it's human nature to dislike being the bearer of bad news. After all, bad news upsets people and makes them confrontational. No wonder people want to avoid it. But in business, communicating the bad news is equally as important as the good news. We like the line from *The Godfather*, said by Tom Hagen, the consigliere played by actor Robert Duvall, when the Hollywood director flatly refuses to do business with "the family." Hagen tells him, "I must go to the airport. The Godfather wants to hear bad news immediately."

Edward Jones' managing partner Jim Weddle says, "The markets are cyclical; they go up and they go down. For this reason, we emphasize to our financial advisors, 'You cement your relationships with clients when you deliver something other than good news.' If a client has purchased a stock, a bond, or a mutual fund, he or she deserves an update on the performance. Certainly clients receive statements and reports, but they also need an explanation. It's disappointing when every investment just doesn't go up, but that never happens. For this reason, I tell the folks who are coming through our training classes what I was told from a veteran when I was a rookie—something that I would say to my clients. 'You know, sir, there are going to be days when your investments are going up in value and you are really feeling good about them, and you are going to be feeling really good about me. And there are going to be days when your investments are not performing very well, and you are not going to be very happy with me. In fact, on those days, you might feel like throwing a brick right through my window. When so, just make sure that when you throw that brick through my window, you tape a check to it. Because that's the exact right time to be adding to your investments because that's when they're low in price.' This speaks so clearly about the emotions of investing, and I think it's important to let clients know that they'll be hearing from you during the bad times."

Weddle recalls how Edward Jones responded on September 11. "I was on the Management Committee at the time, and John Bachmann, Doug Hill, Daryl Pope, and Rich Malone, all very senior people, were attending meetings in New York. John Sloop, one of the other Management Committee members and I were in St. Louis, and we gathered up others and convened a meeting. Our focus was on helping our financial advisors and branch office administrators communicate with their clients. Afterward, John and I sat down at one of our closed-circuit television stations, and we reached out to our field people at their branch offices. 'We don't know any more about the tragedy in New York than what you see on the TV and read in the newspapers,' we said.

'But here's what you need to do. The markets are going to be closed. They are probably going to be closed today and tomorrow. But it doesn't matter because you still need to come to your branch and you need to be there for clients when they call and ask what they should do. And the answer is, you don't do anything quite yet. We're going to monitor the situation. And we are going to get back to you as soon as we have any information to share.'"

6

The Personal Touch

The Internet is unquestionably one of the most innovative advancements in modern technology. With it, we can do online banking and pay our utility bills with a few clicks of the computer mouse. We can search for low rates for hotel rooms and airfares and shop for just about anything ranging from theater tickets to rare books. We can even track our investments in our financial portfolio on the Internet.

Yet in spite of its boundless applications to serve customers, the Internet is being used as a substitute for customer service by many companies, exasperating millions of people. In a nutshell, when it's time to interface with another human being, we do not like having dialogue with computers. Although it's possible to converse with a machine—if you want to call it that—it can't be programmed to address all questions and problems. When we are unable to navigate our way through a company's Web site and need assistance, we become frustrated. According to a 2008 ARG study, *56% of Americans think today's companies are being run by machines and they don't like it*. These individuals have become so disenchanted that *43.1% think the Internet, a tool intended to enhance communication, actually hinders service*. Certainly, companies are not intentionally replacing humans with machines to antagonize anyone. These systems are installed for efficiency, and by replacing salaried employees with technology, costs are reduced. It defeats the purpose, however, when aggravated customers are driven to take their business elsewhere.

The same complaints are heard by customers who call in for information and service but voice-activated machines respond to their questions and complaints. Our research shows that *97.6% of callers prefer speaking to a live person*. It's a sad commentary when today's technology that is designed to serve people triggers so much ill will.

It's not only an aversion to technology that is destroying customer loyalty, it's the need to interface with a company employee when service is needed. Customers also want personal service when they visit retail stores. In fact, *73% say that stores have cut back on employees, making it difficult to get service*. Between the lack of retail help and the impersonal nature of Web sites and voice mail systems, *45% think customer service is a thing of the past and 69.6% think the customer service that their parents received is gone forever*. The same research showed that *73% attribute a decrease in service directly to cutbacks in the number of employees. Interestingly, a corresponding number, approximately 78.8%, replied that they found it difficult to find someone in a store to serve them*.

Fortunately, some companies have resisted cutting back on service and in fact have bucked the trend by increasing it. The good news is that in spite of incurring additional costs for employee wages, these companies are prospering. Unquestionably, it is more expensive to add staff on the floor in a retail store and employ qualified people to handle incoming calls versus a machine. Indeed, companies such as Four Seasons may charge a premium for providing exceptional service. Even so, their guests don't seem to mind paying a premium to get a higher level of service. Nor do those customers of industry leaders such as Chubb, Lexus, NetJets, and Tom James. ARG research reveals that *67.2% of Americans are willing to pay more for VIP service*. How much more will they pay? *This research discloses that they are willing to pay an additional 10% to 20%*. Our interpretation of this data is that it is prudent for those companies catering to a more discriminating clientele to invest in skilled people who will, in turn, provide an added value that justifies a slightly higher price tag. Obviously people, not machines, provide a personal touch that enhances the total customer experience.

We acknowledge that a small owner-operated enterprise has an advantage in this area. There is nothing quite like having the owner of a restaurant thank you by sending over a free drink or dessert as a token of his appreciation. Or for that matter, having the owner come to your table to thank you for your patronage. Likewise, an owner of a haberdashery may say, "I love how you look in that suit. May I suggest you consider these three ties that I think go perfectly with it." Or it might be just a simple, "Thank you for coming in today. With other stores in the area, I appreciate having you choose us." As we mentioned before, nobody can do this personal service better than the owner. Unquestionably this is the small owner's biggest competitive edge. This accounts for why *57.3% of Americans think publicly owned companies are less customer driven than privately held companies.* However, this does not infer that big companies are not capable of providing personal service. After all, large companies are competent with recruiting caring people—and properly training large numbers of them. Surely these people are also capable of having one-on-one relationships with individual customers. Being big should never imply that a company is bureaucratic, uncaring, or impersonal. Admittedly, it's easy to stray away from these qualities when an organization becomes so large that it loses focus on the importance of one-on-one relationships. But customer-driven companies don't let this happen, no matter how big they grow. On the contrary, it is the attention they give to serving individual customers that has spawned their success and growth.

The Sweetest Sound in Any Language

In his classic book *How to Win Friends and Influence People,* Dale Carnegie told us that the sweetest sound in the English language is our own name. It astounds us how many companies fail to train their people to say the customer's name when addressing him or her. There is simply no excuse. After all, how much effort does it take to introduce one's self by saying, "Hi, I'm John Smith and you're...?"

We find it inexcusable in certain industries, especially when the customer's name is literally right under an employee's nose. For example, a bank teller has a customer's name on a check or deposit slip. Yet, more often than not, bank employees don't call a customer by name during a banking transaction. A hotel clerk or an airline ticket agent only has to read the name on the reservation. A maître d' also has the name of customers on a reservation list—names that can be passed on to the server who can then greet customers by name too. This should be a given, but more often than not customers go nameless. An ARG study uncovers that *85.3% of Americans think being greeted by name at a fine restaurant enhances their dining experience. And 84% say that when they are called by name, it motivates them to come back.* For a fine restaurant to know these statistics and not call all customers by name is deplorable.

An ARG study reveals that *88% of Americans are rarely called by name when they shop.* At banks where tellers have the customer's name at their fingertips, *38% of Americans say that they are not called by name.* In the hotel industry, *84% are not addressed by name.* Be assured this will never happen at Four Seasons.

"Name recognition is a very big thing for us at Four Seasons," Ellen du Bellay, vice president of learning and development, says. "We want our employees to know the names of the guests, and to set an example for them, we teach our management team to know employees' names. When our employees feel good about being called by name, they'll understand how a guest will feel. Our hotel general managers generally know the names of all their employees, which can be 300-plus people."

"When Mr. Jones comes in," du Bellay explains, "our people welcome him, 'Good morning, Mr. Jones. Welcome back to Four Seasons.' At either an eight o'clock morning meeting or at late in the afternoon for the following day, most of our hotels have staff meetings at which all arrival and guest information is cascaded through employee shift briefings. A front desk manager, for example, will attend the meeting and review it at a preshift briefing with his people."

"Of course, everyone who comes through our doors at Four Seasons will get a warm welcome," Barbara Talbott, executive vice president of marketing, explains. "We never make judgments about someone's appearance. Every guest is greeted in a friendly way. While our hotels are sumptuous and elaborate, we are not intimidating. Every person who walks through our door will experience comfort and a sense of belonging. This is what keeps people coming back.

"Our regular guests will hear, 'Welcome back. It's been a while,' or 'My goodness, you travel a lot because didn't we just see you here last week.'"

ARG surveyed Americans to find out if it mattered to them that someone would recognize them with a warm "Welcome back." And *82.4% said they were surprised to be remembered.* In fact, *97.1% said that this made them want to go back again.* This illustrates how people like it when they're treated with respect as though they are important.

✳   ✳   ✳

"We encourage our employees to call customers by name," says Arnold Block, former general manager of Harrah's in St. Louis. "We know that people feel good when they walk down the streets in their neighborhood or go to their favorite restaurant and get a warm hello. We want to create the same feeling in our casino." Harrah's can identify who's playing its slot machines and table games because this information shows up on its computers. So even with those customers with whom it is not acquainted, it has the technology to know who they are. "Most people like to be recognized by name," Block adds. "It makes them feel comfortable. They feel more secure. And when they're treated this way, there is a propensity to come back."

❋   ❋   ❋

With large companies, it may not be possible to know all customers by name, especially when you don't see them on a regular basis. Besides, while some people have a knack for connecting the right name with the right face, most people don't. Because Re/MAX has 120,000 real estate associates, plus 50,000 employees, the company's chairman, Dave Liniger, admits that he is unable to remember everybody's name. "It's not intentional, but I even call my sons by the wrong name half the time," he says. "At our conventions and large gatherings, we have everyone wear large name tags, so this helps me give everyone a big hello. When I go on road trips, I attend many broker/agents meetings. For instance, tomorrow, I'll be in New York and the following day, Newark, New Jersey, and the next day in Connecticut. During this three-day period, I'll see a lot of RE/MAX people. To call people by name, I rely on my briefing book that has photos of the people I'll see. I'll spend a good amount of time on the plane studying their names, faces, and a few facts about each of them. I'll take another look at it before I go to bed. My wife, Gail, also takes a briefing book on her trips to our offices."

❋   ❋   ❋

Over the years, hundreds of thousands of Mary Kay Independent Beauty Consultants met founder Mary Kay Ash, a business leader who made a Herculean effort to warmly greet people by their name. A woman with great people skills, Ash believed that every person is special and deserves to be treated accordingly. "Whenever I meet someone," Ash once recalled, "I try to imagine her wearing an invisible sign that says, *Make me feel important!* I respond to this sign immediately, and it works wonders." Ash remembered when, as a young woman, she worked for a large direct sales company and while attending a convention she stood in a long line for hours in order to shake hands with the company's president. "When it was my turn to meet him, he acted as if I didn't exist. He probably had no idea how much that hurt me, but after all those years, I still remember, so it obviously had a powerful impact on me. He made no eye contact with me and kept looking to see how long the line of people was behind me. I felt as if I were invisible. I learned an important lesson about people that day, which I've never forgotten. I promised myself then and there that if I should ever rise to that position, I would never treat people the way I was treated. No matter how busy you are, you must take time to make the other person feel important."

Years later, tens of thousands of Beauty Consultants attended the company's annual Seminar and were given name tags to wear. Ash always repeated the names of whomever she greeted. Sometimes Ash shook hands for hours at a time, and as physically tiring as it was, the petite woman, who was barely taller than five feet, always mustered up her enthusiasm to make everyone feel like the most important person in the room. Ash did it with sincerity and grace, and to this day people who met her recall how good she made them feel. Amazingly, she managed to pass this torch on to the leaders in her company and the independent sales force.

Knowing how exhausting it was for people to stand in long lines to meet her personally, Ash would show lots of empathy, apologizing for personally inconveniencing them. An ARG study shows that *when a company apologizes to a customer for its wrongdoing, 95.6% of those surveyed will accept the apology and continue to do business with the company.* The same survey revealed that *97.7% admire a company's honesty when it apologizes.* This shows that people understand that companies are fallible and know they are capable of erring, so they will accept it—if there is an apology.

In an ARG study, *85% of those surveyed said that they feel better when the cashier apologizes for the long wait.* This proves that most Americans will accept an apology. Conversely, *71% said that when a store is out of an item, they are upset when nobody apologizes about it. When there wasn't an apology, 41% said they never went back to the store again.* The lesson is that you must profusely and convincingly apologize and tell your customers, "We are so sorry. What can we do for you?" Because this fix is so easy to do, it should be automatic with all companies.

✳   ✳   ✳

In its effort to recognize customers by name, Lexus is currently working on a chip that will be installed in a vehicle's dashboard and programmed to flash the owner's name on a screen that can be read on the dealership's service lane. It will also send a message to the customer's salesperson in the showroom who may then come to the service department to say hello. Like other service-driven companies, Lexus is relying on technology to add a personal touch to its treatment of customers. So while people don't like doing business with machines, this illustrates how a proper use of technology can enhance the customer experience.

Getting to Know All about You

While we give kudos to knowing the customer by name, it's just a starting point. Customer-driven companies want to know whatever it takes to enhance the customer experience. The best and most direct way to learn about one's customers is by asking a series of questions. Chubb's former vice chairman, Tom Motamed, explains, "The worst thing an insurance agent can do is come to a prospect's house and say, 'I'm going to tell you all about the construction of your house and why it needs an alarm here, and another one over there.' Instead, our agents are trained to say, 'Tell me about your house,' or ask, 'Can we walk around your home?' People love to talk about their businesses and their stuff. So we ask questions and let them talk. We do the same thing when we recruit agents who we also view as our customers. 'Tell me about yourself,' I'll say. 'Tell me about the people you work with. What are your areas of expertise? What are you trying to do?' By asking a lot of questions and letting them talk, we might find out the agency has an agent who practiced law for 20 years and would be effective at opening accounts with law firms. We might also learn that a brokerage firm has someone who's knowledgeable in fine arts and paintings. Or perhaps there's another person with expertise in manufacturing. When we seek agents to represent Chubb, we also inquire into their values to determine if they match ours. At the end of the day, it's not a negative reflection on any of the 39,000 insurance agencies in the country that do not share our values. But those who don't are not going to sell our products and services.

"Sometimes I'll ask, 'Why do you want to be appointed by Chubb?' Someone may reply, 'Well, I lost an account to a Chubb broker, and if I was with your company, that would not have happened.' After asking a lot of questions, I might learn that the agent lost the business for a good reason. He got outperformed by somebody who actually knows what they are doing."

✳   ✳   ✳

It comes as no surprise that Edward Jones brokers are also trained to ask a lot of questions. As managing partner Jim Weddle explains, "This is how we differentiate ourselves. We go out into the community and meet with individuals, business and professional people, and retired folks by making face-to-face calls. We sit across from them at their desk or kitchen table, and we look them squarely in the eye. During our initial contact, we ask a lot of personal questions and gather confidential information. Being there in person is a far more effective way to learn about their financial affairs and plans for the future than by a telephone interview."

✳   ✳   ✳

A Tom James sales rep asks a lot of questions during the first call on a prospect. "If he's going to become someone's personal clothing consultant," explains former president Jim McEachern, "he must first understand that person's needs and tastes. For starters, he must find out what's in his wardrobe. What he has and doesn't have. Does he have plaid suits? Stripes? This color or that color? This fabric or that fabric? Does he wear traditional suits or high-fashion suits? We have a prepared questionnaire that's used to collect this information. While the first sales call might take as long as two hours, once this data is collected, it speeds up future calls. Afterward, our rep will file this data in his computer and refer to it on future sales calls."

Even with all of our modern technology, there are a lot of business transactions that are conducted the same as they were 200 years ago. People back then met a stranger, and much like we do today, they chat for a while, size each other up, and if they have confidence in each other, they make a deal and hope for the best. Tom James reps ask a lot of questions and are very good listeners. They don't try to dominate conversations, and they give their customers adequate time to explain their needs.

"I stress the importance of giving the customer what he wants, not what you think he should buy," McEachern stresses. "This is why we conduct a fact-finding session during the first call. Later on in the relationship, many of our customers rely on our sales rep to make a specific selection for him, but this happens down the road after we've gotten to know what the customer enjoys wearing."

"After a while, we have a complete inventory of what our customer has in his closet," Steve Adelsberg says, "and we've got all his history. Part of our job is to help him diversify what he wears but without taking him out of his comfort zone." As the Tom James number one salesperson and with 1,400 clients, Adelsberg reviews each customer's file before making a sales call.

Another Tom James clothing consultant, Naresh Khanna, adds, "After I start to work with a customer, I know his likes and dislikes. Soon, I can save a lot of time by showing him inventory that I know he will like. Later, it becomes very personal. I know his wife and children, where they go to school, his hobbies, and so on. The more I know about him and the more he learns to trust me, the better I can serve him. For example, I know what he does at work, whom he sees and meets with, when he attends board meetings, and what's on his social calendar. I know if he has a vacation home(s) and where he travels. By understanding the total person, I know how he dresses for all occasions. In the long term, it's about trust, confidence, and competence. The more competent I am in my customer's eyes, the more confident he feels in his business. And the longer he will stay a client."

✻   ✻   ✻

ARG did a survey to see how customers felt about being asked about their experience with a company, and 80.8% *said they take the time to talk.* So yes, people will take the time to give their opinion, if you're willing to listen to what they have to say. And 88% *say that it makes them madder when they receive a follow-up call for their opinion but nothing is ever done about it.* This makes them feel as though their time has been wasted and their opinion doesn't really matter. *When a company calls to ask a customer about his or her satisfaction, 90% say that this call makes them want to do more business with the company. For those customers that are dissatisfied, 79% are willing to accept a sincere apology.*

Cabela's stays close to its customers through its division Outdoor Adventures. Here, the company arranges hunting and fishing trips, some to exotic places such as an excursion to hunt caribou in Canada or to fish for salmon in a remote area of Alaska. Some of these trips are expensive, complete with a guide service; others are moderately priced and are semiguided or a do-it-yourself adventure. Prior to sending customers to a location, members of Outdoor Adventures' staff visit the destination to determine what kind of equipment will be needed, and certain recommendations are passed on to customers. "We get rave reviews from customers," tells Dennis Highby, Cabela's CEO, "and so many will say, 'I would have never thought I needed this little doodad or that item, but I'm so glad I had it.'"

✻   ✻   ✻

During the early days of RE/MAX, Gail and Dave Liniger entertained employees and brokers in their home. "With a small budget, we started out having ice cream parties," Gail Liniger recalls. "Later we had Tommy

Bahama parties. Everyone came in a Hawaiian shirt, we'd serve margaritas and play Jimmy Buffett music. We had so much fun. Today we spend a lot of our weekends at our home in Scottsdale. We built it with three guest bedrooms so we can entertain our top regional broker/owners who stay with us. I used to do all the cooking, including baking cookies for our guests, but the new house has a staff so, like Dave, I can spend quality time with our guests. This way, we really get to know them."

*　*　*

When a new Lexus model is introduced, the company works overtime during the first three months seeking customers' comments about their new car. "We are absolutely convinced that we are delivering the finest product in its segment," former group vice president and general manager Bob Carter explains, "but something can go wrong, as we learned in the past. For example, once one of our cars had an assembly problem. It was not apparent initially, but became so between 400 and 800 miles. Although today we have a very efficient monitoring system that comes through our dealers, we also want our associates here at the division to be in contact with customers when we introduce a new vehicle. So we require every one of our 400-plus associates who work in our sales and marketing division plus those in the field to call four customers a week. I do it, my personal assistant does it . . . everyone in the customer assistance center, and I mean everyone. We want to be sure we are meeting customers' expectations. If you haven't talked to a customer or haven't been in a dealership in the last 48 hours, you don't know what's going on. This business is so complex and dynamic, staying in tune with marketing is mandatory. These calls are typically made for the first three to four months of a new product launch. If there is any product issue, we want to know so we can fix it immediately. We listen to everything. For instance, a customer might say, 'I love the car except for the color selections on the new LS. I wish you had a medium beige and a dark brown.' We keep records on every comment. We accumulate this information and, along with our product planning people, we put together a summary called 'The Voice of the Customer.' If a couple of customers remark that the brakes squeak, we'll check it out. Others might indicate a fashion trend by conveying they didn't like a light interior because it shows dirt. When we launched the LS in late 2006, it had just been out for 11 weeks, and I can tell you a dozen different features that the customers either told me personally or our associates that we requested to be changed on the car."

*　*　*

World Wide Technology (WWT) received its first government work as a small minority-owned business. Today, it does more business with the federal government than any other minority-owned company in the United States. "We've made it our business to understand the culture of the government," founder and chairman Dave Steward explains, "and we did this by developing close relationships in Washington, D.C. Very few companies are able to do business commercially as well as with the federal government. In order for us to accomplish this, we invested a lot of time and money into understanding the government's contracting process, which is very different than doing business with the private sector. We've learned all the government's regulations, its acronyms, and so on. It took us years to figure out, but we were determined to do it, and we stuck to it. To get these contracts, we had to adjust our modus operandi to comply with government procedures. We knew going in that if we wanted to do business with the government this was a requirement. Then once you get the business, you anticipate that the government is always making changes and you must be willing to make changes to accommodate it. To be in compliance, a government contractor must constantly adapt. We figured that the potential for high-volume business makes it worthwhile. Many companies view those changing rules and regulations as too restrictive and won't compete on government contracts."

Dave Steward and his management team worked hard to know the ins and outs of doing business with the federal government, and their determination has paid off. Today, WWT has contracts with the United States Department of Agriculture (USDA), Department of Defense, Department of Commerce, Department of Transportation, Central Intelligence Agency (CIA), Federal Bureau of Investigation (FBI), Internal Revenue Service (IRS), and several other agencies. WWT is the largest St. Louis–based company doing business with the federal government. With government contracts totaling about $700 million, the company's federal business represents about 25% of its total revenues.

Getting Our Head in the Customer's Tent

"Our objective is to have our head in the tent," Dave Steward at WWT explains. This way we can observe and understand a business far better than anyone looking in from the outside. This gives us a great advantage. How can the competition possibly get to know all the moving parts? We're able to see what's going on and we can make improvements. And if you don't improve on it, shame on you. This also gives you the opportunity to expand and change your business model because you know their needs. You know the personality and the culture of the customer—what they believe in, and all the little nuances. You know where they're going with the business."

Steward states that World Wide Technology is one of a handful of suppliers and vendors that are fully integrated with Cisco. "By developing expertise on their technology," he emphasizes, "so our systems are compatible with theirs, it makes it easy for Cisco to do business with us. Sure, this costs us more money and requires us to do more work. It took us several months to get integrated with Cisco. And it was over a period of years for us to get into AT&T in a way that it works smoothly. Today, we understand one another and how these systems are working together. As a result, it also makes the work in our back office a lot easier. As a consequence, it reduces our costs and enables us to pass along that cost savings to our client. From the customer's vantage, it makes a lot more sense to do business with us versus a company with systems that are not compatible."

In 2007, World Wide Technology invested $65 million upgrading its business systems, which involved a total reengineering of the business. "One of our goals in '07 was to implement an 11i upgrade (Oracle Enterprise Research Planning System). The cut over was so seamless," he explains, "that it was nearly problem free, and we believe this is vital because so many times companies encounter a host of problems that are crippling to both the vendor and the customer. If the whole thing shuts down, it doesn't help anybody! It's really about vision, leadership, and teamwork. And above all else, it's about trust. It's about serving the customer and putting their interests above yours."

The Thank You Note

When was the last time you received a handwritten note that thanked you for your business? If you never received one, you're not alone. An ARG survey reveals that *only 8.7% of Americans have received one in the past two years, and 6.1% in the last three years; 71.5% have never received a thank-you-for-your-business note in their entire lives. Of those who have, 44.2% were very surprised and 49.5% were somewhat surprised. Only 6.3% were not surprised.* We believe a thank you note is such a nice gesture, and anyone in business who wants to build long-term relationships with customers should routinely send them.

So they were surprised to get a thank you note. But what does it mean? Well, *80% said that when they received a thank you note, it made them want to go back to the store.* The customer thinks, "Gosh, I can't believe it. They really do care *after* the sale." Amazingly, *61% who received a thank you note said that they told somebody about it.* This surprising statistic reveals that it was important to them. ARG research reveals that *10% of consumers walk into a store based on word-of-mouth. In the 1950s, 90% of store visits were generated by word-of-mouth.* With the high cost of advertising, this is a strong reason why treating your customers well will make them rave about you to others.

Thanking people goes beyond politeness. Showing appreciation is part of a company's culture. Four Season's founder Isadore Sharp is known to call Four Seasons employees all over the world and shower them with praise. "This past Christmas holiday," Ellen du Bellay says, "Issy Sharp called to thank me for a great year. I know he calls to thank so many employees, including Four Seasons general managers all over the world. He is such a humble, appreciative person. He frequently visits the hotels, and at town hall meetings, he's constantly thanking and praising employees for their contributions. Four Seasons people have such adulation for him, he's their hero. Our people are grateful for all Issy has done. He's the one who should be thanked. Just, the same, he's always thanking everyone else. His style of leadership is to lead by example, and he has taught us to express appreciation to our guests."

When employees are at the receiving end of the many employee events, such as Employee Appreciation Day, they experience the good feeling it gives them, and in turn, they extend their appreciation to customers.

Barbara Talbott concurs that part of the Four Seasons culture is being humble, and when it comes to making mistakes, the better the company does, the higher are guests' expectations, so falling short on service is bound to happen. "When we receive e-mails or letters from guests," she explains, "the president of worldwide operations often personally calls or writes to them. Our general managers do the same thing."

✳   ✳   ✳

Tom James sales reps ask a lot of questions to collect facts about their customers that are put into their computers. "Our reps are trained to review a customer's bio information prior to making a sales call," explains Jim McEachern. "Then they can say, 'How's your wife, Elizabeth?' or 'Congratulations on your son Bill's graduation from state college.' Sure, it's a small thing, but people appreciate knowing someone has taken a personal interest in them. Yes, they probably realize that we have the name written down somewhere, but they still appreciate the fact that we made an effort to do it. From my first days selling Tom James clothing, I always sent a note to thank a customer for his business. Oftentimes, I even sent one to people who didn't buy and thanked them for the time they spent with me. To encourage our salespeople to send thank you notes, we've created a variety of letters to choose from, or they can create their own. It's not so much what is said, it's the expression of appreciation that matters. And while I recommend a handwritten note, a typewritten one or an e-mail is better than nothing."

Naresh Khanna has been sending thank you notes to his customers ever since he joined Tom James in 1974. While he used to handwrite them, his letters are now typewritten, and his signature is always in green ink, the company's color. "Green is also the color of friendship and peace," he explains. For expediency, Naresh will send an e-mail to certain customers, but he still believes the handwritten note is more personal. "While electronic mail is okay, a real letter is more tangible and people keep it longer, so I always follow up with one." There is one thing that Naresh does that makes his thank you letters very personal. "In addition to thanking them for their business, I thank them for their confidence in me and their friendship," he says.

＊   ＊   ＊

An ARG survey revealed that *24.8% of Americans have written letters to companies to thank them.* Of these letter writers, *94.4% tell how an exceptional person was the reason for writing.* We believe this proves the point that when people rave about their experience, it's driven by people. It's not about a magnificent showroom, a beautiful airplane, or a breathtaking ballroom. As Isadore Sharp says, "It's not the property. It's the people inside that make Four Seasons the company we are."

Thanking a customer for his or her business is a simple courtesy that should be a matter of routine. But unless it's done with sincerity, it serves no purpose. For years now, when a customer thanks a Ritz-Carlton employee, the response is, "It's my pleasure." This response was even better than a thank you. And in fact, it was such the right thing to say that other companies trained their employees to also say it to their customers. For a while, it worked, and you'd hear people saying it everywhere. But over time "it's my pleasure" has been repeated so often that it lost its zing. That's because the bored guy behind the McDonald's drive-through window, the uninterested cashier at the 7-Eleven, and the man in the parkway entrance tollbooth keep repeating by rote, "It's my pleasure," and you can tell from his tone of voice, body language, and facial expressions that he got no pleasure whatsoever. We think it's going too far when you thank a restaurant employee for directions to the bathroom and are told, "It's my pleasure." How sincere can he be? No one derives pleasure from telling anyone where a bathroom is.

Four Seasons hotel manager, Rob Hagelberg says, "People say it without feeling and it comes across as insincere. For this reason, we actively avoid having our employees say, 'It's my pleasure.' Better they should say something spontaneously and express how they feel versus what they were trained to say."

Above and Beyond

Certainly, it is the innumerable small things that companies do for their customers that contribute to winning their loyalty. These are the everyday occurrences: an employee warmly greets a customer by name; a housecleaner turns the clock radio on the nightstand to face in the direction of the bed at nighttime; and so on. We can't overemphasize the importance of paying attention to these seemingly unimportant details, tasks that seem insignificant but nonetheless make a difference in winning customer loyalty. Specifically, we're talking about Four Seasons having his favorite soft drink in a guest's refrigerator, a Lexus dealership serving a cappuccino and providing a free car wash. We refer to these little touches as niceties. They are important, and enough of them certainly influence a customer's loyalty. Performing a once-in-a-lifetime spectacular service but none of the everyday niceties won't by itself cut it. The above-and-beyond-the-call-of-duty act won't win many customers by itself. You have to pay attention to the everyday stuff.

When you do, the big ones that were never expected are going to sweep customers off their feet. Here we're referring to the unforeseen that take customers completely by surprise. These are the home runs (and like it's said in baseball parlance, when you hit a home run, you get to walk around the bases). These are the biggies that get customers to rave about companies; it's what converts them into raving fans. Some of them are told so often that they become part of a company's folklore. Perhaps the most famous incident happened in 1975 when a sales clerk at Nordstrom gave a refund on a set of automobile tires even though the store never sold tires. This story has been retold and published so many times that it has generated millions of dollars of positive publicity for the company. We thought this story was so extraordinary that we called Nordstrom's chairman, Blake Nordstrom, and asked if the tale was fact or fiction. "Yes, I know it's hard to believe, but it really happened," he told us.

During the many interviews we conducted, we heard so many of these stories that we could write a book just on them. However, to keep it short and sweet, we are telling a selected few that we believe will adequately illustrate what great customer-focused companies do, and which, hopefully, will trigger some ideas that you can do for your customers.

∗ ∗ ∗

Matt Harris, executive vice president at NetJets, tells a story about a couple who flew to their vacation home and the person who was supposed to pick them up at the airport didn't show up. "It was nearly midnight, and the crew had put in a long day," Harris explains. "They had done their job which was to safely fly them to their destination, but they couldn't just leave them stranded at the airport. Not even giving it a second thought, the two pilots drove the owners to their house but not before stopping at a grocery store along the way to pick up groceries for the couple. 'Their children and grandchildren were visiting in the morning, and they had an empty refrigerator,' one of the pilots told me. Now it's not in the pilot's job description to go grocery shopping for a customer. It was just an automatic response by the two pilots."

Another example, "Two pilots were taking owners to a funeral, and like many owners do, they took their pets with them. Knowing that the owners would be on the ground for an estimated four hours, the account manager arranged for a dog service to be at the airport at the time of the plane's arrival. The service walked and cared for the dogs until the owners returned. We don't just meet our customers' expectations, we exceed them. Our people do it because they care, not because it's in the contract, which of course, it isn't."

When NetJets tells its customers, "You're family," it backs these words up with its actions. The company not only wants its customers to fly safely, it also wants to keep them healthy while they travel. This is why NetJets initiated its Mayo Clinic Executive Travel Response, a program that provides access to medical support from the Mayo Clinic while its customers are on one of its aircraft or at their destination anywhere in the world. This around-the-clock, 365-day service puts customers in touch with highly trained and experienced critical care flight nurses and physicians who are available for consultation.

"They just have to call a dedicated phone number exclusive to Net-Jets owners for health information services," explains the company's president, Jim Christiansen. "This service will also inform them about when and where to seek medical attention. This is particularly useful when flying internationally, since medications differ by country and language barriers can be a problem. In emergency situations, the Mayo person will coordinate medical care with local hospitals and doctors. These medical professionals have a wide selection of resources, including a contact list with data on more than 14,000 Mayo Clinic alumni around the world."

Christiansen mentions that the Mayo program is free to NetJets owners. "It was something Richard came up with when he once said, 'Gee, if I'm traveling in a foreign country with my mother and my children and one of us gets sick, how do I deal with it?' That's how the idea originated. He figured if that would be a problem for him and his family, it could also be one for our owners. As it's turned out, we've had several incidences when it's saved someone's life. In one case, an owner called the Mayo Clinic from his room in an Eastern Bloc country and described his symptoms over the phone. 'Go at once to this physician, who's a Mayo doctor,' the man was instructed. 'We will call him ahead and we'll arrange for you to get into a cab.' As it turned out, they set up a video-conference call and performed the surgery in this Eastern Bloc country supervised by Mayo medical people."

At an additional cost, the Mayo Clinic will arrange for medical transportation and evacuation services on a custom aircraft (not a NetJets aircraft) that's fully equipped with all medical emergency equipment and emergency medical personnel. It's virtually an ambulance–emergency room in the sky!

✳   ✳   ✳

Jim McEachern talks about how a Tom James salesman won a customer's loyalty by doing the unexpected. "It was a new account," McEachern explains, "that needed some clothes we couldn't provide in time for an upcoming trip three days later. After the customer explained what kind of clothes he had to have, our salesman went shopping for him at a fine men's store and later that day returned with the merchandise. Our salesman didn't make a nickel on the transaction. It was just his way of showing the customer that he was there to serve him. The customer was in awe and today is a raving Tom James fan."

✳   ✳   ✳

It was only a matter of a few minutes after sitting down to interview Bob Carter at Lexus, before he proudly talked about an associate at the company's call center. "A call came in on a late Friday afternoon from a customer who was vacationing with his family in San Diego, which is about 120 miles from here. He had taken the car to the local dealer, but the part wasn't available. It appeared as though the family would be stranded in San Diego over the weekend, which wasn't in their plans. The call center associate who had talked to the customer didn't want that to happen. On his own initiative, without seeking his supervisor's permission, he went to our parts depot, got the part, and drove to San Diego in his own car on his own time. His action was above and beyond the call of duty. No company could have ever included that in an employee's job description. It's something that happens because it's part of our company culture. I get so proud when our people do these things, I just want to give them a big hug. Our people here and at our dealerships are always doing good deeds of this nature for customers. We're always hearing stories like this."

Nancy Fein, former vice president of customer satisfaction at Lexus, tells another story about a Lexus associate, this one was a valet at a dealership who also held an entry-level position. "A man had just purchased a Lexus for his wife, and soon after he got home he called to say, 'I can't figure out how to hook up the garage door opener.' The dealer asked one of his valets to go to the customer's house and take care of it. After the valet hooked up the garage door opener, the door opened and the valet saw the man's shiny new BMW parked in the garage. The man said, 'Wow, you did that so quickly. Thank you so much. I greatly appreciate it. You know, I recently had the same problem with my car, and for weeks I've been calling the BMW dealership to fix my opener. Not only haven't they done it, they don't even return my calls.' The valet says, 'I'll hook it up for you.' Fifteen minutes later, both cars' door openers were working. The customer was positively delighted."

"The brand is about the customer—the ownership and the experience," Bob Carter emphasizes. "Not to discount the quality of the car, ownership experience is what ultimately wins customer loyalty."

✳   ✳   ✳

Cabela's CEO, Dennis Highby, delights in telling about a young couple with two small kids who were on their way to a wedding in Omaha. "They were big Cabela's fans and had planned their trip around stopping in our Kansas City store," Highby tells. "They spent a few hours in the store, having a great time, but when they got ready to drive the last few hours to the wedding, their car wouldn't start. When one of our employees found out about their predicament, he went outside and said, 'Here are the keys to my car. Take it.' They said they were going to get a tow truck and have the car repaired. They politely thanked him. 'No, you don't have time and you'll miss the wedding. I insist. Take my car. On your way back, you can drop it off and get yours fixed.' The couple finally agreed to take his vehicle and they didn't miss the wedding. I can't begin to tell you how proud it makes all of us feel to know we have people working for us who are so giving to our customers."

*   *   *

The customers of all of the companies profiled in this book unremittingly rave about how the service they receive continuously exceeds their expectations. We believe Four Seasons epitomizes an organization with a philosophy on doing whatever it takes to go beyond a customer's expectations. This desire to exceed a guest's expectations is deeply ingrained in the company's culture, starting with Isadore Sharp. Sharp's unique style of leadership—one that doesn't dictate but leads by example—has harvested a legion of dedicated Four Seasons employees around the world focused on always doing what's right for the guest.

Dimitrios Zarikos, who is now the general manager of Four Seasons Resort Provence at Terre Blanche, tells a story how Sharp inspired him to do what's best for customers. "I was just new in the Four Seasons family, working in New York, when I received a call on an early August morning from Mr. Sharp asking if he and his wife could reserve a table for dinner that same night. Obviously he could.

"When I showed him to his table, it was the first time we had met. He was very warm and pleasant. Five minutes later, he called me to the table. 'Dimitri, where is the pianist?' I explained that business was slow so we made the decision to cancel the pianist during July and August. 'Terrible idea,' he said in a calm, soft voice. 'Please have a seat, Dimitri, and allow me to tell you a little bit about Four Seasons.' By that time I was hoping for the earth to split in two and swallow me.

" 'Let's suppose that a retired couple from Wisconsin who had heard so much about Four Seasons in New York had saved enough to splurge for a weekend and they arrived here today. Have you or have you not robbed them of the total experience? If business is slow, would you ever think of removing the doorman?' He smiled warmly and added, 'If you found a way to make the same dish in the kitchen with one less cook, I'd say you were a hero. If you find ways to save without affecting the guest experience, go ahead and do it. But do not save at the expense of the guest.' That, in a nutshell told me so much about who we were and how different we were as a company from where I was coming from."

❋ ❋ ❋

On December 26, 2004, Maldives, a chain of small coral islands in the Indian Ocean, was hit by a powerful tsunami. The death toll was 82, small in comparison to other Asian nations where 225,000 lost their lives. The damage to the small republic was severe, especially for the small archipelago nation's tourism industry. "Our Four Seasons was wiped out," Isadore Sharp says. "The tsunami struck so fast, our employees had to act on their own and quickly because there were no orders coming in telling them what to do. However, they did know that we do business by the Golden Rule. Those 300 employees had to act according to their own value system. 'What do I do in a time of crisis? Do I run for cover? Or do I look at what has to be done?' They acted heroically. We have stories about how guests, including many small children, were in the ocean, and how our employees put their lives at risk to swim out and rescue them. It was a scary situation. Nobody had ever been trained to risk his or her life. Thank God, nobody was seriously injured. Our owner was able to get an airplane and fly everyone off the island.

"We reopened it just before Christmas in 2006," Sharp continues. "To keep our people, we transferred more than 200 of them to other hotels around the world. Many of them were kids who had never been off the island. They didn't have to be told how to do their job because they already knew we only had one standard. So whether it was on the Maldives or in New York City, they knew what to do. They knew how to deal with guests."

A mother and daughter had checked into Four Seasons Hotel George V in Paris. The young woman would be studying in France for the year. When the general manager heard about them, he introduced himself to the mother. Realizing her apprehension about leaving her daughter alone in a large foreign city, he said, "Here's my mobile phone number. If there is ever anything I can do, please call me at any time. And please make sure your daughter has my number in case she ever needs to call me." Talk about treating customers like a family member!

Ellen du Bellay tells a story about a female executive who was hosting a lunch when a waiter asked her, "Are you gals ready to order or would you like to chit-chat some more?"

"The waiter noticed his remark had upset the woman who obviously felt as though she and her guests were being treated like frivolous ladies meeting for lunch rather than in a serious business meeting," du Bellay explains. "He immediately reported the incident to his boss, Randy, who was in charge of food and beverage. Randy called the woman to apologize. Her office was nearby, so to further appease her, the next morning, he stopped by her office with some freshly made cappuccino and just-baked muffins. 'I feel just terrible about what happened yesterday,' he said, 'so I would like to offer you some breakfast. Please, may I just leave this on your desk?' She looked up at him and said, 'Do you know what I am doing right now? I am writing to Mr. Sharp and you just ruined it. There is no way I can write to him after this.' She was so grateful that she became a lifelong guest."

Rob Hagelberg was director of rooms at Four Seasons Hotel Houston when the Crown Prince of Saudi Arabia stayed at the hotel while paying a visit to President Bush at his ranch in Crawford, 170 miles northwest. The Crown Prince and his party rented 320 rooms for six nights; there wasn't a hotel around Crawford large enough to accommodate a group of this size. Indeed this was a sizable group with sizable demands.

"On Friday before Monday's arrival, a man who had constructed palaces for the Crown Prince family came in to give us instructions on the preparation of the suites for the Crown Prince. My job was to help him get everything set up. I showed him a recently renovated suite that was magnificent, and he agreed, 'Yes, this is very nice but we need to make changes.'

"For his breakfast meeting, the Crown Prince likes to sit in a big chair with his family and staff on his left and right. Thirteen satellite TV channels were also installed on the roof with cables connected to his suite. Another suite down the hall was converted into a meeting room where he had a large chair in front with 12 chairs along each side. This room was also redecorated with selected rugs and flags. Another room was converted into a dining room. Red carpeting was installed in the hallways between the suites. Rooms were also redone for the staff. All the furniture was removed from one room where they made tea; the walls and floors covered with plastic.

"They placed something like 1,500 room service orders during their stay," Hagelberg continues. "They brought a cook with them and prepared some of the food in their rooms. They ate their meals according to their own time zone, and our kitchen was sending dinners to rooms for 300 people at 3 a.m. That's not a normal routine for a hotel, but that was part of the service we provided.

"They rented five custom motor coaches and an ambulance for transportation back and forth to the President's ranch. At the end of the week, they checked out and our job was to turn the place back to what it normally is. Getting those rooms ready within three days according to those specifications and providing so many unusual services in the middle of the night was a test of our meddle. It took a phenomenal team effort that left us exhausted, but with a sense of pride that we did it as a team. We were especially pleased to be told by the group on its way out that we provided the best guest service experience they've ever had."

Just as Four Seasons employees go above and beyond for the Crown Prince so does an employee in San Francisco to please a little girl who was traveling with her father. The hotel's seamstress made a minicrib for her dolls from wicker baskets, complete with Egyptian cotton bed skirts, sheets, pillows, and blankets. Yes, everyone receives the royal treatment at Four Seasons.

Annoying Telephone and Internet Behavior

It's about time American companies wake up and stop annoying their customers who call in by phone and visit their Web sites. It amazes us that companies will abuse and neglect prospective customers as well as others who *are* their customers. Why can't they realize that they are mistreating customers before, during, and after the sale? Many of these companies score high marks on customer service in other areas — it's as if their phone and online etiquette doesn't count.

Nearly everyone owns a cell phone today, and as a result, large numbers of store employees are talking on them during work hours when they should be taking care of their customers. ARG research shows that *65.5% of Americans have had to wait for a store employee to get off his or her cell phone and they don't like it.* The same survey revealed that *57.5% won't stick around. They are so offended that they walk out the door. The other 42.5% who do wait aren't happy campers either and they tell a friend about their unpleasant experience.* Either way, a company loses. The lesson is: instruct your employees to turn off their cell phones at work.

A high percentage of companies use voice mail to keep their overhead low. Having a machine handle customer calls is definitely cheaper than paying employees wages. But when you consider the lost revenues because customers are hanging up and shopping elsewhere, this is hardly good business. An ARG survey revealed that *43% of Americans who call a company and get a voice mail message think that it's a waste of time to leave their callback number. Another 26.6% expressed that voice mail bothers them so much they hang up.* No business can afford to antagonize a quarter of its customers.

Another way to annoy customers is to have them talk to a telephone operator based in India. In fact, *42.7% of Americans told us that they can't understand what a person from India is saying, and a whooping 21.1% get downright angry.* These numbers verify that if you do this, you're upsetting 60% of your customers. Ask yourself if you have lost your patience when you are forced to talk to an operator whom you can barely understand. Odds are high that you have. ARG research shows that *94.5% of Americans say they are provoked when a person that speaks broken English handles their call.* How bad is it? The same survey reveals that *31.6% of Americans said it's driven them to stop doing business with the company.*

How do consumers interpret the use of voice mail and the hiring of low-waged employees with poor English language skills? They think companies that do it are willing to give less service so they can reduce their overhead. These companies may as well put up big signs that read: "To save money, we are willing to annoy you." Fortunately, there are some companies, although a minority, that are willing to invest whatever money it takes to avoid this inappropriate treatment of customers. For instance, Cabela's has five call centers; not a single call is outsourced. Depending on the time of year, an estimated 900 to 2,500 people are available to handle customer calls. "Every single call is answered by a 'live' person," explains Ron Spath, vice president of customer relations.

"Yes, it does cost more in the short run, but keeping customers satisfied generates repeat orders, so we consider it a good investment," Spath says. "I bet that of the 50 compliments that come in here every day, more than half are from callers who say something like, 'Thank you for having a real person talk to me,' and 'Thank you for speaking English.' Jim Cabela has long said, 'If other people only knew how easy this is. You just have to be willing to invest, answer live, and answer fast.'

"I'll tell you something else," Spath continues. "Every page of our Web site has our phone number prominently displayed. Why do we do this? We want to make it easy to do business with us. If somebody needs information about a product, has a service question, or is confused about how to shop online, we want to hear from that person."

✳   ✳   ✳

Service-driven companies know that annoyed and frustrated customers shop elsewhere. An ARG study revealed that 53.4% *of Americans say that it is virtually impossible to find a telephone number to call when they visit most Web sites.* And what do they think about those companies that don't include a phone number on their Web site? A staggering 70.8% *said that they think these companies purposely make it difficult to contact them!* Imagine having customers believe a company doesn't want to hear their complaints and soothe their frustrations—or worse, doesn't want to give them service. And as evidenced by how many companies ignore protesting customers, we must assume that when phone numbers are missing, it is not an oversight. These companies have intentionally not listed their phone numbers because they don't want to deal with unhappy campers. Interestingly, we visited AT&T's Web site to inquire about a service and we couldn't find a listed telephone number that would make it possible to talk to a live person. It is difficult fathom that of all companies, a telephone company wouldn't want to have its customers communicate with it via the telephone! Not listing a phone number on a Web site is nothing new. Before the Internet, the same companies sent letters to complaining customers sans phone numbers.

To our amazement, when we called AT&T for service and did talk to an employee, an emergency came up, so rather than going through the long ordeal of having to explain our problem to another person again, we requested to have the person on the line call us back in an hour. "I am sorry but I can't do that," she replied. "Why can't you?" we asked. Of course there was no reasonable excuse she could have, so she just replied, "I am not allowed." And, of all companies, why couldn't a telephone company employee call a customer back? This annoyed us so much that we put this in a research study. We found out we were not alone on this score: 84.8% *of our fellow Americans said it upsets them even more when they are told by an operator that she or he can't call them back.* It is clearly logical that an operator who has pulled up your record should call you back rather than have you and another operator start from scratch to solve your problem!

"There is nothing more frustrating to a customer than to have a problem and feel as though he or she has nowhere to turn," Aaron Brown, the former national director of customer relations at Pulte, says. "This is why we listed our phone number on the Web page, and customers could call Pulte's corporate office where someone was always available to talk to them. Pulte wants to hear from its customers, and they particularly want to hear from an unhappy customer."

Typically a Chubb policyholder will call her or his agent to report a claim. But on weekends and in the evenings, when one's agent might not be available, Chubb has a toll-free number that's accessible 24 hours a day, 365 days a year. Calls are taken at two Chubb call centers. Mark Korsgaard, who was responsible for developing and building these centers, says, "We designed the system to assure we'd have people talking to people, not to answering machines or interactive voice recorders. And no client ever talks to an offshore telephone operator. We made a financial commitment in these call centers that there'd always be enough people available to talk to callers. This is part of our cost of doing business to achieve outstanding customer satisfaction."

"Serving the customer is so ingrained in our company's culture that even when former customers call in for advice, Chubb employees are eager to help them," explains Vice President Mark Schussel, the insurer's public relations manager. "This is true throughout the entire organization, including our most senior managers who routinely take these incoming calls. I know this is appreciated by the comments I hear from our agents and brokers."

It's improbable that you'll never hear a complaint about telephone service at NetJets. That's because the company takes extreme measures to ensure a maximum level of customer service. As Matt Harris explains, "When you're a NetJets owner, you are assigned an account management team that consists of six people. You are given a dedicated 1-800 number. Every owner has his or her own phone number. On average, every phone is answered in 12 seconds or less, and calls are received 24/7. Because the owner works with the same team, strong relationships develop."

* * *

We've observed how customer-focused companies recognize that communicating via the telephone and online is as much a part of the total customer experience as is talking to "live" shoppers in a retail store. And because they do recognize that, they work overtime at making them feel valued. As a consequence, their customers respond with repeat orders and referrals.

7

It's about Time

To research this book, we conducted extensive interviews with senior executives of customer-focused companies. We kept hearing recurring comments about how today's customers place a high value on their time. We were told that in order to win a customer's loyalty, it's imperative to respect his or her time and be focused at maximizing it. As a result, we've devoted an entire chapter to cover this important subject.

It started with the downsizing of America in the early 1990s when companies started reducing their workforces. Ever since, Americans have been working longer hours and scratching for more discretionary time. Do the math. The average American today puts in a 46- to 47-hour work-week. Add another 52 minutes for daily commuting time to and from work, and that person has a serious time crunch.

In retailing, the first place you vividly see how customers are reacting to time pressures is at the checkout counter. To reduce costs, many retailers have fewer checkout lines, and when customers see long lines and half the counters aren't open, they fume. In fact, an ARG study reveals that 33.3% *have quit shopping at a store because they thought the lines were too long.* What upsets even more shoppers is when a store has a line for customers with 10 or less items and only a couple of lines for customers with more than 10 items. *This upsets 57.1% of shoppers very much and 37.1% somewhat. Only 5.8% of all shoppers say that it doesn't bother them.* The same study revealed that *78.8% of Americans have stopped shopping a store because its checkout lines were too long, and 59% shop a small grocery store so they can get in and out more quickly.*

The obvious thing to avoid angering customers with long checkout lines is to staff the lines with well-trained employees who can ring up transactions more quickly than poorly trained ones. We give praise to Apple for coming up with a new way to speed things up. In late 2007 the company revamped its 201 stores to accommodate an onrush of shoppers who are snapping up its revolutionary iPhone at a record-breaking pace. To accomplish this, clipboard-carrying concierges greet customers at the door to direct them to the right section of the store. Several others mill the floor in case someone has a question. With cash registers removed, a common question nowadays is, "Where do I pay?" The store employee would instantly reply, "Right here," and whip out a portable scanner from a hip holster. Receipts are e-mailed on the spot or, if the customer prefers, a paper version emerges from printers hidden underneath display tables. The products are usually brought in from storage in the back, but for the holiday season, Apple designated an "express shopping" section, with inventory on the floor ready for purchase. The new procedure worked fine except for the cash customer who experienced some delays.

We thought that it would annoy more shoppers to be stuck in a long checkout line than to be put on hold when they call a company; however, when asked what annoys them more, 59% *said being put on hold is more upsetting versus 41% who were more upset about being in a long checkout line.* If being put on hold isn't bad enough, do you want to know what really angers customers? Put them on hold and then when you finally answer the phone, don't make any attempt to apologize for it. An ARG study shows that 94% *of those surveyed become infuriated when they get no apology for being put on hold.* Many, however, don't express their anger because they are afraid that if they do, the operator will hang up on them!

A 2006 survey by Mystery Shopping Providers Association found average checkout line wait times of 4 minutes, 27 seconds at grocery stores; 4 minutes, 55 seconds at apparel stores; and 5 minutes, 23 seconds at department stores. Still-hurried customers bristle at the wait times and often perceive the delays as longer than they actually were.

To speed things up, Best Buy is employing "personal shopping assis-tants" who are knowledgeable about all merchandise in the store. They wear button-down shirts to set them apart from regular Best Buy sales-people clad in Navy blue polo shirts. Their job is to individually serve time-starved customers making complicated purchases such as home theater systems. In some Circuit City stores, salespeople have computer tablets hung from their shoulders like book bags, again more effective than mandating a dress-in-black dress code. The tablets are used to call product specifications for customers and help customers compare features of merchandise. Target and Wal-Mart have attempted to speed up shopping for new moms by clustering baby clothes, baby food, strollers, diapers, and even maternity clothes in the same department. Lowe's has installed "Need Help" buttons where shoppers often need to summon assistance—key-cutting and shelving areas, for example. The average response time is less than 60 seconds. Rival Home Depot tested the call buttons and is now installing them across the United States.

With Americans collectively making 127 million trips to Wal-Mart each week, the company is focused on having these customers make the best of their time while shopping in its stores. That's because the company knows that the average Wal-Mart shopper spends 21 minutes in the store, but finds only 7 of the 10 items on his or her shopping list. To boost declining sales growth, one key is helping customers find and buy those eighth, ninth, and tenth items before they rush off to their kids' soccer games. So the chain is attempting to make its sprawling stores easier to navigate. Among the changes: better signs to help shoppers find merchandise, more convenient placement of hot-selling items, and staffing changes to speed up the checkout times. "We don't decide how long the people are in the store," Wal-Mart marketing chief Stephen Quinn explains. "What we can decide is how easy it is for you, within the 21 minutes you've allocated, to get what you want."

For years, big discount retailers kept building bigger and bigger boxes, figuring the combination of low prices and huge assortment trumped other considerations. The result is that shoppers all too often spend much of their time trudging from department to department to find elusive items on their shopping list, and some give up without finding them. Now the focus is on getting shoppers to make the best use of their time during their shopping experience. Those retailers who figure it out will be the ones to win market share.

The Value of Time

Seeing irritable customers unable to find their way through a big box store, unable to locate a sales clerk, or stuck in a long checkout line are just the tip of the iceberg. Customers with similar frustrations can also be spotted in long lines at airline ticket counters, banks, fast food restaurants—everywhere that people engage in commerce. They have little patience for slow service, and they are unforgiving to companies that show no sympathy for their plight.

We asked Dave Wilson, the Lexus dealer in Newport Beach, California, about his thinking on why he built a $75 million dealership, the most expensive in the United States. "Our slogan, 'It's About Time,' says it all," Wilson explains. "Of course, we're talking about the customer's time, and everything we do here is focused on the value of the customer's time. There's a certain subset of the population where time is more valuable than money. Here, in the Newport Beach area, we're in the middle of it. This dealership was built to value our customers' time. When you visit us, the most obvious time savers are the 120 stalls we have to get the customer in and out of here as quickly as possible. In between each stall there is a mini–parts department that's restocked nightly. This way, when customers bring their car in for a 30,000-, 60,000-, 90,000-, or 120,000-mile routine maintenance, the technician doesn't have to go from his stall and past 100 other stalls to the parts department to get an oil filter, a set of spark plugs, or an air cleaner. In addition, there may be several different people simultaneously working on different areas of the car to speed things up."

Bob Carter, former group vice president at Lexus' U.S. headquarters, explains, "We've created a process that allows us to get a car serviced so they're in and out in 45 to 60 minutes. It's true that some customers drop off their car for normal maintenance in the morning and come back later in the day to pick it up. Although a dealership may give them a loaner for the day, they still have to come back to get their car. But what they really want is to make only one trip. If we can keep the time to do the work down to an hour, the customer will save time by waiting for his car because he doesn't have to drive back to his office, come back to the dealership, and then drive home from here."

For a dealership with the volume of Wilson's, 500 loaner cars would be required to honor customers' requests so they could avoid waiting for their car to be serviced. If the number of those loaners is reduced, it represents a substantial savings to the dealership. Wilson estimates that the costs he would have to pay in rental fees are reduced by $500,000 a month. So not only does the customer get better service, the speed in which the service is rendered is a big money saver to the dealership. "For those customers who want a loaner," Wilson tells, "we help you unload your car, take you over to the loaner car area, and in 60 seconds, you're on your way out. I know a Mercedes dealership that takes as long as an hour to check your car in and another hour to pick it up. We also save time for our customers by having four cashiers handle the paperwork when it comes time to pay the bill."

Prior to a customer taking possession of his new purchase, the vehicle is given a final inspection in Wilson's delivery room, where there are six stalls, each with high-intensity lights so a technician can examine the car, inch by inch, before it is delivered to the customer. Here, the Lexus dealership motto is: "Get it right the first time." And again, it's about recognizing the value of a customer's time so the vehicle doesn't have to come back unnecessarily for service. It is also in the delivery room where a salesperson spends an hour with a new car owner going over every aspect of the vehicle. This is a service that Wilson provides because today's Lexus has state-of-the-art technology that he feels requires explaining by a knowledgeable salesperson. "Some customers balk and don't want to take the time to be told how to use the equipment on their car," Wilson tells. "'This is the twentieth new car I've had,' a man will say. Of course, the next day his wife is calling back. 'Can you explain how to turn the radio on?' While Lexus has a lot of sophisticated technology, it's not so complicated that you can't figure out how to use most of it. But there are some benefits and features on these cars that didn't exist five years ago, and they do require explaining."

When you consider that Mercedes has a 600-page owner's manual on how to operate some of its expensive models, the time in Wilson's delivery room is well spent. "To maximize your benefit and use for one of BMW's transmissions," Wilson says, "you need to take 7 three-hour courses. Now, nobody is going to do that. Years ago when I was a used car manager, I'd ask people, 'Do you know that you had a tilt wheel and cruise control?' People who owned their car for five years didn't even know they had these options. Without an explanation, some people will spend hours just figuring out how to use their navigation system. So in addition to teaching customers how to maximize the use of the features on their vehicle, they also end up saving time because it will take them much longer to learn on their own what we can teach them in the delivery room."

Wilson didn't cut any corners when he built his $75 million dealership. For starters, he plunked down $30 million for an eight-acre lot and tore down 10 two-story office buildings on it that had been built in the early 1970s. The buildings' 60 tenants had been on month-to-month leases. The property is located at the corner of McArthur and Jamboree in Newport Beach, which is said to be the most prestigious corner in affluent Orange County. Beautifully landscaped, there is an elaborate lighted corner water display and a variety of exotic palm trees line the street frontages. The two-story building is magnificent, looking more like a five-star hotel than a car dealership. Its exterior construction is granite, and it has water walls at both the showroom entrance and service entrance. The main entrance was indeed constructed to give the feeling as if one were approaching a luxury hotel, and, in fact, it comes complete with concierge service. There is a concierge at the main entrance, and another at the service department entrance. Upon being warmly greeted by the concierge at the service entrance, the customer is introduced to a service writer who explains the service work that will be done.

The interior of the building is equally impressive with granite walls and marble floors. Its furnishings are impeccable and beautifully decorated. And the place is spotless. Everything, including the bathrooms and automotive service areas, is hospital clean. Its over-the-top amenities are not what you'd expect to see in a car dealership. In six different waiting areas, some with grand fireplaces, there are 17 high-definition plasma screen televisions. There are quiet rooms with large selections of magazines and daily newspapers. If you come with a laptop computer, there are private places to hook up, but if you didn't bring yours and want to go online, there are three computer workstations. If you are looking for something to do, there is a playroom for adults, complete with pinball machines, car racing games, and so on. If your small children accompany you, there is also a game room for their amusement, while older children can visit a more elaborate video game area. There are also a Tommy Bahama shop and an Oakley store that sells top-of-the-line sports sunglasses. The dealership also has a delicatessen that serves croissants, breakfast rolls, cappuccinos, and coffee each morning. At lunch, the deli serves sandwiches, and later in the day, desserts. Periodically there are wine tasting events. For golfers there is a putting green. And if you have the time, you can take a scheduled tour of the dealership that takes about 90 minutes.

"I recently saw one woman here at nine and I had to attend a meeting in Torrence," Wilson says, "and when I came back at three, she was still here. 'Don't they have your car done?' I asked her. 'It was ready before ten,' she said. 'I bought two of these shirts for my husband and when I got home, he liked them so much, I came back to buy some for my son.' Our idea is that if we can slow you down for an hour or so, we don't have to loan you a car. It boils down to having you spend your time in a way that you think is worthwhile rather than sitting around wasting it."

Bob Carter mentions that a high percentage of Lexus owners today are women. "For this reason, some of our dealers have installed high-end boutiques. Others may have a café, and some will have a Starbucks franchise within the dealership. It's all about providing a way for our customers to make the best use of their time while they're in our store. While we're providing them with amenities, we're always focused on the processes of the Toyota production system, which is considered to be one of the most efficient in the world, and applying them in the service departments at the dealerships. This helps on the efficiency side. Then if I tell you you'll be on your way in 45 minutes, I'm going to try to get you out of here in 35 minutes. But if I tell you 45 minutes and it takes an hour and 15 minutes, no matter how phenomenal that level of service was, I haven't met your expectations."

Germain Lexus has two locations in Columbus, Ohio, one is in Easton, one of the most upscale lifestyle shopping centers in the United States. Like Wilson's, the Germain dealership is a magnificent facility, and it, too, offers many of the same amenities. "This is the highest rent district in the metropolitan area," Rick Germain explains. "We decided it's worth the price because our customers can drop off their cars for service, and if they choose to leave our building, they can walk across the street to the mall.

"The definition of luxury has changed over the years," Germain adds. "People are busy with work and raising their families, so a very important commodity these days is their time. A few years ago, I remember hearing someone say at a Lexus dealership meeting that luxury used to be possessions and later it was experiences. Nowadays, it's time. That's what people value the most because they are so busy doing other things."

For the car owner who is strictly interested in the fastest possible service, and thinks all the amenities are bells and whistles, Lexus Benchmark Service comes into play. "We're just rolling it out to our 223 dealers," Nancy Fein, the division's former vice president of customer satisfaction, explains. "The Toyota production system is very efficient at identifying waste and then coming up with ways through a team approach to do things more productively. The Lexus Benchmark Service helps us to value our customer's time, and by working with dealers, we can identify and train people to do a 30,000-mile service job in less than 25 minutes that used to take two-and-a-half hours. Sure, it takes discipline and dedication, but that's nothing new at Lexus."

When it comes to selling Lexus cars to baby boomers, Group Vice President Mark Templin emphasizes that it's a different ballgame than when selling to Gen X and Y buyers. As mentioned earlier, Templin headed Scion, Toyota's division that caters to Gen X and Gen Y. "You have to remember that these young people are really different from any previous generation," he explains, "because they have the Internet and they are capable of going online and doing their homework far more thoroughly than their parents. There is so much information on the Internet, and they are smart enough to figure out the cost of ownership of any product. Now this changes the dynamics of buying a car. First, we have to recognize that they know as much about the technology and pricing of the car as the people in the dealership who are trying to serve them. So this means we must treat them in a different way by respecting their time. For instance, there are the baby boomers who expect to negotiate on the price when they buy a car because that's the way they've been doing it for the last 50 years and they want to continue to do it that way. But with some of the Gen X and Y customers who have priced the car online, they might say, 'I don't negotiate for anything else I buy, so why do I have to negotiate the price when I buy a car?'

"I think the smartest dealers today are flexible enough to say, 'We will do it any way that you want to do it, Mr. Customer. Here's my fixed price, if you just want to buy a car, but we can negotiate if that's what you'd rather do.' With some customers, it's a matter of 'if you can negotiate quickly, then I don't mind it, but don't make it a waste of my time.' Some of our Lexus dealers have experimented with a full one-price model where the customer can just take it or leave it. But I don't think it necessarily has to be a one-size-fits-all. It goes back to just treating customers the way they want to be treated, or better than they want to be treated and saving them time."

In the past, a high percentage of car buyers dreaded the negotiation phase of purchasing a car. They didn't like to haggle with a car salesperson, never knowing if they were getting a good price. However, in recent years, the U.S. automobile industry has moved in the direction where the manufacturer's suggested retail price and the true transaction price are more compressed, whereas the gap in the two prices was formerly further apart. With this in mind, Templin acknowledges that Americans today are feeling more comfortable about purchasing a car. The automotive executive pauses briefly and reflects, "With customers knowing how to price online by figuring out what the car costs the dealer, the consumer is empowered, and at the very least, by everyone knowing what the starting point is, the negotiation is quicker than it used to be."

Templin emphasizes that one of Lexus' biggest challenges at the time of the purchase of a car, as well as the entire automobile industry, is how to speed up the finance and insurance process. "Today's customers have expressed their annoyances with the time it takes to do the required paperwork," Templin says, "and they say it is a part of the buying experience that most customers dislike," he explains. "Of course, the paperwork has to be done so we have to find ways to speed it up. We are experimenting with an online approval process where the application is more automated to eliminate many of the current steps. Presently, we're recommending to our dealers that they provide more offices to handle the finance and insurance transaction. Another approach is to train every sales consultant to be capable of handling this process. Some of our dealers have their people do the walk-through whereby they explain the features and benefits of the car to the new owner. This way, while the paperwork is being completed, the customer can sign the final documents and more quickly be able to get into his car and drive away."

Selling Time

"My business is about a quality of life," NetJets' CEO Richard Santulli says, "and I sell time. What I give my customer is a quality of life, whether it's business or personal, and it's about time. I go to Columbus on Wednesday, and I know what time I'll be there. It might take me longer to get to Manhattan from my office in New Jersey than it will to Columbus. I have to meet with Bank of America in Columbus, and I have a four o'clock meeting back here in New Jersey. I don't have a problem doing that. It's easy. I sell time.

"The same applies to the guy who takes his family on a vacation. He's thinking about a commercial flight, 'I have to be at the airport two hours before the departure time. Then I have to get a rental car. By the time I get to my destination, I'm exhausted.' Then, the last day, he's dreading the fact that he now has to do it in reverse. With NetJets, you just drive up to the plane. You get there two minutes before, and a few minutes later, you're airborne. I can leave my house in Florida, and three hours and 10 minutes later, be at my house in New Jersey.

"It makes me more competitive," Santulli continues. "You better have three people to compete with me because I'll be in three places in one day. Not only that, when somebody has access to a private plane, they'll travel. They're not going to put off the trip saying, 'I really don't want to go.'"

* * *

NetJets sells time (saving it), and Tom James Company, in an entirely different business, also sells time. "We started our company on the premise that most men don't like to shop," former president Jim McEachern tells. "If we could go to their office, we felt it would appeal to them because they'd save time. We'd provide the convenience of keeping them from getting in their car, driving in traffic to a store, looking to see if what they wanted was available in their size, and after getting it altered, making another trip to pick it up. Oftentimes, a store won't have what the customer is looking for, so he has to repeat the process again (and again) before he actually makes a purchase. We sell our clothes with almost an infinite variety of patterns, colors, fabrics, and styles which include two- or three-button coats that can be single- or double-breasted and so on. We have so many varieties of clothing ranging from the traditional look to the Italian look. It's a rare occasion when we can't provide what a customer is looking for. We can't always compete on price alone, but when the value of a customer's time becomes a part of the equation, we become very competitive."

McEachern recalls a sale that he made early in his career to Ben Weinberg, an attorney who was the president of the Atlanta Bar Association. "When I first met Ben, I told him that I could save him time. 'I'll make it a lot more convenient for you, Mr. Weinberg. You won't have to go shopping and I could offer you a wide selection tailored to your specific tastes and measurements.' 'Okay, I'll take two suits,' he told me. 'You pick them out.' I just took his measurements and came back in a few weeks with his suits. He liked them and said, 'I want you to see me every season and have two suits that you think I'll like. And I want you in and out in five minutes.' That was our arrangement. It was all about saving him time. Weinberg knew the value of his time, and knowing what he billed clients on an hourly basis, he was saving money by buying his suits from me. I sold him suits for many years until he finally retired."

Steve Adelsberg, Tom James' number one salesperson whose annual sales are in the $2.5 million to $3 million range, concurs that his clients are successful people who place a high value on their time. "After a while, I know their tastes and what they already have in their wardrobe, so I don't have to ask them a lot of questions that I did when I first sold them. I don't have to show them different things to find out what they like and dislike."

To conserve his own time, Adelsberg has a driver. This enables him to work in the back seat in between sales calls. Plus, he doesn't waste any time looking for a parking space in downtown Baltimore and Washington, D.C. His clients are affluent, successful professional and business people. When they see how he values his time, they know that he recognizes the value of their time. Adelsberg also points out that with the services of a driver he is able to maximize his time. He sees 10 clients a day, which is a higher number than he'd see if he drove his own car. Another top Tom James producer, Christian Boehm, points out that most successful people surround themselves with professionals such as accountants, lawyers, financial advisors, and other experts. "My clients understand that they must rely on experts in other fields to advise them," he says, "and I'm their professional clothier who consults them about their wardrobe needs. All of their advisors conserve their time. Without them, they'd be required to spend an inordinate amount of time understanding complicated legal, tax, and financial matters. With reliable, trusted advisors, however, they can focus on their own careers. Note that I emphasize 'trusted.' Once you've earned their trust, the selling process is considerably shortened."

Time Well Spent

"When you look at a physician's job," says Joe Scodari, former head of Johnson & Johnson's pharmaceuticals business, "it's quite different today in the U.S. as compared to other countries. In the U.S., there are so many stakeholders that impact a doctor's time. To backtrack, when I started in this business, doctors were more like entrepreneurs who were able to do with their patients whatever they thought was appropriate from their perspective. There wasn't the oversight that exists today that requires input from other stakeholders. Now, we have managed care organizations that dictate practice guidelines. They're telling physicians what they can and can't prescribe. There are also the academics and the societies that make demands on doctors. All of these consume a doctor's time and his or her ability to operate independently."

Scodari emphasizes that with the demands on today's physician's time, the issue of managing time and interfacing with a drug representative has become increasingly more imperative. "It's about having a relationship," Scodari says, "that's based on effective communication between the two parties. If the representative does not communicate in a meaningful and responsive way to that physician's needs and practice, it's unlikely that she will get much time to tell her story. It's as if it becomes an advertising message. You're in there, you make a quick point, and you walk out.

"Today's rep must be able to build a relationship that is founded on adding value to that physician's practice. He or she is providing something that the doctor believes is important. To succeed, the rep must maximize the value of the time spent with the doctor and be able to have a two-way exchange that drives value to both parties."

A pharmaceutical representative must be patient because today's busy physicians are solidly booked with appointments during their office hours. Of course, doctors realize that they must meet with drug reps who serve as an important source of information on current medical occurrences, but during their office hours, patients are their top priority. Consequently, a drug rep will typically spend a major portion of his or her time waiting in the reception area versus interfacing with the physician. "This comes with the territory," Scodari explains, "but because these jobs require a significant amount of technical competency, during this downtime, we encourage our J&J reps to read company learning materials and current medical publications."

＊　＊　＊

"In the insurance business, there are two ways I look at time," says Tom Motamed, Chubb's former chief operating officer. "First, how much time does it take to approve or disapprove an application? This is really an issue between the insurer and the broker. I call it responsiveness. If we are not responsive to our agents and brokers, they will lose faith in Chubb and won't want to deal with us. To them, time is money, and we should not slow down their selling time. With this in mind, if they submit an application for coverage that we don't like, we need to tell them right away, and let them find another underwriter. If the answer is yes, it becomes somewhat more tortuous because we are going to ask a lot of questions. Why? Because we want to understand that customer. When we put together the coverage for the customer, we have to know what the exposures are, what kinds of losses are possible, what kind of policy should be issued, and what should be the terms and conditions of the policy. All this takes time. Agents and brokers aren't happy about that. Then there is a lot of back and forth, but the end result is a better product. All this is necessary because when there is a loss, the client wants to get paid. They don't want to hear that the agent missed something, or that Chubb missed something. Or, 'I thought we had that covered!' This is why we ask a lot of questions up front—it enables us to put the best program together.

"At the end of the day, it took longer to issue a policy, but when the client submits a claim, we pay more promptly than other insurers. I love it when the customer says, 'Gee, I got even more than I thought I'd get.' When I hear that, I say, 'God bless you. The fact is, that's what you deserve. We're not looking to cut back on you.'"

Mark Korsgaard, who's in charge of Chubb's worldwide casualty claims, stresses that while it may take longer to underwrite a policy, the company is in a position to respond faster when a homeowner submits a claim. "We're not one of those insurance companies that require a client to submit his receipts and invoices for what he's purchased," Korsgaard tells. "We don't get into that, and we know most people don't even have the paperwork. We've learned to segment claims from the simplest to the most complex. We can fast-track and simplify a majority of the claims. Those that are straightforward require very little documentation from the insured, and it's a one-day process. With today's technology, we are able to obtain information quickly and without asking the insured a lot of questions, we can just pay the claim. We believe speed is a benefit. Obviously, the speed in which we pay a claim is what's going to satisfy most people."

✳   ✳   ✳

"There have been many marketing books advising that if you're a vice president, director, or general manager, you should be 100% accessible to your customers," former Pulte Homes vice president Eric Pekarski says. "I agree—as long as it's the customer that you serve. But first you must ask, 'Who are my customers?' In management, you should be 100% accessible to the people who work for you because *they* are your customers. But people get confused when they think that their customer is always the consumer. You have to know who your customer is. Let's say that I'm in customer relations in the field at Pulte, and I get promoted to general manager. Chances are I'm going to want to get involved with the customer like I was before, because that's my comfort zone. It's what I'm good at. However, my job changes as general manager. My customers now become the customer relations contacts as opposed to the customer. And as a vice president, my customers are the general managers instead of the customer relations contacts. A company can't have a lot of people who are taking care of the same customer or trying to, because it burns up a ton of labor and a ton of time. It also gets the customer confused. You can't put customers in a position where they bounce back and forth.

"I hear companies talk about how time consuming taking care of customers is. It really isn't—not if there is one point of contact and that person knows exactly what he or she is supposed to do. But when a general manager used to say to me, 'My phone is just ringing off the hook,' my first question was, 'Why are they calling you instead of talking to a customer relations contact?' At Pulte, the customer's liaison is the customer relations contact. That's the person to call whenever a customer needs anything. At companies where a customer has to call a lot of different people every time a question or problem arises, the customer consumes a lot of valuable time that wears him down."

Time: The Ultimate Luxury

"We monitor our customer centers very carefully," Bob Carter explains, "and we are always engaging with our customers when we bring out a new Lexus product. For example, we are currently hearing about how they view our products and our level of service. We've narrowed down how high-end customers define luxury, and they aren't necessarily looking at one or two things. Sure, they're looking at personalized service, but in my view, people are very affluent today and have enough things. Today's true luxury is time. So, if I really want to offer you the highest luxury, it's going to be focused on the value of your time, how to make best use of your time, and I'll respect your time."

"Travelers today are more pressed than ever for time," Rob Hagelberg, Four Seasons' Westlake Village hotel manager, explains. "This is true with our Four Seasons guests on vacation as well as on business trips. That's why we make sure they don't spend much time at the front desk checking in and out. We make sure our room service is on time and accurate. It's also important for everything in the room to be in working order including the shower, phone, television, and Internet service. We know that when something is broken, it wastes our guest's time. When a big event is held at our hotel, we'll bring in more resources for valet parking. Unlike some hotels, you won't see people waiting for 20 minutes for their car at a Four Seasons hotel. If need be, we'll all pitch in and valet park to make sure our customers don't have a long wait."

Employees at all levels place a high value on a Four Seasons' guest's time. An example of how this works is illustrated by what Hakan Uluer, a company area director of finance in Istanbul, did when a guest was pressed for time in an emergency situation. The city had been hit by a heavy snowstorm and all transportation had virtually collapsed. In anticipation of the bad weather, Uluer drove to work early that morning and was able to find his way to the hotel. Upon his arrival, the concierge informed him about a guest who was unable to get a taxi or any other transportation. "It's imperative for him to attend a meeting at the Hyatt hotel," the concierge said. Uluer volunteered to drive the guest to his destination, but along the way, traffic came to a standstill. When they got within walking distance of the Hyatt, the guest said that in order to make his meeting on time, he would go by foot. With the heavy accumulation of snow, however, the guest was not able to walk in snow wearing his fancy pair of shoes. "No problem," said Uluer. "Take my boots." The guest put on the boots, profusely thanked Uluer, and walked the rest of the way to the Hyatt, getting there just before the meeting commenced.

As Barbara Talbott, executive vice president of marketing, explains in her Cornell article, "The Power of Personal Service," "Four Seasons can do much to reduce inevitable stresses that travelers face by offering solutions to ensure comfort, convenience, and control. It can also help travelers to mitigate the absolute scarcity of their time by making the most, and best, of time they do have. That this happens most of all through personal service is evidenced by the priority guests themselves place upon it. Today's hectic lifestyles demand true 24/7 service—comprehensive, reliable, and uncompromising. By making the most of time, personal service helps to address this ever-present source of stress, whether felt as the need to be time efficient in the performance of business, or in the equally pressing desire to make the most of precious leisure time."

In another situation where time was of the essence, a senior female executive who worked for a large multinational company was in London and staying at another luxury hotel where she was conducting seminars. She was originally from Canada and was an avid hockey fan. That night the seventh and last game of the series of the Stanley Cup finals was being broadcast at 2 a.m. London time. However, to her dismay, the game was not being televised in London. When she asked the hotel's general manager if there was anything he could do, he flatly said no. This is when she decided to call the concierge desk at Four Seasons. After all, Four Seasons is a Canadian company, and perhaps someone there would be more understanding about her quandary.

The concierge said he'd check into it and call her back. Thirty minutes later, he said that the hotel could reposition the hotel's satellite to receive the hockey game, and if she was interested, a room was available. The woman was astonished that Four Seasons would accommodate such an unusual request from an unknown guest at a competitive hotel. In particular, she was aware that the concierge had little knowledge of hockey but evidently understood that the game was important to her. She checked into Four Seasons at midnight, and although she watched her home team go down in defeat, she has been a loyal customer of Four Seasons ever since.

Talbott stresses that luxury-hotel guests have high expectations. As stated in "The Power of Personal Service," "They need 24-hour support and an assurance that whatever the hour or request, it will be responded to quickly by someone who takes responsibility to carry through. They also expect exceptional promptness and accuracy; getting things right the first time, most times, and recovering well when mistakes occur."

Four Seasons founder Isadore Sharp said at the American Express Luxury Summit in 2006, "The essential question for us in the early days was, 'What did our guests value most?' Market research said it was luxury. And luxury didn't necessarily mean elegant surroundings and gourmet meals. When we looked closely, it became clear that the greatest luxury for our customer was time, and service could help them make the most of that. Giving them greater productivity, greater enjoyment. What better luxury could there be?" Talbott says that this insight led to the world's first 24-hour luxury hotel, one that operated on guests' timelines rather than dictating its own; one that anticipated services to make their travel easier, including around-the-clock room dining, one-hour pressing, four-hour dry cleaning; and after-hours access to retail shops and other services nearby.

Time Rewards for Best Customers

"I don't understand grocery stores that have the shortest lines for customers who buy the least," says David Norton, senior vice president and chief marketing officer at Caesars Entertainment. "Yes, there are obvious reasons why a person buying eight items wants to get out quickly. But the person who is buying the most groceries is most likely to be the store's most loyal customer, and he has to wait the longest. At Caesars, our strategy is to quickly get our best customers out of the line so they can be out on the gaming floor—which is what they want to do, and it helps make money for us too."

Caesars has a rewards program that recognizes customers based on their gaming activity. The company's most valued customers are those who most frequently gamble the most money in the company's casinos. Incidentally, it has nothing to do with how much a customer loses—it's strictly based on his play time and his wagers. A customer who plays the five-dollar slot machines is a more valued customer than the one who spends the same amount of time playing the nickel slots. Win or lose, it's all about a customer's play time and wagers. The odds are with the house, and over time, the casino is going to win, so a player's wins or losses are not factored into the equation in determining his or her value to the casino.

The acronym THEO is the theoretical value that Caesars uses that is based on the game customers play, their average bet, and how long they play. Applying THEO, the most valued Caesars customers are Seven Stars customers, and then there are Diamond customers, Platinum customers, and Gold customers. Customers issued a Seven Stars card are the most valuable, and its holders are entitled to the most rewards; the Gold cardholders receive the least rewards. The reward cards are inserted into slot machines or given to pit bosses when table games are played. A customer's play is tracked to determine his or her gaming activity.

"We are constantly looking at the mix of our customers," explains John Bruns, former vice president of customer satisfaction. "Our Seven Stars and Diamonds are 5% of our customer population, the Platinums are 10%, and the Golds are 85%. With only 5% of our customer population, Diamonds and Sevens bring in about 60% of our gaming revenues. The Platinums are 10% of the population and bring in about 25%. The total of the remaining 85% of our customers are the Golds, and they generate 15% of our revenues."

Using a mathematical formula to value a company's best customers is reminiscent of Vilfreedo Pareto, the nineteenth-century Italian economist who is famous for the Pareto principle, known also as the 80-20 rule. Pareto noticed that 80% of Italy's wealth was owned by 20% of the population. The Pareto principle has since been applied to many situations. For instance, 80% of a company's sales come from 20% of its customers. People wear 20% of their most favorite clothes about 80% of the time; and so on.

"Knowing that our Seven Stars, Diamond, and Platinum cardholders are 15% of our customer population and generate 85% of our revenues," Bruns says, "are important numbers to us, especially when we know that our Gold cardholders outnumber them by nearly six to one, but only account for 15% of our revenues. This tells us to focus on our most valued customers. And it prompted us to design a delivery system that would differentiate the service to them. We determined that we should serve our best customers based on what we call the measurement of wait time. In other words, how long does a customer wait to be served? For example, we serve customers at the front office, the buffet, and cashiering. We know that a Diamond is worth $100,000 to us (he plays at a value of $10,000 a year with an average lifetime of 10 years), and a Seven Stars is worth about $600,000 over the same time span. It's simply good business to avoid having one of these customers standing in line behind a $2,000 Platinum or a $200 Gold customer. So even though there may be five cashier's windows, three of them may serve the Seven Stars and Diamonds and two are open for Platinums and Golds. We don't want to put our $100,000 and $600,000 customers at risk by having them stand in line behind our $200 customers. Look at it this way, one Diamond at $10,000 a year equals 50 Golds, and one Seven Stars equals 300 Golds. While we want all of our customers to enjoy their experience in our casinos, we don't want our most valued customers standing in line behind customers that represent considerably less predetermined revenues.

"We also know that our Diamonds and Seven Stars are more affluent and probably retired," Bruns continues. "This means they play seven days a week, not just on weekends like our Golds who are working during the weekdays. Of course, having our Diamonds and Seven Stars here seven days a week is factored into our THEO formula. So what happens is that on Fridays, Saturdays, and Sundays, the Gold players come here in droves, and this high volume creates pressure on our capability to serve the Diamonds and Seven Stars. We don't want to upset our most valued customers by having them stand in long lines behind the Golds. We don't want them saying, 'I'm here all the time, and I have to wait behind all of these people. That's it. I'm out of here.' We know that if they go elsewhere, their Monday-through-Thursday business is difficult to replace. That's because there are a limited number of people with the time and money that choose gaming as their preferred form of entertainment. To make sure our employees get it, we tell them, 'One Diamond and Seven Stars equals jobs Monday through Thursday. If we upset this customer on a Saturday night, he's not going to be here during the week.' So we may have six cashiering lines on a packed Saturday night and three lines are open to Diamonds and Seven Stars. This enables them to avoid long waits behind the Golds.

"As I said, it's hard to replace a disgruntled Diamond or Seven Stars customer, but the Golds are indeed replaceable," Bruns adds. "All I have to do is say, 'Come on down, sign up for our Total Rewards card and get a free buffet.' They come down in droves. So I can replace them, and this means I am willing to take a risk with these customers in order to protect the more valued customers. As you can see, our delivery system is designed with a very clear focus on our best customers. Our CEO, Gary Loveman, often says, 'You can't be all things to all people.'"

On occasion, Gold customers object to long waits in lines while preferred customers go to the front of a long line to cash their chips, check in to the hotel, or to be immediately seated in a Caesars restaurant. Bruns states: "Our employees are trained to say, 'First of all, Mr. Smith, I apologize for your wait, and I thank you for playing at our casino. Now let me answer your question about why that gentleman in the shorter Diamond line went through the line faster than you did. The Diamond line is for players that have consolidated their play and come to one of our casinos versus going somewhere else. We reward them for that. I imagine that you probably play at some of the other casinos here, don't you?' They generally nod that they do. 'Well, Mr. Smith, I bet that if you brought all of your play to us, you would be a Diamond member and we would love to see you over in that line. We hope that you will consider that next time you're out.'"

Flextime

In her autobiography, *Miracles Happen*, Mary Kay Ash wrote about her early days in direct sales when she was a single working mother of three children. "I only had room for three things in my life: God, family, and career. I had no social life. Every waking hour was geared to my three children, my work, and my church. My entire day was planned around the children's schedule. I got up at five o'clock so that I could do my housework before they arose. Then I gave them a good breakfast and got them off to school. After they were gone, I left too—for my first party. I'd have another party in the early afternoon, and then I would make certain to be home to greet my children when they came home from school. I gave them their dinner and got them ready for bed. Then at seven o'clock, I would leave for my evening party. My housekeeper would have them asleep long before I got back. It worked out fine. I was able to have my cake and eat it too, because I was a working mother who still made time to be with her children. I was just sure to thank God for my high energy level!"

In 1963, Ash started her business on a shoestring, investing her life savings of $5,000 to start a cosmetics company that would distribute its skin care products via its Independent Beauty Consultants who sell directly to their customers through a "party plan." The Beauty Consultant would conduct skin care classes to small groups consisting of five to eight women at one of their homes. Initially Ash was her company's number one Beauty Consultant, recruiter, and teacher. Ash taught by example, and her strong leadership made her an excellent role model for other women who joined the fledgling sales organization. She practiced what she preached. God and her family were her top priorities. Her career came third.

Over the years, large numbers of women were attracted to Ash's business opportunity because it offered them the opportunity to personally manage their work hours so that they, like she, could work their jobs around their families. "The company has succeeded," Rhonda Shasteen, a senior vice president, explains, "because we provide an opportunity to women allowing them to spend time with their families while enjoying financial rewards. For example, Shirley Hutton, one of our most successful Independent National Sales Directors, used to get a master schedule from her children's principal at the beginning of the school year, and she would write every important event for the upcoming nine months in her date book. She put down football and basketball games, class plays, PTA meetings, teacher-parent days, everything. She never made a business commitment on these days and evenings because those times were reserved for her children. Today, the company has more than 1.7 million Beauty Consultants in well over 30 global markets who are working as independent salespersons, enjoying flexible work hours. Large numbers of women in Russia and China are personally experiencing free enterprise for the first time in their lives, and they too, just like Mary Kay did early on in her career, are working their careers around their families. In some countries where women are not considered equal to men, they are enjoying an empowerment that is otherwise unavailable to them."

Since Mary Kay first began, a woman would invite five or six friends to her house to host a skin care class, and today and every day, all over the world, hundreds of thousands of these and similar selling situations are being conducted. "Due to today's time demands," Rhonda Shasteen explains, "Beauty Consultants also schedule individual facials, because some of their customers don't have the time to attend a skin care class. With so many women working today, these are often office calls rather than a visit to a customer's home. A customer can also visit her Beauty Consultant's Mary Kay personal Web site and place an order online. This is a big timesaver for a customer who might otherwise buy a similar product at a retail store. Her Mary Kay Independent Beauty

Consultant can deliver the merchandise to her door so the customer doesn't have to go anywhere to pick it up."

✳   ✳   ✳

"People are busier than ever," says Aaron Brown, former national director of customer relations at Pulte Homes. "As a consequence, Pulte adapted its contacts' work schedules to accommodate customers so they could provide services to them at their convenience. It used to be that we'd be available from 7 a.m. to 5 p.m., and most people were okay with that. Customers would take a day off or do what they had to do to come in during those hours. Today, a customer relations contact has to have flexible work hours. They can't punch a clock. They have to do what needs to be done. If they wanted to work until 9 p.m. one night and come in the next morning at 11, it was their choice. If they wanted to work on a Saturday to accommodate customers and take off on Monday, that was also their choice."

Prompt Telephone Time

As we mentioned earlier, customers in long checkout lines perceive the wait time longer than it actually is. This is also the case when telephone callers are put on hold. Another thing they dislike. ARG research also revealed that *94.5% of Americans get provoked when a person that handles their call speaks broken English*. Every telephone operator at Cabela's speaks English, and a customer never converses with a machine. "Every single call is answered by a live person," Ron Spath, vice president of customer relations, states. "We don't have any interactive voice recorders and there are no menus. The feedback we get from our customers is very clear about how much they appreciate not having to waste a lot of time talking to a machine. They've also indicated it takes much longer to talk to someone who speaks broken English. We realize that outsourcing these calls to places like India costs less, but we think it's a good investment to pay more in order to save our customers' time. It's this same line of thinking that lead us to prominently display our toll-free telephone number on every page of our Web site. We don't want to frustrate any customers who have questions that they can't find answers to when they visit our Web site."

Knowing how customers want quick responses when they call the Cabela's 800-number, its computer-integrated caller ID system automatically identifies a current customer calling from his home phone number. "It recognizes the phone number," Spath explains, "and the customer's records are simultaneously displayed on the agent's computer screen when he or she picks up the phone receiver. There's a match with 60% of our inbound calls, so with these calls our people know who they are talking to. They then verify some basic information such as, 'Are you still in Atlanta, Georgia?' They do this to make sure they're talking to the right person. Our people are instructed to use tact because some people don't like it when a company knows too much about them. For this reason, they're trained to be subtle. By having mailing and credit card information on file, a lot of time is saved. We are set up to do the same thing on live e-mail chats. Our people are on call 24/7, 365, and average about two-and-a-half hours' response time in returning calls to customers with answers to their inquiries. During the day, it's much faster. On complicated calls, we have 19 advanced representatives who handle incoming calls, e-mails, and chats. These people are quite knowledgeable and capable of promptly handling inquiries."

Cabela's exemplifies how callers should be treated, but sadly as we all know from our personal experiences, a majority of companies are guilty of poor telephone etiquette and show no regard for their customers' time. Every one of us has had the displeasure of being put on hold for long periods of time. Not only is this discourteous, it is very bad for business. In an ARG study, *46.7% of Americans said that they have stopped doing business with a company(s) because they were put on hold for too long.* We view this as inexcusable—and a very poor way to do business. Customers are too hard to come by and too valuable to lose them this way to a competitor.

✳   ✳   ✳

At Lexus, responding to a telephone call is quite simple. "We don't have a whole lot of policies," Nancy Fein says. "There isn't a matrix that says if a customer says this, you say or do this. Everyone is empowered to do what we call 'case managing each customer.' So if you call in to me, I am the only one who is going to call you back. You will deal with me, and I will not refer you to someone else. I am not putting you through the system. I have the responsibility and authority to take care of you."

✳   ✳   ✳

People want fast service when they submit insurance claims. Chubb knows this and has a toll-free number available 24/7, 365. While there will be a menu to choose from, its purpose is to direct customers to the right person, never to a machine. "Our claims people are there to get the necessary information," Frances O'Brien, senior vice president, explains, "and they are able to tell a client, 'Here's a shop in your area where you can take your car. It will make your repairs a priority.' Or, if it's a home-owner's claim, 'Here's a fire expert to call,' or 'Call this water damage guy who can come in, and as a Chubb insured, you will receive priority ser-vice.' It's all about quickly getting the information and understanding that the client is upset with his loss so let's not hassle him. Within 24 to 48 hours, we'll have an adjuster, if necessary, who will visit the location or the car to see what has to be done. With small claims, the first person a claimant converses with on the phone is authorized to make the payment if the claim doesn't need to be adjusted. Generally, this individual can approve a loss up to $15,000. It's as easy as, 'You lost your watch and it's covered in your policy. I'll send you a check.' A claim is especially settled quickly if, say, an expensive piece of jewelry such as a gold Rolex watch is listed on a schedule. It's all about time."

8

Why Selling a Service Differs from Selling a Product

Products and services go together in tandem. A good product with poor service is a recipe for failure. And good service with an inferior product also doesn't work. For example, you wouldn't consider going back to a restaurant that had wonderful food but the service was horrendous. The same applies if the food was terrible; you wouldn't go back no matter how much you liked the waiter.

By the way, we consider ambiance as a part of service. A delicious meal served in a dirty, rundown restaurant leaves a lot to be desired. We believe the atmosphere and presentation of the meal is part of what you pay for in a restaurant. Howard Schultz, founder and chairman of Starbucks, built a worldwide coffee shop on this premise. Certainly Starbucks doles out mouth-watering cappuccinos and lattes—but it's the same product you can make yourself for a fraction of the cost. A cup of Starbucks coffee is also more expensive than what you'd pay for a quality cup of coffee at Dunkin' Donuts or McDonald's. So what is driving millions of people to Starbucks for their caffeine fix? It's the ambiance. They're paying a premium for the experience that comes with the relaxing atmosphere where they can escape for a few minutes from their otherwise hectic lives.

It's also the ambiance at Wilson's dealership in Newport Beach that enhances the experience of owning a Lexus. It puts customers in the mood to own a luxury car. It's part of the package. And quite a unique experience for a customer who got his last car serviced at a dealership where he spent a couple of hours sitting on a plastic chair reading three-month-old frayed magazines and drinking stale coffee in a paper cup. Similarly, once inside a Cabela's store, a customer feels the excitement of the great outdoors and yearns to be camping and fishing. The same thing happens when a Tom James rep visits a client's office. Immaculately dressed, he walks in as if he just stepped out of a *Gentleman's Quarterly* magazine. His appearance sends a message that wearing Tom James clothing makes one look professional, smart, and chic. As Christian Boehm, a company clothing consultant in the Cleveland, Ohio, area, says, "I tell our trainees that when they look the part, 'the person across the desk will aspire to look like you.'"

Getting Started

It's never easy to get a new enterprise off the ground. It's especially diffi-cult when there's not a tangible product involved because the customer doesn't have anything to see or touch. With a tangible product, the cus-tomer has a better idea about what he's getting in exchange for his money. With a service, there is nothing to put one's arms around. So selling a ser-vice boils down to convincing the buyer to trust what the seller says. With an established business, a customer relies on one's reputation, but with a start-up without a track record, there is little on which to determine that the seller will deliver what is promised.

For example, today, the RE/MAX concept is widely accepted by top real estate agents and the general public. RE/MAX is a household name. But imagine the obstacles founder Dave Liniger faced in 1972 when he launched his business. Liniger solicited real estate agents and had to con-vince them to leave their current brokers to become RE/MAX brokers. From the beginning, Liniger focused only on recruiting top producers, who generally worked for the biggest "name" real estate brokers in the area. While they could earn higher commissions with RE/MAX, they would no longer be associated with the local real estate firm that was well known in the local community. It was believed that it was the broker's reputation that prompted homeowners to list their homes with an estab-lished firm. The commission fees were the same everywhere, so why would anyone want to list her or his property with an unknown hole-in-the-wall real estate broker? The larger firms also had superior training programs. Liniger's pitch to top producers was that they no longer needed the training, and most significantly, they were paying a huge premium to their present broker. The real estate broker's take on a transaction was 50% of the agent's commission. With RE/MAX, he or she would pay a fixed monthly fee for office space and other expenses that would be shared with other RE/MAX agents in the office. While there was an element of risk in Liniger's proposition, the top producers would take home bigger paychecks because their expenses plus the fees they paid to RE/MAX would be considerably less than their previous broker's take. Liniger's job was to convince real estate agents that by taking a risk they would earn far more money than they otherwise would by staying put. He also had to convince them that their broker wasn't the reason why they got listings—it was their own doing.

It makes a lot of sense to be a RE/MAX agent today, especially after knowing 120,000 real estate agents have joined its ranks and are indeed earning more commissions. But at a time when nobody ever heard of RE/MAX or Dave Liniger, convincing a top producer to leave his broker was not exactly a walk in the park.

When asked to discuss how difficult it was to sign up the first RE/MAX agents, Liniger doesn't hesitate to say, "It was impossible."

Another obstacle that Liniger initially faced was Article 24, which was in bold print in the Code of Ethics of the National Association of Realtors (NAR). The industry's association claimed that Article 24 was based on its version of its Golden Rule that stated, "Do unto other real estate firms what you would have them do unto you." In this case, the message was that brokers shalt not solicit agents from another broker. However, for RE/MAX to exist, it had to sign up agents who worked for other firms, and it did so by posing the question: "Why split your commission with a broker when you can make 100%?" Bill Echols, a RE/MAX vice president, explains: "The NAR said it was unethical to proselyte real estate agents from other firms. You weren't supposed to actively recruit anyone directly. This meant that Dave could tell them about his company only if they approached him and asked what RE/MAX was. In the beginning, Dave played by these rules. Later on, he challenged the NAR, claiming that Article 24 violated free commerce. Dave told them, 'Slavery ended in the 1860s, and there's no such thing today, folks. We have the right to talk to whomever we want to because nobody owns these people. They have the right to know about other options available to them.' When he said that the NAR was in violation of antitrust laws and talked about suing it, the association convened and decided it would be best if Article

24 was removed from its Code of Ethics. Dave won without ever having to pay legal fees to fight the NAR. It was a good thing, because he didn't have the money to engage in a legal fight."

✳   ✳   ✳

With a fleet of over 700 aircraft worldwide operated through its subsidiaries, NetJets is the world's undisputed leader in private aviation. In fact the size of its fleet is equal to that of the world's second largest airline. Today NetJets operates in excess of 400,000 flights per year to more than 170 countries. In 1984, its CEO, Richard Santulli, bought Columbus-based Executive Jet Aviation for $2.5 million. It was a small charter company that owned five airplanes. He envisioned certain synergies. Santulli had owned a portfolio of helicopters that he leased to oil companies that were drilling offshore wells in the Gulf of Mexico. Executive Jet had a good maintenance crew, and Santulli believed his newly acquired company could service his helicopters. He also leased out some airplanes, and upon their leases expiration, he planned to have Executive Jet charter them. His company lost money in 1984, but the following year it made a small profit. It wasn't until 1986 when Santulli came up with the idea of selling fractional ownership in airplanes that it marked the beginning of an industry that theretofore did not exist.

For years, Santulli had traveled on commercial airplanes to and from the Gulf of Mexico region. He thought the connections from the East Coast to such places as Shreveport and Biloxi were a nightmare. Knowing that other businesspeople had the same problem, he figured that if several people could share an airplane and divide the cost, they'd all benefit. When he talked to other businesspeople, however, Santulli discovered that they all wanted to fly on Tuesdays and Thursdays, so there was no guarantee that the airplane would always be available. This is what prompted Santulli to devise a way for people to own a share of an airplane that could be available when they needed it that would not involve incurring the full 100% of the costs of maintaining and using it. "For this to work," Santulli says, "when somebody bought a share, I had to make sure that nothing would happen to prevent us from picking him up. Because if that were to happen, the word would spread and the company would fail. My first cluster of clients was in Chicago, where a Goldman Sachs partner bought a share from me, and then it was all a referral business. I always promised to give anyone who wasn't satisfied his money back."

"Being a financial guy, I bundled everything and made it simple for people to understand," Santulli continues. "I'd tell them, 'If you buy a quarter of a Citation S2, you pay me $38,000 a month and pay the management fees. You'll have a lease that entitles you to fly 20 hours a month.' Those are not the exact numbers, but that's the concept and it was easy to grasp what you got for your money. But people kept saying that it was too expensive. I thought it made sense, particularly for people who already owned a plane, and that's who I thought would be my clients. I got data from Cessna, and for those guys who were flying 200 or 250 hours, I was going to save them a lot of money. To me, it just made so much logical sense to do it. The problem was that when I'd see people who owned an airplane, they forgot how much they paid for it. Once they bought the asset, they couldn't care less. They didn't think the capital part of my deal made sense. So I took the capital part out. Instead I'd say, 'You could buy the airplane and here's the management fee. Here's the number you pay,' but then people would divide the number by 20 and say, 'Wait a minute, I could charter an airplane for less than that.' I'd regroup and reply, 'You buy the asset, pay me a monthly fixed fee, plus an hourly rate, which is how you charter an airplane.' I changed my initial concept three times during the first 18 months.

"As it turned out, there was something I overlooked. People with planes thought their pilots were the best pilots in the world, and they weren't buying what I was selling. The people who did sign up were those who had never owned an airplane. But it wasn't like we were selling fractional ownership like hotcakes. In 1986, there were four owners of fractionally held aircraft. I broke even in 1987, and I started adding four planes a year. By '89 we turned the corner; then the recession came, and the interest rates went crazy. From '89 to '91, I sold a single one-eighth fractional ownership. That was it, and I was still buying airplanes. I had no partners and a huge overhead. We lost between $38 and $45 million in that two-and-a-half-year period. All of my wealth I accumulated from my years with Goldman Sachs and from my helicopter leasing business was going fast. I personally signed everything, and my chief financial officer kept telling me to declare bankruptcy. I was nearly broke. In the late eighties, when I would try to sell a fraction, they'd say, 'Why would I want to do that?' I'd reply, 'Because I can save you 75% of the cost,' and they'd answer, 'Airplanes go up in value.' Guess what? In the early 1990s, you couldn't sell an airplane. So their value didn't go up, and, in fact, went down. Then, in 1993, I made my first deal on a Hawker Raytheon 1000 that could go nonstop from coast to coast, and I was able to put together some good contracts with manufacturers. From that time on, everything was good."

It is always difficult to launch a new venture that is unlike anything that has ever been previously done. What's more, coming up with a new concept in a service industry is all the more challenging. As a consequence, NetJets struggled during its early years, and for a while it appeared as if the company would go belly up. However, Santulli persevered, and today NetJets is flying high.

Sell the Sizzle with the Steak

Here's an interesting scenario. Imagine being the owner of a retail store on your hometown's Main Street. Although you have some competition in town, every shop owner is making a good living. Then one day—to your dismay—dozens of retailers come to town, and each is selling merchandise identical to your store's. On top of that, each competitor builds a magnificent storefront and decorates its interior with exquisite furnishings. To build market share, each of these merchants sells below cost and lavishes customers with gifts and prizes.

The competitive environment just depicted is not make-believe; it's an accurate description of Las Vegas' main drag. On Las Vegas Boulevard, also known as "the Strip," casinos line both sides of the street for a four-mile stretch, each establishment glitzier and more pretentious than the last.

With 17 out of the world's 24 biggest hotels, Vegas' lineup of megaresorts is an amazing sight to behold. Each establishment competes to attract its share of the 36 million–plus visitors that annually make the pilgrimage to the greatest gambling mecca on the face of the planet. Harrah's, now known as Caesars, which opened its doors in Reno in 1937 as a bingo parlor, came to Las Vegas in 1980. That's when the company converted a former 1,600-room Holiday Inn on the Strip into a casino resort. (With several renovations, the property now has 2,677 rooms.) Directly across the street is Caesars Palace, and within a five-minute walking distance are Bellagio, the Venetian, and Wynn, each of which has been built at a cost estimated at about $2 billion.

The Mirage, also across the street from Harrah's Las Vegas, is equipped with a 70-foot-high volcano that erupts every 15 minutes. Inside the hotel, you can walk through a tropical rain forest, get misted by waterfalls, and press your nose against a 20,000-gallon aquarium stocked with sharks, stingrays, and angelfish. There is also an elaborate habitat, housing magnificent white tigers that until recently appeared nightly in the famed Siegfried &Roy magic show. Next door to the Mirage is Treasure Island Hotel, with its a 65-foot-deep lagoon where every 90 minutes nightly the pirate ship *Hispaniola* engages the HMS *Britannia* in combat in the "Battle of Buccaneer Bay." Twenty dueling actors fight it out in a winner-take-all battle—the defeated vessel does a deep six! Going south on the Strip you'll encounter the pyramid-shaped Luxor where you walk through a 10-story sphinx entranceway; once inside, you view a replica of King Tut's tomb complete with Egyptian statues that dwarf even those found in the original ancient ruins. From there you can drop in at the New York–New York Hotel to gaze in wonder at the skyline of the Big Apple. The property features replicas of the Statue of Liberty and a dozen skyscrapers including the Chrysler Building, a 300-foot-long Brooklyn Bridge, and a Coney Island–style roller coaster that encircles the premises.

There are several other ultradeluxe casinos in Vegas, including MGM Grand, Circus-Circus, Excalibur, and Mandalay Bay. By comparison, Harrah's Las Vegas—the oldest of the major casinos on the Strip—is plain vanilla. Yet, it is one of the most successful in the gaming industry. How does Harrah's compete in an industry where the products—slot machines, gaming tables, roulette wheels—are virtually identical? Harrah's realized that it couldn't be a contender using the competition's approach of making large investments in theme casinos to attract customers. The company simply didn't have the money. Instead, its management determined that another kind of sizzle was needed to win customer loyalty. Its thinking was that erupting volcanoes, battling pirate ships, and full-scale canals with gondola rides were major tourist attractions. But it takes more to build long-term customer loyalty. Novelties are not what generate repeat visits.

It was determined that Harrah's would sell another kind of sizzle, but it would differ from the sizzle at other Vegas casinos that have poured large sums of money in bricks and mortar constructing huge edifices. Instead, Harrah's invested hundreds of millions of dollars in information technology so it could accumulate information on its customers—to remember who they are, record their likes and dislikes, and disseminate this data to the appropriate service personnel.

"Now, when you put your rewards card in a slot machine," David Norton, senior vice president and chief marketing officer, Caesars Entertainment, explains, "we are able to know what games you play, how long you play, and so on. Similarly when you give your card to a dealer, he tracks your time and average bet. Outside the gaming area, we also try to capture customer preferences. We track all the offers and incentives we send to you and which ones you respond to. We know which outlets you go to for your comps, and we've recently started tracking nongaming spending as well. With this information, we know which restaurants our customers prefer, how much of its food and liquor they consume, as well as which retail stores they shop and what entertainment they prefer. Since we know past behavior, we can also understand what our customers' potential value is, and we can determine what their future value is likely to be. We know who's likely to be a long-term customer and who's not. We take a look at their observed behavior, and our team of analysts builds models to show their predicted behavior. We look to see if there's a gap between how many times a person comes here and the share of his wallet we receive now, versus what our models say is possible.

"At our VIP level," Norton adds, "we get even more information so we can customize the experience. For instance, do they like golfing? Do they like boxing? We know what brand of chardonnay they prefer so we can stock it in their room upon arrival."

A record 39.2 million people visited Las Vegas in 2007, making it one of the most popular tourist destinations in the world. With dozens of casinos to visit, we wanted to know why they choose one over another. An ARG survey revealed that 67.3% *choose a casino that they believe will make them feel special versus wanting to go to the newest place that's the talk of the town. Of those customers that choose Harrah's, 46.2% said it's the company's reward program that is the key reason for their choice.* Considering that most loyalty programs will get a 20% response due to their rewards card, this is a remarkable figure.

Knowing the Business You're In

Johnson & Johnson's former head of its pharmaceuticals business, Joe Scodari, explains, "If you are an innovator in the pharmaceutical business, you are not in the pill business. You are not in the injections business. That's the physical form of the product that we sell. But that's not what we're about. What we are selling is the knowledge, all the data that was developed to eventually bring our product to the market. So when our reps present our products to physicians, they aren't selling pills. They're selling what those pills will do for patients."

Johnson & Johnson is a world leader in medical devices. How well Chairman Bill Weldon personally knows that these products are far more than medical mechanisms. "I had a knee replaced," he tells, "and before my knee replacement, I could hardly walk. It's changed my life. Take a look at heart patient recipients of a Cypher stent. Many of them would not be alive today if it weren't for the impact of that device. And with endoscopic surgery today, a gall bladder can be removed without the patient having to be cut open. With the optics and the instruments, a small incision is made to remove a gall bladder and the patient is back to work tomorrow. Then there are advancements that have been made in the central nervous system [CNS] area. Early in my career I was exposed to a person who had been confined to a locked ward in a hospital for 10 or so years. Then he was put on one of our CNS medications. The man was then released from the ward and could function as a normal human being. You see these things and you realize that our products represent incredible medical advances that have a phenomenal impact on people's lives."

Weldon likes to remind J&J employees with jobs in offices, laboratories, and manufacturing plants about how their work affects so many people in a positive way. "To let our scientists and other employees know how much they impact other people's lives, we invite patients who have taken J&J medicines to come in to speak to our employees. Rather than strictly quoting numbers and statistics on how patients are doing with our products, we want our people to hear what patients have to say. This is why I say that there is not a person in the world who could find fault with this industry if he or she ever had the opportunity to sit down and talk with patients whose lives have been changed. I believe that when you put a face on people, it enables you to see how they are so appreciative about what we do to help them. For example, we invited a young man in his early twenties to our Centocor plant to talk about how Remicade changed his life. This man's favorite activity was playing the piano, and he told our people about how he'd do it for hours and hours prior to being stricken with rheumatoid arthritis. 'It was so painful,' he said, 'that I couldn't play the piano. I'd play for 20 minutes and then I'd have to lay down because it hurt so much. Today, I'm able to play for six to seven hours a day, and my dream is to become a concert pianist.' After listening to his story, there wasn't a dry eye in the audience."

✳　✳　✳

"Our competitors have all been aircraft manufacturers," NetJets' president Jim Christiansen stresses. "As a consequence, most of them have a difficult time bridging the manufacturing mentality over to a service mentality.

That's why you see them running their fractional ownership programs like a manufacturing process. We are in the service business. We constantly emphasize this point. We happen to deliver our service using airplanes, but this is a service business first. We don't have an assembly line. We don't have all that automated process stuff. We are a service business. It's all part of our culture and how we work in what is a very open structure."

Added Value

Christiansen is proud of the fact that NetJets has high standards for its pilots and boasts about the fact that they receive more training than any airline. "Yes, continual training is important and helps to assure that the company keeps its unblemished safety record intact, and as such we consider it an added value. Although NetJets may excel in this area, an airline service is expected to train its pilots on a regular basis. Hence, we submit that most companies train their pilots well. But where NetJets goes far beyond its customers' expectations is with the training and instruction its pilots receive in the use of special Mayo Clinic–designed emergency medical supplies and kits. These kits, together with descriptive manuals, emergency oxygen, and automatic electronic defibrillators (AEDs), are aboard every NetJets aircraft. In the event of an emergency, NetJets flight crews are able to contact the Mayo Clinic and its emergency physicians and nurses will provide comprehensive information regarding treatment and possible flight diversion recommendations. When necessary, the Mayo Clinic may arrange assistance utilizing local emergency services that, when necessary, will meet the plane upon landing."

Santulli tells about a NetJets Mayo Clinic–trained pilot. "A lineman was filling the plane with gas in Texas and he keeled over. He had a severe heart attack, and our pilot started giving him mouth-to-mouth resuscitation. Another pilot ran and got the defibrillator that was aboard the plane. They hit the guy with paddles and kept him alive until the paramedics got there. They saved the man's life. Every one of our pilots and flight attendants receives Mayo Clinic training, and as a result, we are saving lives."

It's true that you don't fly an airline because its pilots have experience administrating AED, and with most airlines cutting back on expenses, what NetJets does is a service above and beyond what you expect to receive for the price of an airline ticket. It's an added service that provides the vast majority of people with peace of mind. And to anyone who needs it aboard an aircraft, it's a godsend.

* * *

No product can be more tangible than a car. Just the same, the people at Lexus insist that they sell the experience every bit as much as the car itself. "We have a delivery process," Nancy Fein, former vice president of customer satisfaction at Lexus, explains, "and when our customer rates initial quality, they don't just rate the product. They are also rating whether or not they can use the features which are based on how well they understand the car. This is why we encourage our salespeople and delivery specialists to follow certain guidelines during the 'walk around.' The walk around is conducted at the time when the customer comes in to pick up his or her new car. Customers go through a checklist that covers certain key points so they can maximize their use of the car. For example, there are the personalized settings that are customized to coordinate with customers' tastes and needs. Let's say you like having all the doors unlock when the driver's door is unlocked. Well, your car can be customized to have all the doors unlock with the driver's door. Likewise, you can have your lights come on 15 or 30 seconds after you close the door. There are many features that can be tailored to customers' preferences. The dealership has access to the codes, so you can't do them yourself. Most customers have these customized adjustments made at delivery; however, some want to get used to driving their car, so they bring it in 30 days or so later." Fein points out that, "without the walk around, a customer might own a car for years and never use many of its features that were paid for. Again, it's a matter of not just buying a car but understanding what a newly purchased car can do."

"A customer can learn how to set up other features by reading the directions in the owner's manual," Lexus dealer Rick Germain adds. "But some, such as the navigation system and the satellite radio, are so complicated that I recommend having a salesperson or a delivery specialist demonstrate how to use them during the walk around. Again, this is part of the service we provide to give our customers the most for their money. Anyone can sell a car, but that's just the beginning."

* * *

Ashley's chairman, Ron Wanek, refers to a product's added value as "the magic." The 6,000 furniture retailers that are called on by the company's independent marketing specialists ("furniture reps" as they are known in the industry) and those at the furniture marts such as High Point and Las Vegas marts are the source of the magic that Wanek refers to. "When our reps make a sales call or talk to a customer in one of our showrooms at the mart," Wanek explains, "we are one of many sources of manufacturers so the buyer has a large selection of choices. In addition to providing good values and timely delivery that reduce the retailer's warehousing costs, we have another significant competitive advantage, and this is one that my son, Todd, gets full credit for. Todd's a genius when it comes to anticipating what furniture will sell for in the coming season. This is vital to our success, because in addition to manufacturing furniture, about 40% comes from the Far East where we have products made for us according to our designs and specifications. It generally takes three to five months for these goods to be manufactured and delivered to the States. This means we must make the furniture before we sell it. The furniture business is very stylish, so like the fashion houses in the men's and ladies' clothing industry, we must anticipate what will sell. Our customers know we excel in this area, and they rely on our expertise to pick the right merchandise that their customers will want. There's a magic in our knowing what will be hot before it hits the market, because it's a costly mistake to make large quantities of furniture and find out that the consumer doesn't like it. So far, we've always been right on target. Like I said, Todd excels in this area."

✳   ✳   ✳

Let's compare buying skin care products at a supermarket or department store to the Mary Kay experience. For the purpose of this discussion, we won't debate which products are a better value, but we do think there is an added value in having a Mary Kay Independent Beauty Consultant conduct a skin care class to demonstrate not only the different features of products but also how to apply them. We think this is superior to walking up and down the aisles of a retail store searching and finally selecting a product that you think will best serve your needs. The information in small print on the back of the box isn't sufficient to tell you what you need to know. And when you start comparing a large selection of cosmetics manufactured by different companies, it's bound to cause some confusion. "All women are different," Rhonda Shasteen, senior vice president, explains, "ranging from their skin type to their daily habits. For instance, are they in or out of the sun a lot? Do they have a more active lifestyle? No two women are alike, so it's not as if you can pick something up at the counter and buy a one-size-fits-all. Beauty Consultants are able to tailor each product or regimen to her individual customer's needs. We believe that for a customer to receive maximum value from the use of the product, personal service is essential. In fact, we have a name for it. We call it Golden Rule Customer Service."

Intangible Differences

When it comes to selling an insurance product, Chubb's former vice chairman and chief operating officer, Tom Motamed, says, "An insurance policy is not just the product. Ours is a product that is wrapped with service. That's part of what Chubb sells. People don't call an agent and say, 'I want Chubb.' Our agents and brokers have to sell Chubb to their clients. Also note that insurance is something most people don't want to buy. They understand they need it, but they look at insurance as a commodity. However, in order for Chubb to have survived for 125 years, we had to come out with a compelling story, and it couldn't be a product that could be viewed as a commodity. Service is a big piece of the product. While we don't sell life insurance, it's perhaps the worst intangible because nobody wants to believe they are going to die. Then, all they get is this piece of paper. And they don't get any service with that. Nobody calls them. At best, they might get a birthday card or a Christmas card. With casualty insurance, there is a much larger chance of a loss. People know that there are fires, director and officers (D&O) claims, and car accidents. They understand that they need it. But what they don't understand is that not all policies are the same nor are all companies alike."

"When you buy a car," Chubb's chief operating officer Paul Krump explains, "you can see, touch, and literally smell it. With the exception of taste, all of your senses are involved. You can see how the automatic windows and door locks work. You can see, feel, and smell the beautiful leather. You can read the specs on the engine no matter if the salesperson does or doesn't open the hood. With an insurance policy, you just get a piece of paper, and it's the odd person who reads it in its entirety. Instead the client is relying on the agent for direction."

When you first do business with Chubb, you immediately notice a difference in service by the way the company does its homework to make sure it understands exactly what it's underwriting. With other companies, you can get your house, your car, or your business insured simply by calling an agent, talking to him or her on the telephone, answering some questions, and bingo, you're covered. Yes, Chubb insures more expensive homes than the norm, so the stakes are higher with these properties. So there is a good reason why the company exerts a lot of effort up front. And as a result, when the time comes to file a claim, there are fewer questions asked and quicker claim settlements. Typically a Chubb appraiser will come to your home and ask to be walked through it so he or she can determine its replacement cost, which is based on the price to rebuild it today with similar quality materials and craftsmanship. This approach is vital in the event of a calamity and pursuing claim settlement. Isn't it better to be asked a lot of questions at the time of application rather than to be cross-examined by a claims adjuster and having to haggle to get a satisfactory settlement? Chubb appraisers are the best in the insurance industry. The company has an array of specialists with expertise in such fields ranging from architectural design and fine art to historic preservation and interior design. Chubb appraisers can also offer advice on fire and burglary protection and make recommendations on alarm technology.

When it comes to appraising historic homes, Chubb has no peers. So for good reason the National Trust for Historic Preservation has a program that promotes Chubb as an insurer. Many historic properties are located in the Mid-Atlantic States, New England, and Virginia where insurance premiums can be 50% higher due to the higher construction costs, as well as for true replacement for parts from the historic era, including moldings, antique hardware, and antique glass.

Chubb's affluent clientele can also receive an unusual service that's provided by its collections specialists. "These specialists don't actually go out to appraise expensive art," Frances O'Brien, senior vice president, explains, "but they do make recommendations to clients about when and where to go to have art collections appraised by reputable people. As an added service, they help clients catalog their collections, and they will make recommendations on how to display it as well as how to protect it. And if anything in your collection needs restoration work, they can direct a client to a restoration company. For clients who want to loan pieces of their art collections to a museum, Chubb has experts to advise them on packing and shipping sculptures and paintings." Again, these are atypical services that are not offered by other casualty companies. They are reasons why Chubb dominates the market catering to the affluent.

Still More Intangible Benefits

Michael Callahan, Cabela's former senior vice president of business development and international operations, thinks that an advantage of buying quality outdoor equipment at Cabela's is that "in today's busy world, most people have time constraints, so an avid outdoors person doesn't want to worry about faulty equipment when on a hunting or fishing trip. You don't want to be sitting there in a duck blind when it's five below and you're freezing because the quality of your down jacket is inferior. The same is true about allotting five days of the year for fly fishing and having your waders leak. When you're hundreds or even thousands of miles away from home, you spent a lot of time and money getting there. You want to make sure that everything works like it's supposed to."

✳   ✳   ✳

Jim McEachern, Tom James' former president, remembers what a customer once said to him many years ago about an added benefit he received when he wore a Tom James suit: "This young fellow sold office machines for Burroughs, and a few years after I met him he became the company's number one salesperson in the U.S. One day I asked him, 'What do you attribute your success to?' 'After I started wearing your clothes,' he told me, 'I felt like I was equal to anyone I would call on, and it give me a lot of confidence.'"

Clothing consultant Naresh Khanna says he often hears his clients make similar remarks. "'I could be addressing other members at a board meeting,' they say, 'or making an important presentation to a major customer, and I feel so comfortable in my clothes that I feel nothing can go wrong.' It reminds me about how kids take a bath and getting dressed up for Sunday school or a wedding and their behavior changes. Their manners improve and they politely listen to what they're told. There's something about feeling and looking good that makes us act differently."

Another top Tom James salesperson, Christian Boehm, believes that quality clothing improves how people think about themselves. He advises his clients about what suits to wear for certain occasions. "'This is the suit I think you should wear to your board meeting,' I'll say, 'and be sure to wear this shirt and tie with it. It gives you your power look.' With another client, I'll say, 'When you meet with your banker, you want to wear gray. I recommend this color with this stripe.'

"I had a client call me several weeks after he had placed a big order with me," Boehm continues. "'Christian, I've been invited to attend an event in the Caribbean. Here, let me read the invitation to you. There are going to be some extremely rich people there, and I need to look like I belong in the room. What should I wear?' He was telling me that he didn't want to feel intimidated by the attendees. I had to do a dinner outfit for him. He later called to thank me. 'I felt right at home with everyone,' he said. 'I blended right in.' You see, it's not the tangible clothes that our clients buy, it's how they feel in those clothes.

"We sell how they look and feel in their clothes," Boehm adds. "What gives me a high in my work is when a client tells me about the compliments he received for the way he looked in his Tom Jones clothes. It's those unsolicited compliments that keep them coming back."

9

When Price Rules

If your customers' number one reason for doing business with you is based on your having the lowest prices in town, don't expect their loyalty when someone else comes along with an even lower price. This is especially true if you're in an industry where people are unable to differentiate between your product and someone else's. You know your company is in a lot of trouble when a customer walks into your store to inquire about a certain product, and your employee says, "Yep, we got 'em too."

Most of the big supermarkets in the United States are failing to differentiate their stores and products from their competitors'. As a consequence, consumers are going to the stores that offer the best prices. An ARG survey uncovers that *67.3% of Americans look at the weekly supermarket ads and shop at the store with the lowest prices.* These shoppers' decisions are based in part on their ability to compare the prices of branded goods. Two out of three people think that there is so little difference between supermarkets that price is the determining factor where they shop each week. The same study discloses that *56% of all shoppers say that they only have a little or no loyalty to their local supermarket.*

No company should ever put itself in a position where it must win two out of every three of its customers each week who are going to the cheapest seller. A handful of specialty grocery stores have avoided being put in this position by being different. Most notably are Whole Foods and Wild Oats, each of which sells organic food that is perceived as being healthier; as such, shoppers will pay a premium for it. Trader Joe's is another specialty grocery chain that has separated itself from the herd with specialty foods, quick checkout lines, and well-trained employees.

Many people buy airline tickets today according to which carrier offers the cheapest price. They visit Web sites that list cheap fares and select the cheapest one. This is because air travel has become a commodity. The service doesn't vary no matter which commercial airlines you pick. They have all cut back on service to reduce costs. When you call to make a reservation or inquire about a flight, you must first answer a series of questions via voice-activated computers, then you're put on hold. Eventually you'll get to talk to a ticket agent. We've all gone through the routine enough times that it makes us wish we could afford to fly on a private jet.

An ARG study reveals that *60.4% of Americans prefer to receive frequent flyer points in lieu of a cash discount when they purchase a ticket.* When questioned about why they prefer the frequent flyer points, they replied that receiving a cash discount would reduce their airfare by such a small amount, it would virtually be meaningless. A follow-up question was asked and the answer surprised us. *Only 46% of Americans think that the benefits of an awards program for frequent flyer miles are worth the effort to sign up.* How much influence do frequent flyer programs have on today's traveler? An ARG study shows that *only 27% try to fly the airline that they have a frequent flyer card with.*

✳   ✳   ✳

Wal-Mart is the world's largest company. Its immense growth is a result of building superior distribution and warehousing systems, plus buying large quantities of goods at low prices that, in turn, are sold at low prices. For years, Wal-Mart stayed out of the big cities and concentrated on opening stores in small towns across the United States. These markets were easy pickings. Theretofore, the local merchants had no competition and had become complacent. Being the only game in town, they were able to charge high prices for their goods, and their customers continued to patronize them. Without competition, their stores had not been remodeled for years and looked worn. They hired clerks at minimum wages and gave them minimum training. Their merchandise was poorly displayed. And their selection of merchandise was inadequate. With Wal-Mart in town, the local merchants were no match for "the outsider." It was only a matter of time before these small-time operators started to close their doors. Some people say, "Look what Wal-Mart did to Small Town, U.S.A. They killed off the small merchant." We believe some of the fault lies with the small merchants who failed to offer adequate service and so their customers jumped ship and headed to Wal-Mart.

Over time, Wal-Mart expanded into big cities where it encountered higher overhead for rent, salaries, and taxes, but with certain efficiencies and huge buying power, the company remained strong in this more competitive environment. Consumers shopped Wal-Mart because it offered the best prices in town. And as other stores followed suit and lowered their prices, Wal-Mart became even more efficient and fought fiercely to protect its position as the lowest-priced operator in town. And as long as the Wal-Mart stays this way, its customers will shop their stores. However, Wal-Mart's focus on lowering prices has been followed by a decline in its gross margin, which, at the time of this writing, is 23.65% of sales. In our opinion, Wal-Mart cannot keep dropping its prices because there comes a point when its vendors will tell the company, "We can't sell it to you for less than what we can make it for."

To expand its market, Wal-Mart has tried to lure more affluent shoppers by stocking trendy apparel and home décor merchandise. However, the well-heeled consumer is more particular and demands more service than the less affluent. Nor is this upscale customer willing to endure a Wal-Mart store that is constantly packed with customers and has long checkout lines. While less affluent shoppers might be willing to put up with these inconveniences to save some money, this is not the case with those who could afford to pay more for service.

Wal-Mart continues to have strong sales in groceries and pharmacy items, which are, for the most part, commodities. However, supermarkets are now finding ways to compete with Wal-Mart's lower prices. They are wooing customers with fresh seafood and meat departments that have butchers who cut fish and meat to the customers' specifications. Many supermarkets have upgraded their delis and bakery areas; some have added a Starbucks. Others offer larger selections of organic foods and locally grown fresh fruits and vegetables. We are also seeing supermarkets sell ready-to-go sandwiches so their customers can eat lunch on the run. And more specialty grocery stores and supermarkets are selling deliciously prepared home-style cooking and other gourmet meals for those people with hectic work schedules who want to stay out of the kitchen. While these meals are more expensive than unprepared foods, they cost considerably less than dining at a restaurant. Ideal for the two-income family, these products are great time-savers. Safeway, for example, is currently converting its store into "lifestyle" markets with wood floors, on-site bakeries, and high-end private-label brands. So instead of going head-on in a futile attempt to match Wal-Mart's low prices, these super-markets are winning customer loyalty the good old-fashioned way—by giving them added value.

In every business, there is always an opportunity for a newcomer to beat out a long-established company by offering something other than just the lowest bid. For instance, we recently heard about a large, well-known roofing company that offered a great deal to replace a new roof on a small office building. A young man driving a pickup truck approached the property owner and made a slightly higher bid for the job. He had excellent references and a passion for his work. He promised to be there with a crew every day until the job was finished. The young roofer empha-sized how important it was for his company to do a superior job because he was interested in building a good reputation. The property owner liked his conviction and gave the job to him. As it turned out, it was the right choice. The young roofer did excellent work and the customer got his money's worth.

Don't Commoditize Your Product

"Many people have the perception that airline travel is a commodity," Richard Santulli, NetJets' CEO, states. "The only reason they still like a particular commercial airline is for the frequent flyer miles. In my busi-ness, I tell people we're not selling a commodity. I explain to them that I charge more money because I spend more money on my airplanes. I pay more money to my pilots. I send them to safety school two times every year. I have meteorologists. I have licensed dispatchers. I provide all of these, and my competition doesn't, and I have to charge for it. 'It's not like buying home heating oil,' I tell them. 'It doesn't matter what home heat-ing oil you buy. If it's $3.40 or $3.10, you and I will take the $3.10.' The same applies to natural gas. If someone says, 'I can sell you natural gas at $.40 a cubic foot less,' you're going to take it. Airline travel has become a commodity, and that's what I have to compete with."

✳ ✳ ✳

Ron Wanek, Ashley Furniture's chairman, says that if consumers are unable to determine any differences between two comparable products, furniture becomes a commodity and they'll choose the one with the cheapest price tag. "When people can compare apples with apples," he insists, "Ashley comes out on top every time because consumers buy furniture based on its design, quality, *and* price. Price will be the tiebreaker only when they can't see any other reasons to buy. But when they can compare not only price tags but design and quality, their buying decision is based on the combination of these three considerations. Sure, they may buy something because it's the lowest price, but when they take it home and they're unhappy with the way it looks, believe me, they have no problem about returning it today and asking for their money back. And a retailer with customers that keep coming back for refunds won't be in business very long."

*　　*　　*

Chubb is a leading underwriter of worker's compensation in the United States. While many companies "shop" the lowest rates when choosing an insurer for their coverage, Paul Krump, a company senior vice president, says that this is not the way his company does business. "It's reminiscent of the waiter who comes to your table and immediately rattles off 30 different meals on the regular menu and tells you about all the specials. He's going to annoy most sophisticated people. Well, some insurance agents sell worker's comp the same way. That's not our style at Chubb.

"Prior to visiting a client, we do our homework by reviewing a prospective company's previous experience, analyzing loss control surveys, and even going over available data on the Internet. Then we'll sit down with the client and ask some questions to learn more about the company. After jotting down notes, we'll discover that their needs are radically different than what we had anticipated when we walked in. For example, we may learn that their big concern is employee retention so this shifts our focus to this area. Our conversation may lead to how they can invest in workplace safety and result in skewing their comp program. Later we may discuss return-to-work programs. Here we might point out how working with nurse practitioners can bring people back to work more quickly, or how the longer people stay out, the more likely they are to get hooked on daytime television that, in turn, increases the length of time they'll stay home. Our job is to address what our clients perceive are the issues of the day.

"This is a far cry from walking in and commoditizing your product by just talking about the rates, which is how most agents sell worker's comp. I liken our work to the doctor who sits down with a patient and, rather than asking a lot of questions, starts off by saying, 'What's going on in your life?' and then keeps quiet and listens. You can find out a lot about people when you keep quiet and hear what they have to say."

Krump believes that when worker's compensation is sold correctly, it's not about determining a premium rate based on a client's past claim experience and using actuarial charts to determine the underwriting risk and a corresponding premium. There are other factors to consider in addition to the price, and according to him, there are times when an underwriter may charge a higher premium that is, in fact, the better value. As he points out, Chubb may provide solutions on reducing workers' injuries and the recovery time for claimants unable to work. In such cases, the monetary gain to the client can exceed the higher premium. Chubb's service may also result in higher productivity. It is also possible that in the long run, a company's claim experience decreases and results in lower premiums. "As you can see," Krump concludes, "price is a factor, but a client must also consider such things as coverage, claim certainty, and loss mitigation. But if it's only about price, price, price, we may not be the right people."

Mark Korsgaard, who heads worldwide casualty claims at Chubb, acknowledges that some people buy insurance based strictly on the lowest rates. "It's only when they submit a claim," he says, "that they notice the differences. For instance, we don't have a claims center in India. They will talk to a qualified claims person here in the U.S. And our claims people aren't so overburdened with work that they're unavailable when you need them. It's like that across the board. The price that our clients pay is reflected in the service they receive, because we have staffed and trained people. Our brokers tell clients, 'Chubb may be a little more expensive up front, but this is why you want them,' and then they explain how we differentiate with better service. The product itself is also superior. For instance, when an automobile claim is submitted, and there's a rental involved, the client will get a car that's similar to his rather than a less expensive model. It's the little nuances like this that separate us from our competition."

Selling Peace of Mind

It's hard to put a price tag on buying piece of mind. But it's part of what you buy when you take out an insurance policy. For instance, Paul Krump insists that peace of mind is what companies get when they have Chubb coverage in a foreign country. "You feel comfortable with us because when your broker tells you that your Chubb coverage complies with local laws, you don't have to worry about it," Krump states. "Chubb will give you a wrapper policy that states difference conditions and limits that appear on a cover sheet. You can also read it in English and know that the coverage you have in Thailand is the same as you have in Topeka. And you know that when Thai regulators pay you a visit, you can show them proof of insurance. These are big advantages that few insurance companies provide."

Krump cites an example of a client that was an American company with a plant in Asia. "The client was concerned about the company's assets being expropriated. Our broker called me with the client on the phone and asked, 'Does Chubb do some political risk?' 'We do,' I assured him and explained some details about our coverage we call CEND, which helps protect your assets from confiscation, expropriation, nationalization, and depravation. 'Would you mind if I set up a conference call with my banker?' the client asked. 'He's concerned about our exposure to certain risks at our operations in Asia.' I replied, 'Do you mind if I go down the hall to get one of my specialists for political risks? I'll invite him to join us on the call. Give me 15 minutes, and we'll do a conference call with your banker.' It was only a few minutes later before we were assembled for the call.

"Later that day, the broker called to thank me. 'You were amazing,' he said. 'My client had been talking to other brokers who told him that they'd have to go to Chicago or New York to figure out a solution for his company's CEND problem. And I was able to call the client and tell him that I've got our chief operating officer at Chubb on the phone. I told him that you spent 15 years doing political risk insurance and that if anyone knew how to put this thing together it would be you and our Chubb team. Later in the day, we received a fax with the term sheet. All I can say, Paul, is thank you so much for making me look so good in front of my client.'"

✳   ✳   ✳

When you have the reputation for being a company that jumps through hoops to serve your customers, they'll be willing to pay a little extra knowing that they'll receive exceptional service. "In a recent focus group," Barbara Talbott, Four Seasons' executive vice president of marketing, says, "people told us that when they make a reservation at a Four Seasons resort, they know they won't have to worry about it being a great vacation because that's a given at Four Seasons. It's the confidence and trust they have in us that breeds loyalty.

"On the subject of loyalty, Four Seasons doesn't have a loyalty program," Talbott adds, "which is uncommon in our industry. You know, when people use the word *loyalty* in relation to things that are intrinsic to the product or service, I have to inquire about what they think their customers are being loyal to. Is it the perks? Is it the product? Is it the brand? Is it the loyalty program? We've always focused on intrinsic trust and loyalty, which is something you can't pick up and put down in another place. Everyone and anyone can have a points program. Anyone can play the game of offering more perks. And anyone can compete for price discounting. We don't see that any of those things are ways to engender loyalty that we can protect and enhance over time."

"You cannot create sustainable uniqueness through a loyalty program," Susan Helstab, senior vice president of corporate marketing, adds. "You can only create sustainable uniqueness by what you offer and how you do it."

Unlike other hotel chains, there is not a VIP program at Four Seasons that awards customers that are frequent guests. "Every guest at Four Seasons is a VIP," founder Isadore Sharp insists. "Some of the airline companies wanted to partner with us in a frequent flyer program. 'It's a sweetheart deal,' they said. 'We'll do it at a price so you can only make money on it. Look at these studies we've done,'" Sharp tells. "I replied, 'Of course, when you asked the question about how good it would be for Four Seasons to have a frequent flyer program, you got an affirmative answer.' And why wouldn't they? It's a giveaway. But what about when the right question is asked, which is, 'Would they continue using Four Seasons if we didn't have a frequent flyer program?' That wasn't why our customers were coming, so it wasn't a matter of getting a better deal. We didn't want to get locked into giving things away. Instead we prefer to embellish the service to our customers."

Price Integrity

Tourism around the world plummeted on September 11, 2001, when terrorists obliterated the World Trade Center twin towers. "The one thing we knew for certain was that the terrorist attack had changed the world forever," Sharp tells. "That morning, I met with our senior people. I started the meeting by reminding them about the difficult times we went through two decades earlier when interest rates were north of 20% and the company was in dire financial straits.

"I told them, 'Today, the company is financially strong. This is not like 1981 when we were a small company and I was $300 million in debt.

We have hotels around the world, and we are debt free. Yes, what happened at World Trade Center was horrific, but we will get through this no matter how long it takes. And this will have a devastating effect on our industry, but just like we did in '81, we will survive.' Meanwhile, we had investors who were owners in other hotels that were reducing their work-force by 50%. I understood that other hotel operators could only keep market share by keeping their prices competitive with everybody else. I told our management team, 'Nobody is coming to Four Seasons for price. And for us to drop our prices by 10%, 20%, or 30% is something we can't afford to do. If we do, all we will be doing is giving money away that we don't have to. We will be aggressive in getting business but we will not discount. Let's be creative in how we sell our product.'

"Our owners are very sophisticated and they were no longer people who own hotels because they like them," Sharp continues. "They are pro-fessional owners. Some of them said to me, 'Look, this is my money.' I answered by saying, 'Yes, I know it's your money and I am responsible for it. I am telling you we can do this better if we do it this way.' I made it clear to them that we should not be compared to other hotel companies that were like the airline industry. I emphasized that our customers come to us because of what we give them, and they will continue to do that. Then I traveled to as many as 35 to 40 hotels in a year's time because I wanted our people to hear my message directly from me. I told them what I thought was going to happen and assured them that we'd get through it. I didn't have the answer as to how long it would take because nobody knew. 'We will have to live with terrorism,' I kept repeating, 'and what-ever time it takes, so be it. This will not kill our industry. People will continue to travel. Sure we're scared and people are cutting back on their travel. But we'll get through it.' I think it was reassuring to hear my message directly from me, because nobody was risking more than I. All my wealth was tied up in the company. I was speaking what I believed. So I could say to them, 'Hey, look, I am with you on this.'

"It was my role from the pulpit that I speak from to let people hear directly how I think. 'As dark as the cloud is, and I know you're reading gloom and doom every day in the newspapers,' I said, 'trust me, there is a sun above that cloud. We will have an opportunity.' And we did. In 2000, the company had its best year ever. In comparison, and even after the effects of 9/11, by the end of 2003, we had the highest RevPAR [revenue per available room] and occupancy rates in the industry and in our com-pany's history. Our worldwide rate was slightly higher than the peak we had achieved in 2000, whereas every other hotel company was 20% to 40%

lower. Plus, our market share increased. People preferred Four Seasons even at an extra price because more than ever we gave what was most valuable to them. They felt safe here. The whole attitude of how people think of lifestyle came into focus. Yes, life was not like it was before. Attitudes change when people see that they are no longer in control all the time. But when they stayed at Four Seasons, it was a sanctuary."

✳   ✳   ✳

Jim Christiansen, NetJets' president, tells a story about a major corporation that hired a consultant and was shopping to buy fractional ownership: "They were taking bids and asked us to submit a Request for Proposal (RFP). We turned in our proposal and they wanted to negotiate a better price. I told them that we have a most favored nations clause in our contract, which means all of our customers receive the same terms. 'That's fine,' they told us, 'but all of your competitors give stuff away. They negotiate the price of the airplane, the management fee, and they will give us free hours.' My reply was, 'While they compete on price, we compete on quality.' We went through this whole process, and their purchasing department woman called, 'Congratulations, you win. What do we do now?' I told her to have the binder signed and send it back with a deposit, and she consented. Then she asked, 'We want three airplanes, so what kind of discount do we get?' I referred her to the contract and read the most favored nations clause, and again reminded her that we don't negotiate price. 'Everybody gets treated the same,' I said. 'Everyone gets treated fairly. You will never be embarrassed when your CEO or one of your colleagues talks to another NetJets owner and is told that he didn't get a free 15% of flight time, because we don't do it. If we do it for one, we do it for everybody.' She said, 'Okay, sounds good,' and I sent over the three binders.

"Then the three binders were returned to us. On each one, the price was scratched out with an amendment on the page margin stating that because it was a big purchase, there would be a 20% discount on the airplane, plus a 15% discount on the occupied hourly fee and the management fee for a five-year period.

"I called her and again explained that we don't discount," Christiansen continues, "and with that, the company canceled the order. 'That's it! We're opening the bidding process again,' we were told, and they did. They issued a new RFP, and started the whole thing all over. This time, we got them to visit our operations in Columbus. And like the last time, we won the bidding. Even though we were more expensive and wouldn't give them any of the freebies they wanted, we got their business. It's been over a year now, and I got to know their people. Recently one of them said to me, 'Jim, we are so glad you were persistent. We now know we made the right choice. Your people are phenomenal. The service you give us is unbelievable.' What made believers out of them was having them visit our facilities and see our infrastructure that we put in place to support them. The added value isn't always obvious when you're out there, the airplane shows up, and you don't understand the complexities of this business behind the scenes. Like I heard one of our sales reps tell a customer, 'If you needed a brain surgeon, you wouldn't shop around for the cheapest one you could find.'"

✳   ✳   ✳

Dave Liniger built RE/MAX on the premise that successful real estate agents can earn more money by paying for their own expenses at RE/MAX rather than working with a local broker who receives 50% of the commissions earned on each transaction. With RE/MAX, a good producer has considerably higher earnings because the amount of expenses she or he incurs is far less than what a local broker would otherwise take off the top. While this concept makes such good sense today, 30 years ago it was difficult to convince people to join forces with his start-up company. Over time, Liniger's concept proved to be correct, and it changed the industry. As he puts it, "There was a lot of price fixing back then, and the consumer had little choice but to pay the going rate. The biggest broker in town said, 'We receive x percent commission,' and the second biggest agent said, 'I charge the same thing.' Then the agent was paid 50% of the gross of what the broker received. Today, it's all negotiable. So what we did is we liberated the agent. The homeowner and an RE/MAX agent can do whatever they want. It's up to the agent because it's his business. For instance, if the seller asks, 'How many times will you advertise my property a week?' the agent doesn't have to ask his broker for an answer because it's his decision to make. Depending on the property, he might say, 'I'll do it three times a week,' or, 'I'll do it five times a week.' His name is in big print on the RE/MAX sign, and when a call comes in, it doesn't go through the broker but directly to him. With all the support in advertising and training we give brokers, we like to say, 'RE/MAX agents are in business for themselves, but not by themselves.'

"It's somewhat demeaning when agents can't make these decisions but are required to ask the broker for permission," Liniger continues. "In many cases, top producers know the business better than their boss because the broker hasn't been out in the field for the past 20 years. Our surveys show this independence has resulted in a higher percent of customer satisfaction and agent satisfaction."

The RE/MAX concept works because the company signs up only experienced top producers. Run-of-the-mill agents might not make enough money to cover their expenses, and the 50% of their commission that goes to their broker could work out to be less money.

Liniger doesn't want novice agents because, without experience, they often do a disservice to the seller. "A beginner looks at a home and has no concept of its value," Liniger explains. "He says, 'This home is beautiful. I'll get you $750,000.' He's enthusiastic and the seller says, 'Wow. Let's do it.' A professional comes in and says, 'For your information, this house is worth $600,000.' If that's all the two agents do, the seller might go with the novice. Then what happens is the house sits on the market for months and the seller takes a bath. However, a professional agent backs up what she says. She makes a competitive analysis by comparing the property with others in the area. She might show data on 42 properties, and with this information says, 'Of these properties, two are selling each month, so without adding any more to this inventory, there is a two-year supply. Now, if you price your home at $700,000 or $800,000, the vast majority of buyers will never even look at it.' By putting in hours of preparation to accumulate good information, she is providing a professional service that is far more valuable than the sheer enthusiasm of a naïve salesperson that could in fact really hurt somebody. The seller is paying for the years of experience that the individual has, so those mistakes are avoided."

More Bang for the Customer's Buck

Anderson Companies is one of the largest privately owned companies in the United States. Based in Florence, Alabama, the Anderson Companies employ more than 15,000 people. Included in this $4 billion family-owned empire are Anderson News Company, the largest magazine and book company in the United States; Anderson Merchandisers, the largest distributor of prerecorded music in the United States; Books-A-Million, the nation's third largest bookstore chain; Whitman Publishing; Anderson Press; Dalmatian Press; and TNT Fireworks. TNT Fireworks is the largest distributor of consumer fireworks in the United States. In addition to having 30 company-owned fireworks stores, TNT has products that are sold to 16,000 stores; also, 5,500 nonprofit groups and individuals across the country use TNT products as their primary source for fund-raising around the Fourth of July. The New Year's holiday is a secondary season for the sale of TNT fireworks, and during this period, nonprofit groups and fund-raisers also assemble temporary roadside tents, although fewer in number and mainly in warmer climates.

TNT Fireworks supplies retail outlets that run the gamut from the one-operator tent to the entire Wal-Mart chain (TNT is the exclusive fireworks supplier for Wal-Mart). The company has a full-time sales force that sells fireworks to fund-raising groups such as churches, band boosters, and soccer teams. TNT is headed by Terry Anderson, one of four Anderson sons who run the various Anderson operations.

TNT's extensive line of fireworks includes firecrackers, fountains, rockets, reloadables, roman candles, sparklers, and spinners. Consumers can make small purchases or buy a package with an assortment of fireworks. For years, TNT's most expensive package of assorted fireworks sold for $100. "If the pieces in the package were purchased separately, the total price would have been $200," Terry Anderson explains, "so the customer had an incentive to spend $100 for the opportunity to receive twice as much for his money. We then increased it to $150, and this package sold so well that we decided to test the waters with a $200 package with $400 of individually sold fireworks."

In 2002, TNT hired ARG to conduct research, and in a national survey that did extensive interviews with TNT customers and other fireworks consumers it was determined that there was high demand for a larger, more expensive package than its $200 package. An analysis of the study results recommended that TNT sell a $400 package that would contain $800 worth of fireworks. The new "Big Bang" package doubled the size of the company's "big" package. "Many of our managers balked when we made the announcement that we were introducing the Big Bang," Anderson tells, "but Britt [CEO of ARG] insisted, 'This is what your customers are telling us, so based on this information, this is what you should do.' Big Bang made its debut in 2002 in time for Fourth of July, and it was the biggest introductory product in our company's history. It was an instant success. Our sales volume skyrocketed, and so did our profit margins. It was so successful that in 2006 we came out with a $500 package, and it too has been a big hit."

Anderson points out that Big Bang packages are big hits for groups such as block parties and family reunions, although many individuals also purchase it. "Like any business," he explains, "you have to be careful in how you price your product, because if it's overpriced, your customer base will resist it and shop elsewhere. It's amazing what reliable research did for our company, and ever since ARG has been doing research for other Anderson Companies units. One study revealed how consumers recognize the TNT brand, and with this research we were able to tell retailers that we're the best-known fireworks brand in the U.S. (and U.K). As a result, many retailers exclusively sell TNT fireworks."

In a related ARG study, *49.3% of Americans belong to Sam's Club, Costco, and BJ's. Of these customers, 88.8% often buy merchandise in bulk to save money.* The research also revealed that *67.6% of the customers that buy in bulk do it with the understanding they might not always use all the product.* Still, they are willing to buy in bulk because they are convinced it's less expensive than buying small quantities.

The Price of a Pill

An ARG study shows that *86.8% of Americans think pharmaceutical companies overcharge for prescription medicines.* They are livid about the high cost of health care. As a consequence, pharmaceutical companies have been relentlessly hammered by the media. Why not? With billions of dollars in annual profits, the big pharmaceutical—Big Pharma—have deep pockets. Why shouldn't the government step in and require these companies to reduce prices? The bad press has vilified giant pharmaceuticals, so much so that recent polls that rate the popularity of companies place the Big Pharma almost at rock bottom. Only the oil companies fare worse. Even the tobacco industry gets better marks. In the minds of most Americans, it doesn't matter that the pharmaceutical products save lives and reduce pain and suffering while tobacco products kill and debilitate people. Americans fume when they hear stories about senior citizens being forced to drive to Canada to get their prescriptions filled. This resentment is so high that many people want the government to step in and force the pharmaceuticals to reduce their drug prices.

Interestingly, one pharmaceutical company stands head and shoulders above the others. An ARG study reveals that *only 18.3% of Americans think Johnson & Johnson overcharges.* As we will explain in Chapter 12 on branding, J&J is the world's most admired pharmaceutical company.

One article made an issue about how the cost of raw materials for certain medicines was only pennies, yet prescription prices ranged from several dollars to hundreds of dollars. Of course, the cost of raw materials has little to do with the cost of a finished product. The article's assessment was tantamount to comparing the cost of the raw materials that go into creating a masterpiece oil painting to its multi-million-dollar price tag. The cost of its raw materials—the canvas and oil—is less than a dollar!

While the price of raw materials may indeed be pennies, the article failed to mention the enormous costs of research and development, the hundreds of millions of dollars spent for clinical trials, and the huge up-front investment made to manufacture a new medicine. Nor did it mention the high risk in making a drug: only one in hundreds of molecule candidates discovered in a laboratory ever makes it to the marketplace. Nor was it noted that the FDA requires a company to have its manufacturing facility built and operating prior to the approval of a new medicine—for good reason. Consider the consequences of switching to a life-saving drug only to later be told by your pharmacist, "We are sorry, but we can't fill your prescription today. Come back in a week or two and maybe it will be available then." Your reply might be, "Without it, I could very well be dead in two weeks."

Consider too the value of a life-saving medicine or one that reduces horrific pain and suffering. If your pain is constant and severe enough, what you shell out for the medicine might be priceless. Ponder the cost of insulin for a diabetic and the alternative if not treated. Or think about the cost of a medicine that inhibits HIV as compared to forgoing treatment.

Those people who complain about the high cost of medicines should consider how modern drugs significantly reduce the period of time patients are confined to hospitals. Today's medicines get the patient out of the hospital sooner and into the comfort of his or her own home. Hence, the number of days of hospital confinement is substantially reduced. For example, breakthrough medicines for treatment of mental disorders such as schizophrenia and bipolar mania have given a new lease on life to patients that were formerly confined to institutions. With medication, many of these individuals are now able to live productive lives.

Once a 20-year patent expires, a generic drug company can make a drug for pennies on the dollar. The generic firm can do this because it doesn't have to spend an estimated $1 billion to make a new drug, so its investment in comparison to the company that develops the drug is minuscule. And because pharmaceutical companies want to protect their patents, one is often filed years before FDA approval, so there may be only five or ten years remaining before the drug goes off patent. This reduces the remaining time to recoup its investment. Furthermore, there is a lot of competition out there from other pharmaceutical companies, so even with approval, many drugs fail in the marketplace.

If the media continue lambasting Big Pharma, it's possible that politicians will react to public opinion and regulatory bodies will change laws that take away the incentive for these companies to make new medicines. If that were to happen, who would then make them domestically? The only alternatives would be the government or our nation's universities. Does anyone seriously think those are viable options? The lesson that we can learn from the plight of the pharmaceutical companies is that they collectively have done a poor job in communicating why the prices of their products are so high.

The pharmaceutical industry is so highly regulated that companies are running scared and have become gun shy about telling their story for fear of censorship. This situation has prompted ARG to ask the question, "Do you think more favorably about the price of medicine when you know how much it costs the company to develop it?" Responses revealed that *76.4% of those who were adequately informed replied that they were willing to accept the high price of their medicines.* With this information, our advice to pharmaceutical companies is to better educate the general public about their high costs of R&D.

Trust-Based Relationships

Caesars Entertainment chairman, president, and CEO Gary Loveman describes casino customers as "promiscuous" because when they visit destination markets they go from casino to casino. "I'm in the business of fostering customer monogamy," he says half-seriously, "like the Ladies' Temperance Movement."

A former Harvard Business School professor, Loveman explains, "When you look at the dry-cleaning industry, people don't go to a different dry cleaner every time their clothes need to be cleaned. Nor do people go to a different auto mechanic every time their car needs repair. The same thing is true with your pharmacist or hairdresser. Women go to the same beauty parlor for 10 years and never consider going someplace else. It's not price that wins the loyalty of these customers. It's more about trust-based relationships."

While it may be a great sale or a lowball price that gets a prospect to walk through your door and make an initial purchase, to win a lifetime customer, it will take a trust-based relationship. You will earn customer loyalty by extending outstanding service coupled with your integrity that demonstrates that you sincerely care about him or her. This is why you are loyal to your barber, beautician, dry cleaner, and pharmacist. It's why Four Seasons has an incredibly loyal clientele. And why tens of millions of women call their Mary Kay Independent Beauty Consultants when they need more products. It's why Chubb policyholders renew their policies and seek additional coverage with their broker. And it's why Tom James customers reorder clothes year after year from their clothing consultants.

As Jim McEachern, former president of Tom James, points out, "There are three things that a Tom James customer must be happy with: the product, the service, and his personal relationship with the clothing consultant. We hardly ever advertise, so the vast majority of our new customers come by referral. For example, years ago I made a call on a managing partner of a large law firm in Atlanta. He bought a suit and several more over the next couple of years. By then, I had earned his trust and confidence, and one day he said to me, 'Jim, here's a list of the names of all my partners and associates that I think could use your services. I am going to buy the first suit for each of them, but I want them to hear your full presentation.' I said that his generosity would be appreciated, and I asked him why he was doing it. 'They represent this firm, and how they look is a reflection on our professionalism,' he said. I thanked him for the business and expressed how much I valued our relationship."

✳   ✳   ✳

Edward Jones is a company with principles, and when need be, it will turn down business rather than violating what it believes is best for its customers. Edward Jones' managing partner, Jim Weddle, explains, "We will not accept an order in options, futures, penny stocks, or commodities. Those are not long-term investments. We view them as wagers with the odds stacked against the investor. Yes, we might give up some business, but if so, so be it. We focus on keeping people out of investments where they are likely to have a bad experience."

Weddle emphasizes that the firm's clients consider a financial advisor as a trusted advisor, "and a person who has his or her best interests at heart. Over time, a strong relationship is formed."

John Bachmann, a senior partner and former managing partner of the firm, says, "An Edward Jones client is a serious long-term investor, and our business model has been built on establishing face-to-face personal relationships with our clients. This is why we don't do online trading. Sure, we pay our bills online and our people use it as a tool. But our value added is the relationship. Our client knows that we deliver what we promise, and we consider this our competitive advantage."

10

Multiple Tiers of Customers

Unless you sell a commodity directly to consumers, you're probably selling to multiple tiers of customers. For instance, Johnson & Johnson's drug reps sell prescription medicines to physicians and hospitals. These medicines are prescribed to patients, who, in turn, go to a pharmacy that dispenses the prescriptions. There may also be layers of middlemen in the distribution system.

J&J's consumer health-care products segment, another business of the giant international company, consists of a wide range of products such as baby powder, shampoos, baby oil, mouthwash, and so on. These products are sold through different channels of distribution as are its medical devices and diagnostics products. So, a multi-billion-dollar company such as J&J has many tiers of customers. And then there is the company's ultimate customer—the consumer.

Again, it goes back to the J&J credo: "We believe our first responsibility is to the doctors, nurses, and patients, to mothers and fathers, and all the others who use our products and services." The company recognizes that to succeed, it must serve all of its customers. It's not enough for a medicine to be well received by the medical profession but fail to inhibit or cure a patient's disease. However, a medicine can cure a patient only if a physician prescribes it. So if the medical profession doesn't believe in it, a medicine will not be consumed by its end user, the patient.

Companies with multiple tiers of customers must take caution to avoid conflicts by serving one tier to the detriment of another. For example, a pharmaceutical company may think it is serving in the best interest of the consumer when it advertises a product to a wide audience in print and on television. Some companies consider it as a public service because it educates the general public. Critics think they are pushing their drugs on persons who are not medically trained who, in turn, challenge their physicians' treatment. Doctors object because it undermines their authority and consumes valuable time to explain why the patient should be treated with a different drug. Pfizer's Viagra ads are a classic example. Treatment for erectile dysfunction is not an option for all men, but many who saw Viagra television commercials started asking their doctors to prescribe it. Many doctors expressed their anger in having to give long explanations to their patients on why they should not take Viagra. Some medical people told stories about how angered men became confrontational and belligerent. When we learned how displeased doctors are about pharmaceutical companies that advertise prescription drugs, we decided to see what the consumer thought about these ads. An ARG study showed that *72.8% of Americans are in favor of having pharmaceutical companies advertise their products.* When ARG surveyors questioned those in favor of these ads, *77.8% said it prompted them to ask their doctor to prescribe the advertised drug.* So while the end user thinks there is a benefit to this form of advertising, the drug companies' first-tier customer opposes it. Herein is the dilemma. There is not one good answer. All companies that sell to multiple tiers of customers should consider all angles to circumvent potential conflicts.

There is another kind of customer tier that categorizes customers according to their monetary value to a company. Here, a most valued customer receives preferential treatment. For instance, a large food manufacturer will expend more service catering to a large supermarket chain than to a small mom-and-pop grocery store. While some people may espouse that all customers be treated equal, common sense dictates that one should concentrate more time and effort on larger accounts. Likewise, the resources of a law firm are better used serving a Fortune 500 client. Similarly, an owner of a fine jewelry store will personally show expensive designer jewelry to wealthy customers while the job of selling lower-priced merchandise is handled by a sales clerk. It's more probable that a manufacturer with a network of dealerships would spend more time wining and dining large dealers in major markets versus its low-volume dealers in sparsely populated areas. This does not imply that small customers are unimportant. Instead, it is a matter of large customers being considered more important.

Of course, the whole idea behind customer loyalty programs is for companies to award their best customers for their business. While the airline industry has been the first to offer frequent flyer points to their customers, many other industries have since followed with similar programs. With so many of these programs out there and considering the hassle that exists for redeeming frequent flyer points, we wanted to know what today's consumers think about them. An ARG study shows that *46% think the benefits of a frequent flyer rewards program are worth the effort it takes to join.* While we don't have comparison figures from previous years, it's our hunch that today's consumers are less enamored with frequent flyer programs than in past years. This is evidenced by an ARG study that disclosed that only *27% of all travelers will make an effort to buy a ticket from the airline that issued their card.* Well, so much for loyalty programs in the airlines industry!

In another ARG study, *35.7% of Americans expressed that they will stop doing business with a company when being a member of its customer loyalty program doesn't result in receiving more recognition as a good customer. However, when a customer loyalty program does work, and nonmembers observe all the perks that VIP members receive, 50.3% of them are motivated to consolidate all of their business so they too can be given VIP treatment in the future.*

Choose the Right Partners

Whether you refer to your first-tier customers as agents, dealers, franchise owners, or distributors, we discovered that customer-focused companies treat them as partners, and they carefully select them as if one would choose a spouse. Ideally it will be a long-term relationship—turnover is expensive, much like getting a divorce. Not only is it costly to go through the process of terminating a business relationship with one party, it's time consuming to find a replacement. And when there's a new party brought in, it's confusing to the end user, the consumer. So ideally, it's best to do it right the first time. The bigger the investment that's required by the partner, the more complex is the selection process.

Consider, for example, the large investment required to open a new car dealership. As we discussed earlier, Dave Wilson's Lexus dealership in

Newport Beach cost $75 million to build. This doesn't include Wilson's inventory and payroll overhead. With such high stakes, both Lexus and Wilson had a vested interest in making sure it would be a good marriage—one that would last for a lifetime. The company is very selective about who is granted the right to put the Lexus sign on its rooftop. And since 1989, when Wilson opened one of the first Lexus dealerships, the number has grown to 223 dealers. Lexus dealerships have the highest return on investment in the industry, and as the most profitable, the demand for these dealerships is high. Bob Carter, former group vice president of Lexus, talks about the high number of applicants who contact the company when the word gets out that Lexus is interested in a dealership in a particular area. "In 2007 when we announced we were interested in opening in San Luis Obispo, California, an upscale retirement community on the coast, west of Fresno, within the first 60 days after we started our candidate selection 59 applications came in. This is a high-growth market, one that we consider a smaller market with projected sales of about 500 new cars a year. All of these applicants were viable candidates with years of experience in the business. It's rewarding to see how the demand for a Lexus dealership has soared in the past 20 years."

A major advantage Lexus enjoyed at the time of its debut in 1989 was being a member of the Toyota family. "It was the confidence that people had in the strength of the Toyota Motor Corporation," Carter emphasizes, "that attracted them."

Back in the late 1980s, Dave Wilson had already established himself as a star Toyota dealer. He owned and operated the company's second-largest dealership in the United States. Based on his past experiences with Toyota, he had complete faith that its entry into the luxury car business was destined to be a huge success. "I had the honor of opening one of the first Lexus dealerships," Wilson proudly tells. "I bought Toyota of Orange in 1982, and by 1985, it had become the company's sixth largest dealership in the U.S. However at the time when I signed the Lexus initial dealer agreement in 1987, I was buried in debt. In fact, I barely had any equity. I was burdened with a five-year loan and was making double payments. I was getting close to paying off the loan, but to open the Lexus dealership, I bought a piece of property and constructed a building. I was doing this based on my complete faith in Toyota. This was prior to ever seeing a Lexus car.

"Believe me, I had more than my share of sleepless nights," Wilson continues, "but the Toyota people were wonderful. Whatever they said every month was what happened. It was not this way when I had been a Ford and Lincoln-Mercury dealer for 13 years. Ford Motor Company had the idea that the product costs x to produce and the customer would pay y. However, there was a delta between x and y that was an ongoing struggle to see whether the manufacturer or the dealer would get that money. In contrast, Toyota recognized a relationship between the dealer and manufacturer. Toyota viewed the dealer as its customer.

"The company has a wonderful IT system that's set up to serve the dealer," Wilson adds. "I only have to push a computer button and Lexus puts the car in my inventory. At the same time, my bank sends them an electronic fund transfer. Just as Toyota always 'got it,' so does Lexus. In order for the company to be successful, the dealer needs to be successful. Every dealer knows that the company wants him or her to succeed. The company knows that if I'm fighting to keep the lights on and am only mowing the grass every other week, it's a bad reflection on the company."

Wilson pauses to reflect and continues. "There is no other automobile manufacturer that I would have risked putting $75 million into a building. I built a single-purpose building. If this doesn't work out, we're not going to bulldoze it and build a high rise. This is either going to work as a Lexus dealership or it's not going to work. There's already a Mercedes store right down the street and a nearby BMW store. GM and Ford don't have the product. There is not another franchise that can support the overhead we have here. While I didn't invest the farm in this place, if I had to close the doors and just keep paying $500,000 a month for rent on an empty building, I'd take a big hit. I went into this with both eyes wide open, having complete faith in this company. That comes from working with Toyota for a quarter of a century. In my mind, my faith is not misplaced. This is a company that does what it says it's going to do."

The Germain Lexus dealerships are owned and operated today by the three grandsons of Warren Germain: Bob Jr., Rick, and Steve. Warren Germain was an accountant who retired at Ford Motor Company in 1947 and the following year opened a Mercury dealership in Columbus, Ohio. His son, Bob, ran the family business that has been passed down to his three sons. The Germain automobile empire now consists of 14 dealerships. Bob Germain obtained a Toyota franchise in 1969. Today there are two Germain Lexus dealerships in Columbus and one in Naples, Florida. Like Dave Wilson, the Germains were in on the ground floor in 1989, when they opened one of the first Lexus dealerships in the United States. "There were a lot of dealers in '89 that didn't believe Lexus could compete with the luxury companies like Mercedes, BMW, Cadillac, and Lincoln," Rick Germain explains. "They had no interest in a Lexus dealership and thought it would be a poor investment. But guys like Dave Wilson and my father who had a long history with Toyota knew better. My brothers and I were very confident that Toyota would be a strong competitor in the luxury car arena. Back then, Lexus was an unknown brand, and we looked at owning the dealership as a unique opportunity to start from scratch. We would be able to develop a brand and reputation in our market as opposed to getting awarded an existing franchise."

Being the most profitable dealerships in the industry was an integral part of the Lexus strategy from the start. To assure their success, the company carefully selected experienced dealers with pedigreed reputations. Wilson and Germain are representative of the quality of dealers the company seeks. Of course, producing an excellent product and backing it up with superior service is also part of its winning formula. Then, unlike other luxury car manufacturers, Lexus was careful to avoid flooding the market with an excessive amount of dealerships. "Other automobile manufacturers tend to put too many dealerships in the same market, and consequently none is able to make much money," Germain tells. "Lexus started off with fewer dealers and grew it slower."

Of course, the early Lexus dealers that had been associated with Toyota were true believers that the company would be trustworthy. "When I became a Toyota dealer in 1982, the company had 1,200 dealerships," Wilson tells. "Back then the company was selling 500,000 cars. This year, it will sell more than 2.5 million cars, and there are still 1,200 Toyota dealerships. If one is taken out of the market, another one replaces it, but the company is not overloading the market with dealerships."

It's interesting how Lexus stated in its mission statement that the company would do things right from the start, including having the finest dealer network in the industry.

"Our direct customer is the dealer," Bob Carter says. "Like other automobile manufacturers, we have a franchise agreement with each of them. It's very spelled out—very specific requirements. But in the real world, the dealers are our customers. Our half of the partnership is to deliver product, and we strive to deliver it as close to perfect as we can. The dealer's half of the partnership is to provide the facility, and we ask them to have the best facility and best people in their market. It's the dealer's job to create the best customer experience for the ultimate car owner."

✳   ✳   ✳

Dave Liniger, CEO of RE/MAX, also understands how to serve multiple client tiers. "All RE/MAX franchises consist of independently owned and operated offices," Liniger explains. "With this structure, none assumes any liability for another. Just the same, they are interdependent on each other's reputations. For example, we can have 10 offices in town and one bad office that goes bankrupt. The newspaper doesn't say RE/MAX so-and-so went bankrupt. It reports that RE/MAX went bankrupt and it reflects on the other offices. Customer calls start pouring in: 'You guys are going under.' And the broker has to explain, 'Oh no, that was an office that's 20 miles away that has nothing to do with our office.' Today, we have to be more selective than ever to protect our reputation as well as our brokers' reputations. Our selectivity has paid off in spades. More than half of our sales today are from existing brokers who are buying a second, third, or fourth office. This is commonplace in franchising today. McDonald's rarely sells a single franchise. Their existing ones open new McDonald's."

The quality of its people is reflected in the fact that RE/MAX brokers have the most professional designations per capita in the real estate industry. "Nobody comes into the business and plans to fail," Liniger says. "We stress to our people, 'The more you learn, the more you earn,' and we offer courses to our brokers to acquire Certified Residential Specialist (CRS) and Graduate Realtor Institute (GRI) designations. We also have conventions and training sessions covering everything from how to use the latest in technology to how to deal with seniors. We even use RE/MAX DVDs and our own satellite television network to educate and improve our brokers' skills."

The Consequences of Choosing the Wrong Partners

A recurring theme in this book is to do things right the first time—it's expensive to replace lost customers, employees, and dealers. With this in mind, make the effort to line up the right partners early on so you can avoid having to get rid of them and finding new ones.

Founded in 1837, Deere & Co. has been selling farm equipment through independent dealers for more than a century. Deere dealers like to brag that they "bleed green," the company's trademark. But even as the farm boom helps Deere harvest record profits, dozens of North American dealerships are getting sent out to pasture, including some that have been passed through families for generations. The man behind the cuts is CEO Robert Lane who insists times have changed. In an age where tractors use satellites to track the location of every seed, he says, dealers must match the sophistication and size of agribusiness customers.

"For years we've talked about Deere as a family," says Lane. "The fact is we are not a family. What we are is a high-performance team.... If someone is not pulling their weight, you're not on the high-performance team anymore."

Deere's overhaul is one answer to a challenge faced by many large businesses that distribute through independent retailers. These retailers are supposed to know the local turf and market the product more effectively than a big corporation could. But if the retailers are too small scale, their inefficiencies could outweigh the advantages. Lane fears that small dealers don't have the wherewithal to hire enough skilled staff or track inventories. Also Deere is trying to wean itself from years of overproduction at its factories, and it needs dealers who can manage inventory well.

By contract, dealers have to meet Deere's performance targets or face losing their right to sell Deere products. If someone wants to transfer his dealership to a child or anyone else, Deere must approve. As of the end of 2006, the company has 2,934 dealer locations in the United States and Canada, down 12% from the 3,400 dealers it had in 1996. The actual number of dealers is even lower due to big dealers having multiple locations and acquiring small dealerships. The company's motive to terminate small dealerships is to enhance customer service. According to Deere, technology is a key reason why size matters. On some of today's tractors, farmers needn't even touch the steering wheel: the machines turn themselves on, to ensure that no patch of soil is covered twice. Their computers can be programmed to track soil temperature and control fertilizer spraying. The bigger Deere dealers can afford more skilled managers and technicians. The small units don't have the volume to employ the talent needed to serve their customers. By eliminating the small dealers, the surviving big ones have larger territories. This decreases the odds of a price war.

Of course, when Deere set up small dealerships in small farming communities across the country more than 100 years ago, there was no way of knowing how vastly different the marketplace would be in the twenty-first century. Likewise, companies such as Lexus, Edward Jones, Chubb, Ashley, and others that are doing all the right things to establish strong distribution channels today may have to make adjustments like Deere has made. One thing is certain: today's customer tiers will be different in the distant future.

Taking Good Care of Your Customers' Customers

When the first Lexus dealerships opened, the company sent a poster with a message that the company had never had a dissatisfied customer, and *it didn't intend to have one.* "It let all the dealers know that the company was starting on a clean sheet of paper," Germain tells.

In 2006, Lexus introduced Bluetooth, a hands-free phone system. Customers were very receptive to having this state-of-the-art technology in their new cars, but it wasn't long after Bluetooth was available that it shot right to the number one spot for complaints at the company's call center. "It is not intuitive technology," Nancy Fein, former vice president of customer satisfaction at Lexus, explains. "In fact, it's quite complicated, and our salespeople were unable to explain to customers how the address book gets loaded in and what button then gets pushed. The problem for most users was figuring out what phones pair up with what cars. While some customers were able to follow the manual, many couldn't. To solve the problem, we teamed up with Letstalk.com, a Web site set up by two young entrepreneurs to provide information on what to do. Our customers can now go to Lexus.com and receive instructions on how to do it. Our call center people will walk them through it just as our dealer personnel can now do. It wasn't on my annual plan to come up with a fix for Bluetooth, because I had no idea it would be a problem. But once it surfaced, we had to find a way to fix this customer experience that was a source of a lot of frustration. The Web site did the trick. The Bluetooth problem dropped down from number one on our top 10 complaints to around number 20."

* * *

All automobile manufacturers provide training for their dealerships' salespeople. So does Lexus. But the company goes far beyond what its competitors do. "We train every associate in a Lexus dealership," Bob Carter explains. "This includes the sales associate, the service technician, the service consultant, the valet, the receptionist—every person in the dealership. In 2007, we trained nearly 11,000 associates. Let's take an entry-level position that is critically important at one of our dealerships—the receptionist. We think this position is key to a dealership's success, because no one there talks to more customers. We want the receptionist to understand a product like our new LS 460, and we want him or her to be enthusiastic about it. We want him or her to experience driving the Mercedes S class, the Cadillac STS, and the BMW 7 series. We want this person to know the strengths and weaknesses of the competition, and knowing the differences, we are confident that he or she will become as passionate about the brand and our products as I am. Yes, it's a major investment for us to give this kind of training, and it takes three months or so a year to execute. Starting on both coasts, we send our people out in the field in August and they're finished by November."

In an ARG survey, *75.7% of Americans said they believed that the dealer, not the automobile manufacturer is responsible for serving a new car.* Consumers feel that they bought the car from the dealership, so it should take care of them when there is a problem.

* * *

Frances O'Brien, senior vice president, explains that Chubb agents and brokers have more contact with policyholders than the company, and she emphasizes, "They are their clients. They own the clients. Our job is to serve the agents and brokers well, and in turn, they will tell their clients, 'This is why I am recommending Chubb, and this is why you are going to pay a little bit more for this coverage.' We are the product, and for our brokers and agents to fulfill their promise to their clients, we have to be there for them."

"At the end of the day, we're talking about your assets being protected," Tom Motamed, former vice chairman and chief operating officer, says. "Our business is about asset protection, and because it's personal, you probably want to discuss your assets with your agent or broker whom you have a relationship with.

"We do not sell directly to clients," Motamed explains. "We are not licensed to do that, so we depend on our distribution model to sell our products. To be successful, we have to first sell the agent and broker on what Chubb is all about. This involves our integrity, ratings, balance sheet, location, and so on. We're competing with 2,200 insurance companies in the U.S., so it's not what you'd call a walk in the park. Second, we have to sell them on our products and services. This means they've got to be able to give their clients a reason why Chubb is worth paying a little more for. As you can see, it's a double sale."

* * *

There are 360 licensees that operate Ashley Furniture stores today, and the number is growing. In addition, Ashley sells its extensive line of furniture to more than 6,000 retailers that represent approximately 12,000 stores. "We are very selective on who we partner up with," says company chairman Ron Wanek. "Our success depends on how well they do. We have a lot of furniture-store owners that come to us to see if they can convert their existing store to be an Ashley store. Generally, if somebody hasn't been running a good store, he or she probably won't be a good operator of an Ashley store either." An Ashley store licensee is an independent owner-operator, and his or her license is good for a certain number of years. The licensee must meet certain company standards in order to have the license renewed.

In addition to providing a large selection of furniture (more than 6,000 stock furniture items) at low prices, there are other reasons why independent furniture-store owners choose to sell Ashley products. With its distribution centers strategically located across the United States, Ashley has the capacity to deliver furniture within two days to a high percentage of its customers. Only in remote areas in such places as Wyoming or Montana does delivery take perhaps seven days, which is still considerably faster than other furniture manufacturers. Ashley's state-of-the-art distribution centers serve as a great competitive advantage. A customer can purchase a piece of furniture such as a sofa or a bedroom group that he or she sees on display in a store, and with the implementation of compatible technology, the order is instantaneously processed at the Ashley distribution center. This assures fast delivery time, often made the same or following day. It can take several weeks for competing retailers from the time of placing the order with a manufacturer until the time when the furniture is delivered to the customer's home. In fact, it's not unusual for other companies to take as much as three months to make deliveries of out-of-stock merchandise. "Our whole value proposition in the marketplace," explains Todd Wanek, Ashley's president and CEO, "is really fast delivery to the store and getting it to the customer very fast. To make this happen, we have a fleet of more than 800 tractors and 2,000 trailers. We have trucks on the road every single week. There was one peak week when we delivered 2,500 truckloads of furniture."

Like in other areas of retailing, the mom-and-pop furniture stores lack the buying power and economies of scale of the big chain stores. The small-store owner can't afford to hire high-priced executives with expertise in such areas as warehousing, distribution, marketing, and advertising. Here too, Ashley helps its army of 6,000 independent furniture-store owners operate at a high level of efficiency. The company has top marketing specialists to advise and assist them with advertising, store layouts, and computer systems services. Other services include everything from use of proprietary software to manuals on how to run their businesses. Licensees and independent-store owners also attend Ashley conferences that are conducted throughout the year. "It's almost impossible for the little guy to do all of these things independently today," Ron Wanek insists.

At the end of the day, what makes Ashley excel is its ability to select the right merchandise that the consumer wants, because no matter how fast the company can deliver competitively priced furniture, if nobody wants to buy it, the business model is a bust. In this area, Ron Wanek credits his son, Todd, who he refers to as a genius when it comes to forecasting what will sell in the marketplace. Because most of its furniture is manufactured in the Pacific Rim, Ashley must place enormously large orders in advance so that it can have tens of millions of dollars of merchandise in its warehouses to meet the demand of the American consumer when it comes time to furnish his or her house. Without its ability to forecast what styles will sell for the upcoming season, the lag time between replenishing hot-selling merchandise would take three to five months; hence Ashley would lose its competitive advantage.

"We do a lot of studying on demographic analyses," Todd Wanek explains. "I spend much of my time in this area, plus we have a team of designers and salespeople who are very focused on what the consumer is going to want in the future. For example, we're constantly studying what's happening in other industries such as in fashions so we can forecast color palettes. We're routinely looking at buying trends in housing, keeping an eye on what colors are being used for such products as kitchen cabinets and bathroom fixtures. We want to know how people are decorating their homes. And we're always talking to the people in our stores and our customers' stores, accumulating and then analyzing the feedback we receive from them. Our challenge is to constantly keep on top of what our customers want. Then we must communicate this information to our licensees and retail accounts and then instruct them on how to train their salespeople."

A major advantage that Ashley has over other furniture manufacturers is that it's been in the retail business since the opening of its first home store in 1996. Ashley operates a few company-owned stores, which helps keep its management close to the consumer.

A Perpetual Source for New Ideas

Prior to launching Lexus, Toyota sent its people into the field to find out what American luxury car owners wanted. The Lexus was originally designed to satisfy this segment of the market in the United States. "The European automobile manufacturers built their cars for what the European owners wanted," Rick Germain explains. "I don't think they really cared about what interested American luxury car buyers. Toyota found out that

Americans wanted a quieter, smoother, more comfortable car. European drivers and European manufacturers are more concerned with cornering, handling, and feeling the road. But there were a lot of Cadillac and Lincoln owners that were used to a softer, cushier ride. Lexus people focused on interior comfort too. For example, I remember how Lexus installed cup holders but the European didn't think it was important for their product. But it was. Lexus engineered and built in a lot of creature comforts to cater to the luxury car owners that were surveyed. The Lexus was $10,000 to $15,000 less than other luxury cars on the market in '89, so with the comfort features, the car was a great value. Then, when they owned their Lexus, they found out that the quality was better."

✳   ✳   ✳

"There are approximately 650,000 women in the United States who sell Mary Kay products," Rhonda Shasteen, senior vice president of corporate brand strategy and sales support, tells, "and they all know they can call here at a moment's notice and let us know if something isn't right in the field. They are all independent businesswomen, and if there's an issue of any kind, they aren't shy about telling us about it. The company's founder, Mary Kay Ash, was always so proud about how the people in our independent sales force feel they have this connection and know we work with them. Of course, that's the way it is today. Not only do we instantly get feedback on potential problems, they help to keep us current on new ideas."

✳   ✳   ✳

Throughout the year, there are RE/MAX conferences and seminars conducted at national, regional, and local levels. Again, with an organization consisting of 120,000 independent real estate brokers and agents, there is a constant flow of ideas from the sales field. By and large, these are not shy individuals. They represent the cream of the crop in the real estate field. And because they know that RE/MAX respects and welcomes their suggestions, they supply the company with a steady stream of fresh ideas. The most sophisticated RE/MAX producers are members of the Chairman's Club. To qualify for this elite group, an individual must generate a minimum of $500,000 in annual commissions. There are about 2,500 members in this group, and they are invited to two to three seminars each year. "We listen very carefully to what they say," Dave Liniger emphasizes. "All of our senior officers and I make sure we are accessible to them. Then there's the Chairman's Leadership Advisory Counsel. To qualify for this group, a broker must have a minimum of 175 agents. There are 170 members of this counsel, and in addition to meeting with them at our summer and winter conventions, we invite them to an annual retreat. It's in someplace like Hawaii; last year it was in Spain. Here, they have unlimited access to 12 senior officers for its entire six days. They put together the entire agenda, and we get all their input. We constantly ask them, 'What do you want to do?' and of course, we inform them about where we're going and what changes we foresee."

Liniger spends 270 days a year on the road meeting with RE/MAX people. Everyone in the organization has his e-mail address. While it's not possible for him to respond to every one personally, he makes sure that everyone gets answered.

✳ ✳ ✳

The Cabela's catalogs are superbly done on high-quality paper with graphic, full-color photography. A recipient, an avid outdoors person, looks forward to its arrival and eagerly flips through the pages as a sports fan would read *Sports Illustrated*. Just as the company emphasizes quality in its products and service, no corners are cut to produce the catalog. "When you consider all the costs to make and mail the catalog, I estimate each side of a single page costs us about $10,000," Dennis Highby, Cabela's president and CEO, says. "We carry too many items to put every one of them in the catalog, so we must carefully select which ones make the cut. This applies to everything sold with the Cabela's brand, which today represents about one-third of everything we sell. This is a high percentage considering that for years we didn't sell anything with our own brand. To determine which products with the Cabela's brand are included, we listen carefully to our customers on how much they enjoy using our branded merchandise. We do this by measuring every square inch of these catalogs for profitability.

"For instance," the CEO continues, flipping through a fly fishing catalog, "the first two pages have Cabela's fly rods. But then, each of the items on it has to make a profit, based on the square inches they occupy in the book. It's the customers who determine what will be in next year's catalog."

Not All Customers Are Created Equal

Equality works fine in a democracy. But in the business world, it should not be expected that all customers be treated the same without regard to revenue. It is not practical to treat all your customers alike, nor is it good for business. Certainly, every customer deserves courtesy and respect, regardless of size. The most profitable customers should be prioritized and be recipients of a higher level of service. Customers who buy a first-class airline ticket pay a premium for better service. Why? The carrier makes more money on first-class fares. It's quite simple. This does not mean economy-class passengers are treated discourteously. Airline employees still treat them with politeness. Still there are amenities they do not receive, ranging from more comfortable, roomy seating to meals that are not served to other passengers. First-class passengers also have faster check-in lines and access to the airline's private club. Economy travelers have the opportunity to buy a more expensive seat but choose otherwise; they choose to tolerate less service in exchange for paying less. Likewise, customers who pay higher prices for hotel and cruise line rooms receive better service. There are more services for people who buy skyboxes at sports arenas. So it should come as no surprise when a company extends more service to a loyal customer versus an infrequent customer. It's good business. The steady customer generates more revenues.

Perhaps nowhere is there more extensive and more lavish service showered on valued customers than in the gaming industry. As mentioned earlier, Caesars has a ranking system that values its most profitable customers in its rewards program, and in turn, they receive certain perks ranging from faster check-in lines to free drinks and meals, all dependent on their casino gambling activity. "We are able to see very quickly, even on the first visit," John Bruns, former vice president of customer satisfaction, explains, "what a customer's potential play might be. With the slots, our technology tracks a customer's play, and our pit managers can record this customer's play at table games. Based on an individual's play and behavior we can say, 'Here's a high-value, high-frequency potential customer.' And once such a customer is identified, it doesn't take us long to send an ambassador to greet him or her. If a high-potential player is experiencing a fast loss, we want to intervene by welcoming the player to Caesars and perhaps offering a complimentary dinner or show tickets—the value of the comp is determined on mathematical models we use. A host might say, 'We know you've had some unfortunate luck here, so let me buy your dinner today to show that we appreciate your business.' By doing this, the customer doesn't leave without something of value, which we think is very important in our business."

In the gaming industry, it's an accepted fact of life that a customer's gambling activity determines how he or she is treated. Casino patrons accept this favoritism as standard procedure. No matter what a person's net worth, if he or she is not a player no special treatment is given. Caesars doesn't know how much money a customer has—that only becomes a consideration if an individual requests a line of credit. Otherwise, the company makes no attempt to find out, because it doesn't matter.

On rare occasions, it may upset some customers who stand in slower-moving cashier and restaurant lines. If so, a customer might receive some sympathy, but he or she won't get anything else. It's an equitable system and executed with a total lack of prejudice. It doesn't matter if a person is male or female, young or old, white or black. Every Caesars customer is evaluated and treated by the same standard, which is according to how much money is put at risk. The company doesn't care if a customer wins or loses—as long as he or she plays for certain periods of time and at certain stakes.

Once you get past the facades in Las Vegas, there isn't much difference in the gaming tables and the slot machines. Yes, lavish settings, big-time entertainment, fine dining, and special events are main drawing cards. The list of special events includes boxing matches, concerts, and poker and slot machine tournaments, and their main purpose is to attract customers to spend their time and money in the casinos. If it were possible to fill the casinos to maximum capacity without these attractions, none of these enhancements would exist. Under such a scenario, there would be only gaming tables and slot machines; additional trimmings would be unnecessary overhead. But on the famous Strip in Las Vegas, where the competition is fierce, enhancements are necessary. And one of the oldest and most reliable is the "comp," short for complimentary, as in complimentary drink, complimentary dinner, complimentary room, and so on.

The practice of comping customers began in the early days of Nevada back in the 1940s, when free alcoholic beverages were "on the house" to preferred customers. To keep a customer from wandering down the street, complimentary meals were provided, and when the free room was thrown in, even more time was spent on the premise. The purpose of all comps is to fill seats at the gaming tables and slot machines. Executed by astute businesspeople, the costs of comps are built into the casino's business model. Conceptually, this requires casino management to calculate comps as routine expenses to acquire and retain customers. Properly done, it's no different from building in other expenses such as advertising and payroll. While other businesses have a budget for entertaining customers and clients, casino companies have taken it to another level.

In the early 1960s, many casino resorts began flying players from across the country on junkets. Customers were rated according to their casino activity, and the expense of flying them to Vegas to spend a certain amount of time at the tables was calculated into the cost of business. Later, in addition to flying in a planeload of customers on a chartered airplane, airfare on commercial aircraft was provided to rated players, and the high rollers received first-class tickets. Over time, casino resorts sent their own private jets to transport their best customers to and from Las Vegas. With other casinos competing for the same customers, the level of comps kept rising. Dinners and golf outings with celebrity entertainers were used to induce a high roller to come to Vegas for the weekend. Bigger and more deluxe rooms were built to accommodate deserving customers. Today, the top-tier casinos such as Bellagio, Wynn, Caesars Palace, MGM Grand, and Rio have suites (also known as villas) that range from a few thousand square feet to as much as 45,000 square feet. These incredible accommodations are reserved for the highest of the high rollers known as whales, the biggest fish in the ocean (never mind that a whale is a mammal). Whales have credit lines in the millions.

These customers expect and receive red-carpet treatment comparable to that normally reserved for royalty and heads of state. In fact, royalty and heads of state would envy how the whales are treated in Las Vegas. The customer experience is so grand that the superrich from Hong Kong, Taiwan, and Tokyo are attracted to this remote oasis in the Nevada desert to place their bets. Whales normally arrive on their own private jets, or if they prefer, a casino dispatches its own jet to fly them in. On arrival, they are chauffeur-driven in a stretch limousine to one of the world's largest and most spectacular hotels. Suites have their own concierge and an on-call host, 24 hours a day. Each suite has a staff of housekeepers, a full-time chauffeur, and chefs that are available to prepare gourmet meals in the suite's kitchen. Some of the larger suites have their own butler's quarters that provide 24-hour service, assuring an available butler during the guest's entire stay. Anything a whale requests, if it's possible, is given, gratis. For instance, if a whale's wardrobe is missing something, it will be delivered—a dozen expensive imported shirts, a dozen silk ties, even a different Italian suit or sports jacket for every day of the week.

You can't rent a suite—they are only available to high rollers with high credit lines. Microsoft's Bill Gates once came to Las Vegas to attend the Comdex Convention (Consumer Electronics Convention). His offer to pay $20,000 to $25,000 a night for a five-day stay in one of Rio's Palazzo suites was turned down. Why? Bill Gates was not a rated player; he plays $3 to $6 hold-'em poker. "Those rooms were available only to very high-level players who had credit lines of $2 million to $3 million and up,"

Gary Thompson, director of communications, Caesars Entertainment, explains. "There was a time when we believed that we couldn't afford to tie up a room for $100,000 and take the risk of losing a whale because we couldn't accommodate him. Our thinking has since changed. Today, we'd be delighted to have Bill Gates as one of our guests."

Las Vegas epitomizes a place where all customers are not created equal. The comp system works best in Las Vegas because gaming has a mathematical model based on certain odds that favor the casino. Simply put, comps are factored in as part of the cost of doing business. It doesn't matter how much money you have. The only thing that matters is how much you gamble. Comps are only given to gamblers based on their play activity. Otherwise, even Bill Gates is treated as an average Joe.

11

Satisfy Main Street First, Then Wall Street

Too often, companies are so concerned about meeting short-term earnings goals to satisfy the investment community that they neglect their customers. In retailing, same-store monthly sales figures are regularly compared to last year's numbers, a sad commentary on measuring performance. In the American automobile industry, weekly sales numbers are compared to the previous year's weekly numbers! With Japanese automakers' market share steadily rising, Chrysler, Ford, and General Motors should have better things to do than comparing short-term performance numbers. Not only is it a poor way to keep score, it takes the focus off long-term thinking.

It is true that a company should be managed in the best interests of its owners or, in the case of a publicly traded corporation, its shareholders. Oftentimes, however, many of these investors are traders who want immediate profits that boost the current market price of its traded stock. These temporary "in-and-out" owners have different investment objectives than long-term investors; in fact, they may be in conflict with the best interest of the company. Interim quick fixes to ongoing problems may appear to work well today but can turn out to be the root of a dreadful outcome down the road. For example, to produce an enviable year-end profit, a company might reduce expenditures by trimming its workforce. Needed capital investments in technology are postponed, consumer research budgets are slashed, and advertising is reduced. There is a long list of ways to lower overhead, and yes, these cutbacks may indeed increase current year-end earnings. But over time, these reductions are likely to play a heavy toll, jeopardizing the company's future by gravely weakening its competitive position.

When employees are laid off to fatten a company's bottom line, don't think for one moment that customers don't notice it. An ARG study shows that 71.8% of Americans *think that most retailers make shopping difficult by not having enough employees to serve them.* Interestingly, about the same percentage (54.8%) has stopped shopping a store because they have had difficulty finding what they wanted. Being short staffed is not a solution to improving one's bottom line. On the contrary, it decreases revenues. The same study reveals that 80.3% *think retailers are more concerned about their profits than about providing good service.* For obvious reasons, this is no way to win customer loyalty. You don't want to drive them out of your store thinking, "If I'm second fiddle to their profits, I'll find another company that values me as a customer."

As we've mentioned, another way to drive customers out the door is to require them to have a receipt in order to return merchandise. An ARG survey shows that 36% *of Americans are less likely to shop at stores like Target or Best Buy as a direct result of their strict no-return policies of merchandise without a receipt.* ARG also turned up another interesting finding: 44.3% *of consumers will stop shopping a store that does not have a 30-day satisfaction guarantee.* As we mentioned earlier, 2.8% of all Americans are jerks—these are the ones who will return a camcorder after they used it at their daughter's wedding or on a vacation. It's not good business to penalize 100% of your customers for this small percentage of jerks who take advantage of your satisfaction guarantee.

How do seemingly capable managers make such bad decisions to have no-return policies and refrain from offering a 30-day satisfaction guarantee? They get caught up in trying to please the securities analysts that they neglect their customers. This leads them to make unwise decisions that hurt their business. An ARG survey uncovered the fact that 27% *of consumers have stopped shopping at a store because they were unimpressed with its exterior appearance.* Again, in an effort to look good for Wall Street, retailers are prone to allow their stores to become run-down or out of date in order to save money. Not fixing your store may improve short-term earnings, but long-term, fewer customers mean lower revenues.

We've all experienced having a favorite, once-popular restaurant go out of business. This might happen when existing or new management decides to make changes to improve its bottom line. To increase margins, the chef is instructed to purchase a less expensive quality of food. Or perhaps a new chef is hired at a lower salary to replace a popular chef. It might even be that the portion sizes of meals are reduced, or menu prices are increased. For the record, we're all in favor for growing revenues to increase profits. Just remember: a company can't cut expenses and grow market share.

In the area of long-term planning, American business leaders would do well to emulate the Japanese, a nation of long-term thinkers. The Japanese culture plays a strong rule on how its businesspeople think. To understand the Japanese culture, the word *mottainai* must be understood. Its definition is that all things are precious, and to waste is a sin. Consider too that the contrasts between Japan and the United States are striking: Japan is a land of limited resources, and the United States is a land of plenty that has evolved into a disposable society.

Japan is an overcrowded land about the size of California with a population of 128 million. Its population density of 343 people per square kilometer is 11 times that of the United States and even 2.5 times that of heavily populated China. Japan's population is slightly less than half the U.S. population but in an area about one twenty-fifth the size. With vast shortages in both natural resources and real estate, the Japanese think, live, and work differently. They must; their survival depends on it. Japan has almost no raw materials except water, and because its terrain is jagged and mountainous, only 17% of the land is habitable or arable. The awareness of space, or the lack thereof, has been deeply engrained in the Japanese culture. By the early 1600s, Japan had a population density about twice that of the present-day United States. Or look at it this way: if Japan had the same population density as the United States, there would only be 9 million Japanese.

The shortage of space caused the late-nineteenth-century farmers in Japan to work collectively to improve efficiency. This teamwork approach formed the basis of the consensus management system that prevails in Japanese business circles in the twenty-first century. The Japanese are known to establish a strong identity as part of a group (that is, a family, a corporation). A large Japanese corporation often is considered more than just a place to work and to generate profits. In contrast, during the nineteenth century, adventurous Americans pioneered a vast virgin land, building farms and ranches often miles from the nearest neighbor.

Isolated, these settlers became zealously independent—a characteristic that epitomizes the American spirit to this day.

The independence of Americans is evident in how our nation's workforce changes jobs at a significantly higher rate than the Japanese. A young Japanese manager expects to stay with the same company for 20 or 30 years and has plans to move up the ranks during this period. Consequently, he or she is thinking toward the future and isn't interested in achieving short-term gains that will jeopardize the company's long-term picture. With low turnover, the company's employees buy into its philosophy. In contrast to American companies, there is less chance of the Japanese seeking a new CEO from the outside who comes in with his own team to clean house—and to make drastic changes to turn the business around. It is not that we object to change. We do however object to change that plays havoc with employee morale. Nor do we favor change that promotes what's convenient to improve a profit-and-loss statement but is detrimental to customer service.

When "made in Japan" was stamped on a product following World War II, it automatically meant to nearly everyone that it was cheap, shoddy merchandise. Then in 1950, a group of about 50 Japanese industrialists began to enroll in W. Edwards Deming's quality-control conferences. Deming, an American business consultant, lectured on statistical process control, and he espoused to his audience that if they would do as he instructed them, within five years Japanese quality would be known the world over and that other nations' manufacturers would be screaming for protection. As it turned out, it only took four years before the Japanese's reputation stood for quality-made products. To this day, Japanese manufacturers stress constant improvement, always striving for continual improvement. In an ARG study, *57.5% of Americans think that due to the Japanese commitment to long-term planning, their companies have an advantage over U.S. companies.* The same study revealed that *56% of Americans think Japanese companies are more customer-focused than American companies.* This comes as no surprise, because in order for a company to think long-term, its focus must be on its customers.

The Right Priorities

We have drawn attention to the huge amounts of money pharmaceutical companies spend to introduce a new medicine. The staggering costs are in the $1 billion range, and this figure does not include the thousands of molecules that are leads in a laboratory test tube but fail during the early stages of research. A molecule may show promise in a test tube but fail to work in a living organism. Even a high percentage of those that show potential when tested on laboratory animals are likely to fail in the human body. The investment costs add up during the six or so years a compound goes through its early stages of development; highly skilled and highly paid scientists work diligently in their attempts to make it a viable medicine. When the drug finally makes it to Phase I, the earliest stage of testing it in human volunteers, there may be $100 million or more invested in a single drug that still shows promise while the cost of the failed attempts is money down the drain. Still, 70% of the molecules that make it this far will never reach the market—the big question still remains: will it work in patients?

To find out, a drug candidate still has several more years to be scrutinized during the second and third phases of the costly clinical trials. It is estimated that 40% to 50% of drug candidates that enter the third and final phase of trials won't receive FDA approval. During the final phases of the clinical trials, a pharmaceutical company is required to invest large sums of money in its manufacturing facility before receiving FDA approval. A new plant can add another several hundred million dollars to the cost of a new drug. Many manufacturing facilities have been built and hundreds of employees must be hired and trained. Still, the FDA may reject a drug's application. Johnson & Johnson's CEO, Bill Weldon, says, "If you start out with 10,000 molecules, maybe only a few of them will move through the pipeline. The others drop out because of concerns with safety or efficacy. Then, after you get them approved, only one in three will ever pay for the investment."

In a highly competitive field, there are also other pharmaceutical companies that might come out with a better drug. It is also possible that an approved drug might have its patients experience previously unknown side effects. This can lead to its withdrawal from the market. This is what happened to Merck's Vioxx and Pfizer's Celebrex, both multi-billion-dollar Cox 2 inhibitor blockbuster drugs. Also, outlandish product-liability lawsuits add to the cost of medicines. Merck has been defending against claims that Vioxx caused heart attacks on a case-by-case basis, winning about two of every three, but so far its defense has exceeded $1 billion, and the meter is still running.

Then there are the generic drug companies. Without incurring a billion-dollar cost for research and development, a generic drug manufacturer is able to produce a copied version of a medicine for pennies on the dollar. Hence, once a big-selling drug's patent expires, it ceases to be a significant source of revenue to the original manufacturer. With the competitiveness in being the first to make a lab discovery, pharmaceutical companies often file for a patent early on in the game. And since it may take years to make and test before a drug receives FDA approval and is launched in the marketplace, the period of time that it is actually sold and protected by patent law may be considerably less than 20 years. "We have one product in our pipeline that we haven't launched, and its patent expires in six years," explains Bob Sheroff, president of J&J's global biologics supply chain. "Now with Remicade, we received FDA approval for an indication to treat Crohn's disease in 1998, but it wasn't until later when the FDA approved Remicade to treat other immune-mediated disorders such as rheumatoid arthritis, psoriasis, ulcerative colitis, and ankylosing spondylitis. Still, our patent on Remicade expires in 2018 for all indications. The date of a patent begins with the filing of the original protein or compound."

With all of these risks, one must ask why pharmaceutical companies continue to make new medicines. CEO Bill Weldon explains: "What we do is different from other businesses because people depend on our products for their health and even their lives. We are willing to take these risks because people have such a strong need for these medicines. For example, we are spending a lot of money on a medicine that can revolutionize the treatment of tuberculosis. It's probable that we will never make money on this product, but rather our intent will be, if it works, to eradicate tuberculosis. A few years ago, we started to develop a vaginal microbicide to help prevent the sexual transmission of HIV [human immunodeficiency virus, the virus that causes AIDS]. As the majority of new infections of HIV are in Africa, we provided a royalty-free license to the International Partnership for Microbicides so that they can develop and commercialize the product for use in resource-poor countries in order to help slow the spread of HIV.

"An older product, Vermox, a medicine for deworming children, is made by Janssen Pharmaceutica, a Belgium company J&J acquired in 1961. Vermox was approved by the FDA in 1968 when the costs of making a medicine were significantly less. Over the years, we've given millions and millions of free doses of Vermox to children's funds in different countries around the world. But when you spend a billion dollars on a product and have 10 years invested in getting it to the market, you need a pretty good product for a long period of time to realize a profit."

After a brief pause, Weldon adds, "I can't say it enough about men and women who come into this industry to help people. They are dedicated to bring better health care to people around the world. For all the things that have been written in the newspapers about this industry, I feel the media has been amiss for not visiting our research labs to sit and talk with J&J people as well as those at other pharmaceutical companies. If they did, they'd realize that these scientists are there to bring value and help people in their lives. You just have to look at the dramatic changes that have been brought about and the impacts that are being made in such areas as cancer and metabolic diseases. People are being kept out of the hospitals and longevity has risen. This is a direct reflection on scientific research and people who have committed their lives to helping others.

"At one meeting, a reporter made reference to the pharmaceutical companies being profit mongers," Weldon continues. "'You don't really want to find cures,' he said, 'you just want to make people feel better and continue paying for your drugs.' I told him that there will always be enough diseases and needs in this world for us to have things to do. Another reporter talked about the side effects caused by certain medicines, implying that pharmaceutical companies knowingly keep drugs in the market even though they cause unacceptable side effects. This is sheer nonsense. I strongly believe in this industry and its people. They work hard to do good things, and despite what the media might say, I don't think anyone in this industry would want to bring a product to the market that would do damage to somebody. On a related subject, our diagnostics group is working with our pharmaceutical group and making progress in the personalized medicine area. In the future, medical people will be able to give you a diagnostic that will be able to determine that a particular drug will be effective without a side effect. We're moving in that direction and hope to get there soon."

We find it interesting that whenever we talked to J&J people, the company credo habitually became a part of the conversation. This illustrates how deeply ingrained the credo is in the company's day-to-day business. This is the way it is supposed to be according to Denise McGinn, who is a J&J vice president of business development. McGinn's job is to find business opportunities for the company's biotech business group. In this capacity, she and her team are constantly looking for sources for new products. As she explains, "Our two sources are either within our internal R&D or going outside the company. This requires my team to scour the outside for potential products in their very early stages that we might acquire, including a medicine's intellectual properties and even its patents that might be applied to our own work. Other times we might do a merger and acquisition." Constantly on the go, in a period of a year McGinn and her team might review as many as 200 companies as candidates for an acquisition; if all goes well, one or two deals will be executed.

"It's always about the patients first," she emphasizes. "Our overall goal is to alleviate suffering and hopefully cure their disease. We are always thinking about this when we are working long hours on difficult assignments. First, we look at the science of a potential medicine and how it will serve the patient. Then we look at its commercial aspects such as the market for the product and how much we can make. However, our top priority is to look at the patient and how we can take care of an unmet need."

Like other high-level people we met at J&J, Bob Sheroff, president of global biologics supply chain, emphasizes that the company's credo is its guiding force that keeps management focused on its priorities. "Number one is the patient," he explains, "and number four is the shareholder. It's interesting that when General Robert Johnson wrote the credo in 1943, he was the company's only shareholder. He owned the entire company, and yet he put the shareholder's interest fourth, after the customers (doctors, nurses, patients, mothers and fathers, and all others who use our products), employees, and the community.

"In 1942, shortly after the bombing of Pearl Harbor, Johnson had volunteered for the army," Sheroff continues. "With his business acumen, it was decided that he would be better used in Washington. President Roosevelt asked him to serve as chairman of the Smaller War Plants Corporation. His job was to champion the cause of small companies in the contract-bidding process. In this position, he was given the honorary title of "brigadier general," and afterward was referred to as General Johnson, or simply as "the general." Shortly after he wrote the company's credo, he petitioned to have a credo that would be followed by major U.S. corporations. In addition to a credo, Johnson crusaded for a minimum wage. A minimum wage was passed, but his idea that American industry needed a credo or a conduct of ethics to follow was unacceptable to business leaders, most notably those in the railroad and petroleum industries. 'We can't put our stockholders last,' his opponents insisted.

"The general's credo lives on," Sheroff adds. "Each year, our CEO, Bill Weldon, meets with the top 120 managers of J&J. I've been lucky enough to attend these meetings. Bill always spends a minimum of two hours discussing the credo. Russell Deyo, the company's chief compliance officer, also participates in the discussion. Now you have to remember, Bill is preaching to the choir because each of those present has been around for a long time. But it emphasizes how important our credo is that our CEO revisits it at each one of these high-level meetings. He always finds a way to make it seem fresh, but it's always the same message."

Long-Term Partners

Now and then, privately owned companies join forces with large, financially strong companies that share their same values. This has been a strong attraction for the 250-plus companies that have become members of the J&J family. It is also what attracted NetJets' CEO Richard Santulli to Warren Buffett's Berkshire Hathaway.

"A big mistake that most people make," Santulli explains, "is that they either plan to sell before the company has sufficiently matured, or they go public. I'm always telling people that if you run a business to sell it, it's going to be a bad business. 'Take care of your business,' I say, 'and the value that you will create will be the right value.' For example, NetJets had 80 customers in Europe five years ago. We added 600 owners in the last two years. We have no competition in the fractional ownership in Europe. Had I gone public, our European operations would be out of business. That's because after losing $40 million back to back during the first two years, Wall Street would have said, 'You're making money in America and you're throwing it away in Europe. Get out of the business over there.'

"That's the problem. You can't think long term. That's why I sold out to Berkshire Hathaway. At the time, Goldman Sachs, who owned 20% of NetJets, was not happy about it. They kept saying that we can go public and get more money. I said, 'I'm not going public. Had we done an IPO, I wouldn't have been able to continue building the business. With Berkshire Hathaway, I am able to run my business not short term, but long term. I don't have to cater to the shareholders. The shareholder is Warren. He sees my financial results, but he's never seen a financial projection. I don't have to ask for his permission to buy airplanes. He has confidence in me and he trusts me. He also allows me to build my business in Europe. I speak to Warren a lot. Naturally, he wasn't happy that we were losing money in Europe. But I kept telling him, 'In 10 years (it came out to be less than 10 years), we'll be profitable, and we don't have any fractional competition over there.' That's what happened. Warren is perfect for us. Number one, he's brilliant and I talk to him all the time. I ask him for advice. Number two, he leaves me alone. He lets me build my business. Number three, being part of Berkshire Hathaway allows

NetJets to borrow money at a lot cheaper rate. Not having capital restraints in this business is very important for our long-term growth."

Santulli explains that being a Berkshire Hathaway company is very prestigious. "It elevates our brand a notch. Our customers know that we stand for safety. They know we stand for quality. We tell everyone, Warren and his family fly with us, and so do my family and I. We know it's the safest operation in the world."

* * *

In 2007, Four Seasons Hotels, a publicly traded company, was taken private in a negotiated transaction for a price of $3.7 billion. The purchasers were an affiliate of a trust created by HRH Prince Alwaleed for the benefit of HRH Prince Alwaleed and his family, an affiliate of the private investment entity of William H. Gates III, and the family holding company of Isadore Sharp.

Sharp had spent more than 45 years building Four Seasons into one of the world's leading managers of luxury hotels and resorts. The company had achieved this success by focusing on the long-term best interests of all its key stakeholders: its guests, its employees, the owners of the properties it managed, and its shareholders. While the company had been private and public at various points in its history, it was always able to maintain its long-term focus on the best interests of its stakeholders as a result of Sharp's controlling ownership position. For Sharp, the privatization was another step in this long-term approach.

As Sharp explained, "I had reached the stage where I thought it would be desirable to assess the possibility of pursuing an ownership transition with a small number of investors who would share my long-term vision for Four Seasons. You see, a change in ownership was ultimately inevitable, because someday my children would have needed to sell my family's ownership position. Pursuing a transition while I could continue to be fully engaged in running the business would help to ensure that the company's long-term vision and strategy were preserved." Key to realizing this objective was, of course, attracting like-minded partners.

The new investors fit the bill. They each have the ability to take a long-term financial view, and that investment orientation permits Four Seasons to stay true to its vision and core values.

Sharp continues to believe that the long-term view has served and will always serve Four Seasons well. The new ownership group is another example of that perspective. It means that, "if something happens to me, it's no longer an open question about what will happen to control of the company."

Staying Private

Edward Jones is the largest of the major full-service investment brokerage firms that is not a publicly owned company. Its owners are its top-performing home-office associates, financial advisors, and branch office administrators. Based on certain criteria, the company has a formula for acquiring equity as either a limited partner or general partner. "With ownership in the company," Jim Weddle, managing partner, explains, "our people have an incentive to do what's in the long-term best interests of Edward Jones and our clients. They also want to make sure the people around them are doing the right things. We think owners act differently from employees. They stop thinking about short-term gains because they have a stake in the company's future. They're not interested in realizing an immediate profit that will hurt their equity position down the road. We like having our brokers and our clients in it for the long haul."

John Bachmann, senior partner, points out that when the firm sent its first financial advisors to the United Kingdom, there was no pressure from Wall Street to generate immediate profits. "It was a big investment," he explains, "and we knew it would be years before we'd see a profit. As a publicly owned company, we would have had to be more focused on short-term results that could have influenced our decision making. We might have paid more attention to controlling our budget in order to keep costs down. For example, there have been times when all we'd have to do is stop training our people and we would have made a lot of money in a hurry. But when you do that, you're mortgaging your future."

✳ ✳ ✳

According to Dave Liniger, chairman and CEO, RE/MAX has never had a need to raise any outside capital. "The company is profitable," he explains, "so we've been able to build through our annual growth. Being a privately owned company with a limited number of shareholders allows us to make long-term plans and not have to worry about quarterly reporting that would have an effect on the stock values. We think this gives us a tremendous competitive advantage. And we are not required to do extensive reporting that would let our competitors know our future plans. By not having to be concerned about satisfying Wall Street with our quarterly performance, we have never had to cut back on any of our over-head such as advertising during a downturn.

"With mergers and acquisitions, companies will cut back on the overhead," Liniger adds, "to pay off the loans that they incurred to make the deal. I like being where we are—we've never been bought out, and we don't have to make payments on money we owe. We can just go about doing our day-to-day business."

✳ ✳ ✳

We talked about Dave Steward earlier and how he applied biblical principles to build World Wide Technology, a $2.4 billion company that today is the largest African American–owned company. Dave says the scriptures teach WWT to think long-term. "The seeds we wisely sow today will be repeated one hundredfold in years to come," Steward asserts. "As a privately held corporation, our company is not subject to pressures that the investment community exerts on management. With a publicly held company, investors and analysts make demands on management to produce short-term gains that will boost quarterly financial statements. Short-term investors' interests may be best served by a temporary increase in the price of a traded stock. For example, a favorable announcement will enable them to sell their holdings and realize a quick profit. This type of investor is not concerned about the future of the company. Accordingly, this same investor resists long-term capital expenditures that decrease short-term profits but enhance the welfare of the company in years to come.

"Unquestionably, there were times when we had to make difficult decisions that required us to sacrifice short-term profits in order to someday realize long-term gains. I won't kid you and say it was easy. Being able to generate short-term profits is tempting, especially for a start-up company in dire need of cash. But we refused to compromise our principles and we patiently bided our time, believing that we would someday be rewarded. As the Bible tells us, faith is having a belief in the unforeseen.

"At WWT, we keep focused on making sure we have the ability to continue to bring more value to our customer tomorrow versus what we did today. If we can do this, it will always keep us in the game."

12

The Power of a Strong Brand

A husband goes to the supermarket with a shopping list that his wife prepared for him to pick up the following six items: box of tissues, salt, chocolate syrup, frozen peas, ketchup, and mayonnaise. The chances are that he'll come home with the following: Kleenex, Morton's, Hershey's, Birds Eye, Heinz, and Hellmann's. Why are we so sure a husband would buy these items? Our logic is based on the theory that when in doubt people buy the most familiar brands. This behavior reduces the risk of making a bad buying decision. Consumers like to know what they are getting.

Of the above brands, Heinz's reputation as the number one ketchup is so strong that it's found in 97% of households. Even more impressive is the fact that Heinz ketchup monopolizes the restaurant industry. It's rare to find a restaurant that serves another brand. Heinz ketchup is perceived as the best by the majority of Americans, and no restaurateur dares having his customers think he's cutting corners by serving another brand of ketchup.

A recent ARG study reveals that *67.6% of American consumers will buy a recognized brand product in preference to a less expensive unknown brand*. The fact is that two out of three people are willing to spend more money to buy a product that they know emphasizes the value of a good brand. However, the bigger the difference in the price of the two products, the more consumers will lean toward buying a nonbrand product. Price elasticity works in favor of the nonbrand product.

Depending on the product, brand awareness varies. For instance, ARG research determined that *when we buy apparel, 60.9% of us will buy only brands we know.* Our reasons for strong brand loyalty, however, fluctuate from product to product. For example, trust is particularly important when it comes to buying baby formula. People aren't interested in saving money when it comes to their baby's health. This is why Similac and Enfamil command 86% of the American market. Even when educated mothers read the labels of generic baby formula products and find that the ingredients are identical, they stick with Similac and Enfamil.

There is no doubt that people will pay more for a brand product. Here's how it works on a more pricey product: an ARG study shows that *a Maytag washer has 40% brand recognition versus a White Westinghouse washer with 7% brand recognition.* Based on these numbers, a Maytag ad featuring a $499 washer will have more sales than an ad featuring a $399 White Westinghouse washer. To have the same impact on customers, White Westinghouse would have to sell its washer at an ad price point under $299 to reach the same amount of shoppers as Maytag. This comparison illustrates the value of a good brand versus an unknown brand.

Becoming a recognized brand is no easy matter, but it's definitely worthwhile because it is quite valuable. Interbrand, a division of Omnicom, is a premier branding company. Each year in cooperation with *BusinessWeek*, using a sophisticated five-step discounted economic value-added methodology, Interbrand ranks the top 100 company brands. The following are the top 10 companies with their 2007 brand values:

2007 Rank	2007 Brand	Brand Value ($m)
1	Coca-Cola	65,324
2	Microsoft	58,709
3	IBM	57,091
4	GE	51,589
5	Nokia	33,696
6	Toyota	32,070
7	Intel	30,954
8	McDonald's	29,398
9	Disney	29,210
10	Mercedes	23,568

Coca-Cola is perennially recognized as the world's leading brand. The value of its brand is approximately 52% of its market capitalization (currently $126 billion). Amazing, isn't it, that the value of Coca-Cola's brand is worth more than all of its tangible assets?

The company's own number crunchers are fond of saying that a Coca-Cola beverage of some sort is swallowed 1.4 billion times a day in various spots on the planet. (That translates to 58,333,333 servings an hour, or 972,322 a minute, or 16,204 a second.) The liters per capita consumed in the United States are 31.3. Coke's U.S. market share is 41% of the cola market compared to second-place Pepsi's 33%.

Americans have an addiction to Coke, or putting it another way, a love affair. In May 2007, Coke officially opened its new 92,000-square-foot museum, replacing the old World of Coca-Cola museum. What is remarkable about the museum is that visitors pay to walk through a building full of Coke ads, albeit interactive and slickly displayed. Museum officials say they expect more than one million visitors a year. (Admission is $15 for adults, $9 for children.)

How a brand is perceived has much to do with its worth. Consumers' perception causes them to crave a Coke to quench their thirst, even though dozens of imitators have knocked off the product and some have succeeded in manufacturing a product that is nearly indistinguishable from Coca-Cola. In the early 1900s, figuring out the exact formula was hard to do, so the company wisely didn't file for a patent. Had Coca-Cola done so, based on patent law at the time, it would have expired in 17 years and the formula would have become public domain. Today, however, sophisticated laboratories have the capacity to break it down, analyze it, and come up with a beverage to challenge the "real thing." But try to get a Coke fan to settle for a Pepsi and see how unhappy he or she becomes. Granted, the taste is important, but we know what really matters is the Coca-Cola name. How many consumers do you think would buy an identical tasting beverage called Fred's Cola?

Although Coca-Cola continues to hold its top position, when it comes to branding no company can rest on its laurels. Like other ubiquitous American brands, from Ford to Polaroid to McDonald's and Budweiser, Coca-Cola has lost some of its magic. It seemed to happen overnight, as if unseen forces were conspiring against the company: the stock market bubble burst and foreign economies deflated; tainted cans of Coke made Belgian schoolchildren sick; and some of Coke's African American employees sued, citing an ugly history of discrimination. Worse yet, soft drinks became a prime target in the national debate about why many Americans were fat. Drinking Coke wasn't so "fun" anymore, and Americans started reaching for bottled water and an expanding variety of other noncarbonated drinks that offered new tastes and better nutrition. All of this proves that no brand is immune to changes in the marketplace that can tarnish its luster. While Coca-Cola still holds the number one spot, its bright star has slightly faded, and no doubt this has caused some sleepless nights for the company's executives in Atlanta.

Johnson & Johnson's CEO Bill Weldon concurs, "People ask me, 'What would cause you to lose sleep at night?' I always answer, 'Anybody, anyplace doing anything that would tarnish the Johnson & Johnson brand.'"

Dallas Kersey, who recently retired as senior marketing officer at Edward Jones, poetically describes the fragileness of a brand: "A brand has the delicateness of butterfly wings because it can be injured at any moment in time. So a company's brand must be nurtured and requires constant care. This translates to how we treat our customers. An Edward Jones client is the serious, long-term individual investor. As far as we're concerned, we only have one customer. As one of our financial advisors so aptly said, 'I'm always in touching distance of my client.' This is who we are. Our brand is built on that face-to-face relationship."

"It takes 20 years to build a reputation and five minutes to ruin it," Warren Buffett says. "If you think about that, you'll do things differently."

The Trust Factor

Branding dates back to 500 BC during the Roman Empire when products such as cheese, wine, medicine, pottery, and glass vessels were stamped with a maker's mark. The people then were able to buy goods made by reputable craftsmen. Later, in Europe, between the fourteenth and seventeenth centuries, a "merchant's mark" served as evidence that a merchant's traded goods were acquired from reliable sources. Today, intellectual properties (patents, trademarks, and copyrights) provide adequate protection against having one's product copied. Intellectual properties also offer assurance that the consumer is buying the real McCoy, notwithstanding "knocked-off goods."

Depending on the product, a company's reputation is a focal concern in determining who gets your business. Naturally, what you're buying is relevant. For example, when shopping for commodities such as paper clips, screwdrivers, or barbells, we are not particular about who makes them. In other situations, the brand name is a significant factor.

For example, brand products like J&J's baby powder, baby oil, and Band-Aids are so well established that most loving parents would automatically buy them over another brand. Likewise, Similac, Gerber, and Enfamil have high market share because mothers don't want to take any chances with an unfamiliar brand that might jeopardize their baby's growth and development. Once parents find a formula or food for their babies that they like and trust, they tend to stick to it and are willing to pay higher prices for it. As a result, it's difficult for new companies to break into the business without buying an established brand.

A product that has no obvious correlation with infant food is an automobile tire. However, Michelin shares a commonality with Similac and Enfamil—Michelin built its marketing strategy with a focus on female buyers whose biggest concern about tires is safety. Michelin's marketing campaign broke the tradition of placing ads mainly in TV programming and print media geared to sports-minded male buyers. Instead, Michelin's advertising was placed with media that catered to a female-dominated market. Its early commercials showed babies inside the Michelin tire with a message stressing their security. Appealing to a mother's instinct to protect her offspring, the company sold peace of mind. Prior to Michelin's marketing campaign, automobile tires were sold as a commodity—the American consumer typically shopped for the lowest-priced tire. Michelin won the hearts of millions of American car owners by selling them a tire that they trusted would provide safety for their loved ones.

Trust plays a major role in the strength of a brand. And while an effective advertising campaign helps to build strong brand loyalty for a superior product, a personal recommendation will strongly influence what we buy. ARG research reveals that *91% of Americans will listen to a family member, friend, or associate when they recommend where we should go to buy big-ticket items such as cars, jewelry, and furniture.* This illustrates the importance in having loyal and delighted customers serve as a company's goodwill ambassadors. Remember: you can't buy a vigorous word-of-mouth campaign—it must be earned.

An ARG study tells us that *66.1% of Americans place more value on a recommendation from a family member, friend, or associate than one from the Better Business Bureau.* The survey also discloses that *85% of Americans think that a high rating by J.D. Power is meaningful.*

✳ ✳ ✳

The names of many banks and insurance companies contain the word *trust,* and for good reason. People place their money and their future with companies that they trust. This is why one's reputation is so essential in business. Chubb's former vice chairman and chief operating officer, Tom Motamed, emphasizes, "When I visit our offices around the world, I tell our people, 'The most important thing you have is your reputation. That's what you sell every day. Don't ever let your reputation be tarnished.' I'd like to think it's this way in every business, whether it's a CEO of a big corporation or the fellow who comes to take care of your landscaping. If he does a poor job, it reflects on his reputation. If he tells you he's going to be there on Tuesday and shows up three days later, you don't think so highly of him. I think one of our keys at Chubb is our reputation—this is applicable to the product, the service, and the relationships we establish. What you say and what you stand for has a strong impact on the value of your product and service. They are intertwined."

At the end of the day, the way an insurance company handles and pays claims speaks volumes about what its brand stands for. "Our main concern is our customer," Frances O'Brien, Chubb's senior vice president, says. "We make a promise to every client who does business with us, and when a claim comes in, we are going to be there to support that promise. Whenever there is any doubt regarding a claim, we will bend in favor of the customer as opposed to ourselves." How true. An insurance policy, like all contracts, is a promise that two parties make to each other. And like any promise, it is only as good as the party who makes it.

✳ ✳ ✳

"We don't look at the Four Seasons brand as a label," explains Barbara Talbott, executive vice president of marketing. "We view our brand as a promise, which we believe is considerably more substantive than a line that you tag on. We feel the brand itself must represent what's most important to our customers. Then it's our job to make sure we do the right things so it carries through in every experience they have with us. For instance, you may talk to a reservations person who answers the phone or have contact with an employee by e-mail—everyone, including those behind the scenes, is recruited with the same idea in mind. They are service minded. They are committed to excellence. It's the same with our reservations sales agents who are interacting with customers. They are all representatives of our brand. They are courteous and respectful, and they extend a warm welcome to our guests. Our guests are treated this way by every Four Seasons employee. There is a consistency that they sense, and they feel good about it. I also believe that a truly great brand such as Four Seasons delivers on more than one level. It touches your logic and also your emotion. You trust the brand. You trust it logically because you know you'll get everything that you need. We will try to exceed your expectations. When we do this and you personally experience it, you know that we care about you. As one guest said, 'Four Seasons is in the business of saying yes.' Other than one's personal experience, customers hear about the Four Seasons brand from people they trust who say good things about us. This is a powerful reason for them to choose Four Seasons."

Your first impression of a Four Seasons property is that you are swept away by its beauty, especially if you happen to visit one of its resorts in one of its exotic faraway locations. Each resort has its own unique magnificent scenic location, and whether it's on the Caribbean Sea or the Red Sea, you are assured of a breathtaking view, one that you will remember forever. Everything at Four Seasons is first class—your hotel room, the dining room, the spa. But what else you will always remember is the way you are treated. People also rave about the service they receive during a Four Seasons visit. And even more than the bricks and mortar, it's the service that brings guests back again and again.

Back in 1986 Four Seasons had its IPO, founder and CEO Isadore Sharp recounts what he told Wall Street analysts: "'I believe that within 10 years, we will be as well known for what we represent as are Hilton and Hyatt for what they represent.' This statement prompted the analysts to ask, 'What is it that your company will be known for?'

"'We will build a brand name that will be synonymous with quality.' I replied. That is exactly what we set out to do. At the time, it was a monumental goal. When I spoke about quality, it was more than the property in the physical sense. Sure, we were determined to have a consistency of product, meaning that every hotel would have a certain level of quality. And we do, in our designs of properties from the most modern to the most traditional. Our hotels are indigenous to the country. We try to be respectful to the local community. Today we have irreplaceable buildings in irreplaceable locations. We have better buildings and better locations than any company in the world. But this is only half of the equation. The other half is our people. I don't deny that others can copy the physical product—and they do. But to create a service culture that is consistent worldwide is what we think is something special. You can visit any Four Seasons all over the world, and you will find this commitment by our people. To have this commitment *and* the product is what Four Seasons stands for. It is one that I believe cannot be duplicated."

ARG surveyed people and asked them what they think about the Four Seasons brand: *65% said they think about quality and 35% think about its service*. This tells us that Four Seasons has two great strengths. People look at their hotels and think it's a quality place to stay and service is what makes the quality work. In a survey of this nature, what a company doesn't want to hear is having 80% say quality and 20% say service. This would mean that it's a beautiful property but the service is mediocre. In this survey, a perfect score is 50-50. When compared to previous ARG studies, Four Seasons 65%–35% quality-to-service findings are the highest score ever attained in the hotel/resort industry. What makes this score exceptional is that typically 25% to 35% of the responses answer, "I don't know."

✳ ✳ ✳

The Johnson & Johnson brand is one of the world's most respected brands, and one that has been popular since the late 1800s when Robert Wood Johnson and his two younger brothers, James Wood and Edward Mead, founded the company. One of the company's most innovative early products was packaged gauze and cotton complete with medications in a bottle. They were sold primarily to hospitals and doctors' offices, which, at the time, were not sterilized. The cotton was wrapped in blue paper, the same to this day. In the early 1890s the company introduced its famous baby powder and soon was also selling baby oil and baby shampoo. Ever since, generations of American parents have used these products that they apply with tender loving care on their small children. And it's likely that ever since the J&J Band-Aid was introduced in 1921, every child growing up in America has had one applied to a scraped knee, a bruised elbow, a cut finger. These and many other J&J products bring back warm memories, ones that we cherish all of our lives. There is a sense of nostalgia that makes us care about J&J because we grew up knowing that the company made products that took care of us in times of need. We have good reason for us to trust its brand. Over the years, a host of many other J&J products have entered our daily lives, including Stayfree, Band-Aid Brand Adhesive Bandages, Neutrogena, and Tylenol.

"We view the Johnson & Johnson brand as a trust fund," says the company's CEO, Bill Weldon, "and in my estimation, there isn't a more important brand in the world. We place a high value on our reputation, which opens many doors for us that provide many opportunities to engage in discussions around the world with government officials and other pharmaceutical companies."

Bill Weldon points out that while the brand recognition of the company's consumer products is so strong, many of its pharmaceutical and medical devices made by various units of the J&J family are not known to the general public but highly recognized and regarded within the medical profession. "For example, you couldn't walk into an operating room anywhere in the world and not find Ethicon sutures. I think Ethicon Endo is synonymous with most instruments for endoscopic surgery. Likewise, when it comes to pharmaceutical tranquilizers used for central nervous system treatment, our Janssen unit comes to mind with most medical professionals. And it's the same in the area of sports medicine and with the application of joint replacement and spinal fusions with our DePuy Orthopaedics' products. While the consumer doesn't need to recognize these brands, we like the fact that physicians and surgeons first think of these J&J companies for their trustworthiness and high quality of product."

✳ ✳ ✳

When the first Lexus rolled off the assembly lines in 1988, its early success had a lot to do with Toyota's reputation for being a brand standing for reliability. For years Toyota had built a vehicle known for durability and low maintenance. In fact, if you were driving off road into the wilderness, your life might depend on what brand of vehicle you drove. This point was made perfectly clear in an Australian television commercial that showed a competitor's vehicle with its hood up in the Outback. In view just a few feet away, there was a skeleton of the driver. The ad's message was: *Drive a Land Cruiser or drink your own urine.* "Our company came to fruition because we were an export company," former Lexus group vice president James Farley explains, "that was building commodity products that were used in very harsh conditions around the world and they had to work. For many of our customers it could be life or death situations. Or maybe it meant walking 50 miles. So this was our company's DNA, and it extended into the service world with Lexus.

"When we first introduced the Lexus as a luxury car in the U.S., our parent company, Toyota, had built a reputation on quality, safety, and fuel economy. Over a period of 20 years, Toyota had established a reputation built on trust. We didn't disappoint people," Farley continues. "Admittedly, it wasn't very sexy initially in the sixties and seventies; it had a tremendous impact on our launching of the Lexus. Then the first Lexus recall with the rear-window brake light was our first test of trust. We were so fearful of breaking people's trust. We gave them a free tank of gas and washed their cars. We gave them champagne and roses. We humbly apologized, and our apologies were accepted. And that's the way it's been with Lexus ever since—we just keep trying to build equity in the idea of trusting us."

✳ ✳ ✳

Chubb. Four Seasons. Johnson & Johnson. Lexus. Each of these brands has built a reputation for keeping its promise to its customers. Each company is the highest-regarded brand in its industry. This situation illustrates that it doesn't matter what the product is. It could be insurance, hospitality, or pharmaceutical and health-care products. The same principle of winning customer loyalty by building trust is applicable in every business—from D&O insurance to luxury lodging to baby powder to cars and trucks.

Two Different Business Models

If you want your brand to stand above the crowd, you must separate it from the rest of the pack. Edward Jones separates itself from other security firms with its unique business model that has more than 10,000 offices located across North America and the United Kingdom. Each office is staffed with one financial advisor and a branch office administrator. No other securities firm comes even close to having so many branch offices. "Our business model is having our folks go out to meet people face-to-face," explains Jim Weddle, the firm's managing partner. "Our people look them in the eye and find out who they are by asking questions. During this initial contact, we are looking for a need. 'How can I be helpful to this person?' By being there in person, our financial advisor might think, 'He's in his 30s and there are photos of two small children on the desk credenza. Here's an opportunity to help him with his need to save for their college educations. Perhaps he hasn't even thought about it yet or he may be procrastinating.' With this in mind, he talks a 529 education savings plan. With another person, we might talk investments in a retirement account. Or if the individual is already retired, his need might be having his money in municipal bonds or corporate bonds.

"Later on, our folks come back with a solution to a particular need," Weddle continues. "This is how we train our people and how they position a repeat contact. What is different about our approach is that our financial advisor doesn't meet with people to sell a specific product. For example, he doesn't start his sales presentation by talking about why the client should buy XYZ stock. So rather than leading with the product, he's leading with the solution to a need. Old-time stockbrokers used to call clients and lead with a product. They'd call and start pitching, 'XYZ stock is trading at $18 and I think it will go to $50. Here's why . . .' That's the old way, and we think it's not effective today. We want to improve a client's financial situation, and everyone has a different set of objectives. It might be that someone is annoyed with the amount of taxes he's paying on investment returns, so an IRA might be the right solution. Or perhaps his money should be put into tax-free bonds, or we might look at a tax-sheltered annuity. So the need is: 'I've got to address my tax situation.' By doing it this way, our people can go back and help somebody, and it will eventually result in a lot more business in those products rather than leading with a product itself."

Like Chubb, Four Seasons, and Johnson & Johnson, Edward Jones is a company with a sterling reputation that has been built on trust. "Our people want to be known as a trusted advisor," Weddle emphasizes. "They earn this reputation over time by working closely with people one on one and taking the time to give each client a tailored solution, not a one size fits all. It is one client at a time, and when a financial advisor has earned a customer's trust, other accounts with be opened due to a referral. Our most successful people build their careers this way—their clients tell their family members, friends, and business associates about the exceptional service they received. The best accounts and future clients come from referrals. Naturally, nobody is going to refer anyone to a company that he or she doesn't trust. This is exactly how I came to go to my personal doctor as well as the attorney who does my estate work. These were referred to me."

❋ ❋ ❋

Can you name a company that has a minimum advertising budget yet is a household word in the United States? Give up? It's Mary Kay. Your mind probably goes immediately to the pink Cadillacs. The company's founder, Mary Kay Ash, came up with the idea in the autumn of 1968, five years after she started the company. Her young enterprise had a good year and she headed to a Cadillac dealership to buy a new car. After the salesman went over the options and the price, he asked, "What color do you want, ma'am?"

She pulled the company's lip palette out of her purse and, pointing to a pale pink, said, "This color." He quoted her a price to have it repainted and warned, "When the car gets here, you're not going to like it!"

Mary Kay loved it. So did the independent sales force. "What do we have to do to get one of those?" they asked. Her son Richard did the math and came up with what sales figures were needed to be awarded a pink Cadillac. Five top producers earned the use of one in 1969. The following year, 10 earned the use of a car, and in 1972 so did the top 20 producers. The company has since awarded other pink cars ranging from Mercedes in Germany to top-of-the-line Toyotas in the Pacific Rim. The company has awarded the use of more than 100,000 "Career Cars" since 1969.

Today, a pink Cadillac is synonymous with Mary Kay. General Motors officially named the color "Mary Kay pink." The original car was a pink de Ville, a model that has since been discontinued; it has been replaced with a pink DTS, and in keeping with the times, other models are made available, including the Escalade, XLR, and CTS. Under the company's agreement with GM, no one can purchase a pink Cadillac, nor can a GM dealer paint one in Mary Kay pink without permission. Mary Kay owns the color exclusively. GM considers Mary Kay pink Cadillacs a real coup. As one GM marketing executive has said, "The Mary Kay pink Caddy is one of the best-known icons in corporate America. It's great for the Cadillac brand."

This unique award has drawn so much attention that Bruce Springsteen came out with a hit song, "Pink Cadillac," in 1983. Six years later, Clint Eastwood and Bernadette Peters starred in a 1989 movie with the same title, and several other related titles have appeared down through the years. As the awareness of a pink Cadillac has become a symbol of the Independent Beauty Consultant's personal business success, it also has become a powerful incentive for other independent sales force members to strive to earn the use of one. Whenever a pink Cadillac passes, heads still turn. Every year at the company's annual meeting, known as the "Seminar," pink Cadillacs are awarded. An arena packed with thousands of peers approvingly applaud and cheer. Those who are not awarded are inspired and determine that next year will be their turn on center stage to receive their own pink Cadillac. And as Mary Kay Ash used to say, "Once you drive a pink Cadillac, you never want to go back to having something else parked in your driveway for all your neighbors to see."

Rhonda Shasteen, Mary Kay's senior vice president of corporate brand strategy and sales support, says that the pink Cadillac has helped build the company's strong brand name. "But it's only one of many things. Although she passed away on Thanksgiving Day, her favorite holiday, in 2001, people associate the brand with Mary Kay, the person. Mary Kay was one of the most successful and dynamic businesswomen in our nation's history. There have been books written about her, and even a movie was made. She serves as an inspiration to women all over the world. I don't think any other woman in business has ever had such a positive influence on so many other women.

"Our company's general counsel once said to me, 'Rhonda, if I could sell you all the physical assets of the company and you could start your business tomorrow, or I could sell you only the trade name and you would have nothing else but the Mary Kay name, what would it be?' I answered, 'I would take the name in a heartbeat. I can replace the building, I can hire employees, but there will never be another brand like Mary Kay.'"

Prior to her death, Mary Kay Ash had become a living legend. Her legend continues to live on. "Mary Kay believed that women could soar to great heights, if given the opportunity," says Yvonne Pendleton, who serves as the company's director of corporate heritage. "Over the years, hundreds of thousands heard her repeatedly urge them on to greatness, spurred by her belief in them. She would say: 'All that you send into the lives of others comes back into your own. Expect great things and great things will happen. You can have anything in this world, if you want it badly enough and are willing to pay the price.' More than any tangible assets of this company, it is Mary Kay's philosophy and teachings that will long be remembered and passed down to future generations. And truly, her teachings influence many women and leaders beyond our company today."

Over the years, Mary Kay has built a wonderful reputation for having excellent merchandise and a knowledgeable independent sales force of women who teach other women how to use skin-care and color cosmetics products. In an ARG survey taken of women who use Mary Kay products, *67% of these consumers say that it is very important to be instructed on how to use the products and have an informed person make recommendations on which to buy*. With two out of three consumers acknowledging the important role that the Mary Kay Independent Beauty Consultant plays, it reaffirms our emphasis on the difference there is in simply having a salesclerk behind a counter and a well-informed person you trust demonstrate a product and make specific recommendations.

Dealing with the Unexpected

In business you must deal with the unexpected. When it happens, make sure you are ready. How companies react in unforeseen circumstances truly tests the mettle of its management. A textbook example is how

Johnson & Johnson reacted in 1982 when an unknown person tampered with capsules of Extra Strength Tylenol and filled them with cyanide. Seven victims who had bought the product off retail shelves in the Chicago area were killed. At the time, Tylenol was J&J's number one product, but more was at stake than lost sales—the company's reputation was on the line. Overnight, Johnson & Johnson was faced with a catastrophic and completely unprecedented public confidence nightmare. Literally within minutes of being informed of the incident, Chairman James E. Burke took immediate action to protect the public. Burke and other company executives worked into the night with the news media and with authorities in an all-out effort to warn and to keep the public informed. Wherever there was even the slightest of chance that consumers were in danger, products were withdrawn. This action resulted in more than 31 million Tylenol products removed from stores and homes across the United States. All advertising of Tylenol was curtailed. The cyanide-laced Tylenol was reported on the evening news by all national networks. It was the headline story by newspapers across the country. The impact it had on the nation was frightening.

The following week, the price of J&J's stock dropped 18%. Sales of its top two competitors skyrocketed. Meanwhile, Burke and other senior managers continued to inform a wary public not to use Tylenol. Working closely with the media as well as placing a one-time ad in newspapers across the country, J&J explained how to exchange Tylenol capsules for tablets or refunds. The company also placed a $2.50 coupon in newspaper ads to reimburse consumers who might have thrown away Tylenol during the tampering incident. The ad also offered an incentive to purchase Tylenol in other forms. Weeks following the poisoning episode, the FDA came out with guidelines for tamper-resistant packaging for the entire food and drug industry. When Tylenol was put back on the shelves, J&J had taken additional precautions by using new triple-safety-sealed packaging to thwart tampering—two more than the FDA recommendations. By the following year, Tylenol was again the best-selling analgesic brand.

J&J had fully gained the public's confidence, and then, in early January 1986, another person in the state of New York died from cyanide poisoning as a result of a Tylenol contamination. J&J repeated the same course of action it had taken in 1982. When a second contaminated bottle of Tylenol was discovered two days later, the company alerted the nation not to use Tylenol capsules. This time the company made the decision to discontinue the manufacturing and sale of all over-the-counter medications in capsule form. During a press conference, Burke stated, "We feel the company can no longer guarantee the safety of capsules to a degree consistent with Johnson & Johnson's standards of responsibility to its consumers." J&J had earned the trust of the nation, and it only took one week to turn around the second Tylenol calamity. This time, it took only five months before the Tylenol brand was again the leading pain reliever in the United States.

In both the 1982 and 1986 tampering incidents, J&J offered no cover-ups, denials, or lame excuses. No employees were advised to respond to the media with a "no comment" answer. Management stepped up to the plate to inform and protect the public. The leadership at J&J provided unprecedented access to the media, and in turn, the media was cooperative and, yes, supportive. The public's response was overwhelmingly positive. Ever since Johnson & Johnson is ranked as one of the world's most admired companies.

"J&J's reputation isn't a result of some public relations campaign," Joe Scodari, former head of J&J's pharmaceuticals business, explains. "The company's credibility has been earned by what we've done over time. We place a high value on our reputation, and we fiercely protect it. We believe the J&J trust mark is our most valuable asset." J&J's response to the tampering of Tylenol demonstrates how action speaks louder than words.

We previously discussed that the pharmaceutical companies rank only above the oil companies on a recent list of least admired industries. Despite the public distrust of the pharmaceutical industry, Johnson & Johnson perennially ranks among the top 10 of all American companies. A recent ARG survey revealed that *84% of all consumers believe Johnson & Johnson is a brand they could trust.* Based on other ARG studies, 90% is a perfect score. This rating puts the J&J brand in the top 10 most admired in America. For the past few years, Americans have been up in arms over the high costs of medicines, and to a major extent it's the reason why pharmaceutical companies are not trusted. In short, the American public believes they are being gored by an industry driven by greed. As a consequence, an ARG survey stated that *87% of consumers think that pharmaceutical companies overcharge. In comparison, only 18.3% think that J&J does.* How well these numbers confirm the strength of the Johnson & Johnson brand—a brand people trust.

Expand the Brand

Caesars Entertainment, Inc., known as Harrah's Entertainment, Inc. until the company's name was changed in 2008, is the largest gaming company in the world. It is a much different company today than when Bill Harrah owned it. Back then he owned two casinos, the original in Reno and a sister casino in Lake Tahoe. Today the company has casinos across the United States, including Atlantic City, Kansas City, St. Louis, Chicago, New Orleans, as well as on Native American reservations in California, Arizona, and North Carolina. The company has acquired some of the biggest names in the gaming industry such as Rio, Caesars, Bally's Horseshoe, Paris, Flamingo, and Showboat.

"The integrity of the brand and what it stands for today," says Ginny Shanks, former Senior Vice President, Brand Marketing, "is what Bill Harrah stood for and it has become imbedded in our company culture. We take good care of our employees and our customers. This has been and remains the fabric of what the brand has been since the very beginning. Today we have a portfolio of casinos that operate under different brands, and we've tied them all together with our Total Rewards program that recognizes our loyal customers at any of our properties. Our customers have the opportunity to be rewarded for their loyalty when they visit any of our casinos across the U.S. It's true that a customer might have a different experience at Harrah's on the Strip than across the street at Caesars Palace or next door at Flamingo. But with a diverse portfolio of casinos, the customer has choices on where to go to gamble, dine, lodge, shop, and take in a show. And he or she will receive the same warm, friendly service at all of our properties."

"We have a lot of brands today," explains David Norton, senior vice president and chief marketing officer, Caesars Entertainment, "and they stand for a lot of different things. Here in Vegas, there's Caesars Palace and Paris at the high end, with Rio and Harrah's close behind, followed by Bally's and Flamingo. We think this is good distribution, and with each of these brands having its own individual personality we feel there is value in being able to offer something different because we know customers like to visit other casinos in town. The nice thing is that when you present your Diamond card, all of our casinos will recognize you as a Diamond member because Total Rewards is used at all of our properties. With this in mind, they'll go to one of our casinos because they know they'll be rewarded for their play there whereas they are not at that level elsewhere in town."

In addition to expanding the brand to include an array of casinos, the company acquired the World Series of Poker (WSOP) in early 2004. Its roots trace back to 1949 when gambling legend Nicholas "Nick the Greek" Dandolos asked Benny Binion, owner of the famous Horseshoe in downtown Las Vegas, to sponsor a high-stakes poker marathon. Binion, a great promoter, consented and arranged for the Greek to play Johnny Moss, a legendary personality in the world of high-stake gambling. Knowing that it would attract large crowds, Binion insisted that the game must be open to the public to view at the Horseshoe. The Greek and Moss played a marathon that lasted for six months, taking breaks to sleep and answer to calls from Mother Nature. Moss eventually won an estimated $2 million. When the Greek lost the final pot, his famous last words were, "Mr. Moss, I have to let you go." He then went upstairs to his room to sleep. The crowds that came to watch the marathon had the fervor of dedicated sports fans, and in 1970, Binion decided to re-create the event featuring a battle of the poker giants; he called it the "World Series of Poker." In the beginning, the winner was chosen by popular vote, and again Johnny Moss was hailed as the world's best all-around poker player. Back then, all poker games were played, ranging from draw poker to five-card stud. Today, no-limit Texas Hold 'em is the most popular game, but the WSOP offers events in at least eight different versions of poker. The following year, the winner would be determined by a freeze-out tournament, which meant that players were systematically eliminated until one player had all the chips. Moss won again. In 1972, Thomas "Amarillo Slim" Preston, won the title. A colorful man, Amarillo Slim appeared on national television talk shows and became a celebrity. He also wrote a bestselling book and appeared in several movies. Amarillo Slim was the game's ambassador. The WSOP was on its way to becoming a major national event.

The 1980s introduced preliminary satellite competitions where players bought in with small stakes. NBC Sports dispatched a crew to cover the 1981 WSOP, and millions of viewers were introduced to the game. By the middle of the decade, an estimated 2,000 participants competed. As more entries joined in, the prize money increased proportionately. Chris Moneymaker, a 29-year-old accountant from Atlanta, was the winner of the 2003 WSOP, taking home $2.5 million. An amateur, Moneymaker achieved instant superstar status with his winnings. He was a personable young man, and millions of viewers could identify with him, so the game's popularity soared. The following year, another amateur, patent attorney Greg Raymer, won $5 million, and his win let it be known that you don't have to be a professional poker player to go home with the top prize. The winner of the 2005 event took home $7.5 million. In 2006, another amateur, Jamie Gold, a 37-year-old movie director from Malibu, came in first out of 8,772 players and won $12 million, surpassing the combined payout of events such as Wimbledon, The Masters, and the Kentucky Derby.

The 2007 WSOP event was held at the Rio in Las Vegas in July. The winner, Jerry Yang, a native of Laos, is a 39-year-old psychologist from Temecula, California. The father of six had just been playing poker for two years. The nine participants at the final table ranged in age from 22 to 62 and represented five countries—the United States, Canada, the United Kingdom, South Africa, and Russia—it was truly a world series. Yang was victorious over 6,358 players. His first-prize winnings were $8.25 million. Many celebrities played, and Tobey "Spider-Man" Maguire finished in 292nd place and received $39,445 in winnings. Other celebrities, including Oscar nominee Don Cheadle, Matt Damon, Adam Sandler, Charles Barkley, Ray Romano, and Jennifer Tilly, played in a charity tournament at the WSOP that raised more than $700,000 for survivors of the genocide in Darfur, Sudan.

The popularity of poker has never been so high. "More people today play poker than golf, bowl, or go to movies," explains Gary Thompson, director of communications for Caesars Entertainment. "It's a popular pastime for an estimated 50 to 70 million Americans, and its popularity overseas is growing rapidly. It's a game that adult men and women can play together no matter their age or physical condition. While top professional poker players enter the WSOP's main event, anyone who enters—whether amateur or pro—has a chance to win. If you want to get lucky playing poker, you want to get lucky at the World Series of Poker Main Event because you can win an enormous amount of money. You can't play golf or basketball against a Tiger Woods or a Shaquille O'Neal, but at the WSOP you can play poker with a world champion player and beat him.

"One way to become good at poker is by logging on to www.aol.com," Thompson adds, "where you can play for free and have a chance to win a $10,000 seat in the WSOP Main Event. It's a great way to learn the game and sharpen up your skill."

After acquiring WSOP in 2004, Harrah's hired three key marketing executives. One was Jeffrey Pollack, a former top marketing executive with the National Basketball Association (NBA), who later served in a similar position at the National Association for Stock Car Racing (NASCAR). Pollack came on board Harrah's as vice president of sports and entertainment marketing. The other top recruits were Ty Stewart, former director of integrated marketing for the National Football League (NFL), and Craig Abrams, who did an internship with the company while attending Harvard Business School. In January 2007, Pollack was named the first commissioner of the WSOP. In 2007, more than 54,000 participated in the WSOP 55-event tournament. In addition to revenues from the take that WSOP receives from the buy-ins—which range from $1,000 to $50,000—from each player, other proceeds are generated from food and beverage purchases, retail merchandise, hotel rooms, food charges, and vendors' fees. Of course, the tournament also draws large crowds that visit the casino—and they spend time at the slot machines and table games. "The average stay for a WSOP player is 6.6 days," Thompson says, "versus 3.6 days for the average Las Vegas visitor. But the biggest value is how the WSOP brand enhances the company's brand. A lot of young people who never played poker before are watching our tournaments on television, and they're learning how to play. It's exposing them to gaming as a form of entertainment, and they're coming out to Las Vegas as well as casinos in other areas. In this respect, it's benefiting not only us but our gaming industry as well."

Caesars Entertainment has a reputation of hiring smart people from outside the gaming industry. For example, the company's CEO, Gary Loveman, is a former Harvard Business School professor, and its previous CEO, Phil Satre, had practiced law. Going to the outside to hire Pollack and Stewart was a stroke of genius. With their previous NBA, NASCAR, and NFL backgrounds, the dynamic duo was able to land national sponsors for the audience of 30 million viewers that tune in to watch WSOP tournaments on ESPN. These sponsors include AOL, Activision, Corum, Hershey's Chocolates, Kraft Foods, Milwaukee's Best Light, Planters Peanuts, and Verizon. "These are major consumer products companies that understand how poker has become a mainstream form of entertainment," Thompson reveals. "Interestingly, WSOP is the third-highest-rated programming on ESPN, trailing only NFL football and NASCAR racing. As you can see, a sponsor can reach the demographics it wants. ESPN does 32 hours of original programming, and the same events are repeated more than 500 hours a year on other ESPN channels such as ESPN Classic and ESPN II. What's particularly interesting is that unlike other taped sporting events, people will watch poker tournaments even though they already know who won. That's because they want to watch the strategy so they can improve their own poker skills."

"People like to watch the action on TV," Ginny Shanks says. "It's very entertaining, and it whets their appetite to visit our casinos. Of course, it gives some of the viewers a taste of what the World Series of Poker is like and creates a desire to play in the big event in Vegas."

Due to the large audience that is created by repeat WSOP events, companies such as Hershey's and Milwaukee's Best Light are doing year-round promotional tie-ins that offer chances to win a seat in the WSOP. So, in addition to the vast exposure that Caesars Entertainment receives from the television audiences, consumers are seeing the brand in convenience stores, supermarkets, and everywhere where candy and beer are sold.

An Above-the-Crowd Logo

Bill Echols was a RE/MAX regional co-owner in New Mexico prior to working at the company's Denver headquarters, where today he is a vice president. When he first joined the company in 1977, Echols and his partner, Darrel Stilwell, began setting up RE/MAX offices in New Mexico, Arizona, and Nevada. The company was only four years old, and while it was becoming known in Colorado, there was zero brand aware- ness elsewhere. Echols and Stilwell loved RE/MAX's 100% commission concept, and it intrigued most real estate agents who worked on a 50-50 split with their broker. Still, it was hard to recruit new agents because they had never heard about RE/MAX. But, just as important, home buyers didn't know about RE/MAX either—and agents were sensitive to the cus- tomers' point of view. Every region went through the same steep climb. Until you reached that tipping point, and people started knowing who you were, it was a constant, agent-by-agent battle to build the business and spread the dream.

At a 1978 quarterly regional directors' meeting held in Lake Tahoe and attended by Echols with eight of his peers from different regions, there was a heated discussion on the need to come up with an effective logo to promote the unknown RE/MAX brand. Someone suggested, "We need something that will make us a household word like Century 21." And another director said, "We need a slogan that tells who we are." The meet- ing adjourned, and everyone went home with the assignment to think of something clever that could put RE/MAX on the map.

A week later, Echols was driving with a real estate agent and head- ing back to her office after lunch to drop her off. Suddenly, in the middle of their conversation, from the corner of his eye he caught a glimpse of four hot air balloons in the sky. "That's it!" he said out loud. "That's what?" she asked. "Oh, you wouldn't understand. Just an idea I had," he replied in a soft voice.

What Echols had seen in the sky was not so unusual in Albuquerque, which had been the home of the Albuquerque International Balloon

Fiesta since the early 1970s. But outside New Mexico, anywhere else in the United States, it was certainly an eye-catcher. Echols rushed back to his office to tell Darrel Stilwell about how a hot air balloon could be used as a great logo for RE/MAX. When he got there and started to talk about it, Stilwell said, "Tell me later, we've got a meeting with Tommy Thompson, and I told him as soon as you got here, we'd meet with him."

"Tommy had just joined our first Albuquerque RE/MAX office as sales manager," Echols tells, "so rather than keep him waiting, we met with him. A few minutes into the meeting, Tommy said, 'My next-door neighbor, a Kodak district representative, is a sport balloon pilot who sold his balloon last year. He asked me if I'd like to go partners with him on a new one. I told him I didn't have an interest, but my new bosses might.'

"Having just visualized a hot air balloon with RE/MAX on it while I was in my car, I immediately said, 'Yes! We will absolutely do it.' Darrel gave me one of those looks and said, 'What are you talking about?' I said, 'I can't believe this is happening,' and I told them about what I had just seen in the sky and my visualization about it.

"Back in those days, the RE/MAX logo was the red, white, and blue yard sign," Echols continues. 'Can't you just see this hot air balloon up there with red, white, and blue and RE/MAX right in the middle?' I paused and added, 'Just picture a seven-story-high hot air balloon soaring overhead in the company's colors with the name on it. We have to do this. Even if nobody else in the company likes it, we'll fly it in the fiesta every October. We can always use it for promotions here in New Mexico where hot air balloons are so popular.'"

"Let's go for it," Stilwell and Thompson said in unison.

By October, the balloon fiesta was underway, and a RE/MAX hot air balloon was up, up, and away with more than 1,000 others soaring high above in the sky. The fiesta started each morning at sunup when all the balloons do a mass ascension and compete in different events. More than one million people attended throughout the 10-day happening. The 1978 fiesta was sponsored by Kodak and hailed as the second-most-photographed event in the world right behind the Rose Bowl Parade. Echols and Stilwell had left the fiesta a few days before it ended to attend a RE/MAX meeting of regional managers that was held at the Marriott O'Hara International Airport.

"We showed a film of our seven-story-tall balloon with the RE/MAX name on it," Echols tells. "The other managers cheered and yelled when they saw it, but that wasn't anything so unusual. They reacted the same way about practically anything with our name on it. After the film was shown, Dave [Liniger] was the only one who was not excited about it. He told us that we could use it in Albuquerque as a promotional tool, but it wasn't for RE/MAX. After the meeting ended, we all went to the hotel bar to have a drink. Dave always picked up the tab, and always a perfect host, he would go back and forth to the bar retrieving drinks to our table. While waiting for the bartender to fill his order, Dave watched *The Dinah Shore Show* being broadcast live from the Albuquerque balloon fiesta. During every commercial break, the cameras showed a full view of the RE/MAX balloon.

"Dave came running back to the table shouting, 'Come here, look, you've got to see what's on TV.' All of us rushed to the bar, and again at the commercial break, our seven-story-high RE/MAX balloon was shown on national television. Again, our guys went wild, high-fiving and screaming. I just kept quiet and didn't say a word. A few months later, the company decided to show the balloon in a commercial in Denver, and it wasn't long before RE/MAX was the most recognizable real estate name in Denver. 'Above the Crowd' was the byline, and that says it all."

In 1977, RE/MAX became the top-selling real estate firm in Denver, but when a survey was taken, it showed that the general population ranked RE/MAX in the number eight spot. With a budget of $150,000, enough to cover the cost of paying for airtime, there was little left for its production costs, so Dave Liniger volunteered to stand in front of a RE/MAX sign and say, "We're number one in Denver. Buy from RE/MAX."

"Nobody liked the idea, and neither did I," Echols says, "so we decided to shoot an image of the balloon in the sky with a voiceover saying, 'RE/MAX is number one in Denver,' and another voiceover saying, 'Above the Crowd.' We made this ad for $5,000, and when we did our yearly survey a couple of weeks later, we moved up from the eighth best-known firm to the number one best-known firm in town. That was from just one TV campaign!"

It wasn't long afterward that the RE/MAX hot air balloon appeared on all yard signs, stationary, business cards, company newsletters, and wherever else anyone saw the company's name. There are 123 hot air balloons in the RE/MAX fleet today, and each one averages about 100 appearances a year. It's estimated that each time it's either tethered or in flight, an estimated 50,000 people see the balloon.

To date, more than $6 billion has been spent on the RE/MAX brand. According to Mike Reagan, the company's senior vice president of brand marketing, there are an estimated 14 billion impressions generated that show the RE/MAX brand—this includes everything ranging from yard signs and letterheads to the company's Internet publication and TV commercials. For example, Reagan points out that there is an audience of millions of viewers watching *NFL Sunday Night Football* that carries a RE/MAX commercial.

"Our brand is our most valuable asset," Reagan asserts. "Unlike how difficult it was for the company to recruit new agents when it was first launched back in the 1970s, we can look someone right in the eye and say, 'When you pick up the phone and identify yourself as an agent with RE/MAX, the person may not know who you are but he or she will know who RE/MAX is. This is true with any consumer you call. So other than the fact that the brand is working for you 24 hours a day, seven days a week, it allows you to start on day one and be able to take advantage of more than three decades of brand awareness.'"

In an ARG survey, *64.3% of Americans recognize the RE/MAX brand*. Based on previous studies, any brand that scores over 40% is a winner. This same survey revealed that *45.9% of all people think of RE/MAX whenever they see a hot air balloon*. This is a remarkable statistic and shows how well the company has done in building consumer awareness of its logo. Perhaps only the Goodyear blimp would score higher in brand association if consumers were to be asked if they think of Goodyear when they see a blimp. But, then, we seldom see a blimp in the sky compared to how many hot air balloons are up there.

Doing Good Is Good Business

As we anticipated prior to conducting our research for this book, all of the companies featured in this book are outstanding corporate citizens. Our assumption was correct: companies that care for their employees and customers also care about their communities. They willingly give to worthy charities and support their communities. They encourage their employees to be involved and allow them to serve civic and charitable organizations on company time. Their giving includes financial contributions, volunteer time, and taking leadership roles. They view giving as a responsibility, and they give willingly—during good times and bad times.

The grandson of Johnson & Johnson's founder, Robert Wood Johnson, wrote the company credo in 1944 that established the company's priorities. In addition to serving customers, it included another responsibility: *We are responsible to the communities in which we live and work and to the world community as well. We must be good citizens—support good works and charities.* Johnson's commitment to do good is evidenced by his leaving the bulk of his estate, a sum of $400 million when he died in 1968, to create the Robert Wood Johnson Foundation. Its mission is to improve the health and health care of all Americans. At present, the Robert Wood Johnson Foundation is the fourth largest foundation in the United States with more than $9 billion in assets. Operated as an independent organization, the foundation in 2006 contributed $403 million to different health-related projects and programs. Johnson's legacy of giving lives on at J&J. The people there are on a mission to make this a better world, and that's what they are doing on and off the job.

The other companies featured in this book are relatively new companies in comparison to J&J and Chubb, which both have roots going back to the late 1800s. All are involved in giving back to the community. We won't attempt to tell all the good deeds these companies do—that would require a separate book, but we will mention a few of their good deeds that we find of interest.

RE/MAX's founders Gail and Dave Liniger bought 221 acres of grassy, hilly ranch land just 15 minutes outside of Denver that's surrounded by 4,000 government-owned acres of open space land, surrounded by majestic mountains. The Linigers originally bought the land to raise Arabian horses but then changed their minds and built a Professional Golf Association quality golf course. It's called The Sanctuary, and *Golf Digest* called it "the best private course in America." Neither Gail nor Dave played golf until after they bought the land, and they're both so busy that they rarely take in a round. The course is used exclusively for charitable fund-raisers and top relocation agents. All fund-raising proceeds go to the charities and their beneficiaries. The Linigers also created and built a wildlife conversation museum that's located 10 miles south of Denver and opened in 2002. The 110,000-square-foot museum houses an extensive collection of natural history exhibits, paintings and sculpture, photography, and large-format films. Its mission is to instill respect for habitat and wildlife and inspire efforts to conserve for future generations. Also a nonprofit organization, it is used to host fund-raising events. It is open to the general public and invites children and adults to participate in art and conversation classes. It is also a popular destination for school tours in Colorado. It has 200,000 visitors each year.

In 2005, Liniger organized a group of people to fly with him to visit the Walter Reed National Military Medical Center in Bethesda, Maryland. Accompanying Liniger were five Denver Broncos players—quarterback Jake Plummer and cornerback Champ Bailey, and three other team superstars—plus four Bronco cheerleaders who also volunteered for the trip. They spent a day talking to soldiers disabled in the Iraq war. Realizing there was so much to do to help severely injured soldiers in their adjustment to life after their discharge from the military, Liniger decided to do something about it. "We wanted to help amputees get on with their lives," he explains. "We hear the numbers of the military who are killed in Iraq, but there's not enough being said about the amputees. So what could we do for them to fill a void? Well, we could raise funds to help a vet have his house customized so it's wheelchair accessible. We could see to it that a vehicle was equipped for a handicapped person. We could work with local colleges to have them waive fees for a vet's education. There are lots we can do. With the contacts that RE/MAX has with builders, we could get them involved too. We also have 700 offices that are run by ex-military people, so I knew a lot of them would come on board. We made a commitment to be the primary sponsor. We're calling it Sentinels of Freedom. We're not going to put the RE/MAX name on it because we want hundreds of other companies to get involved. With our network of brokers across America, we have the ability take this national relatively fast and that's what we plan to do."

RE/MAX is also a major player in two other charities that Liniger says he and his wife have a passion for. "We are big supporters in the fight against breast cancer," he tells. "During the past few years, we've had our share of RE/MAX people diagnosed with breast cancer, including our president, Margaret Kelly, who is our CEO. Another pet project of ours is Children's Miracle Network, a wonderful organization that serves children's hospitals across the United States and Canada and, in turn, benefits more than 17 million children. One month each year, our agents pledge x amount of dollars out of every closing they have that goes to Children's Miracle Network. So far, we've raised more than $70 million for Children's Miracle Network, and we anticipate raising considerably more."

* * *

NetJets' CEO Richard Santulli serves as the board chairman of Intrepid Fallen Heroes Fund, a not-for-profit organization dedicated to honoring and supporting the men and women in our military who serve in defense of our nation. Santulli became involved shortly after the September 11, 2001, attacks. Under his leadership, $60 million in funds have been raised to build a state-of-the-art 60,000-square-foot physical rehabilitation center at Brooke Army Medical Center in San Antonio, Texas, that was completed in early 2007. The "Center for the Intrepid" serves military personnel who have been catastrophically disabled in operations in Iraq and Afghanistan, and veterans severely injured in other operations and in the normal performance of their duties. Benefits are also provided to needy widows and children of troops. For instance, many of these families receive financial support to help them bridge the gap when they vacate the military base to move elsewhere.

NetJets encourages its people to be actively involved in their communities. "We support their efforts," Santulli explains. "For example, each salesperson can donate to two charitable or civic groups every year by having x number of hours auctioned at fund-raising events. Our only stipulations are that they must do this in conjunction with our customers and the proceeds must go to a worthy charity."

✳ ✳ ✳

While we highlight what Johnson & Johnson, RE/MAX, and NetJets are doing, all of the companies featured in this book are actively involved in giving back in their communities. Giving is deeply ingrained in their corporate culture. What's more, they care. In St. Louis, for example, World Wide Technology's founder and chairman, Dave Steward, is the current chairman of the United Way (UW) board. Edward Jones' former managing partner John Bachmann had chaired the UW board in St. Louis, and current managing partner Jim Weddle is on schedule to serve as its chairman. Dave Steward, a devout Christian, has tithed throughout his business career, and so does Tom James' Jim McEachern. Mary Kay Ash was an early supporter of breast cancer research. That giving is formalized today through the Mary Kay Ash Charitable Foundation, whose outreach is cancers affecting women and domestic violence prevention. Even though it is a privately held, family-owned company and its size pales in comparison to some of the Fortune 500 companies headquartered in Dallas, a 2007 ranking by the *Dallas Business Journal* found Mary Kay number two on the corporate philanthropy list that included such corporate giants as Texas Instruments, Exxon Mobil, Bank of America, and JPMorgan Chase. Mary Kay CEO David Holl says giving is part of the company's DNA. Companies like these consider it a blessing to give, and their giving spirit has spilled over to others. Cabela's is by far the biggest employer in Sidney, Nebraska, and in this capacity, is the town's biggest benefactor in making it a better place to live. RE/MAX encourages its 120,000 agents to support their local communities, and they are active participants in many good causes ranging from Little League to the Susan G. Koman Find the Cure breast cancer organization. Likewise, Four Seasons people are doing their part wherever the company has hotels and resorts, and the same is true of Lexus dealers across the country. A high percentage of Chubb insurance agents are leaders in their community, and Caesars Entertainment people are involved in the hometowns where their casinos are located. Mary Kay independent sales force members throughout the world are actively giving back in their communities—from a Georgia trail ride to benefit the Mary Kay Ash Charitable Foundation's cancer outreach to a California professional hockey team's "Pink at the Rink" that benefits the foundation's domestic violence prevention programs.

We stated earlier that great brands are synonymous with a company's reputation, which is about trust. An ARG survey report recounts that *78% of Americans trust a company that is active in the community. And 53% said they would drive 10 minutes out of their way to buy from a retailer with a good reputation for serving the community. And 68% said they are willing to pay more for a product associated with a good cause.* As we say, doing good is good business.

A Source of Pride

People feel good about themselves when they are either customers or employees for a company known for being the best in its class in its industry. As a Johnson & Johnson employee told us, "It's like the pride a player had who played for the New York Yankees back in the '50s. Being in Yankee pinstripes meant that you were playing for the world's best baseball team. That's what it's like working for J&J."

Chuck Smock, who works in corporate communications at Cabela's, knows the feeling. "I was in Oregon on a fishing trip, and I was wearing my Cabela's cap," he tells. "This huge man who also was wearing a Cabela's hat was at the fish-cleaning station expertly taking apart a halibut with a 12-inch filet knife. When I walked past him, he stopped and pointed the knife at me. I stopped dead in my tracks. Then he spoke, 'Hey man, I like your hat.' 'I like yours too,' I replied. 'Where'd you get it?' he asked. 'I work for Cabela's at the corporate headquarters in Sidney, Nebraska.' He smiled, looked me straight in the eye, and said, 'I love you, man.' He was still pointing the knife at me, but I couldn't help but laugh. And then I thanked him for being a Cabela's customer."

In 2004, Cabela's started sending a special edition of a hardcover catalog to its VIP customers. An estimated 300,000 customers receive this singular publication that's mailed once every spring and again in the autumn. A customer is given VIP status based primarily on the dollar amount of his or her purchases and on frequency of orders. "It's really a beautiful book," Ron Spath, vice president of customer relations, explains, "and some of our customers place it on their coffee tables in the family room. Some people take it to work, and in fact, one customer sent a letter to me saying, 'So many of the guys in my office want to borrow it that my secretary has them sign in for it. This way it gets returned.' Because it's a limited edition, there's a certain amount of pride people take in receiving one."

When Mike Reagan's wife, Cinda, was working on a Habitat for Humanity house in Argentina, he wanted her to have a contact in Argentina. "I called a RE/MAX couple that has an office there," he tells, "and their first response was, 'She's welcome to stay with us at our home, and we'll meet her at the airport to make sure her travels are safe.' I think any RE/MAX associate could walk into one of our offices anywhere in the 65 countries where we are, and he or she would receive a warm greeting. All he'd have to do would be to go online to our Web roster and find a RE/MAX person wherever he or she was going."

Barbara Talbott has a favorite story about the time she was going through U.S. customs in Toronto. "When asked by the customs officer my reason for traveling to the U.S., I replied, 'I have several meetings to attend with the hotel I work for.' 'Which hotel do you work for?' he asked. Generally, there are no questions asked, and I was a bit apprehensive. 'Four Seasons,' I answered. 'Four Seasons! That's my favorite. Whenever my wife and I have a really special occasion, that's where we always go,' he said. I know it was just a little thing, but his comment made my day."

Our favorite story about branding was the one about a Chubb agent in Westchester County in New York that Mark Korsgaard, senior vice president, worldwide casualty claim manager, told us. "A second-generation Chubb agent came home for dinner, and when his wife asked about his day, he told her about being with a client who owned the local bookstore that had burned down. The couple's eight-year-old son was doing his homework and didn't seem as if he was listening. Then without even looking up, he said, 'I hope they have Chubb.' The agent told me, 'It was as if we were in a TV commercial.' What a message, I thought to myself, when a child understands that service makes a difference and that the company providing it makes a difference. Wow, there is something special about the Chubb brand."

✳ ✳ ✳

While it is hard to quantify on a financial statement, there is definitely a value to be placed on employees' pride in their company. It's an intangible quality that permeates an organization and carries over to the customer. One of the best ways to instill this pride in your people is by giving back to the community. It also instills trust in the customer. An ARG study reveals that *78% of consumers state that they trust a company that is actively involved in the community.*

13

The Value of a Customer

Making the first sale is only a starting point. When a customer is revered and pampered, revenues generated from repeat orders will far exceed the initial order. But when customers are neglected, they don't come back and more money must be spent to attract new customers.

This point is made clear by comparing shoppers from the 1950s with today's shoppers. Back then, the majority of Americans were highly loyal to their neighborhood and downtown stores on Main Street. It was a time when the store was usually owned by the person who operated it, and the owner had a personal relationship with his customers. The owner was a neighbor, fellow church member, an old school buddy, or perhaps a friend of a friend. Everyone knew that if something went wrong, he'd fix it. His word was his bond. As a consequence, retailers only put 1% of their sales into advertising. The ad's message was to tell customers of new arrivals of merchandise in their stores. The ad was informational about new products or about the retailer itself.

Today's retailer budgets from 6% to 12% for advertising. The 1950s' retailers didn't have to advertise what makes their stores a good place to shop because their customers already knew, and they'd tell others about it. So they only advertised occasionally to remind people that their stores were great places to shop so "come on in and visit us." Their advertising worked because their customers trusted them.

When today's retailer sends out the same advertising message, there is little or no response. That's because nobody believes it. "Anyone can say that about themselves," consumers say, "but when I was in there last time, they didn't do it." As a result, retailers have increased their advertising budgets up to tenfold so they can inform customers that an event such as a big sale or clearance sale is going on. They are getting hit with a double whammy. Their margins are down because they are spending five times as much to advertise, and when people do shop their store, they are buying merchandise at reduced prices. Following 9/11, hotels around the world offered large discounts to attract guests; an exception was Four Seasons. As we previously discussed, Isadore Sharp, chairman and CEO, didn't reduce room rates because he knew that price was never why people stayed at Four Seasons. Companies like Four Seasons that provide exceptional value can charge a premium for their goods. Their customers are willing to pay more for outstanding service. A company with a reputation for excellent service develops a large following of loyal customers; in addition, it is more likely to be a profitable business. This is true because its base of dedicated customers represents a valued asset. As you will see in this chapter, they are "money in the bank."

A Lincoln-Mercury dealer told us how he once calculated that his dealership spent an average of $100 on advertising and promotion for each potential customer that walked into his showroom. "With a closing rate of 25%, we're spending $400 on advertising and promotion on every car we sell," he determined. When he looked at it this way, he realized how much he was losing from the customers that didn't come back. This thinking led him to stop putting all of his dealership's efforts into making initial car sales and to focus on increasing customer satisfaction.

An ARG study showed that *63% of new car owners do not go back to the same dealership to buy their next car*. When advertising and promotional costs are factored in, just imagine how this affects the bottom line. The same study reported that *of the 40% who did come back, 56.3% of them never shopped at another dealership*. Exceptional service will vastly improve these numbers. Having owned a Toyota dealership in Orange County, California, for 25 years, Dave Wilson says, "Even when I factor in media inflation, I'm now spending about half as much money on my monthly advertising. Why? Our dealership has 70% of the people coming back to buy their second, third, fourth, tenth, or fifteenth car. Talk about dropping to the bottom line. It costs a whole lot less to sell a car the second time and the fifteenth time around."

Here's an interesting bit we gathered from our research: *35.5% of Americans were dissatisfied with a real estate agent because they felt she failed to do her homework.* By not doing her homework, we're talking about such things as not having the comparable prices on other homes recently sold in the area, not doing a walk-through prior to showing it, not knowing information about the school system, the community, and so on. The walk-through takes about one hour, and all the other pertinent information can be obtained online in an hour or less. When it's broken down to a couple of hours, the cost of being prepared as compared to the lost commissions makes it an easy choice. It appalls us when we hear about real estate agents neglecting to do their homework. Sadly, a high percentage of them falls into this category as does a like number of so-called sales professionals in other fields.

Every company can come up with a similar formula to determine its "acquisition cost" of a new customer. A successful stockbroker told us that during his first two years in the business, he made 100 cold calls a day, and at the end of the week, he averaged two new clients. When he calculated the cost in both time and money to make 500 cold calls, he realized how expensive it was to obtain clients. "The first orders were averaging 200 shares, and as I built a relationship with my clients, the size of their orders increased. Many clients had accounts with other brokers, and when I earned their trust, they transferred funds to their accounts with my firm. Knowing the time and energy it takes to open a new account, I can't afford to lose a single client as a result of poor service. It's a given that there will be a certain amount of natural attrition due to death, bankruptcy, or maybe it's a son-in-law who comes into the business. Today, for everyone I lose, I pick up 10 more that are referred to me by satisfied clients."

The true value of a customer isn't the revenue made on the first sale. If the customer is treated right, the first sale will be just the beginning. A real estate agent who sells a $500,000 home to a young couple must look at their long-term potential. Over the years, if they receive outstanding service, they could be the source of millions of dollars. Pulte Homes has satisfied customers that have bought many homes from the company over the past 40 years. Those same loyal customers have recommended the company to their friends and relatives.

According to ARG research, *73.8% of Americans who have bought more than one home in the same area where they live used the same real estate agent again.* This substantiates that satisfied homeowners remain loyal to brokers who took good care of them. Hard work is required to establish one's reputation as a top real estate agent, and it takes time to prove one's self. However, over the years, satisfied customers move to more expensive homes and they are loyal to the agent who earned their trust on a former transaction. They also recommend their agent to friends and relatives who move into the community. And they talk about their good experience with their neighbors. The high turnover of salespeople in the real estate industry is directly related to the lack of repeat business and referrals by satisfied customers.

How well great service companies understand the value of their customers. At Starbucks, a customer represents more than a single cup of coffee. The company is successful because loyal customers come to Starbucks every day—sometimes even more than once a day, week after week. If satisfied customers didn't come back, the company would not be opening stores in the same office buildings and across the street from other Starbucks across the United States and around the world.

Every successful company is built on the premise that loyal customers will buy again. A young married couple that buys a sofa from Ashley Furniture has the potential to buy several housefuls of furniture over their lifetime. Four Seasons doesn't view a guest who stays in a $500 room for two nights as a $1,000 customer. That's because Four Seasons isn't interested in having one-night stands with its customers. It wants to establish long-term relationships with its guests so they will visit again and again.

An ARG study asked Americans *if they'd go back to a restaurant that had great food but poor service: 40.6% said they would; 45.2% would not.* The same survey asked what they'd do *if the food was poor but the service was great. This time 82% would not go back.* This study tells us that if the product is exceptional, half the people will endure poor service, but with a poor quality product, you'll lose 82% of your customers. While it's true that more people may tolerate poor service in comparison to a shabby product, either way, if a business comes up short in either area, it is just a matter of time before it is dead in the water.

The Law of Recurring Revenues

In the world of mergers and acquisitions, a key consideration in determining the value of a target company is to evaluate its earnings before interest, taxes, depreciation, and amortization, also known as EBITDA in business circles. To forecast EBITDA, a company's future revenues are assessed by projecting how much business its current customers will generate in addition to new sales. Again, we point out that there is an acquisition cost to put a new customer on the books that is not incurred with an existing customer. Some companies have high acquisition costs to initially open a new account, but after the sale, they can depend on their customers to send in regular payments for long periods of time. For instance, a high percentage of people make payments on the anniversary of the first year and subsequent years to renew their life insurance policies. So while a life insurance company initially incurs heavy expenses to cover high first-year commissions and underwriting costs, these expenditures are not repeated when premium notices are forwarded to policyholders. Other companies such as magazines and newspapers also have recurring revenues. So do pharmaceutical companies. Once a medicine is prescribed, a patient is likely to take it for a long period of time, in some cases for the rest of his or her life. Then too, we pay for cable television, telephone services, and Internet services, all of which generate recurring revenues to the providers of these services. These are competitive industries that require up-front investments to sign up customers. Utility companies also have recurring revenues, but unlike the above-mentioned companies, water, gas, and electric companies have little or no competition.

We spoke to Bill Bresnan, one of the cable television industry's most respected leaders. In 1958, at age 25, Bresnan entered the business when he designed and built a cable system in Rochester, Minnesota. In 1965, Jack Kent Cooke bought the Rochester cable system and hired Bresnan as vice president of engineering. Cooke was one of the cable industry's early pioneers and one of America's highest profile sports entrepreneurs who, at the time, owned the Washington Redskins and, later, the Los Angeles Lakers and L.A. Kings. He also made regular appearances on the Forbes 400 Richest Americans list. In 1968 Cooke merged his company with H&B American Corporation to form the nation's largest cable television company, a firm that then was merged into Teleprompter Corporation in 1970. Later, Bresnan was named the company's president. In 1981, Westinghouse Broadcasting purchased Teleprompter and Bresnan was named CEO of Group W Cable. In 1984, he started his own company, Bresnan Communications, partnering with John Malone, another cable industry giant.

Headquartered in Purchase, New York, 25 minutes from Bresnan's home in Greenwich, Connecticut, the company served 690,000 customers in 540 communities in Michigan, Minnesota, Nebraska, and Wisconsin. In another venture, Bresnan co-owned and operated cable television systems in Poland and Chile, each serving approximately 330,000 subscribers. The two foreign cable systems were sold in the late 1990s. In 2000, Bresnan Communications was acquired by Charter Communications, a company owned by Paul Allen, cofounder with Bill Gates of Microsoft. Charter paid $3.1 billion.

When we asked Bresnan how the $3.1 billion purchase price was determined, he talked about the law of recurring revenues. "Customers are very valuable," he explains, "and recurring income is what everyone wants. We have no long-term contracts with our customers. They make decisions month to month on whether they are going to stay with our services. In fact, they can disconnect during the month and get a prorated refund for that month. There is competition out there, so an unhappy customer can drop one video provider and replace it with another. This is a service business, and to retain customers, we must excel in servicing our customers.

"In the cable business, new customers are costly in terms of marketing and installation expenditures to hook up their service. What you don't want in our business is what we call 'churn.' That's when a customer hooks up, disconnects, another hooks up, disconnects, and so on. When this happens, in addition to the high initial costs to get a new customer on the books, there are lost revenues. A way to determine what to pay for a cable system company is to place a value on its average subscriber. A buyer will pay a premium for a company with a low churn rate. When we sold the company to Paul Allen in 2000, we got a high price at that time, which was $4,500 per subscriber."

In the late 1990s, Microsoft's cofounder and multibillionaire Paul Allen had a vision that a high percentage of commerce and banking would be transacted over the Internet and the transition would occur quickly. Allen visualized what would be a "last big buffalo hunt," and his vision prompted him to invest large sums of money in buying up video providers, and he was willing to pay a premium to acquire strong companies. Bresnan Communications had a low churn rate.

The acquisition price was based on an average customer paying approximately $36 in monthly fees that included services other than cable television because packages are available that bundle cable, Internet, and telephone services (home-based telephones and cell phones) for a flat monthly fee. The combined package represents a significant savings versus purchasing the same services individually from different providers. The total sales price of a cable company is based on calculating what the average customer pays and for how long he or she pays. The expenses run approximately 60%, so the monthly cash flow on $36 is $14.40 per month, or $173 in annual cash flow for each customer. Since the average acquisition price per cable customer is 10 to 12 times cash flow, Allen was willing to pay a high premium over the $2,100-per-customer value (at 12 times cash flow) that Bresnan Communications would likely have gone for. However Allen was making a strategic investment versus what was going on in the marketplace at the time. Some cable industry experts have said that Allen was willing to overspend so that he could establish a strong foothold in the industry in order to place his flags in many markets in order to reap future profits.

At the time, Bill Bresnan had no interest in selling his business, but he did have a responsibility to his partners to discuss Allen's high offer. "We listened to his offer and agreed to bring in Goldman Sachs to serve as our investment banker," says Bresnan. "Allen originally offered $3,900, but we were not anxious to sell. But when the offer was raised to $4,500, we finally agreed to sell our company."

Many factors are considered in determining the price per customer. Obviously the demographics come into play. For example, in an affluent community, customers sign up for bigger packages that include options such as high-speed Internet and video on demand. High-income subscribers are less likely to discontinue their services. And like in any business, there are bad debts. In high-income areas, there are fewer people living beyond their means. Customers who don't make their payments have their service disconnected. Bresnan points out that the sale of a cable company in Princeton, New Jersey, fetched $6,000 per customer. "Princeton is a high demographic market," he tells.

A customer-focused cable company will have a low churn and consequently a higher value per customer. Bresnan Communications has long been known in the industry as a company that takes good care of its customers; this reputation earned it a high price. "We always provided on-time service," Bresnan explains. "When a customer signed up, we'd guarantee to install service within a two- to four-hour window. In some of the more rural areas way out in the mountains, we couldn't do this, but we did in urban areas. If we arrived late, there was no charge for the installation, and if it was a service call, we'd give them a $30 credit that was applied to their monthly fee. People don't like to sit around all day waiting for their cable guy, so they really appreciated our prompt service. We had service people scattered throughout the state, and this enabled us to have somebody there sooner rather than later. Some cable companies put on less manpower to lower their overhead. We never cut corners that would lessen customer service. We also had training programs for our technicians on courteousness. For example, we instructed them to take off their shoes before entering a customer's house, and they never left a mess.

They were equipped with portable vacuums to clean up the plaster if a hole was drilled in the wall. We also empowered our customer service reps to make adjustments on the spot in the field. Of course, there were certain perimeters, but we gave them a lot of leeway. If a customer didn't feel as though he'd been treated right, the rep could do what he thought was right to solve a problem. Employees become frustrated when they have to run to a supervisor for permission to fix a minor issue and then have to tell the customer, 'I'm sorry but the boss says we can't do a thing.'"

The service that Bresnan Communications provided to its customers in Poland in comparison to what the Poles were used to under communist rule was viewed as simply unbelievable. "We'd install their service within a week after receiving their order," Bresnan tells. "Prior to the uprising in '89 there were horror stories about people who had to make no-interest deposits on a telephone and waited 20 years for it to be installed. The deposit was equivalent to 100 U.S. dollars, a lot of money to millions of poor people in Poland. Under communist rule, when a Polish customer received a phone bill, there was no itemization for long-distance calls. The invoice would only list the total charges. If a customer had a complaint, there was nothing he could do; if he didn't pay the bill, the service was disconnected. There were only two channels of TV service. In the mid-1990s, when we moved in, we offered 60 channels and later added more channels. In many South American countries, citizens often pay under the table to get the telephone company to install phone service. Otherwise, they must wait for months or even years."

After selling his company to Charter, Bill Bresnan, a youthful, energetic man, wasn't interested in retirement. In 2003, operating under the name Bresnan Communications, he headed a group that purchased a cable systems company that services 317,000 subscribers in 197 communities in Colorado, Montana, and Wyoming. The company's revenues are now running more than $400 per customer annually, with a cash flow of an estimated $200. In addition to providing the "triple-play" services (cable, Internet, and telephone), the new company offers commercial phone services to businesses and institutions. Included are high-speed data transmissions to commercial customers such as service stations and fast-food chains. "It's all about saving time for the hurried consumer," Bresnan tells. "Instead of waiting 10 to 20 seconds for your credit card to be approved at the pump, it takes a second with us. You get the same instant credit card approval at a McDonald's. While saving 10 to 20 seconds might not seem like much time, it is when you're standing in line behind several customers." With Bresnan operating his new company with the same intensity of focus on customer service, Bresnan Communications is gaining market share in the mountain states.

✳ ✳ ✳

A catalog company is able to determine the value of its customers in the same way as a cable TV company can. For example, a well-run catalog company will have proven formulas that can predict with reasonable accuracy how much monthly revenues a catalog mailing will generate. Here, too, by analyzing repeat orders that one anticipates loyal customers to place based on past catalog mailings, a value can be determined on an individual customer as well as the entire company. "We have data available today," Cabela's chief financial officer, Ralph Castner, explains, "that tells us what a customer is worth based upon his past catalog orders."

"We have statisticians who measure the long-term value of customers," Dennis Highby, Cabela's CEO, adds, "and knowing their value reminds us to keep treating them like gold because they are so hard to get and we can't afford to lose them. It's very expensive to replace somebody who has been loyal."

We Are Family

When visiting NetJets, you become aware of a sense of family in the way the people there feel about each other. Again, we get back to the culture of a company; it starts with how its leaders treat subordinates, and the attitude permeates throughout the organization and out the door to the customer. "When you see the way Richard [Santulli] treats the employees, there is very much a family feeling," Jim Christiansen, NetJets' president, emphasizes. "He's compassionate and always looks out for our people. It's been this way when we were a small company, and even with nearly 7,000 employees worldwide and growing, it's still this way. This is important to Richard, and he is very focused on it.

"He is very supportive of the people who work in this organization, and he empowers everyone by telling them, 'Just do the right thing.' We're in the service business, and we will do whatever it takes to serve our customers. We will jump through hoops. But, at the same time, we expect our customers to treat our people with respect. It doesn't happen often, but when a customer abuses our people, we will ask him to leave the program.

A couple of months ago this happened when someone called in and was absolutely abusive to one of our people. Our people don't deserve to be treated this way. It's the family aspect. People can become frustrated, and we're not perfect. But everyone should be treated with respect. With this particular individual, we didn't ask Richard if we could fire this customer. But we did. We told Richard about it afterward, and his comment was, 'What took you so long?' as if he were saying, 'Why are you asking me?' We treat our customers with respect, but when an owner doesn't fit in the NetJets family we say something like, 'It's obvious that this isn't going to work out.' It's only happened a few times in the history of our company, but it's something that Richard will back us up on. He'll just say, 'It's okay. This is not the kind of person we want in the program.'

"We've had some customers over the years that have pushed our crews," Christiansen continues, "and this is a problem you have in private aviation. A guy gets on, he owns the airplane, and he demands, 'Hey, I own this airplane, let's go fly.' The captain is nervous and so is the crew. We've heard about many tragedies over the years that have happened due to that. We have excellent buffers here on several levels. One is the safety culture, and two is the knowledge that Richard will support people for upholding safety. He often tells us, 'I have no problem with dealing with an owner who is upset because one of you has followed the safety rules.'"

"Our owners trust us with their lives," explains Matt Harris, executive vice president of owner and employee services. "We take that responsibility very seriously, and that's something that's nonnegotiable." He pauses briefly and adds, "We talk a lot about family here with our employees, but we also talk a lot about it with our customers. That's because we feel they are family. It's not just a contrived phrase when a customer signs a contract with NetJets and we say, 'Welcome to the family.'"

From Tiny Acorns Mighty Oaks Grow

In Chapter 10, we discussed why customers are not treated equally. World Wide Technology's founder and chairman, Dave Steward, thinks differently. As far as he's concerned, he treats every customer equally. "I've visited small clients that do very little business with us," Steward maintains, "and appeared to have very little potential to be a big client. But guess what? These small companies can say some wonderful things about us in the marketplace that can result in a lot of business. Simply put, you don't know who your small customers know. Nor for that matter, can you really know for sure how big a small company may someday become. Sure, we spend a tremendous amount of time with our large clients, but it doesn't take away from the fact that we treat our small clients with the same honor and respect as we do with a $500 million customer.

"I remember how we were treated by some companies when we were in our infancy. There were people that wouldn't give me the time of day. Then there were others who couldn't have been nicer. Well, when you do become bigger, these are things you never forget when you're in a position to place a big order. You're definitely going to go out of your way to do business with those people. There's a story about how Coca-Cola wouldn't sell to Bill Marriott when he opened his first hotel. They were worried about his credit. But Pepsi was willing to take a chance. As a result, when Marriott became one of the world's largest hotel chains, it remained loyal to Pepsi. The scriptures tell us to be faithful with a little and the Lord will bless you with much.

"It takes patience, and sometimes years of it before a door opens with a customer," Steward continues. "Enterprise Leasing is right here in our backyard in St. Louis, and for years I've been good friends with Andrew Taylor, the company's chairman and CEO. Ever since our first year in business, we've tried to do some business with Enterprise. Well, we just recently got a $75,000 order from the company. We're excited and hope it's just the beginning. One of our biggest clients today is AT&T, but it took years before we received an order from them. And it took us seven years before we did business with the State of Missouri—they were doing business with GE out of Tennessee. It didn't matter that we were based in Missouri and a company that was employing Missourians and paying taxes to the state. Nor did it matter that we were supporting the governor and other politicians in Missouri. But when GE was unable to deliver certain solutions to the state, a door opened for us to come in and we were right there. That's because we were persistent, and even though we weren't doing business with the state, we wanted to keep in their faces. Over the years, I've learned that there are times when you don't think you're making any progress, but when you keep yourself in front of people, and they become aware of your passion and commitment, they start to think, 'He keeps coming back, and I keep saying no, but he's adamant about how he can improve the way we are doing things.' It took us somewhere between five to seven years to get some business from the state, and we've had the account now for about seven years. It's about a $70 million account today."

✳ ✳ ✳

Richard Santulli, CEO, recalls the difficult times that NetJets had in 1989 to 1991. "That's when we lost $40 million in three years. I was going broke. It looked like I was done. That was it. Then there was Joe, a gas and oil vendor who stuck by us back then. Today, we're paying him 10 cents more than what everybody else charges for fuel. 'Hey, Rich, why are you doing business with Joe?' I'm sometimes asked. They think I must be married to his daughter. I tell them, 'For three months, I didn't have to pay Joe for fuel. Other vendors wouldn't give me any credit—I had to give them credit cards. I don't do business with those people today. But I do with Joe.' Joe had compassion and he took a chance with NetJets. He stuck by the company when it was a small account with a few airplanes." Now with a fleet of 700-plus airplanes worldwide operated through its subsidiaries, NetJets is a large account. There's a lesson to be learned here.

✳ ✳ ✳

Jim McEachern, former president of Tom James Clothiers, says that many of his customers started buying a shirt or two on the first call and only after buying several did they buy a suit. Later they bought several suits on a regular yearly basis. "One customer was a young associate at a law firm when I first called on him. He was still paying off college debt and just starting a family, struggling to make payments on their first home. My first sale with him was a pair of pants. I didn't look at him as a $50 or $100 customer. I understood his present situation. I looked at him as the customer he could be over the next 5 to 20 years. He later became a senior partner in the law firm and a big customer. He appreciated how I treated him early in his career and introduced me to many other attorneys over the years. Of course, there are some people who just want to test the waters, so they place a small order the first time and buy larger quantities after they are satisfied with the product. Then there are customers who buy $5,000 to $15,000 of clothes on the first presentation. A 40-year-old man who places an order of this size is a $250,000 customer over the next 25 years. So you have to treat him like a $250,000 customer right from the get-go, not like somebody who bought two or three or four suits."

When McEachern places a value on a satisfied customer, he says that it's not just how much he buys but also the number of people he refers that determines his true value. "One of our salesman's first customers was a lawyer in Dallas," McEachern explains, "who loved our product. We once calculated how many other customers he brought to our salesman. The customer was a grandfather, and his children and their children became

Tom James customers. He also introduced the salesman to some of his friends, clients, and attorneys in his firm. Then we calculated who his referrals referred to him, and we put together what resembled a family tree. There were more than 200 names of customers on it who, in total, placed orders for more than a half million dollars of clothes."

In 1971 when McEachern opened an office in Dallas, there wasn't a single Tom James in the entire state of Texas. Later, in the early 1990s, he made a speech at the CEO Club of Dallas. "There were about 50 CEOs in attendance and after I was introduced, I asked, 'How many of you here today are Tom James customers?' About half of them raised their hands. The same thing happened when I addressed another group of business-people in Fort Worth. And in Abilene, a town of about 110,000, I'd estimate that 75% of the successful business and professional people there are our customers. I can't begin to tell you how this makes me feel. It seems like ages ago when nobody in Texas knew who we were."

You Build a Business with Loyal Customers

"My first full year with Tom James was 1967," McEachern tells, "and my income in 1968 increased by 23%. The following year, it went up more than 60%. By the end of the tenth year, I made more than 10 times what I did in my first year. When I used to recruit new salespeople, I'd show them my production numbers and even my income tax returns. 'If you take good care of your customers,' I'd say, 'you'll enjoy big increases in your earnings every year.' I'd then add, 'I never worked so hard in my life during my first two years in this business, but by the tenth year, I was making 10 times more money with a lot less time and effort than I exerted in the beginning.' The reason my earnings increased and the workload got easier was due to the relationships I built with my customers. In the early years, I had to call on a lot more people to make a sale because I didn't have established accounts that would place steady orders every year. Later I didn't have to make as many cold calls because my satisfied customers referred people to me, and my closing ratio was much higher because they were 'presold' on me. 'Come right in,' they'd say, 'I told Bill Brown how good he looked in his suit, and Bill told me how he bought it from you.' The people referred to me were also informed that I was professional, dependable, and trustworthy. By knowing this in advance, they knew I was a person with integrity. They didn't have to worry about if what I said was too good to be true. There was no worry that I would take their money and run. They knew I would do everything I said I would do. This is why referrals are such excellent leads.

"After being in business for a few years," McEachern continues, "I had a block of business that would order new suits every year. It got even better. As my customers became more successful in their careers, they were able to afford to spend more on my merchandise. I also knew what they had in their wardrobes, so I knew what they needed to add. As a consequence, it didn't take as much time to sell my regular customers, and I was able to see more people each day which also increased my earnings. As my number of customers increased, I was more occupied serving my existing customers with a high percent of them placing orders. While I never lost my desire to add new customers, I had to squeeze them in between appointments with my existing customers. Like I said, my workload got easier and my income kept going up. As an added bonus, I was enjoying my work more than ever."

✳ ✳ ✳

Edward Jones has more than 10,000 offices, and according to John Bachmann, senior partner, the firm's most successful financial advisors all start out the same way. "We expect a new financial advisor to spend 80% of his time out of the office. When he's in the office, he's writing thank you notes, looking up information, and answering questions. By spending the majority of his time out in the field in front of prospects, a time will come, perhaps a year or two later, when a transition occurs. In time he will spend 80% of his time in the office and 20% in the field. However, in the beginning, the only way a financial advisor will build his business is by going out and seeing the people. We want that first contact to be face-to-face so the financial advisor can start building a strong relationship. It doesn't happen over the phone or through the mail."

"This is what the Edward Jones brand stands for," Jim Weddle, managing partner, concurs. "We deliver on the promise, which is having convenient locations, convenient to where you live or work. You will have access to a highly trained professional who is willing and actually anxious to work with you face-to-face on a one-on-one basis. That's what our brand stands for. Our financial advisor wants to be the top-of-the-mind choice for the individual who says, 'I need help with my investing.' If our financial advisor does it right, he will build a foundation and succeed in this industry."

An ARG study shows that *94.9% of Americans chose their financial advisor, insurance agent, and real estate agent based on his or her reputation, and 57.6% said that a personal recommendation by a third party had a strong influence on their decision.*

✳ ✳ ✳

When it comes to underwriting an insurance risk, Chubb's former vice chairman and COO, Tom Motamed, says, "It's like getting married. You want to get it right the first time, because if you go into a second marriage, the first one is going to cost you a lot of money. The key in our business is to serve your customer well because, as industry surveys show, after you've had a client for seven to eight years it's very hard for another agent to take that account away from you."

"If you treat people right," Paul Krump, senior vice president and chief operating officer of Chubb Commercial Insurance, adds, "they will want to insure with you. You want them to stay with you because, clearly, the first acquisition of a client is fairly expensive. For instance, we have a lot of life science customers who roll out new pharmaceutical products and medical devices. Once we've got a relationship with these clients, it's significantly easier to update our underwriting as opposed to starting out fresh. The renewal years should be more profitable once those acquisition costs come out of the picture."

✳ ✳ ✳

"Over the years we've done some great marketing," says Lexus' group vice president and general manager, Mark Templin, "but the company didn't succeed because of our marketing. The company grew and succeeded because the first people that came in and bought a Lexus in 1989 loved the product, and they loved the experience they had at their dealership even more. Those customers went out and told their friends, their family, and their coworkers about us, and those people came in to buy our products. Then those customers told more people about the experience they had. It was the word of mouth that drove Lexus success. The same thing is happening today with young people who are buying the IS 250s, the IS 350s, and the GSs. And now the LX is one of our bestselling models to our youngest customers. People are continuing to tell others about their experience at the dealership—it's not just about the product."

✳ ✳ ✳

RE/MAX's vice president, Gail Liniger, explains that with multiple listings every real estate agent sells the same product. "Our business is all about service," she emphasizes. "If you do a good job, you get referrals and repeat business. This happens when you provide the service and then stay in contact with your customers."

✳ ✳ ✳

If you take good care of your customers, your customers will take care of you. Your reward will be repeat orders and referrals. In time, your business will grow and prosper. If you don't serve your customers well, however, there will be no building process. Each year will be like your first year—you will work relentlessly to open new accounts only to lose them and have to start all over again. Ask anyone who ever succeeded at selling real estate, insurance, or investments. Like Jim McEachern, they will tell you how hard they worked to break into their business, dialing for dollars and making cold calls to make new customers. Those who stuck to it and gave exceptional service succeeded by building a loyal customer base, and they, like McEachern, were soon making more money and taking less time and effort to do it. Those who failed to provide good service generally quit because they eventually burned out from hard work and nothing to show for it. Then there were those who kept spinning their wheels, pounding the pavement without noticeable progress. For the most part, they are the ones that spend a lifetime at jobs they can't stand; waiting for the day when they can retire. We've all known cynical people with chips on their shoulder, thinking the world owes them a living.

As Somerset Maugham said, "The common idea that success spoils people by making them vain, egotistical, and self-complacent is erroneous; on the contrary, it makes them, for the most part, humble, tolerant, and kind. Failure makes them bitter and cruel."

14

Change Is Constant

After Professor Albert Einstein passed out final examination papers to the class, a student asked him, "Dr. Einstein, why are you giving us this test? These are the same questions as last year's exam." "It is true that the questions are the same," the famous scientist replied, "but this year the answers are different."

The answers to ARG survey questions also differ from previous years' responses. In a 1986 ARG study, *44% of Americans said they had all the free time they needed. In 1992, 34% had enough free time, and by 2008, only 19.5% didn't feel a time crunch.* This shortage of time has many ramifications on consumer behavior.

When comparing shopping patterns of consumers making a major purchase such as a large appliance or electronics product, we reviewed ARG research dating back to 1980. By being able to assess a current trend with a 27-year history, we were able to enjoy a rare luxury in the field of consumer research. *In 1980, the American consumer shopped at an average of 3.5 stores. In 1990, 2.8 stores were visited. In 1999, 1.5 stores were visited, and in 2007, only 1.3 stores were visited.* These current numbers reveal that only 40% of American shoppers will even visit a second store. The two prevalent reasons for visiting fewer stores are: (1) the merchandise looks the same, and (2) having a less-than-satisfactory experience in retail stores. The lesson to be learned here emphasizes the importance of making sure you're the first store shopped. Being second means that you're in serious trouble, and being third puts you out of business.

A big change we observed was that 90% of store visits in the 1950s were generated by word of mouth. As we stated earlier, ARG's 2007 research reveals that *only 10% of consumers walk into a store based on word of mouth.* Fifty years ago there was less need to advertise—a company's reputation spoke volumes about what it stood for. With 6% to 12% now being spent on advertising to bring shoppers in the door as compared to a mere 1% in the 1950s, many companies have cut back on many services in an attempt to juice up their bottom line. While these cost-cutting measures may produce temporary short-term profits, over time it's a sure way to dig one's own grave.

Here's an interesting ARG finding: the recent abundance of television advertisements by hospitals has impacted patients' relationships with their doctors. *In 2007, 48% of Americans tell their doctor what hospital they want to be treated in, whereas in 1997, only 22% made the decision on where they wanted to be admitted because they felt their doctor knew best.* This research emphasizes the impact of advertising, which in this case is viewed as detrimental by physicians.

The companies featured in this book have built strong reputations by focusing on taking exceptional good care of their customers; consequently, the word on them spreads from customer to customer. Because customers refer other customers to them, less advertising costs are required. Companies like Tom James and World Wide Technology have virtually no advertising budgets. Nor traditionally has Mary Kay regularly appeared in beauty magazines or television ads, preferring instead to invest those dollars in its independent sales force that, in turn, provide invaluable word-of-mouth advertising. The exception is when there's a major product launch. The company's television ads are so rare that you probably have not seen one. Still, Mary Kay is one of the best-known brands in the United States. Chubb is another company with a relatively small advertising budget, yet it's ranked as the 176th largest company on the Fortune 500 list. Chubb is about the same size as the AFLAC insurance company, which is ranked 164th on the Fortune 500 list. AFLAC is a company with a high profile mainly due to its cheesy duck commercials. With Chubb being one of the most respected companies in the insurance industry, the word has spread among insurance brokers and agents that it ranks among the industry's best.

Embracing Change

Capturing and maintaining high market share requires aggressive marketing strategies. You can't wait to see what your competition is doing and follow the pack. You either lead or get out of the way. And once you attain a certain degree of success, you can't rest on your laurels. Surviving in today's competitive marketplace depends on adapting to constant change—and at times, it requires swift action. As a Japanese proverb tells us, "You can't cross a chasm in two small steps."

When Richard Santulli, CEO of NetJets, came up with his concept of fractional ownership as a way for executives and affluent individuals to fly via private jets, NetJets only operated five airplanes. After Santulli did the math, knowing that he needed more planes to make the numbers work, he purchased eight additional airplanes. "I needed enough planes," he explains, "so when an owner wanted to be picked up at a particular airport, there would always be an available plane to accommodate him. If we couldn't guarantee a plane to our customers whenever they needed one, this company would have never been able to get off the ground." For a while it didn't look like NetJets ever would take off. After breaking even in its first year and adding four additional aircraft each year, the company turned the corner in 1989. Then the combination of high interest rates and a recession nearly bankrupted the company. During a grueling two-and-a-half-year period, NetJets lost about $40 million and only a single one-eighth ownership had been sold. Signing personally to obtain more funds to keep his company afloat, Santulli in 1993 purchased a Hawker 1000 from Raytheon, an aircraft capable of flying coast to coast nonstop. "Being able to offer nonstop service," Santulli says, "was a great selling point. Then, from there, we were out of the woods, and business has been good ever since."

Prior to NetJets, there was no fractional aircraft industry, and for a while, it looked like there would never be one. NetJets succeeded because Santulli refused to give up. NetJets, a hugely successful enterprise, is a testament to his tenacity and willingness to adapt to change. Today's NetJets, a company with over 700 aircraft operated worldwide by its subsidiaries, has the world's largest private jet fleet. In 2007, NetJets flew over 380,000 flights to more than 150 countries. Santulli is hailed an industry pioneer, and like all pioneers, he dared to sail on uncharted waters, or in his case, uncharted skyways.

✳ ✳ ✳

Cabela's boldly ventured into uncharted waters when it opened retail stores after having established itself as a big-time catalog company and the world's leading purveyor of hunting, fishing, and camping gear. When the company announced the opening of its first retail store, doomsayers warned that Cabela's customers were conditioned to shopping its catalogs and retail stores would be a distraction to its core business. The company opened its first brick-and-mortar retail operation in Kearney, Nebraska, with 35,000 square feet of space, a big store for a small town with a population of 27,000. Four years later, another opened next door to the company's headquarters in Sidney—this time an 85,000-square-foot store in a town of 5,000. Encouraged by the success of these first two stores, a 150,000-square-foot store was unveiled in 1998 in Owatonna, Minnesota (pop. 24,000). The size of the stores is now averaging 150,000 square feet, the biggest in Hamburg, Pennsylvania, with 250,000 square feet. Cabela's is currently opening as many as 8 stores a year, and it is slated to have more than 30 in operation by the end of 2008. All are different, however; a common theme is that each retail showroom has such features as a restaurant, gun library, lifelike game trophies ranging from elk to elephants, freshwater 25,000-plus gallon aquariums stocked with fish native to the local lakes and streams, plus a huge selection of merchandise. No corners were cut on making each of its stores a bigger-than-all-outdoors shopping experience. But then Cabela's has no shortage of potential customers. In 2006 more than 87 million Americans age 16 and up spent $120 billion hunting, fishing, observing wildlife, and engaging in related activities, according to the U.S. Fish and Wildlife Service.

"Ten years ago, we were strictly a catalog company," says Ron Spath, vice president of customer relations, "and our call centers were the heart of the whole company. In fact, everything we did was focused around the call centers. Then the Internet arrived, and it changed everything. At first, nobody knew how it would affect catalog companies. Some of us, like a lot of people at other companies thought the Internet was just a fad, and the attitude was to 'be careful so we don't put too much into it because it's probably not going to last.' But of course the Internet did last, and it became a great tool that complemented our catalog business. Our decision to open stores was based on what a lot of research was telling us about the high percent of people who don't buy by catalog or online. These are consumers who don't want to buy something that they can't see and touch. Some of the studies said that as many as 80% of the population are this way. If we wanted to grow our business, it would have to come from these consumers. Our best hope of getting close to these people was through retail stores where they could actually come in, pick up the merchandise, feel it, try it on, or whatever. This was our number one reason for getting into the brick-and-mortar business.

"We now reach out to the cross-channel shopper, the individual who wants to see it in the catalog and buy it in the retail store. And vice versa, the person who sees it in a store, goes home, thinks about it, and makes a purchase on the Internet or via our catalog," Spath tells. "That's what we're able to do now, and the different channels, which are the catalog, Internet, and retail store, complement one another."

Spath emphasizes that the company had absolutely no experience in running a chain of retail stores. "In order to serve our customers who want an in-store experience, we knew this was something we had to do. It's really a totally different business, and we're just learning about it." He adds, "We're fast learners."

At first blush, one might be under the impression that a company based in a sleepy rural town in the Nebraska Panhandle would move slowly in reinventing itself. But when Cabela's started opening retail stores, its management showed no signs of shyness when it came to making big and bold decisions Unlike other established catalog companies such as Lands' End, L.L. Bean, J. Crew, and J. Peterman, all of which opened small stores in shopping centers and discount malls, Cabela's wanted its customers to have the option to buy the same large selection of merchandise that appears in its catalog. To accommodate its customers, instead of opening 5,000- to 10,000-square-foot stores, the company built huge destination stores, each with all the bells and whistles that would eventually destine them as major tourist attractions. With companies selling from more than 11,000 different catalogs in the United States, Cabela's wanted to distinguish itself from so many others that opened undersized stores with comparatively small selections of products. In order for its giant-sized stores to work, the company opened four distribution centers with a combined total of more than 3 million square feet of warehousing space that serve both its catalog and store operations. The company uses common carriers to deliver inventory two to three times a week to its retail stores. Here, too, thinking big, Cabela's focused on keeping its stores well stocked with large selections of merchandise for its customers.

※ ※ ※

After operating under the name of its founder Bill Harrah for more than 60 years, Harrah's Entertainment changed its business model when, through a series of mergers and acquisitions, it became the world's largest gaming company. Harrah's added such brand names as Caesars Palace, Paris, Rio, Flamingo, Bally's, as well as the World Series of Poker to its fold, and within a relatively short period of time, it had emerged from a stodgy, plain-vanilla casino to an industry giant. The story of Harrah's is truly amazing, especially because it was one of the first casinos in Nevada with roots dating back to 1936. While nearly all of its contemporaries are long since gone, the company founded by Bill Harrah, now operating under the name Caesars Entertainment, Inc., is clearly today's industry leader. While its customer-focused culture has remained intact, everything else about the company has patently changed. Perhaps more than anything else, technology has been the catalyst. Clearly, the company is the industry's leader in its use of technology, which comes as a surprise considering the company is one of the nation's oldest casinos. Unlike other companies that have been around since the 1930s, it is seldom that one enjoys a competitive advantage directly as a result of being its industry's biggest user of technology.

The success that Caesars Entertainment enjoys today can be attributed to management's ability to acquire other casinos with different business models such as Caesars Palace and Horseshoe and then, with its technological infrastructure and operations and marketing prowess, make the acquisitions more profitable. "We've focused more energy on intellectual capital," David Norton, senior vice president and chief marketing officer of Caesars Entertainment, explains in reference to the company's use of technology. "We obviously want our facilities to be competitive, so we put a lot of money into them, but when you go up and down the Strip, it's obvious that others have spent far more. It's safe to say that our competition has focused more on their properties rather than on marketing technology, which has been our domain."

Change Is Constant—and It's Getting Faster

In Lewis Carroll's *Through the Looking Glass*, the Red Queen cautions Alice, "Now, here, you see, it takes all the running you can do, to keep in the same place. If you want to get somewhere else, you must run at least twice as fast as that." Although Carroll wrote his classic in 1872, the Red Queen's advice is as applicable today in our highly competitive world because remaining stationery is the same as going backward. Be assured that if your company doesn't go forward, others will pass you up.

We live in an ever-changing world, and events are forever happening that change all aspects of our lives. Look at some of the major exterior events that have occurred during the past 50 years that affect our lives of which we have little or no control. The civil rights movement. The Kennedy and King assassinations. Vietnam. Watergate. Women's liberation. The end of the Cold War. Consumerism. The energy crisis. 9/11. The Iraqi War. The Internet. A global economy. High-priced oil. Terrorism. The Aging of the Baby Boomers. Generation X. Generation Y.

The world of technology illustrates how the pace of change has increased over the years. For example, it took 38 years after radio came out until there were 50 million listeners. It took television 13 years to hit the 50 million mark. The number of Internet users to total 50 million took only 4 years. In 1994, only 3 million people were Internet connected; by 1999, 67.5 million were online. In 2004, 180 million Americans used the Internet, and by 2007, 211 million of us go online.

❋ ❋ ❋

"Change is constant," says Johnson & Johnson's CEO, Bill Weldon, "and it's getting faster. Whether you look at patents, the competition, or the regulatory environment, everything is changing so rapidly. Around here, we always say, 'The only product that we have is our capacity to continue to innovate. We must bring new and better products to patients because the environment and science is in a constant state of change.' All you have to do is take a look at the advances that are being made in our labs and see the extraordinary things people are doing.

"I was with a scientist this morning in Boston," Weldon continues, "and I mentioned to her about how I studied science in college that my son is studying in grammar school today. This scientist is doing things that are so far off the charts that it's hard for me to comprehend what she's doing. It's moving so fast today that you must do your best to stay ahead of it. I marvel at the tools we have today that allow us to look at the safety to assure that the tools we bring to the market today are effective as well as safe. The use of the computer allows us to do things we could never previously imagine. The use of engineering of molecules on a screen and advances being made in large peptides and biotechnology—it's like a speeding freight train. All of these changes are enabling us to bring better-than-ever products to patients that have extraordinary impacts on their lives."

❋ ❋ ❋

Susan Helstab, senior vice president of corporate marketing, worked in the consumer products area prior to joining Four Seasons. "A big difference in what we do here," she explains, "is that we are able to interact with our guests on a daily basis. Being on the front line gives us a sense of what kinds of requests are being made and enables us to examine what we did to take care of our guests in anticipation of their needs. As a company, we've always had the ability to take this information, analyze it, and share it across the organization. We've been able to observe this direct feedback and figure out what potential trends it represents. For instance, if you don't have a spa, your guests will tell you all the reasons why the spa experience is so important to them. It helps to inform both service and business decisions."

"By hearing what our guests were telling us," Barbara Talbott, executive vice president of marketing, adds, "we learned that the number one motivation about the spa experience is relaxation, after a long flight for example, to help with jet lag. In recent years at our resorts, we saw that couples were no longer leaving their kids at home with the babysitter—they were taking them along, and oftentimes, the grandparents as well. So we have added special amenities, programs, and facilities for kids and families. Many of our guests also conduct business, even on a leisure trip. So we provide a workspace and high-speed Internet connectivity even for guests vacationing in an exotic, tropical resort. These are just a few changes in our industry, and they will continue as lifestyles evolve."

"It's really a combination of an affluent society and higher expectations," Helstab emphasizes. "At Four Seasons, we've also observed that people today value experiences more than anything else, because, at some point they've become surrounded by all of the things that they need or that they want. Their ability to have and be able to share unforgettable experiences—and to create meaningful memories for themselves—is priceless."

The Customers Are Constantly Changing

We've known for a while that American women buy more than men, even more new cars and trucks. But what has changed is that women now understand their purchasing power and are beginning to demand better treatment, and they're getting it. The Internet is also a resource for women taking charge of their own finances. It was only a few decades ago that women—who now buy a big share of products like tires, power tools, lawn mowers, computers, consumer electronics, and, of course, homes—could not get a bank loan without a male cosigner, regardless of whether they had their own accounts.

As we discussed in Chapter 6, customers like to do business with people who care about them. Treating people with respect and letting them know that their business is appreciated, of course, is nothing new, and, in fact, is as old as the hills. But somehow, in today's high-tech world, we've drifted away from reaching out and touching people personally. As a result, people are now craving the personal touch, and perhaps more than ever, it's become a competitive advantage for those who can provide it. When customers change and crave what is no longer available, companies must also change to accommodate them. In Chapter 7, we talked about how Americans have less discretionary time today than they had in the past. This shortage of time is the root of major change in consumer behavior. It affects everything from where they shop to why brand-name products are increasingly popular. Of course, we can write an entire book on how customers change—but you get the point. Customer-focused companies must adapt to the needs and whims of their customers.

✳ ✳ ✳

"We've made this brand for baby boomers that are now in their fifties and sixties," explains Jim Farley, former group vice president at Lexus, "and remember, there are few brands in the 300,000- to 400,000-unit market that have ever been successful to parents and children simultaneously. Going back, Buick, Oldsmobile, and Cadillac each had a 20-year run. They followed their customer by listening to them, and then they extinguished the brand. Our future challenge is to approach this segment with humbleness and apply our covenant—without alienating the parents. Not many brands have been able to do this, and none have done it in our volume. Looking ahead, in a short seven- to eight-year time frame, 50% of the luxury car market will be people in their thirties and forties. The Generation X and Generation Y buy personalized products. The buying experience has to be totally different than what their parents want. Gen X and Gen Y are time efficient. Their idea of time is completely different than their parents' idea of time."

Mark Templin, Lexus' group vice president and general manager, concurs. "I think a key consideration with Gen X and Gen Y is that they grew up being able to personalize everything they do with their life. Think about it. They can personalize their music choices on their iPod today. They can go to Starbucks and buy coffee a million different ways.

They can buy a computer and order exactly what they want. People can even put a ring tone or wallpaper on their cell phone. They can go online and buy a pair of Nike athletic shoes and customize them. That's right, even their shoes can be personalized!

"These young people have lived in a world where they can personalize everything they do," Templin continues. "We did this very effectively for our Scion customers. Here at Lexus, we've always strived to do the same thing, but the emphasis is more about personalizing the experience rather than trying to have all customers receive it the same way. While I don't think we need to offer as big a variety as we do at Scion, Lexus is starting to offer more personal choices with the car itself that appeals to Gen X and Gen Y. Bear in mind that as people go through different stages of life, such as getting married and having kids, they need different kinds of vehicles as their needs and tastes change."

Templin points out that young people also use their time differently than their parents. "It's interesting to observe them," he says. "For example, they don't sit down to read a long story in the newspaper. They just want to read two or three sentences. 'Tell me what it says and let me get into the next news item,' they say. This all comes from growing up on the Internet. They can go online to pick and choose what they want, plus they can get that information very quickly and then go on to something else. They've developed this ability to do so many things with a lot happening simultaneously. What's more, they're making us be the same way. We are going to end up more like them rather than they ending up like us. So we must adapt to their world and provide information to them the way they want it. We must give them the products and services they want. And we have to do it within the time frame when they want them. They are going to be the future of our business as well as all industries."

Jim Farley refers to it as a complete paradigm shift. To illustrate his point, he tells a story about when he visited a Mini dealership in Las Vegas a while ago. "I said to the dealer," Farley tells, "'I know the Mini is an expensive small hatchback model, and it's a small niche brand that has attracted a lot of 30- and 40-year-old professionals. How do you guys do it? Who did you hire? And do they really have to be trendy-looking young people?' The dealer replied, 'I hired a bunch of young, attractive people who all knew about the history of the Mini, and guess what? I had to let every one of them go.'

"'Why?' I asked. 'They knew the product. They knew the history, and they knew the brand.' 'Yes,' the dealer answered, 'but the people in their thirties and forties who want to buy my product have been sold before they even get to the dealership. All they want out of me is to fill out the paperwork. They want to come in, and they want a customized product. They want to spend the little discretionary time they have talking about what they should get. Then they just want to sign the paper and get the heck out of here.

" 'The problem was that the salespeople were forcing every customer to hear the car's history and making sure he got a walk-around presentation,' the dealer continued. 'It was really frustrating them. Customers complained, "This is ridiculous. You're forcing me to listen to the salesperson and do these nonsensical walk-arounds. These salespeople know less than I do about the car. They want to tell me that the Mini Cooper has a 175-horsepower engine, and it has multiple ABS systems." The customers were like, "I know the product. I just want to buy it. Please leave me alone and let me buy it."

"The dealer shook his head and added, 'Those young salespeople were horrible with the paperwork. After I let them all go, I hired really organized salespeople. All their folders were preprinted out with all the necessary data, and they had the customer's information on the forms before he came into the store. With this information already prepared, they didn't have to get data such as the customer's address, phone number, and so on. Later, when it was time to go over the financing and insurance, which requires filling out a lot of different forms, most of them were already partially completed. All in all, it was a very efficient, personalized process.'

"Visiting that Mini dealership was a real learning experience," Farley explains. "We're now coming out with a big project that will take our original covenant that applies the same principles about world-class products to treating everyone like a guest in your home, and we'll apply it to a new group of customers. We're discovering that the business tactics and practices that we get out of the other end of the sausage machine are very different than their parents'. The parents came out with kielbasa and we are getting bratwurst. Gen X and Gen Y want a customized product, which means offering them more accessories. They're not like their parents were when they bought cars in the lot where it might not have been their first choice of color. They want the exact spec, and they're used to going online to get exactly what they want."

"We're also investigating pricing schemes," Templin emphasizes. "We learned from our experience with pricing the Scion that when there's no negotiation, it saves about 45 minutes. And we're looking at prepaid maintenance, because the customers appreciate the fact that they won't have to budget for maintenance down the road—by paying for it up front, they never have to worry about it again. They don't have to ask, 'Do I go to Jiffy Lube to save money or should I go to the dealer?' Prepaid maintenance by companies such as BMW took a lot of hassle out of the process. We're looking at everything from what's our follow-up with e-mails to what do our dealerships' Web sites look like? We're scrutinizing everything we do because today's customer is different. It's almost like we are back in 1988 again when we first introduced the Lexus."

An ARG study discloses that *52.8% of all Americans prefer to negotiate the price they pay for a new car rather than have a preset price where everyone pays the same amount.* The percentage of people who do not want to negotiate is rising, especially among young people with little time on their hands. The older folk have always haggled over the price when buying a new car, and they're more set in their ways. We suspect that over time, the price negotiation aspect of buying a new car will be a thing of the past.

The main reason why people don't like to negotiate the price when buying a car is because they want to be treated fairly. It upsets them to think that someone else might be buying the same product at a lower price. Basically, they feel this is unfair. For this reason, some Lexus dealers are coming out with a fixed-price policy. "Many people prefer a predetermined price that's fair and nonnegotiable," Templin explains. "We're doing the same thing when people bring in their car for service. When customers are sitting in their car in the service drive, some dealers are now boldly posting a list of charges for everything from oil changes to tire rotations. This way a customer knows that what he pays for service is the same as everyone else. Our customers are willing to pay a fair price for our products and services that we sell them. They just want to know that they pay the same price as everyone else. We've all been on an airplane where a group of customers are talking about how much they paid for their tickets, and they find out that there are 10 of them who each spent a different amount for the identical trip, and sometimes the most expensive ticket is several times more than the cheapest ticket. This infuriates the ones who paid the highest fares. Well, we don't want any of our customers feeling as though we overcharged them."

To illustrate how consumers change, ARG did a study that revealed that *40.3% of Americans who once vowed to never own a foreign car now own one.* A figure this high is a remarkable change of heart in consumer attitude. It tells us how much better foreign-made cars must be viewed in comparison to domestic-made cars. In the same survey, Americans were asked if they thought our domestic automakers could ever regain a quality advantage over the Japanese. The response was that *71.4% expressed that the American automobile industry can make a comeback and recapture the lead from the Japanese.* This survey also tells us that a majority of us still have confidence in American ingenuity.

✳ ✳ ✳

When Mary Kay opened its doors in 1963, its business model focused on catering to women that attended skin care classes in the home of another customer who served as a hostess. It was a time when dual-income families were an anomaly. For a high percentage of women who became Independent Beauty Consultants, it was a part-time job to earn some pocket money to finance a family vacation or perhaps to make monthly payments on a new car. Many of the skin care classes were conducted during the daytime while the women's children were in school. Later, as women en masse entered the workforce, it became necessary to schedule a higher percentage of skin care classes in the evening. However, the independent sales force continued to enjoy financial success not only because more women became interested in working full-time at their Mary Kay careers but also because, as independent business owners, they were free to adjust their work hours as appropriate to meet their own needs as well as their customers'. This flexibility has remained one of the greatest strengths of this business opportunity. "Beauty Consultants used to sell products only at skin care classes at a hostess's home," Rhonda Shasteen says. "It has evolved to include other ways, such as an individual one-on-one skin facial or a quick 15-minute appointment on the go, outside the home. Consumers are also using the convenience of online shopping through their Beauty Consultant's Mary Kay personal Web site as well as direct mail marketing. The company's objective is to offer Beauty Consultants many opportunities to reach out to their customers in the way that best fits their customers' needs."

✳ ✳ ✳

When it comes to fashion, consumers are quite fickle. Since it was founded, Tom James has weathered many trends in men's clothing ranging from leisure suits to bell-bottom trousers. More recently, in men's fashions, casual dress has replaced suits and ties, not only in the workplace but socially as well. Rarely, for example, can a man be spotted at a fine restaurant wearing a suit and tie. During the summer months, it's a rare sighting to see a man in a sports jacket. "The casual dress trend goes back several years," explains Tom James clothing consultant Steve Adelsberg, "with the guys in the tech business who were so laid back.

We had to adapt to that arena. More recently, the trend is moving back to suits."

Christian Boehm, the Tom James clothing consultant in Cleveland, concurs. "The coming of the dot-com rage brought a wave of more casual clothing. Since Tom James specialized in custom-made suits and dress shirts, there was a period when we had to figure out what our role would be in filling our customers' needs. Our company adapted nicely and soon was offering tailored casual clothing to be worn in the office. Today, we're starting to see customers who wear suits on days when they meet with clients, bankers, or perhaps attend board meetings, and then on other days they wear dress slacks with a shirt or sweater."

After a brief pause, Boehm adds, "There are a lot of men who prefer suits to the casual look because it's easier to know what goes with what as compared to trying to match dress slacks with a sports shirt and sweater. And when you're going to a meeting and aren't sure how other people will be dressed, you'll feel more comfortable being overdressed versus being the only one in the room dressed casually."

※ ※ ※

Changes in customers' tastes are also common in the furniture industry. "There used to be an heirloom mentality," explains Ron Wanek, chairman of Ashley Furniture, "and there was a day when a furniture salesman would say, 'This is something you can pass on to your grandchildren.' That doesn't happen anymore. The business is so trendy today. And with furniture being made in China today, the values are unbelievable. The customer is likely to pay more for a suit of clothes today than he will for a sofa. Furniture in the U.S. today is an $80 billion industry, but if you look at what customers are getting now, it's probably double what they were getting 20 years ago. For instance, a group of bedroom furniture made of wood that costs $1,000 was more than $2,000 in the late 1980s. And look at the price of leather today. The price of leather is about one-third of what it was 20 years ago. Today we buy our leather from all over the world—from Australia to Argentina and from the Far East to Italy. A lot of the leather comes from the U.S., but it's no longer tanned or processed here. The global market has changed everything with leather in this industry.

"If you buy leather goods in Italy, the salesperson will tell you a story about what you're buying that will pique your interest," Wanek continues, "but in this country, the salesperson does a poor job at romancing it. One of the problems in the U.S. is that the furniture stores have male-dominated sales forces that make no attempt to talk about the details that the female shopper wants to hear. A female-dominated sales force would fix this problem."

How One Gigantic Company Changed America

ARG Research shows that *more than 50% of all Americans shop at a Wal-Mart each month*. Using a combination of low prices and relentless expansion, Wal-Mart stores emerged from rural Arkansas in the 1970s to reshape the world's largest economy. Its founder, Sam Walton, taught Americans to demand ever-lower prices and instructed vendors and suppliers on running a lean company. Walton's company helped boost America's overall productivity, lowered the inflation rate, and strengthened the buying power for millions of people. Over time, it also accelerated the drive to manufacture products in Asia, drove countless small companies out of business, and sped the decline of Main Street. Those changes are permanent.

In the beginning, Walton opened what was considered a relatively large store in a small town, one that promptly became the dominant store in the area. Logistically, Walton built stores close to his distribution centers, which meant being within a day's drive, and methodically over a period of 30 years Wal-Mart evolved into a national chain. Always on the lookout for better deals from his suppliers, Walton developed a formula to pass the savings on to his customers and, in turn, generate more sales volume. In 1987, when the company celebrated its twenty-fifth anniversary, Wal-Mart's sales were $15.9 billion.

In 1988, the same year that Sam Walton stepped down as the CEO, the first Wal-Mart SuperCenter opened in Washington, Missouri. The SuperCenter concept offers everything that's offered in a standard Wal-Mart discount and grocery store, plus a tire and oil change shop, optical center, one-hour photo processing lab, portrait studio, and many alcove shops such as banks, cellular telephone stores, hair and nail salons, video rental stores, and fast-food outlets.

"What we are is a 'SuperCenter' with one-stop shopping," says Wal-Mart's vice chairman John Menzer. The company expects to build another 170 to 190 of the 200,000-square-foot SuperCenters that are its hallmark and convert 500 smaller discount stores to the bigger format over the next five years. "We would love to wave a magic wand and [make] every one of our discount stores, a SuperCenter," he says.

An ARG study reports that *93.5% of all Americans have shopped at a Wal-Mart SuperCenter.*

Wal-Mart's great insight was perfecting the so-called value loop in retailing. At its most basic, the system works like this: Lower prices generate healthy sales gains and profits. Some of those profits go into further price cuts, generating more sales. The lower the price, the more consumers flock to Wal-Mart. But the value loop is beginning to unravel. For 10 years through 2005, Wal-Mart's sales gains at stores open at least one year averaged 5.2%. The pricing gap between Wal-Mart and rivals has narrowed, and more customers prefer a speedier checkout and to not wait in a line that is five people deep.

"We are going to sell for less," Wal-Mart's CEO Lee Scott says. "I believe that after we are gone, the person who sells for less will do more business than the person who doesn't. If you look at it, the core issue at Wal-Mart is how you can create a value for the consumer where a brand name doesn't exist. Because we don't need to evolve this company when it comes to selling Tide or All or selling Advil—things where the customer knows, here's what the price is, here's the value. We can drive that business and we can create the separation that we need if we have the wherewithal to do that on pricing. But where we really have our challenge is to create the price perception on those things that are not branded."

In 2007, Wal-Mart racked up $378.8 billion in sales, making it the world's largest company. Its worldwide sales are almost three times those of France's Carrefour SA, the world's second-largest publicly traded retailer. Wal-Mart's U.S. revenue is $4\frac{1}{2}$ times that of discount store rival Target, and four times that of second-largest U.S. food retailer Kroger. Its clothing and shoe sales last year alone exceeded the total revenues of Macy's Inc., parent of Macy's and Bloomingdale's department stores. The company's unquenchable thirst for scale has been the secret to its market-changing power.

One Employee Can Change a Company

We've all heard people say, "What's the use? I can't make a difference in the workplace." Probably a person with such a negative attitude can't make a difference, but most of us can if we really try. For example, Denny Flanagan, an airline pilot, is a person who is making a big difference at United Airlines (UAL). What Captain Flanagan does is so impressive that he was the subject of a front-page *Wall Street Journal* feature story in August 2007. The article stated: "Capt. Denny Flanagan is a rare bird in today's frustration-filled air travel world—a pilot who goes out of his way to make flying fun for passengers." What he's been doing throughout his UAL career attracted so much attention that later in the week after the article appeared Flanagan was invited to appear on several national television shows including *Good Morning America* and *The Larry King Show*. We were so intrigued by the article that we interviewed him for this book.

Flanagan told us that air travel has become increasingly more difficult for travelers. He emphasized that in addition to extra measures that have created long lines at the security gates, storms, computer errors, mechanical breakdowns, lost baggage, fewer services on board (lack of meals, pillows, etc.), and crowded skyways have all contributed to taking the joy out of air travel. As a consequence, dispirited travelers have become difficult too. "The customer deserves a good experience," the 56-year-old Navy veteran declares. "I treat everyone as if it's the first time he or she has ever flown. My goal on every flight is to get the flight attendants involved emotionally by reenergizing them. Before the flight I brief them about the air marshals aboard, the weather, any problems such as a malfunctioning coffee pot, and so on.

"After the briefing period, I'll say, 'Oh, by the way, I want to give you my credit card,' and I'll take it out of my pocket. Inevitably, they'll tease me, 'Great, I'm going on a shopping spree in the *Sky Mall* magazine,' and then they'll hand it back to me. 'No, you keep it,' I insist. 'There's a small child flying on board, and I want you to go back there and swipe my card on the air phone after we're in the air so she can call home.' I ask the attendant to say to the child that she should tell her mother, 'Mom, I'm okay and I'm sitting next to someone really nice.' The flight attendants usually get all teary-eyed when I say this, and that's great. It means they're emotionally involved."

Actually, United has discontinued payphone service on board its flights because people preferred to use their cell phones. So nowadays Flanagan takes out his own cell phone and calls parents when flights are stacked up on the runway, running behind schedule. "I get their cell phone numbers from the child and I call the parent. 'Hi, I'm Denny Flanagan, the United Airlines captain of the flight your son, Jacob, is on. We're running about 50 minutes late, and I am calling to let you know so you wouldn't worry.'"

Since airlines have stopped serving meals on nearly all domestic flights, when there is a long delay, Flanagan routinely buys pizzas, apples, bananas, and other snacks for his passengers. Some of his orders have been as many as 200 McDonald's hamburgers, all of which he paid for out of his own pocket. When a passenger's pet is traveling in cargo compartments, he uses his cell-phone camera to take pictures of the pet and shows the owner that his or her animal is safely on board and comfortable. Once in flight, he instructs the flight attendants to raffle off leftover unopened bottles of wine from first class. He often writes notes on his business cards that are handed to first-class passengers and elite-level frequent flyers, addressing them by name, thanking them for flying United. He encourages passengers to write comments on their cocktail napkins about the flight—good and bad. The flight attendant announces that four napkins will be randomly selected and the responses will be read. As an incentive for passengers to voice their opinions, they are rewarded with coupons worth a discount on a future flight. Flanagan posts their comments in crew rooms or mails them to airport managers as well as UAL managers.

Before the plane departs, he will announce on the intercom, "Good morning ladies and gentlemen. I'm your captain, Denny Flanagan." He'll then describe the weather conditions and the flight's route. "We are flying a Boeing 757 this morning. If you have any questions during our flight about the aircraft or flight, I'll be happy to answer them. Our plane this morning is in great shape." He will pause and add, "I'm in good shape." This is followed by laughter and he'll continue, "Oh, I almost forgot to tell you, this is my first flight." Then after a brief pause, he adds, "Today."

In celebration of the company's seventy-fifth anniversary in 2001, UAL published a book titled *The Age of Flight: The History of United Airlines*. However, after 9/11 thousands of UAL employees were laid off, and sales of the $40 coffee table book were slim. "When I heard there were tens of thousands of copies stored in a hanger," Flanagan says, "I asked if I could have some of them. They gave me an ample supply that I use to award a flight attendant or crew member who does something extraordinary during a flight. When a retired company employee is on board, I'll sign a book with the inscription, 'Thank you for your dedication and years of hard work. Your professionalism made a difference for all of us.' I'm careful not to just give copies away. What's more, when I give one to an employee, I present it in front of other employees and make a big deal out of it. 'It's because of you, our customers fly United,' I'll say."

Customers' reaction has been so positive to Captain Flanagan's one-man goodwill campaign that UAL is now reimbursing him for what he spends on snacks to feed his passengers. The company is also having him speak to groups of employees so that others will emulate what he does.

An ARG study reveals that *86.6% of Americans think an individual can make a difference at work.* What's more, *86.5% think a new employee with the right attitude can make an impact on the company.* We hope the word of this spreads to young people who are just entering the workplace, to help spread the word that they *can* make a difference.

Every Marketing Strategy Ultimately Fails

For obvious reasons, an explanation of why a mediocre marketing strategy fails is superfluous. Even an excellent marketing strategy is certain to eventually fail. In our fast-paced world, the cycle of a strong marketing strategy is becoming shorter and shorter. It is certain that the competition will copy a successful marketing strategy and improve it, thereby rendering the original obsolete.

For years the department stores were located in downtowns in cities across the United States and they dominated the retailing industry. Many of the nation's best-known of these downtown department stores have since fallen by the wayside. To name a few, famous stores like Gimbels, Allied Stores, Associated Dry Goods, Carter-Hawley-Hale, Woodward & Lothop, Philadelphia's two great landmarks Garfinkel's and Wanamaker's, and San Francisco's I. Magnin are gone. In New York City alone, 31 major department stores thrived in the 1950s, and now only a handful remain. Even the surviving ones have been acquired or merged with former competitors. In their heyday, these grand department stores dominated their respective marketplaces; other retailers could fare well by merely following the lead of these trendsetters. Yesteryears' department stores were more than simply stores—they were institutions. They reigned supremely, and their leadership was unchallenged. The community's leading department store was often the heart and soul of the city's downtown shopping area. In the larger cities, where there was plenty of business to go around, this prestigious role could be shared by two or three department stores.

The big downtown department store was the original big box store. This giant store offered many products to its customers, and in apparel, it was the trendsetter. As a consequence, shopping in a department store had a certain amount of prestige. Additionally, each store had its own credit card, a powerful sales tool. ARG research reveals that *when a person has a store charge card in hand, there is an 80% chance it will be the first store shopped, and when shopping for apparel there is a 90%*

chance that once in the store, shoppers will make a purchase before leaving if they can find something in their size.

The demise of the American department store started in the 1980s as a result of specific changes that took away three major advantages these retailers enjoyed. First, the category killers came into being. These were the oversized electronics and appliances stores, furniture stores, bookstores, toy stores, sporting goods stores, and others that opened their own big boxes in the suburbs. They offered more selections than the department stores, and with lower overhead, their prices were lower. Then stores like The Limited, The Gap, and Benetton entered the scene, and with their offshore resources they were able to knock off current fashions quickly. Over time, the department stores were no longer perceived as fashion trendsetters. Then along came Wal-Mart and Target with their big boxes, again with more selection at discounted prices. Being the big downtown store was no longer an advantage because their locations boxed them in with no room to add on additional space. Their departments were small in comparison to the much larger box stores that had 50,000-plus square feet of selling space. To add to their woes, the department stores lost their charge card advantage when MasterCard, Visa, and American Express with huge credit card bases started offering perks to their cardholders. Whether it was extra values such as frequent shopper awards or points that could be converted into cash credits, the department store's core strength—its customer-based credit card—was eroded. Today's department store still has a presence in shopping malls and lifestyle centers in the United States, but it is no longer the dominant force it once was.

※ ※ ※

Business history is littered with companies that grew to enormous size and used their girth to rearrange the world to fit their strengths. Think International Business Machines in the mainframe business, or Microsoft in personal computers. For a time, their success bred an ecosystem that sustained their status. In the 1970s, independent software companies piggybacked on IBM's mainframes, resulting in greater demand for mainframe computers. Such orchestration can produce solid growth for decades. But it can also produce corporate blinders. Over time, IBM's grip on the corporate data center left it unable to anticipate the decentralizing effects of personal computing. General Motors' knack at brand creation and frequent model changes left it vulnerable to the incremental quality approach of the Japanese automakers. Microsoft was so busy cramming features into its Windows operating software that it lagged others in the shift to the Internet. Each remains among the top in its industry; yet each has relinquished the role of industry definer—IBM to Intel, GM to Toyota Motor, and Microsoft to Google.

Is it now Wal-Mart's turn to relinquish big chunks of market share? Certainly, there is a long list of great companies that have succumbed to this fate. In the early 1970s, Sears, Roebuck was known as "the big store," accounting for over 1% of the gross national product. And the Great Atlantic & Pacific Tea Company (A&P) totally dominated the U.S. market back in the 1920s and 1930s. At its peak, there were more than 15,000 A&P stores.

Retailing is a mirror to how we live and work. Big box stores thrived by selling highly recognizable national brands, which themselves were fed by two phenomena: the growth of mass media and freeways, which encouraged large stores in remote areas. Stores and brands together achieved scale efficiencies that allowed them to overwhelm local chain stores and regional brands.

But the Internet is transforming the retail definition of scale. The once-stunning compilation of items found in a Wal-Mart SuperCenter doesn't seem so vast alongside the millions of products available on the Internet. At the same time, the cost of creating and sustaining a national brand is rising because of media fragmentation. Niche brands, created by Internet word of mouth, are winning shelf space and sapping profits required to fund big brands' advertising. Manufacturers such as Apple and Phillips–Van Heusen, lacking the retail distribution or presentation they crave, are opening their own stores. One result is that retail giants hold less sway over their customers—and over their suppliers.

The American consumers' lifestyle is changing, and these changes are having an impact on Wal-Mart. Today's consumers are going online to check prices before visiting retailers, and many are avoiding Super-Centers that take too much time to get what they want. Due to their shortage of time, these consumers are willing to pay more if it means saving time that could otherwise be spent with their families and friends.

Wal-Mart is indeed a formidable foe, but be assured its competition isn't sitting around idly, resigned to obliteration. Certainly, there has been a thinning of the herd, but some of those that have survived have grown stronger and have come up with better ways to serve their customers.

For example, supermarkets such as Kroger and Whole Foods are offering prepared or semicooked meals that can be picked up on the way home from work. Best Buy now employs trained specialists who have expertise in its big-ticket electronic products, a service that isn't presently provided in a Wal-Mart. It is also offering installation and other services to sell its flat-panel TVs and PCs. PetSmart now has pet grooming and kennel stays. CVS Caremark and Walgreens are selling basic health services such as school physicals, diagnostic tests, and flu treatment. These and more innovative services are being provided by retailers across the United States—services that SuperCenters are perhaps not equipped to readily provide. Meanwhile, Wal-Mart is building more SuperCenters with one-stop shopping. The company plans to open another 170 to 190 of these 200,000-square-foot SuperCenters each year, and plans are on the drawing board to convert 500 smaller discount stores to the bigger format over the next five years. Vice chairman John Menzer said at a 2007 investors' conference, "We would love to wave a magic wand and [make] every one of our discount stores a SuperCenter."

But that very focus on scale is now a weakness, for the world has changed on Wal-Mart. The big box retailing formula that drove Wal-Mart's success is making it difficult for the retailer to evolve. Consumers are demanding more freshness and choice, which means that foods and new clothing designs must appear on shelves more frequently. They are also demanding more personalized service. Making such changes is difficult for Wal-Mart's SuperCenters, which ascended to the top of retailing by superior efficiency, uniformity, and scale.

For the record, we have not joined forces with the Wal-Mart bashers. Instead we highlight Wal-Mart because, as the world's biggest company, it has an extraordinary impact not only on retailing but also on all facets of commerce including manufacturing, warehousing, and distribution. And although we have accentuated how formerly great companies have lost touch with their customer base with corresponding market share declines, we are not implying the demise of Wal-Mart. Our intent is to emphasize that regardless of its success, or for that matter, any company's, none is immune to market share deterioration. Rest assured, there will always be competitors out there that are willing to work overtime to take away an industry leader's customers.

Luring customers away from a competitor is fair game, and aggressive competitors are willing to work overtime to capture small bits and pieces of market share. At the end of the day, however, it will be the customer that determines which company is deserving of his or her business, and this is what will ultimately govern those that succeed and those that fail. This is the way of a free enterprise system. The customer rules.

Afterword

Go to almost any company and its people will say how customer focused they are. But as we all know from our personal experiences as consumers, few companies really are. This is what prompted us to write *The Customer Rules*. We wanted to find out what the very best customer-focused companies do that keeps getting their customers to come back. And since there is such a disparity between what companies say they do for their customers and what they actually do, we decided to conduct a series of interviews with consumers to find out what it takes to earn their loyalty. And while we were at it, we also interviewed company employees, because we knew that if they aren't sold on their employers, their empathy would carry over to customers.

During the 15-month period we worked on our book, America's Research Group conducted nine studies, each of which consisted of either 1,000 consumers or 1,000 employees. The surveys were conducted on the dates listed below. A final research study was conducted in March 2008 just days prior to submitting our final draft of our manuscript to our editor at McGraw-Hill. This way *The Customer Rules* would have current data upon its autumn publication.

Dates of the Nine ARG Studies

Date Started	Date Completed
September 7, 2006	September 14, 2006
November 16, 2006	November 20, 2006
January 9, 2007	January 12, 2007
March 2, 2007	March 5, 2007
May 18, 2007	May 21, 2007
July 5, 2007	July 9, 2007
September 6, 2007	September 11, 2007
November 9, 2007	November 12, 2007
March 6, 2008	March 11, 2008

The America's Research Group is located in Charleston, South Carolina. The firm has conducted over 8.5 million interviews since 1979. The error factor for each study is $+/-3.8\%$.

Each survey cited in this book consisted of 100-plus questions, and these 9,000-plus total interviews would have a value of $450,000.

It was our desire to give *The Customer Rules* readers a truly informative book with current data to support our premise that the great companies of America are customer focused.

For further information on the research, please contact us at www.americasresearchgroup.com.

Endnotes

Chapter 1

3   "*My serving starts with the 1,200-plus people associated with my company,*" David Steward, founder and chairman, World Wide Technology, interview on October 16, 2006.

4   "*I want you to understand this,*" R.T. King, ed., *Every Light Was On*, University of Nevada, Oral History Program, Reno, Nevada, 1999, p. 181.

4   "*each employee was rated especially for the attention,*" ibid., p. 215.

4   "*You couldn't have an ashtray on the table for five or ten minutes,*" ibid., p. 206.

5   "*I want to have two bathrooms so that when a gentleman,*" ibid., p. 189.

8   "*Our founder, Isadore Sharp,*" Ellen du Bellay, vice president of learning and development, Four Seasons Hotels and Resorts, interview on January 22, 2007.

9   "*opened his own brokerage firm in downtown St. Louis, Missouri,*" Gregory C. Bond, "Edward Jones," *Harvard Business Review*, July 20, 1999.

9   "*operated as a conventional brokerage firm,*" ibid.

10   "*to get ahead in this business, I would have to succeed in the sales side,*" John Bachmann, senior partner, Edward Jones, interview on December 15, 2006.

10   "*I put on the one suit I owned,*" Jim Weddle, managing partner, Edward Jones, interview on December 22, 2006.

11   *"We'd visit the Chamber of Commerce,"* ibid.

12   *"We developed a service index questionnaire,"* Phil Satre, former CEO and chairman, Harrah's, interview on July 18, 2000.

12   *"You can't take someone who doesn't have the right attitude,"* Marilyn Winn, president of Bally's, Rio, and Paris-Las Vegas (divisions of Caesars Entertainment Corporation), interview on May 3, 2000.

13   *"In the gaming industry, a company enjoys a competitive advantage,"* Marilyn Winn, interview on May 3, 2000.

13   *"During an interview we'll ask probing questions,"* Marilyn Winn, interview on July 18, 2000.

13   *"For example, if a woman wants to be a cocktail server,"* Marilyn Winn, interview on May 3, 2000.

14   *"When asked what made him leave a top-notch position,"* Thomas Schaible, vice president of medical affairs, immunology, Centocor, interview on January 16, 2006.

14   *"My friends and colleagues told me that I had to be crazy,"* Joe Scodari, former worldwide chairman, pharmaceuticals group, Johnson & Johnson, interview on December 12, 2005.

14   *"I was intrigued by the incredibly passionate scientists,"* Julie McHugh, company group chair, Johnson & Johnson's Virology business unit, interview on December 7, 2005.

Chapter 2

21   *"At Google you can do your laundry,"* Anne Fisher, "Playing for Keeps," *Fortune,* January 22, 2007, p. 85.

22   *"SAS saves about $85 million a year,"* Richard Florida and Jim Goodnight, "Managing for Creativity," *Harvard Business Review,* Boston, Mass., July–August 2005, p. 128.

24   *"When people are owners, they don't act like employees,"* Jim Weddle, managing partner, Edward Jones, interview on December 15, 2006.

24   *"An estimated 80% of all agents,"* David Liniger, CEO and chairman of the board, RE/MAX, interview on November 13, 2006.

25   *"In 1978, my partner and I opened a RE/MAX office,"* Bill Echols, vice president, public relations, RE/MAX, interview on November 13, 2006.

26   *"It took everyone by surprise,"* Bob Carter, former group vice president, Lexus, interview on January 31, 2007.

27   *"Growing up on a farm in Iowa,"* David Wilson, owner of Lexus dealership in Newport Beach, California, interview on January 31, 2007.

29   *"The traditional thinking in the industry"* Bob Carter, interview on January 31, 2007.

31   *"Our employees are our number one consideration,"* Bill Pulte, founder and chairman of the board, Pulte Homes, interview on February 27, 2007.

31   *"We're not in the coffee business serving people,"* Matthew Rees, "The Fresh-Roasted Smell of Success," *The Wall Street Journal*, November 7, 2007, p. D9.

32   *"We don't hire sales managers and general managers,"* David Wilson, interview on January 31, 2007.

34   *"I believe that the opportunity,"* Rob Hagelberg, hotel manager, Four Seasons Hotel, Westlake Village, interview on February 2, 2007.

34   *"the company regularly invites patients"* Remo J. Colarusso, vice president of worldwide manufacturing, Johnson & Johnson, interview on January 15, 2006.

35   *"Mr. Scodari, I want to thank you,"* Robert L. Shook, *Miracle Medicines*, Portfolio, New York, 2007, p. 233.

35   *"Hearing a story about how one of our products,"* Joe Scodari, former worldwide chairman, pharmaceuticals group, Johnson & Johnson, interview on July 10, 2007.

35   *"Mary Kay sells two things to its customers,"* Rhonda Shasteen, senior vice president, corporate brand strategy and sales support, Mary Kay, interview on February 22, 2007.

38   *"Every single person in this organization,"* Nancy Fein, vice president, customer satisfaction, Toyota, interview on January 31, 2007.

39   *"It's called a familiarization stay,"* Ellen du Bellay, vice president, learning and development, Four Seasons Hotels and Resorts, interview on January 22, 2007.

40   *"We have a saying,"* Michael Callahan, former senior vice president, business development and international operations, Cabela's, interview on April 20, 2007.

41   *"We require them to submit field-test reports,"* Dennis Highby, president and CEO, Cabela's, interview on April 19, 2007.

Chapter 3

46   *"She lived her personal and business life by the Golden Rule,"* Yvonne Pendleton, director of corporate heritage, Mary Kay, interview on March 28, 2007.

47   *"Our company thinks it's important,"* ibid.

48   *"I spent much of my high school and college days,"* Isadore Sharp, CEO and chairman, Four Seasons Hotels and Resorts, interview on February 5, 2007.

49   *"I wanted to be a good host,"* ibid.

49   *"After spending two summers in between semesters,"* Bill Pulte, founder and chairman of the board, Pulte Homes, interview on February 28, 2007.

51   *"His grandfather had been an accountant,"* Rick Germain, owner of Lexus dealership in Columbus, Ohio, interview on February 27, 2007.

52   *"A former mathematician at Goldman Sachs,"* Richard Santulli, CEO, NetJets, interview on March 19, 2007.

54   *"Many companies give a lot of lip service,"* James Christiansen, president, NetJets, interview on April 5, 2007.

54   *"Family and safety are integral parts of our culture,"* Matt Harris, executive vice president, owner and employee services, NetJets, interview on April 5, 2007.

54   *"Richard is incredibly supportive of the people,"* James Christiansen, interview on April 5, 2007.

55   *"When your company is down to its last $300,"* David Steward, founder and chairman, World Wide Technology, interview on December 14, 2006.

57   *"With the recent corporate governance scandals,"* Joe Scodari, former worldwide chairman, pharmaceuticals group, Johnson & Johnson, interview on July 10, 2007.

58   *"I worked at Herter's, an outdoor catalog company,"* Dennis Highby, president and CEO, Cabela's, interview on April 19, 2007.

60   *"You can call in an order,"* Ralph Castner, chief financial officer, Cabela's, interview on April 19, 2007.

60   *"It's built into our system that when someone,"* Michael Callahan, former senior vice president, business development and international operations, Cabela's, interview on April 10, 2007.

61   *"They collected $1,000 apiece from 100 prominent merchants,"* "The Specialists," *Best's Review*, January 2004, p. 4.

62   *"I was in my office when someone came in and said,"* Tom Motamed, former vice chairman and chief operating officer, Chubb, interview on April 26, 2007.

63   *"We have a lot of clientele in the New York financial district,"* Mark Korsgaard, senior vice president and worldwide casualty claim manager, Chubb, interview on April 26, 2007.

64   *"You can't mandate a culture,"* Isadore Sharp, interview on February 5, 2007.

66   *"Our culture is ingrained in the company,"* David Norton, senior vice president and chief marketing officer, Caesars Entertainment, Inc., interview on May 16, 2007.

66   *"Loveman is very visible in the organization,"* John Bruns, former vice president of customer satisfaction, Harrah's, interview on May 1, 2007.

66   *"Centocor was founded with the premise,"* Robert L. Shook, *Miracle Medicines*, Portfolio, New York, 2007, p. 195.

67   *"In late 1998, when Centocor was still an independent company,"* Joe Scodari, interview on July 10, 2007.

67   *"Once we made the decision,"* Shook, *Miracle Medicines*, p. 236.

68 *"The starting point when we do due diligence to acquire a company,"* Bill Weldon, chairman of the board and CEO, Johnson & Johnson, interview on July 10, 2007.

69 *"Did you know that the word* scion *means 'descendant'?"* Mark Templin, group vice president and general manager, Lexus, interview on December 14, 2007.

70 *"We worked with the London School of Business,"* Jim Weddle, managing partner, Edward Jones, interview on December 22, 2006.

71 *"Thank heavens Katie took the initiative,"* ibid.

Chapter 4

75 *"Last night I helped my kids with their 4-H calf,"* Ralph Castner, chief financial officer, Cabela's, interview on April 19, 2007.

76 *"Out of the 6,000 people who live in this town,"* Dennis Highby, president and CEO, Cabela's, interview on April 19, 2007.

77 *"We expect our financial advisors to spend 80% of their time,"* John Bachmann, senior partner, Edward Jones, interview on December 15, 2006.

78 *"Peter challenged us on our assumptions,"* Jim Weddle, managing partner, Edward Jones, interview on December 15, 2006.

79 *"We were small and out in Wisconsin,"* Ron Wanek, chairman, Ashley Furniture, interview on August 7, 2007.

80 *"Knowing that 80% of all agents fail,"* David Liniger, CEO and chairman of the board, RE/MAX, interview on November 13, 2007.

82 *"In the late 1970s, we made a conscious decision,"* Tom Motamed, former vice chairman and chief operating officer, Chubb, interview on April 26, 2007.

83 *"Back in the '70s we were a small company,"* Frances O'Brien, senior vice president, Chubb, interview on April 26, 2007.

84 *"We view life sciences as a growth area,"* Mark Korsgaard, senior vice president and worldwide casualty claim manager, Chubb, interview on April 26, 2007.

85 *"We're not doing construction,"* Tom Motamed, interview on April 26, 2007.

86 *"I am confident that if you talk to any Lexus associate,"* Bob Carter, former group vice president, Lexus, interview on January 31, 2007.

86 *"We are very proud of this achievement,"* Nancy Fein, vice president, customer satisfaction, Toyota, interview on January 31, 2007.

87 *"While less than 3% of their new customers,"* Jim McEachern, former president, Tom James Clothiers, interview on December 2, 2006.

87 *"You can buy a blue suit anywhere,"* Naresh Khanna, clothing consultant, Tom James Clothiers, interview on December 19, 2006.

89   *"We don't have a whole lot of policies,"* Nancy Fein, interview on January 31, 2007.

89   *"It's in my blood,"* Arnold Block, former general manager, Harrah's, St. Louis, interview on December 14, 2006.

90   *"If there's a crunch in the front drive,"* Rob Hagelberg, hotel manager, Four Seasons Hotel, WestlakeVillage, interview on February 2, 2007.

90   *"The store was packed with customers,"* Ralph Castner, interview on April 19, 2007.

91   *"This is what could have happened at NetJets,"* Richard Santulli, CEO, NetJets, interview on March 19, 2007.

91   *"As the world's most comprehensive and broadly based health-care company,"* Bill Weldon, chairman of the board and CEO, Johnson & Johnson, interview on July 10, 2007.

92   *"When you talk to the leaders of J&J's different businesses,"* Ray Jordan, vice president, public affairs and corporate communications, Johnson & Johnson, interview on July 10, 2007.

92   *"With 250 companies, an individual can aspire,"* Bill Weldon, interview on July 10, 2007.

93   *"Being broadly based in human health care,"* Joe Scodari, former worldwide chairman, pharmaceuticals group, Johnson & Johnson, interview on July 10, 2007.

Chapter 5

97   *"Build it and they will come,"* Michael Callahan, former senior vice president of business development and international operations, Cabela's, interview on April 10, 2007.

97   *"Based on our catalog sales,"* Ralph Castner, chief financial officer, Cabela's, interview on April 19, 2007.

98   *"We became accustomed to a 15% to 20% annual growth rate,"* Michael Callahan, interview on April 10, 2007.

100   *"Obviously, the kids don't spend anything,"* ibid.

100   *"We have that initial drop in our catalog sales,"* Ron Spath, vice president of customer relations, Cabela's, interview on April 19, 2007.

100   *"Everyone makes a big fuss about customer satisfaction,"* Bill Pulte, founder and chairman of the board, Pulte Homes, interview on February 28, 2007.

100   *"Bill differentiated a long time ago when he said,"* Eric Pekarski, former national vice president of strategic initiatives, Pulte Homes, interview on March 23, 2007.

101   *"I'm really not in business to satisfy you,"* Bob Carter, former group vice president, Lexus, interview on January 11, 2007.

102   *"Advocates are the customers that talk about us,"* Nancy Fein, vice president of customer satisfaction, Toyota, interview on January 11, 2007.

102   *"Our guests are accustomed to our personal service,"* Susan Helstab, senior vice president, corporate marketing, Four Seasons Hotels and Resorts, interview on January 10, 2007.

102   *"It could be stocking the private bar with specific items,"* Barbara Talbott, executive vice president, marketing, Four Seasons Hotels and Resorts, interview on January 10, 2007.

103   *"There is more aggressiveness to all interactions,"* Susan Helstab, interview on January 10, 2007.

103   *"To celebrate the occasion,"* Ibid.

104   *"It's also the thoughtfulness,"* Barbara Talbott, interview on January 10, 2007.

105   *"What would you want as a customer who is traveling,"* Jim Christiansen, president, NetJets, interview on April 5, 2007.

106   *"When you buy into NetJets,"* Matthew Harris, executive president, owner and employee services, NetJets, interview on April 5, 2007.

106   *"We're constantly modifying schedules,"* Al Peters, vice president, systems operation control center, NetJets, interview on April 5, 2007.

108   *"It's a business that's dependent,"* Rhonda Shasteen, senior vice president, corporate brand strategy and sales support, Mary Kay, interview on February 22, 2007.

108   *"My people know how much I care about this company,"* Richard Santulli, CEO, NetJets, interview on March 19, 2007.

109   *"People mostly get a letter from their insurance company,"* Frances O'Brien, senior vice president, Chubb, interview on April 26, 2007.

109   *"We seek out people who can solve problems,"* Mark Korsgaard, senior vice president and worldwide casualty claim manager, Chubb, interview on April 26, 2007.

110   *"We are the product,"* Frances O'Brien, interview on April 26, 2007.

110   *"The company has 400 loss control engineers around the globe,"* Paul Krump, senior vice president and chief operating officer, Chubb Commercial Insurance, interview on April 26, 2007.

110   *"For most people, they have never experienced a loss,"* Mark Korsgaard, interview on April 26, 2007.

111   *"Most home builders have a customer service department,"* Aaron Brown, former national director of customer relations, Pulte Homes, interview on March 23, 2007.

113   *"Pulte does it because it's the right thing to do,"* Eric Pekarski, interview on April 27, 2007.

114   *"The program is named after Jim Goodknight,"* Jim Weddle, managing partner, Edward Jones, interview on December 22, 2006.

115   *"It's a given that we're all going to make mistakes,"* Eric Pekarski, interview on April 27, 2007.

115   *"We're not infallible and we do make mistakes,"* David Steward, founder and chairman, World Wide Technology, December 14, 2006.

116   *"The markets are cyclical,"* Jim Weddle, interview on December 22, 2006.

Chapter 6

122   *"Name recognition is a very big thing for us,"* Ellen du Bellay, vice president of learning and development, Four Seasons Resorts and Hotels, interview on January 22, 2007.

122   *"Of course, everyone who comes through our doors,"* Barbara Talbott, executive vice president, marketing, Four Seasons Hotels and Resorts, interview on January 20, 2007.

122   *"We encourage our employees to call customers,"* Arnold Block, former general manager of Harrah's, St. Louis, interview on December 14, 2006.

123   *"It's not intentional, but I even call my sons,"* David Liniger, CEO and chairman of the board, RE/MAX, interview on November 11, 2006.

123   *"Whenever I meet someone,"* Mary Kay Ash, *Mary Kay on People Management*, Warner Books, New York, 1984, p. 15.

125   *"The worst thing an insurance agent can do,"* Tom Motamed, former vice chairman and chief operating officer, Chubb, interview on April 26, 2007.

126   *"This is how we differentiate ourselves,"* Jim Weddle, managing partner, Edward Jones, interview on December 22, 2006.

126   *"If he's going to become someone's personal clothing consultant,"* Jim McEachern, former president, Tom James Clothiers, interview on December 2, 2007.

126   *"After a while, we have a complete inventory,"* Steve Adelsberg, clothing consultant, Tom James Clothiers, interview on December 9, 2006.

127   *"After I start to work with a customer,"* Naresh Khanna, clothing consultant, Tom James Clothiers, interview on December 19, 2006.

127   *"We get rave reviews from customers,"* Dennis Highby, president and CEO, Cabela's, interview on April 10, 2007.

127   *"With a small budget, we started out having ice cream parties,"* Gail Liniger, vice president, RE/MAX, interview on November 13, 2006.

128   *"We are absolutely convinced,"* Bob Carter, former group vice president, Lexus, interview on January 31, 2007.

129   *"We've made it our business to understand,"* David Steward, founder and chairman, World Wide Technology, interview on December 14, 2006.

129   *"Our objective is to have our head in the tent,"* ibid.

131   *"This past Christmas holiday,"* Ellen du Bellay, interview on January 22, 2007.

131   *"When we receive e-mails or letters from guests,"* Barbara Talbott, interview on January 20, 2007.

131   *"Our reps are trained to review a customer's bio information,"* Jim McEachern, interview on December 2, 2007.

132   *"Green is also the color of friendship and peace,"* Naresh Khanna, interview on December 19, 2006.

133   *"People say it without feeling and it comes across,"* Rob Hagelberg, hotel manager, Four Seasons Hotel, Westlake Village, interview on February 2, 2007.

134   *"It was nearly midnight, and the crew had put in a long day,"* Matt Harris, executive vice president, owner and employee services, NetJets, interview on April 5, 2007.

135   *"They just have to call a dedicated phone number,"* Jim Christiansen, president, NetJets, interview on April 5, 2007.

135   *"It was a new account,"* Jim McEachern, interview on December 2, 2007.

136   *"A call came in on a late Friday afternoon,"* Bob Carter, interview on January 31, 2007.

136   *"A man had just purchased a Lexus for his wife,"* Nancy Fein, vice president of customer satisfaction, Toyota, interview on January 31, 2007.

136   *"The brand is about the customer,"* Bob Carter, interview on January 31, 2007.

136   *"They were big Cabela's fans,"* Dennis Highby, interview on April 10, 2007.

137   *"I was just new in the Four Seasons family,"* Dimitrios Zarikos, general manager, Four Seasons Resort Provence at Terre Blanche, "Shared Values," collection of stories by Four Seasons employees.

138   *"Our Four Seasons was wiped out,"* Isadore Sharp, CEO and chairman, Four Seasons Hotels and Resorts, interview on February 5, 2007.

138   *"A story about a female executive who was hosting,"* Ellen du Bellay, interview on January 22, 2007.

139   *"The Crown Prince of Saudi Arabia stayed at the hotel,"* Rob Hagelberg, interview on February 2, 2007.

141   *"Every single call is answered by a 'live' person,"* Ron Spath, vice president, customer relations, Cabela's, interview on April 19, 2007.

142   *"There is nothing more frustrating to a customer,"* Aaron Brown, former national director of customer relations, Pulte Homes, interview on March 23, 2007.

143   *"We designed the system to assure we'd have people talking to people,"* Mark Korsgaard, senior vice president and worldwide casualty claim manager, Chubb, interview on April 26, 2007.

143   *"Serving the customer is so ingrained in our company's culture,"* Mark Schussel, vice president, public relations, Chubb, April 26, 2007.

143   *"When you're a NetJets owner,"* Matt Harris, interview on April 5, 2007.

Chapter 7

146   "*. . . clipboard-carrying concierges greet customers,*" May Wong, "*Apple Stores Try New Sales Tactics,*" Associated Press/*The Columbus Dispatch*, November 26, 2007, p. C11.

146   "*A 2006 survey by Mystery Shopping Providers Association,*" Kris Hudson and Ann Zimmerman, "Big Boxes Aim to Speed Up Shopping," *The Wall Street Journal*, June 27, 2007, p. B1.

146   "*They wear button-down shirts to set them apart,*" ibid.

147   "*Among the changes: better signs,*" ibid.

148   "*Our slogan, 'It's About Time,' says it all,*" David Wilson, Lexus dealer in Newport Beach, California, interview on January 31, 2007.

148   "*We've created a process,*" Bob Carter, former group vice president, Lexus, interview on January 31, 2007.

148   "*For those customers who want a loaner,*" David Wilson, interview on January 31, 2007.

151   "*For this reason, some of our dealers,*" Bob Carter, interview on January 31, 2007.

151   "*This is the highest rent district,*" Rick Germain, owner of Lexus dealership in Columbus, Ohio, interview on February 27, 2007.

151   "*We're just rolling it out to our 223 dealers,*" Nancy Fein, vice president, customer satisfaction, Toyota, interview on January 31, 2007.

152   "*When it comes to selling Lexus cars to baby boomers,*" Mark Templin, group vice president and general manager, Lexus, interview on December 14, 2007.

153   "*My business is about a quality of life,*" Richard Santulli, CEO, NetJets, interview on March 19, 2007.

154   "*We started our company on the premise,*" Jim McEachern, former president, Tom James Clothiers, interview on December 2, 2006.

154   "*After a while, I know their tastes,*" Steve Adelsberg, clothing consultant, Tom James Clothiers, interview on December 9, 2006.

155   "*My clients understand that they must rely on expert,*" Christian Boehm, clothing consultant, Tom James Clothiers, interview on December 9, 2006.

155   "*When you look at a physician's job,*" Joe Scodari, former worldwide chairman, pharmaceuticals group, Johnson & Johnson, interview on July 10, 2007.

156   "*In the insurance business, there are two ways I look at time,*" Tom Motamed, former vice chairman and chief operating officer, Chubb, interview on April 26, 2007.

157   "*We're not one of those insurance companies,*" Mark Korsgaard, senior vice president and worldwide casualty claim manager, Chubb, interview on April 26, 2007.

157   *"There have been many marketing books,"* Eric Pekarski, former national vice president, strategic initiatives, Pulte Homes, interview on April 27, 2007.

158   *"We monitor our customer centers very carefully,"* Bob Carter, interview on January 31, 2007.

158   *"Travelers today are more pressed than ever for time,"* Rob Hagelberg, hotel manager, Four Seasons Hotel, Westlake Village, interview on February 2, 2007.

159   *"Four Seasons can do much to reduce inevitable stresses,"* Barbara Talbott, executive vice president of marketing, Four Seasons Hotels and Resorts, interview on January 10, 2007.

160   *"The essential question for us in the early days,"* Isadore Sharp, CEO and chairman, Four Seasons Hotels and Resorts, from a speech given at the American Express Luxury Summit, April 2006.

160   *"I don't understand grocery stores,"* David Norton, senior vice president and chief marketing officer, Caesars Entertainment, Inc., interview on May 16, 2007.

161   *"We are constantly looking at the mix,"* John Bruns, former vice president of customer satisfaction, Harrah's Entertainment, Inc., interview on May 1, 2006.

163   *"I only had room for three things in my life,"* Mary Kay Ash, *Miracles Happen*, Harper & Row, New York, 1981, p. 58.

164   *"The company has succeeded,"* Rhonda Shasteen, senior vice president, corporate brand strategy and sales support, Mary Kay, interview on February 22, 2007.

165   *"People are busier than ever,"* Aaron Brown, former national director of customer relations, Pulte Homes, interview on March 23, 2007.

165   *"Every single call is answered by a live person,"* Ron Spath, vice president of customer relations, Cabela's, interview on April 19, 2007.

166   *"We don't have a whole lot of policies,"* Nancy Fein, interview on January 31, 2007.

167   *"Our claims people are there to get the necessary information,"* Frances O'Brien, senior vice president, Chubb, interview on April 26, 2007.

Chapter 8

170   *"I tell our trainees that when they look the part,"* Christian Boehm, clothing consultant, Tom James Clothiers, interview on December 12, 2006.

170   *"From the beginning, Liniger focused only on recruiting top producers,"* David Liniger, CEO and chairman of the board, RE/MAX, interview on November 13, 2006.

171   *"The NAR said it was unethical,"* Bill Echols, vice president, public relations, RE/MAX, interview on November 14, 2007.

172   *"It was a small charter company that owned five airplanes,"* Richard Santulli, CEO, NetJets, interview on March 19, 2007.

174   *"Imagine being the owner of a retail store,"* Robert L. Shook, *Jackpot*, Wiley & Sons, Inc., Hoboken, NJ, 2003, p. xi.

175   *"Now, when you put your rewards card in a slot,"* David Norton, senior vice president and chief marketing officer, Caesars Entertainment, Inc., interview on May 16, 2007.

176   *"If you are an innovator in the pharmaceutical business,"* Joe Scodari, former worldwide chairman, pharmaceuticals group, Johnson & Johnson, interview on July 10, 2007.

177   *"I had a knee replaced,"* Bill Weldon, chairman of the board and CEO, Johnson & Johnson, interview on July 10, 2007.

178   *"NetJets has high standards,"* ibid.

178   *"A lineman was filling the plane with gas in Texas,"* Richard Santulli, interview on March 19, 2007.

179   *"We have a delivery process,"* Nancy Fein, vice president, customer satisfaction, Toyota, interview on January 31, 2007.

179   *"A customer can learn how to set up other features,"* Rick Germain, owner of Lexus dealership in Columbus, Ohio, interview on February 27, 2007.

180   *"When our reps make a sales call,"* Ron Wanek, chairman, Ashley Furniture, interview on August 7, 2007.

180   *"All women are different,"* Rhonda Shasteen, senior vice president, corporate brand strategy and sales support, Mary Kay, interview on February 22, 2007.

181   *"An insurance policy is not just the product,"* Tom Motamed, former vice chairman and chief operating officer, Chubb, interview on April 26, 2007.

181   *"When you buy a car,"* Paul Krump, senior vice president and chief operating officer, Chubb Commercial Insurance, interview on April 26, 2007.

183   *"In today's busy world,"* Michael Callahan, former senior vice president of business development and international operations, Cabela's, interview on April 10, 2007.

183   *"This young fellow sold office machines,"* Jim McEachern, former president, Tom James Clothiers, interview on December 2, 2006.

183   *"This is the suit I think you should wear to your board meeting,"* Christian Boehm, interview on December 12, 2006.

Chapter 9

187   *"... to lure more affluent shoppers,"* Kris Hudson & James Covert, "Wal-Mart Recovery Dealt a Blow," *The Wall Street Journal*, August 15, 2007, p. A2.

188   *"Many people have the perception,"* Richard Santulli, CEO, NetJets, interview on March 19, 2007.

188   *"... if consumers are unable to determine any differences,"* Ron Wanek, chairman, Ashley Furniture, interview on August 7, 2007.

189   *"It's reminiscent of the waiter who comes to your table,"* Paul Krump, senior vice president and chief operating officer, Chubb Commercial Insurance, interview on April 26, 2007.

190   *"It's only when they submit a claim,"* Mark Korsgaard, senior vice president and worldwide casualty claim manager, Chubb, interview on April 26, 2007.

190   *"You feel comfortable with us,"* Paul Krump, interview on April 26, 2007.

191   *"In a recent focus group,"* Barbara Talbott, executive vice president, marketing, Four Seasons Hotels and Resorts, interview on January 10, 2007.

192   *"Every guest at Four Seasons is a VIP,"* Isadore Sharp, CEO and chairman, Four Seasons Hotels and Resorts, interview on February 5, 2007.

192   *"The one thing we knew for certain,"* ibid.

194   *"They were taking bids and asked us,"* Jim Christiansen, president, NetJets, interview on April 5, 2007.

195   *"... built RE/MAX on the premise,"* David Liniger, CEO and chairman of the board, RE/MAX, interview on December 2, 2007.

196   *"A beginner looks at a home and has no concept of its value,"* ibid.

197   *"If the pieces in the package were purchased separately,"* Terry Anderson, president, TNT Fireworks, interview on August 18, 2007.

198   *"... how the cost of raw materials for certain medicines was only pennies,"* Robert L. Shook, *Miracle Medicines*, Portfolio, New York, 2007, p. 7.

200   *"I'm in the business of fostering customer monogamy,"* Robert L. Shook, *Jackpot*, Wiley & Sons, Inc., Hoboken, NJ, 2003, p. 150.

201   *"There are three things that a Tom James customer,"* Jim McEachern, former president, Tom James Clothiers, interview on December 2, 2006.

201   *"We will not accept an order in options,"* Jim Weddle, managing partner, Edward Jones, interview on December 22, 2006.

201   *"An Edward Jones client is a serious long-term investor,"* John Bachmann, senior partner, Edward Jones, interview on December 15, 2006.

Chapter 10

206   *"With such high stakes, both Lexus and Wilson,"* David Wilson, owner of Lexus dealership in Newport Beach, California, interview on January 31, 2007.

206   *"In 2007 when we announced,"* Bob Carter, former group vice president, Lexus, interview on January 31, 2007.

206 *"Based on his past experiences with Toyota,"* David Wilson, interview on January 31, 2007.

207 *"The Germain Lexus dealerships are owned and operated today,"* Rick Germain, owner of Lexus dealership in Columbus, Ohio, interview on February 27, 2007.

208 *"When I became a Toyota dealer in 1982,"* David Wilson, interview on January 31, 2007.

208 *"Our direct customer is the dealer,"* Bob Carter, interview on January 31, 2007.

208 *"All RE/MAX franchises consist of independently owned and operated offices,"* Dave Liniger, CEO and chairman of the board, RE/MAX, interview on November 13, 2006.

209 *"But even as the farm boom helps Deere harvest record profits,"* Ilan Beat and Timothy Aeppel, "Why Deere Is Weeding Out Dealers Even as Farms Boom," *The Wall Street Journal*, August 14, 2007, p. A1.

210 *"By contract, dealers have to meet,"* ibid.

211 *"When the first Lexus dealerships opened,"* Rick Germain, interview on February 27, 2007.

211 *"It is not intuitive technology,"* Nancy Fein, vice president of customer satisfaction, Toyota, interview on January 31, 2007.

211 *"We train every associate in a Lexus dealership,"* Bob Carter, interview on January 31, 2007.

212 *"Chubb agents and brokers have more contact with policyholders,"* Frances O'Brien, senior vice president, Chubb, interview on April 26, 2007.

212 *"We do not sell directly to clients,"* Tom Motamed, former vice chairman and chief operating officer, Chubb, interview on April 26, 2007.

212 *"We are very selective on who we partner up with,"* Ron Wanek, chairman, Ashley Furniture, interview on August 7, 2007.

213 *"Our whole value proposition in the marketplace,"* Todd Wanek, president and CEO, Ashley Furniture, interview on April 27, 2007.

214 *"The European automobile manufacturers built their cars,"* Rick Germain, interview on February 27, 2007.

215 *"There are approximately 650,000 women in the United States,"* Rhonda Shasteen, senior vice president, corporate brand strategy and sales support, Mary Kay, interview on February 22, 2007.

215 *"Throughout the year, there are RE/MAX conferences,"* David Liniger, interview on November 13, 2006.

216 *"When you consider all the costs,"* Dennis Highby, president and CEO, Cabela's, interview on April 19, 2007.

217 *"We are able to see very quickly,"* John Bruns, senior vice president, customer satisfaction, Harrah's Entertainment, interview on May 1, 2007.

219 *"Those rooms were available only to very high-level players,"* Gary Thompson, director of communications, Caesars Entertainment, Inc., interview on June 6, 2007.

Chapter 11

223 *"Its definition is that all things are precious,"* Robert L. Shook, *Honda: An American Success Story*, Prentice Hall Press, New York, 1988, p. 26.

225 *"70% of the molecules that make it this far,"* Robert L. Shook, *Miracle Medicines*, Portfolio, New York, 2007, p. 3.

225 *"If you start out with 10,000 molecules,"* Bill Weldon, chairman of the board and CEO, Johnson & Johnson, interview on July 10, 2007.

226 *"We have one product in our pipeline,"* Robert Sheroff, president, global biologics supply chain, Johnson & Johnson, interview on August 17, 2007.

226 *"What we do is different from other businesses,"* Bill Weldon, interview on July 10, 2007.

227 *"This is the way it is supposed to be,"* Denise McGinn, vice president of business development, Johnson & Johnson, interview on August 17, 2007.

228 *"...the company's credo is its guiding force,"* Robert Sheroff, interview on August 17, 2007.

229 *"A big mistake that most people make,"* Richard Santulli, CEO, NetJets, interview on March 19, 2007.

230 *"I had reached the stage where I thought it would be desirable,"* Isadore Sharp, CEO and chairman, Four Seasons Hotels and Resorts, interview on February 5, 2007.

231 *"With ownership in the company,"* Jim Weddle, managing partner, Edward Jones, interview on December 22, 2007.

231 *"...when the firm sent its first financial advisors to the United Kingdom,"* John Bachmann, senior partner, Edward Jones, interview on December 22, 2007.

231 *"RE/MAX has never had a need to raise any outside capital,"* David Liniger, CEO and chairman of the board, RE/MAX, interview on November 13, 2007.

232 *"The seeds we wisely sow today,"* David Steward, founder and chairman, World Wide Technology, interview on December 14, 2006.

Chapter 12

233 *"It's rare to find a restaurant that serves another,"* C. Britt Beemer and Robert L. Shook, *It Takes a Prophet to Make a Profit*, Simon & Schuster, New York, 2001, p. 200.

234 *"This is why Similac and Enfamil command,"* ibid, p. 193.

235 *"The company's own number crunchers are fond of saying,"* Andrew Martin, "Does Coke Need a Refill?" *The New York Times*, May 27, 2007, Section 3, p. 1.

235 *"Coke officially opened its new 92,000-square-foot museum,"* ibid.

235   *"Like other ubiquitous American brands,"* ibid.

236   *"People ask me,"* Bill Weldon, chairman of the board and CEO, Johnson & Johnson, interview on July 10, 2007.

236   *"A brand has the delicateness of butterfly wings,"* Dallas Kersey, former senior marketing officer, Edward Jones, interview on December 15, 2007.

236   *"... a 'merchant's mark' served as evidence,"* David Steward and Robert L. Shook, *Doing Business by the Good Book,* Hyperion, New York, 2004, p. 122.

237   *"Once parents find a formula or food for their babies that they like and trust,"* Jason Singer and Dennis K. Berman, "Novartis, Focused on Medicine, May Shed Gerber," *The Wall Street Journal,* November 29, 2006, p. A3.

237   *"... commercials showed babies inside the Michelin tire,"* C. Britt Beemer with Robert L. Shook, *Predatory Marketing,* William Morrow and Company, New York, 1997, p. 60.

238   *"When I visit our offices around the world,"* Tom Motamed, former vice chairman and chief operating officer, Chubb, interview on April 26, 2007.

238   *"Our main concern is our customer,"* Frances O'Brien, senior vice president, Chubb, interview on April 26, 2007.

238   *"We don't look at the Four Seasons brand,"* Barbara Talbott, executive vice president, marketing, Four Seasons Hotels and Resorts, interview on January 10, 2007.

239   *"I believe that within 10 years,"* Isadore Sharp, CEO and chairman, Four Seasons Hotels and Resorts, interview on February 5, 2007.

240   *"We view the Johnson & Johnson brand as a trust fund,"* Bill Weldon, interview on July 10, 2007.

241   *"When we first introduced the Lexus as a luxury car in the U.S.,"* James Farley, former group vice president, Lexus, interview on September 21, 2007.

242   *"Our business model is having our folks,"* Jim Weddle, managing partner, Edward Jones, interview on August 20, 2007.

243   *"After the salesman went over the options,"* Mary Kay Ash, *Mary Kay: You Can Have It All,* Prima Publishing, Rocklin, CA, 1995, p. 198.

244   *"Her son Richard did the math,"* Yvonne Pendleton, director of corporate heritage, Mary Kay, interview on March 28, 2007.

244   *"General Motors officially named the color,"* Yvonne Pendleton, interview on March 28, 2007.

244   *"... the pink Cadillac has helped build,"* Rhonda Shasteen, senior vice president of corporate brand strategy and sales support, Mary Kay, interview on February 22, 2007.

246   *"... with the news media and with authorities in an all-out effort,"* Lawrence G. Foster, *A Company That Cares,* Johnson & Johnson, New Brunswick, NJ, 1986, p. 154.

247 *"J&J's reputation isn't a result of some public relations campaign,"* Joe Scodari, former worldwide chairman, pharmaceuticals group, Johnson & Johnson, interview on July 10, 2007.

248 *"The integrity of the brand and what it stands for today,"* Ginny Shanks, former senior vice president, brand marketing, Harrah's Entertainment, interview on May 29, 2007.

248 *"We have a lot of brands today,"* David Norton, senior vice president and chief marketing officer, Caesars Entertainment, Inc., interview on May 16, 2007.

248 *"Its roots trace back to 1949,"* Gary Thompson, director of communications, Caesars Entertainment, Inc., interview on June 6, 2007.

250 *"More people today play poker than golf, bowl, or go to movies,"* ibid.

252 *"When he first joined the company in 1977,"* Bill Echols, vice president, public relations, RE/MAX, interview on November 13, 2006.

252 *"But, just as important, home buyers didn't know about RE/MAX,"* Phil Harkins and Keith Hollihan, *Everybody Wins: The Story and Lessons Behind RE/MAX*, John Wiley & Sons, Hoboken, NJ, 2005, p. 86.

254 *"In 1977, RE/MAX became the top-selling real estate firm in Denver,"* David Liniger, CEO and chairman of the board, RE/MAX, interview on November 13, 2006.

254 *"... there are an estimated 14 billion impressions generated,"* Mike Reagan, senior vice president, brand marketing, RE/MAX, interview on November 13, 2006.

255 *"The grandson of Johnson & Johnson's founder, Robert Wood Johnson,"* Ray Jordan, vice president, public affairs and corporate communications, Johnson & Johnson, interview on July 10, 2007.

256 *"RE/MAX's founders Gail and Dave Liniger bought 221 acres,"* David Liniger, interview on November 13, 2006.

256 *"The Linigers also created and built a wildlife conversation museum,"* Gail Liniger, vice president, RE/MAX, interview on November 13, 2006.

256 *"In 2005, Liniger organized a group of people,"* David Liniger, interview on November 13, 2006.

257 *"Santulli became involved shortly after the September 11, 2001, attacks,"* Richard Santulli, CEO, NetJets, interview on March 19, 2007.

259 *"I was in Oregon on a fishing trip,"* Chuck Smock, director of communications, Cabela's, interview on April 19, 2007.

259 *"In 2004, Cabela's started sending a special edition,"* Ron Spath, vice president, customer relations, Cabela's, interview on April 19, 2007.

260 *"When Mike Reagan's wife, Cinda,"* Mike Reagan, interview on December 13, 2006.

260 *"When asked by the customs officer,"* Barbara Talbott, interview on January 10, 2007.

260   "*A second-generation Chubb agent*," Mark Korsgaard, senior vice president and worldwide casualty claim manager, Chubb, interview on April 26, 2007.

Chapter 13

267   "*In 1958, at age 25, Bresnan entered the business*," Bill Bresnan, CEO and chairman of the board, Bresnan Communications, interview on September 26, 2007.

271   "*We have statisticians who measure*," Dennis Highby, president and CEO, Cabela's, interview on April 19, 2007.

271   "*When you see the way Richard [Santulli] treats the employees*," Jim Christiansen, president, NetJets, interview on April 5, 2007.

272   "*Our owners trust us with their lives*," Matt Harris, executive vice president of owner and employee services, NetJets, interview on April 5, 2007.

272   "*I've visited small clients that do very little business with us*," David Steward, founder and chairman, World Wide Technology, interview on December 14, 2006.

274   "*That's when we lost $40 million in three years*," Richard Santulli, CEO, NetJets, interview on March 19, 2007.

274   "*. . . that many of his customers started buying a shirt or two*," Jim McEachern, former president, Tom James Clothiers, interview on December 2, 2006.

275   "*My first full year with Tom James was 1967*," ibid.

276   "*We expect a new financial advisor to spend 80% of his time*," John Bachmann, senior partner, Edward Jones, interview on December 15, 2006.

276   "*This is what the Edward Jones brand stands for*," Jim Weddle, managing partner, Edward Jones, interview on August 20, 2007.

277   "*It's like getting married*," Tom Motamed, former vice chairman and chief operating officer, Chubb, interview on April 26, 2007.

277   "*If you treat people right*," Paul Krump, senior vice president and chief operating officer, Chubb Commercial Insurance, interview on April 26, 2007.

277   "*Over the years we've done some great marketing*," Mark Templin, group vice president and general manager, Lexus, interview on December 14, 2007.

277   "*Our business is all about service*," Gail Liniger, vice president, RE/MAX, interview on November 13, 2006.

Chapter 14

281   "*I needed enough planes*," Richard Santulli, CEO, NetJets, interview on March 19, 2007.

282   *"In 2006 more than 87 million Americans age 16 and up,"* Jim McTague, "Cabela's: Ready to Hit a Bull's Eye," *Barron's*, August 20, 2007, p. 18.

282   *"Ten years ago, we were strictly a catalog company,"* Ron Spath, vice president, customer relations, Cabela's, interview on October 8, 2007.

284   *"We've focused more energy on intellectual capital,"* David Norton, senior vice president and chief marketing officer, Caesars Entertainment, Inc., interview on May 16, 2007.

285   *"Change is constant,"* Bill Weldon, chairman of the board and CEO, Johnson & Johnson, interview on July 10, 2007.

286   *"A big difference in what we do here,"* Susan Helstab, senior vice president, corporate marketing, Four Seasons Hotels and Resorts, January 10, 2007.

286   *"By hearing what our guests were telling us,"* Barbara Talbott, executive vice president, marketing, Four Seasons Hotels and Resorts, January 10, 2007.

286   *"It was only a few decades ago that women,"* Mickey Meece, "What Do Woman Want? Just Ask," *The New York Times*, October 29, 2006, Sunday Business, p. 1.

287   *"We've made this brand for baby boomers,"* James Farley, former group vice president, Lexus, interview on September 21, 2007.

287   *"I think a key consideration with Gen X and Gen Y,"* Mark Templin, group vice president and general manager, Lexus, interview on December 14, 2007.

288   *"I said to the dealer,"* James Farley, interview on September 21, 2007.

289   *"We're also investigating pricing schemes,"* Mark Templin, interview on December 14, 2007.

291   *"Beauty Consultants used to sell products,"* Rhonda Shasteen, senior vice president, corporate brand strategy and sales support, Mary Kay, interview on February 22, 2007.

291   *"The casual dress trend goes back several years,"* Steve Adelsberg, clothing consultant, Tom James Clothiers, interview on December 9, 2006.

292   *"The coming of the dot-com rage,"* Christian Boehm, clothing consultant, Tom James Clothiers, interview on December 12, 2006.

292   *"There used to be an heirloom mentality,"* Ron Wanek, chairman, Ashley Furniture, interview on August 7, 2007.

294   *"Wal-Mart's great insight was perfecting,"* Gary McWilliams, "Wal-Mart Era Wanes Amid Big Shifts in Retail," *The Wall Street Journal*, October 3, 2007, p. A1.

294   *"We are going to sell for less,"* "An Interview with Lee Scott, CEO of Wal-Mart," *BusinessWeek*, March 30, 2007.

294   *"The company's unquenchable thirst for scale,"* McWilliams, "Wal-Mart Era Wanes Amid Big Shifts in Retail," p. A1.

295   *"Capt. Denny Flanagan is a rare bird,"* Scott McCartney, "To a United Pilot, The Friendly Skies Are a Point of Pride," *The Wall Street Journal*, August 28, 2007, p. A1.

295   *"The customer deserves a good experience,"* Denny Flanagan, United Airlines pilot, interview on September 4, 2007.

297   *"In their heyday, these grand department stores,"* C. Britt Beemer and Robert L. Shook, *Predatory Marketing,* William Morrow and Company, New York, 1993, p. 59.

298   *"Business history is littered with companies,"* McWilliams, "Wal-Mart Era Wanes Amid Big Shifts in Retail," p. A1.

299   *"Retailing is a mirror to how we live and work,"* ibid.

300   *"We would love to wave a magic wand,"* ibid.

300   *"But that very focus on scale,"* ibid.

Index

About the Authors

C. Britt Beemer is the founder and CEO of America's Research Group (ARG), a national consumer research firm that has interviewed more than 8 million consumers. His clients include companies with revenues ranging from $3 million to tens of billions of dollars in industries such as retailing, manufacturing, consumer products, financial services, real estate, and medical services. Beemer is renown for his accuracy in predicting consumer trends and, in particular, sales for the coming retail Christmas season. For more information, visit www.americasresearchgroup.com.

Robert L. Shook is a bestselling author of many business books, five of which have appeared on the *New York Times* bestseller list, including *Longaberger*, which reached the number-one spot. His most recent book is *The Pep Talk*, his first work of fiction, which was released earlier this year.

The Customer Rules is Beemer and Shook's third collaboration. They also coauthored *It Takes a Prophet to Make a Profit* and *Predatory Marketing*.